D1535660

drylands

*sustainable use of rangelands
into the twenty-first century*

Edited by Victor R. Squires and Ahmed E. Sidahmed

IFAD SERIES: Technical Reports

© 1998 by the International Fund for Agricultural Development (IFAD)

The opinions expressed in this volume are those of the authors and do not necessarily reflect official views or policies of the International Fund for Agricultural Development, except as explicitly stated.

The designations employed and the presentation of material in this publication do not imply the expression of any opinion whatsoever on the part of the International Fund for Agricultural Development (IFAD) of the United Nations concerning the legal status of any country, territory, city or area or of its authorities, or concerning the delimitation of its frontiers or boundaries. The designations "developed" and "developing " economies are intended for statistical convenience and do not necessarily express a judgement about the stage reached by a particular country or area in the development process.

All rights reserved.

ISBN 92-9072-006-9

Joint Editors: Victor R. Squires and Ahmed E. Sidahmed
Prepared by: The Technical Advisory Division of IFAD
Produced by: The Publications and Desktop Publishing Team of IFAD
Design: Marie Slater
Printed by: U.Quintily S.p.A., Rome, Italy
January 1998

IFAD - INTERNATIONAL FUND FOR
AGRICULTURAL DEVELOPMENT
Via del Serafico, 107 - 00142 Rome, Italy
Tel +39-6-54591 - Fax +39-6-5043463 - Telex 620330 IFAD-I
E-mail IFAD@IFAD.ORG

Preface

Dryland areas are a major focus of attention for the International Fund for Agricultural Development. Such areas occupy about one half of the land surface of the earth. It is often thought that drylands and semi-arid zones are wastelands of little use. But for the inhabitants of these zones, even of deserts, this has never been true. Historically, deserts and drylands have provided livelihood to large numbers of human beings and continue to do so. Unfortunately, because of inappropriate policies, these vulnerable zones have been subject to progressive – in some cases what was thought irreversible – deterioration.

These issues are of considerable significance for the Kingdom of Saudi Arabia. Commercialization of livestock production and the transport of livestock and water, together with the erosion of communal systems of managing pasture and rangelands have had serious consequences for dryland areas. Nomads, as well as policy makers, face serious constraints in addressing these problems in spite of advances in technology for monitoring and predicting changes in vegetation and precipitation patterns.

The Meteorology and Environmental Protection Administration (MEPA) and the Ministry of Agriculture and Water (MAW) of the Kingdom, in collaboration with IFAD, organized a four-day workshop in Jeddah, 3 to 6 November 1996 on sustainable use of rangelands and desertification control. The workshop was attended by senior government representatives from the countries of the region as well as over 140 experts from universities and other institutions in Australia, Europe, the Near East and North Africa, and the United States.

The workshop was held under the high patronage of His Royal Highness Prince Sultan Ibn Abdulaziz. It was inaugurated by His Royal Highness Prince Magid Ibn Abdulaziz Ibn Al-Saud, the President of the Saudi Meteorology and Environmental Protection Administration and keynote speeches were made by the President of the Islamic Development Bank and by myself.

The workshop reviewed in depth the capacity and potential of satellite imagery, remote sensing and related technologies advances for monitoring trends and changes in rangelands, livestock and movements of human population. The discussion examined how such advances in technology could provide management early warning tools responsive to the needs of the pastoralists while respecting their cultural traditions and values.

The venue of the workshop in Jeddah was particularly appropriate since a significant proportion of the land surface in the countries of the region is characterized by low and variable rainfall and heavy pressure on limited range and pasture lands. In consequence, the interaction between the environment and the livestock production system is complex and has a strong impact on the livelihoods of nomadic and semi-nomadic dwellers and rangeland inhabitants.

IFAD's mission is precisely to respond to the needs of poor rural communities such as these. The opportunity presented in this workshop through the good offices of the Government of the Kingdom of Saudi Arabia is therefore greatly welcomed by IFAD. It is my sincere hope that the outcome of this workshop will benefit not only dryland inhabitants in Saudi Arabia and its immediate neighbours but be of value to dryland users and managers throughout the world.

Fawzi H. Al-Sultan
President of IFAD

Contents

PART I
Restoring ecological stability in range/livestock production systems

PART II
Modelling and other aids to rangeland management

PART III
*Processing multitemporal imagery for natural resources estimation
and monitoring*

PART IV
Experience in sustainable rangeland development

PART V
Setting the parameters for the twenty-first century

ANNEXES

Foreword

Meeting the needs of nomads through assessing environmental change

IFAD is committed to poverty alleviation and the world's drylands are a major focus. Since it began its operations in 1978, IFAD has recognized that land degradation, particularly in dry zones, poses a major constraint to poverty alleviation and rural development.

An International workshop was convened by IFAD and the key Saudi Arabian agencies (MEPA and MAW) to develop an up-to-date record of the capacity and potential of remote sensing and related technological advances for monitoring trends and changes in rangelands and pastoral livestock and human populations.

I am pleased to present the proceedings of this workshop at a time which coincides with 20th anniversary of IFAD.

The most important objective of the workshop was to ensure that researchers and administrators in different fields became acquainted with findings in other disciplines. Discussions focused on how such techniques could provide highly vulnerable pastoralists with management and early warning tools responsive to their changing needs while fully understanding and embracing their cultural and historic values. It also focused on how such information can contribute to higher levels of sustainability and assist in the battle against poverty.

It was timely and entirely appropriate that Saudi Arabia was the host for this important meeting since the dryland regions of the Gulf and the WANA region are undergoing major changes that will impact on the lives of traditional pastoralists and the urban dweller alike.

The recommendations of this workshop should assist both IFAD and countries in dryland regions in developing programmes of sustainable development.

Abdelmajid Slama
Director, Technical Advisory Division, IFAD

Acknowledgements

Throughout the planning, preparation and production of these proceedings many people became involved, some substantially, others peripherally. To all, the Editors extend their gratitude; several however, merit a particular expression of thanks.

They are: Dr Abdul Bar Algain, President of MEPA; Mr Shigeaki Tomita, Assistant President of the International Fund for Agricultural Development (IFAD); Mr Abdulmajid Slama, Director, Technical Advisory Division, IFAD; Mr Esa Engawi and Dr Abdulazziz Al-Eisa, Meteorology and Environmental Protection Administration (MEPA) and Mr Abdu Gasim Al-Shareef, Ministry of Agriculture and Water (MAW). Other members of the Organizing Committee provided valuable support.

Appreciation is expressed to the King Abdul Azziz University Medical Centre for its provision of a wonderful venue for the workshop.

The staff of IFAD played a crucial role in the arrangements for the workshop and in processing of the proceedings. Special thanks go to Ms Isabella Mazzarella who assisted with the collection of manuscripts, liaison with the participants, travel agents and countless other vital details. Mr Roberto Montalto and Mr Riccardo Valentino looked after the technical details of registration and assisted in many other ways.

Thanks are due to the speakers, the Recommendations Committee and to all those who attended the workshop and whose presence contributed to the success of the workshop. It is to the authors that we owe special thanks. Without their cooperation, and productivity the book would never have progressed beyond the manuscript stage. As the authors are responsible for providing the scientific substance of the proceedings, they deserve special credit.

Editing a book on such a wide range of topics, written by authors who have come to the subject from several disciplines and perspectives, is not an easy task. We take full responsibility for the material that was finally selected for inclusion.

Special thanks go to Mr Mahfouz and staff of IFAD Translation Unit and to the IFAD/Document Management staff of Ms Theresa Panuccio and to Ms Maria Elisa Pinzon who supervised and supported editing and publishing this book and to Ms Marie Slater for the design and typesetting.

Victor R. Squires
Adelaide, Australia (Joint Editor)

Ahmed E. Sidahmed
Rome, Italy (Joint Editor)

Introduction

Change is the key word in today's world. Global change will affect us all. Populations are increasing, the climate is changing, economic systems are altering, communication nets are expanding. People are more mobile than ever before. Traditional range/livestock systems on the world's arid and semi-arid drylands are changing too. At the dawn of the twenty-first century, the whole world is undergoing a metamorphosis. This publication aims at providing the reader with analyis of the changes on the sustainable use of the drylands, especially those where livestock raising depends on grazing natural vegetation.

Drylands - regions under threat

Drylands occupy about one half of the world's land surface. They have been defined by FAO on the basis of the length of the growing season. The zones falling between 1-74 and 75-119 growing days represent the arid and semi-arid drylands respectively. They are characterized by low, erratic and highly inconsistent rainfall levels. These areas receive between 100 and 600 mm of rainfall annually. The main feature of "dryness" is the negative balance between the annual rainfall and evapo-transpiration rate.

Many of the world's drylands are grazed rangelands. All rangelands are characterized by the need to manage and cope with episodic events that constrain opportunities for development. Unlike most cropping systems, rangelands are multi-state systems which tend to flow from one state to another.

Traditional nomadic pastoralism fully exploits these characteristics, typically by moving from one area to another in response to seasonal conditions. Sometimes, cropping is pursued on an opportunistic basis. Significantly, there is mounting evidence that these forms of use were more economically efficient (productive) and less ecologically damaging than the sedentary systems that characterize other landscapes.

There is a clear need to understand the limited potential of semi-arid rangelands to produce products of value to people. Too many rangelands are subjected to a management regime that continually seeks to extract more from these ecosystems than is physically possible. Given the recurring uncertainties about the development potential of rangelands, it is necessary to devise a set of effective land-use policies which can only be formulated after land classification and a realistic evaluation of land capability. This is particularly important in areas where there is a high probability of land degradation from the breakdown of existing management systems, market-induced overstocking or opportunistic cultivation.

Clearly, the problems of rangeland management and of pastoral development are much more complex than the reduction of land degradation through the control of livestock numbers, based on some ill-defined and unenforceable concept of carrying capacity of the rangelands. Grazing systems cannot be replaced easily by prescriptions to reduce land degradation through the control of excessive livestock numbers. Such prescriptions are usually ignored.

Sustainability is the key

The challenge is to put in place management systems which ensure sustainability in the face of the wide variations in both temporal and spatial dimensions. We recognize that in order to achieve such endeavor a comprehensive monitoring system acceptable and understandable by policy makers as well as resource users must be developed and implemented.

"Sustainability" is a concept that most people know about but opinions differ as to what it means. The concept of sustainable agriculture (in its broadest sense) is still evolving and its operational content remains notoriously difficult to define. But there is agreement that systems need to move toward environmental sustainability. This involves developing production systems that maximize the positive synergisms between the various elements in the system and reduce reliance on external inputs that have a negative effect on people and ecosystems.

The ecological, sociological and biophysical causes of land degradation are well known and fully documented elsewhere. Some of them will be dealt with at length in this volume. There are a few key factors which control land use in the rangelands. Mostly these can be viewed as constraints.

Constraints on rangelands utilization

Rainfall amount, occurrence and location influence the spatial and temporal occurrence of vegetation and species composition which in turn largely controls the timing and location of grazing. Climate variability is associated with both drought and flood.

Surface and near-surface water supplies influence distribution of grazing. Water resources can be both limited and limiting. One of the greatest constraints on human activity in the rangelands is the availability, reliability and accessibility of water supplies.

There is much to be said in favor of the traditional strategy of livestock movements for the maximization of livestock production and returns based on the spatial and temporal distribution of forage. Such an "opportunitistic" movement of livestock can come about in response to rainfall variability or other episodic events, like rangeland fires or the outbreak of diseases. In reality, the grazing systems in a region are essentially event-driven.

Because herders live or languish according to how well they can assess risk and uncertainty, they are more sensitive and more sensitized to natural changes than most other population groups. This is why rangeland monitoring and its evolving techniques are potentially of such critical importance to them. Measures for the sustainable development of rangelands, and certainly of anti-desertification programmes, must take a close look at both directly related variables (changes in vegetation cover, depths of topsoil, species composition, etc.) and indirectly related variables (intensity and distribution of precipitation, prices of agricultural commodities, human immigration, etc.) as the basis for remedial action. But authorities must also proceed on the basis of a cost/benefit analysis of how to respond to the perceived threats.

A number of decision-making problems arise as we try to balance the costs of early action against delayed or no action. One way to deal with this problem of uncertainty is to adopt the precautionary principle "when there are threats of serious or irreversible damage, lack of full scientific certainty should not be used as a reason for postponing such measures". Information exchange and transportation have always been, and still remain the major instruments for rangeland management. For this reason, there is little doubt that in due course the pastoral communities will become more involved and participate directly in the adaptation and use of the new technologies for rangeland monitoring.

Scope and content

All of the above issues were the focus of discussion at the international workshop. The workshop aimed at presenting an up-to-date record of the capacity and potential of remote sensing and related technological advances for monitoring trends and changes in rangelands and the pastoral livestock and human populations. The discussions examined how such advanced techniques could provide highly vulnerable pastoralists with management and early warning tools responsive to their changing needs while fully understanding and embracing their cultural and historic values.

Apart from highlighting the immediate relevance for pastoral people in the Arabian Gulf, the aim of the workshop was to propose recommendations supporting pastoral development strategies across the WANA region and the developing world.

The specific objectives of the workshop were to:
1. identify more precisely the situation and development needs of pastoral nomads in rapidly changing economic circumstances;
2. present an up-to-date record of the capacity and potential of remote-sensing techniques to provide environmental data to planners, administrators and hence to pastoralists;

3. explore how these technologies can be adapted to pastoral development within an integrated land management strategy and make cost-effective suggestions for their future adaptation to the needs of pastoral nomads; and
4. draw lessons from the experiences gained in designing strategies and programmes for sustainable use, improvement and management of the rangeland resources.

The workshop had two major themes:

A. Recent technological advances in rangeland monitoring
   • Satellite imagery
   • Low-level aerial survey; videography, still photography
   • Data collection, modelling and early warning systems
   • Setting parameters for the future generation

B. Experience in sustainable rangeland development and desertification control
   • Socio-economics of pastoralism
     - cultural and social values
     - integrated development strategies
   • Applied Research
   • Gulf Cooperation Council (GCC) country experiences

The proceedings are organized into five parts. In the first six chapters the question of how to restore ecological stability to range/livestock production system is examined. Part II (7 chapters) considers the use of modelling and other management tools while Part III (10 chapters) is an overview of the role of remote sensing and related technologies to natural estimation and monitoring. Part IV (8 chapters) is an analysis of sustainable development as applied in arid or semi-arid regions, with special emphasis on those in which it was traditional for livestock producers to be nomads or semi-nomads. A case study approach is used in Parts III and IV to illustrate the application of these newer technologies and to assess the experience in sustainable rangeland management from a number of countries in North Africa, the Middle East and the Arabian Gulf region.

Some principles for the sustainable use of rangelands which will help set the parameters for future generations are discussed in Part V. The question of whether traditional nomadic systems can survive into the twenty-first century is also addressed.

Victor Squires   *Ahmed Sidahmed*

part I

*Restoring ecological stability
in range/livestock production systems*

Dryland degradation issues are complex and controversial. An assessment of more than two decades of monitoring by Lund University and others was not able to verify the confirmed lack of a commonly accepted paradigm of desertification. The papers presented in this section outline the criteria for monitoring dryland degradation and discuss and outline policy implications and sustainability. A case study approach demonstrates and exemplifies the points made. Examples are drawn from Africa, the Near East and West Asia. Issues of dryland degradation are discussed in six chapters.

Sustainable development: a dream or an economic and environmental imperative?

1

V. R. Squires

Synopsis

This paper examines the concepts of "environment", "sustainability" and "sustainable development". The twin problems of rural poverty and resource degradation are highlighted. Equity considerations are discussed, especially inter-generational equity.

Key points

1. *Sustainable development is defined as "development to meet the needs of the present, without compromising the ability of future generations to meet their own needs". Sustainable development assumes the alignment of development decisions with environmental considerations.*

2. *The key question is just what do we want to sustain? Many possibilities exist. Although the concept of sustainable agriculture (in its broadest sense) is still evolving and its operational content remains notoriously difficult to define, there is need to move in the direction of environmental sustainability. In the context of the fragile resource base and limited potential for high productivity gains characterizing marginal areas, it can be expected that a major emphasis must be placed on reducing the vulnerability of smallholders to resource fragility and natural hazards such as droughts, floods and wildfires.*

1. INTRODUCTION – SOME DEFINITIONS AND CHALLENGES

One of the most fundamental problems confronting humans at present is how to meet the basic needs and goals of all peoples on earth without simultaneously destroying the resource base, i.e., the "environment" from which ultimately these needs must be met (Young and Solbrig, 1993). This is why nations have turned to the idea of sustainable development, which was defined by the Brundtland Commission as "development to meet the needs of the present without compromising the ability of future generations to meet their own needs...as a process of change in which the exploitation or resources, the direction of investments, the orientation of technological development are made consistent with future as well as present needs" (WCED,1987).

Among other things, the concept of sustainable development requires the preservation and enhancement of the productive capacity of natural resources, an equitable land distribution, a redistribution of wealth to the poor and the maintenance of natural ecological processes.

FAO (1991) defined sustainable agriculture as "the management and conservation of the natural resource base, and the orientation of technological and institutional change in such a manner as to ensure the attainment and continued satisfaction of human needs for present and future generations. Such sustainable development (in agriculture, forestry and fisheries sectors) conserves land, water, plant and animal genetic resources, is environmentally non-degrading, technically appropriate, economically viable, and socially acceptable". This definition acknowledges the key role that humans play now and in the future in sustainable agriculture. Until there is consensus about what sustainable development is, however, it will be difficult to implement.

What do we wish to sustain? Many possibilities exist. Do we want to sustain:
(i)   the rural population and community structure at existing levels?
(ii)   the biological and ecological integrity of the region?
(iii)   the financial viability of farmers and pastoralists/herders?
(iv)   the people and their traditional lifestyle?

Once a decision is made as to which of these (singularly or in combination) is the main aim, then the action taken to achieve this aim can be better specified. But what does sustainable development mean in practice?

Essentially, sustainable development is a set of strategies and tools to achieve the following:
- integrate conservation and development;
- ensure satisfaction of basic human needs;
- achieve equity and social justice;
- provide for social self-determination and cultural diversity; and
- maintain ecological integrity.

Each of the above is a major goal in itself and a condition for achieving the others, thus underlining the interdependence of the different dimensions of sustainability and the need for an integrated, interdisciplinary approach to achievement of growth that is sustainable. Many groups of researchers are trying to define sustainability indicators and to devise methods to monitor them under field conditions (Busby, 1995). Sustainability indicators can be of two kinds: physico-biotic or socio-economic.

Land resource management, in its narrowest sense, is the actual practice of using land by the local human populations in a sustainable way (Geerken et al., this volume). People are the instruments and beneficiaries, as well as the victims, of all development activities. Their active involvement in the development process is the key to success (Andrew and Fargher, this volume). Furthermore, unless we keep foremost in our minds the need to continue to improve the welfare of people, environmental programmes will certainly fail.

The poor, in particular, tend to be hardest hit by environmental degradation and are the least well-equipped to protect themselves. Yet, at the same time, the poor cause much environmental damage out of short-term necessity, ignorance or lack of resources.

The challenge is to make participation more than an empty catchword. Practical progress is required at three levels. First, those potentially affected by development projects need to be more involved at the design stage. Second, local knowledge needs to be better used in the design and implementation of programmes. Third, we need to build our capacity to assess the social impact of policies and investments – a particularly important, but difficult, task, requiring a different skill mix and a different way of doing business (Ngaido et al., this volume).

2. WILL THE FUTURE WORK?

The world is changing rapidly. There are three basic drivers of change:

Population growth. Although slowing, population growth is still rising and the highest rates are in those countries which are least able to sustain them. Further analysis of the population growth pattern shows that three categories of nations exist: (i) those in which population growth is below replacement (e.g., parts of Europe); (ii) those at replacement fertility (e.g., North America); and (iii) those above replacement level (e.g., Asia, Africa, South America). In these countries this means that populations will double in less than 25 years (Ngaido et al., this volume). The subject of population growth is complex and controversial and must be approached with respect for various religious and ethical values and cultural backgrounds.

Economic growth. Industrial production has already grown 50-fold during the twentieth century and the World Bank estimates that it could well increase by another 350% by the year 2030 (Serageldin and Steer, 1994). If present production trends and population growth continue, the earth's carrying capacity will be exceeded before long.

Technological innovation. The pace of change defies belief. Just consider the changes in the past century or so. The Industrial Revolution, important though it was, has been overshadowed by the so-called "Information Revolution".

2.1 Social factors affecting the future

Trends are occurring which will have profound effects on society and, in turn, on the struggle to achieve sustainable development.

Urbanization is a major factor, especially in less developed countries and newly industrialized countries. By the year 2000, almost half the world's population will live in urban areas and while urban population growth in developing countries as a whole has been slowing, a further three-quarters of a billion people will have been added to urban areas by the turn of the century. This shift is in response to changing methods in agriculture and, to a large extent, to the fact that the demographic profile has shifted. Yet, it is imperative that agriculture be modernized if there is to be food security. The change from subsistence agriculture to a full market economy is inevitable, but it begs the question "Will there be enough jobs?" (Jazairy, Alamgir and Panuccio, 1992).

Human investment patterns, family structure and education are also changing globally. Families are getting smaller as the burden of dependents on parents of working age increases. Women are assuming greater economic responsibility of families and there is a reduction in the quantity of resources invested in the next generation.

Social stability, violence and disorder are worrying trends. There are doubts about the stability of cities because of the rapid population increases, slow pace of infrastructure development and provision of services such as health, education and welfare. There are many teenagers who are restless and mobile. Regrettably, the job market is saturated and this leads to restlessness, violence and lawlessness. Because many in this age bracket are unskilled, they are "stranded" in a technological society that has few uses for manual labour at the levels which present themselves.

Equity patterns are also a cause for continuing concern. The gap between the bottom one-fifth and the top one-fifth of society is widening. Equity considerations loom large. Inter-generational equity is also a factor, bearing in mind the definition of sustainable development as including the provision for future generations. We could be like Groucho Marx and say " Why should I care about future generations – what have they ever done for me?", or instead consider what might be the fate of our children's children. However, we should act in way that ensures that they all have opportunities to be at least as well off as we are (Young, 1993).

2.2 Environmental factors affecting the future

Resource depletion. Everything that we need, want, use, abuse or consume comes from nature. Will it last? Ironically enough, the debate about resource depletion has shifted from concerns about non-renewable resources (e.g., fossil fuels and minerals), to fears that we will run out of renewable resources. There is a growing scarcity of renewable resources such as fresh water, food and fibre, forest products, fish and shellfish (WRI, 1996). As populations rise we will need more of these resources. The rush to develop the world has damaged the natural systems that sustain renewable resources (Tolba, 1982).

Examples of this depletion are reflected in:
- land degradation and soil loss;
- spread of deserts;
- build-up of pollutants in the air, water and soil;
- damage to watersheds; and
- loss of biodiversity.

Sustainable use places the focus on two groups of disenfranchised people: the poor of today and the generations of tomorrow. The rapid degradation of the natural resource base of the rural poor is significantly worsening their poverty. Yet many of the threats to the environment in the developing world occur as a result of poverty. Indeed, rural poverty and degradation of the environment are mutually reinforcing. When people's survival is at stake they are forced to over-stock fragile grazing lands, cut trees for firewood and overuse ground waters (Ayoub, this volume).

Few aspects of development have been found to be so complex as the need to reconcile anti-poverty and pro-environment goals. The policy linkages and choices to be made have yet to be articulated. One pivotal point is that no long-term strategy of poverty alleviation can succeed in the face of environmental forces that promote persistent erosion of the natural resources upon which we all depend (Geerken et al., this volume).

Economic, social and political conditions have changed dramatically and profoundly over the past 20 years and the changes are far reaching (Al Eisa, this volume; Blench, this volume).

3. SUMMARY

The following questions have been raised:

- Is nomadism still a viable option?
- Can forage and water resources be sustained?
- Are there alternative uses for the land?
- What are the biodiversity implications of a change in land use?
- How do we measure and monitor change?
- What are cost-effective techniques and tools to do this monitoring?
- How do we ensure involvement and participation by local people?

The ultimate question must be "Is nomadism justifiable in the light of concerns about sustainable use of rangelands?" The papers presented in this volume address some of these issues in the context of nomadic and semi-nomadic herders living in marginal lands in the Arabian Gulf and the Near East. The issues raised and the opinions expressed will have relevance to similar situations elsewhere in the world, such as central Asia, parts of Africa and the Indian sub-continent (Chapter 33).

References

Al-Eisa, A. (in press) Changes and factors affecting Bedouin movement for grazing (this volume).

Andrew, M.H. and Fargher, J. D. (in press) Meeting the needs of nomads: the usefulness of the Farming Systems Research (FSR) approach (this volume).

Ayoub, A.T. (in press) Development of indicators for monitoring and assessment of rangeland desertification (this volume).

Blench, R. (in press) Rangeland degradation and socio-economic change among the Bedu in Jordan: results of the 1995 IFAD Survey (this volume).

Busby, F.E. 1995. Sustainable use and management of the world's rangelands. p. 1-5, in Omar S., Razzaque M.A., and Fozia Alsdirawi (eds), *Range management in arid zones*. Keegan Paul, London.

Food and Agriculture Organization of the United Nations (FAO) 1991. The FAO/Netherlands Conference on Agriculture and the Environment. Hertogenbosch, (The Netherlands. 15-19 April 1991. Report of the Conference, Vol. 2.

Geerken, R., Ilawi, M., Japa, M., Kaufmann, H., Roeder, H., Sankary, A.M. and Segl, K. (in press) Monitoring desertification to define and implement suitable measures towards sustainable rangeland management (this volume).

Jazairy, I., Alamgir, M. and Panuccio,T. 1992. *The State of World Rural Poverty: an inquiry into its causes and consequences*. IFAD and New York University Press, New York.

Ngaido, T., Nordblom, T. Osman, A.E. and Gintzburger, G. (in press). A policy shift toward sustainable resource development (this volume).

Serageldin, I and Steer, A. 1994. *Making Development Sustainable*. Environmentally Sustainable Development Occasional paper, No. 2. World Bank, Washington D.C.

Tolba, M. 1992. *Development without destruction: evolving environmental perceptions*. Tycooly Press, Dublin.

World Commission on Environment and Development (WCED) 1987. *Our Common Future.* Oxford University Press, Oxford.

World Resources Institute (WRI). 1996. World Resources 1996-97. (WRI/UNEP). Oxford University Press, Oxford.

Young, M.D. 1993. *For our children's children: some practical implications of inter-generational equity and the precautionary principle.* Resource Assessment Commission, (Australia) Occasional Paper, No. 6, AGPS, Canberra.

Young, M.D. and Solbrig, O.T. 1993. The world's savannas: Economic driving forces, ecological constraints and policy options for sustainable land use. MAB/UNESCO Volume 12. Parthenon Publishing, Carnforth and Paris.

Indicators of dryland degradation

A. T. Ayoub

2

Synopsis

This chapter reviews the current status of thinking on desertification, its causes and control measures.

Key Points

1. *The rangelands are high-risk areas with respect to sustainability due, to the fragility of the resource base. One serious difficulty of examining sustainability in these areas is their inherent variability. Several global attempts at rangeland degradation/desertification assessments have been made by the United Nations Environment Programme (UNEP) and others, but there are still considerable differences in opinion on the global extent, severity and trend of land degradation.*

2. *Vegetation degradation (i.e. denseness, diversity) is prevalent in almost 70% of global rangelands, but on the return of rains the vegetation may re-establish itself very quickly in areas where soil degradation is not serious. Within the drylands, water is clearly the decisive resource affecting rangelands, and plant cover is primarily a reflection of precipitation.*

3. *Human activities that can cause rangeland degradation include: overgrazing, often selectively; the over-exploitation of woody resources for fuelwood; and the uncontrolled use of fire (e.g., for regenerating pasture). The degradation of soil conditions can be distinguished by the following: loss of topsoil through water or wind erosion; terrain deformation and mass movement through water or wind erosion; and overblowing. The degradation of the surface hydrological conditions is closely related to vegetational degradation and soil surface crusting and sealing.*

4. *Four types of vulnerability of rangeland to desertification processes can be identified, namely: surfaces subject to sand movement; stony or rocky surfaces subject to stripping of topsoil by deflation or sheet wash; areas subject to accelerated runoff; and surfaces subject to salinization or alkalinization.*

1. INTRODUCTION

Desertification has been with us for over a thousand years, but it went unrecognized for a very long time (Dregne, 1991). It was not until the twentieth century that governments and people finally realized that land degradation/desertification threatened their future. It is now recognized that desertification is one of the central problems in sustainable development of the dryland ecosystems. Rainfall variability both in time and space, coupled with the inherent ecological fragility of the drylands, weakens the resilience of the ecosystem and its ability to return to its original condition.

Desertification of land resources endangers basic production systems, as well as natural ecosystems. It places some one billion people in 110 countries at risk, mainly in developing regions. The drylands comprise an estimated one-third of the earth's surface, of which three-fourths have suffered some degree of desertification (UNCOD, 1977; FAO/UNEP, 1984; Mabbut, 1984; UNEP, 1992a). The cost of losses due to desertification was estimated at five times the cost of halting desertification (UNEP, 1992b). The reclamation of only 50% of these lands may be economically viable due to climate and soil limitations (Table 2.1). Projections indicated that desertification in rangelands will continue to increase at existing rates. The causes of dryland degradation are complex, including: the impacts of drought and desiccation; overgrazing of rangelands; unsustainable agricultural practices; deforestation; unfavourable land-tenure rights; undervaluation of land resources and pricing failures; and numerous other social and economic processes (Box 1).

Table 2.1

Extent of desertification/land degradation in rangelands of the world in million hectares, and estimated indicative average global cost of direct anti-desertification measures

Desertification	Total rangeland	Slight to none	Moderate	Severe	Very severe
	4 556	1 223	1 267	1 984	72
Loss of productivity (%)		0-25	25-50	50-75	75-100
Major target		A. Prevention of desertification	B. Corrective measures to sustain productivity	C. Rehabilitation of degraded land and its return to productive use	
Main preventive, corrective or reclamative actions		Monitoring of vegetation, introduction of improved rangeland management and pastoralism	Reduction of stock number per unit area of rangeland plus, as in A.	Artificial revegetation with appropriate rest period later on, as in A.	Continuous rest period for natural recovery with full protection
Cost per ha in USD		5-15	10-30	40-60	3-7

Source: (UNEP 1992)

Box 1

Some causes of rangeland degradation

Rangelands are impacted by:

Drought (extent, frequency and severity);

Livestock pressure (too much for too long);

Crops (encroachment onto grazing lands);

Fires (natural and deliberately lit);

Boreholes (too many and too close together);

Locusts (extent, frequency and severity of outbreaks); and

Human factors (social, economic and political).

The link between desertification and poverty is direct and intimate. It is the main reason for the steady decline in rural income resulting in complex demographic, economic and social changes. The process affects all those who depend on the land as a basic resource, whether for crops, livestock or fuelwood.

The situation on the current magnitude of the desertification problem as presented above has been evaluated in general terms. However, more precise data and methods are required on the status, trends and hazards. In chapters 10, 12, 14 and 38 of Agenda 21, and in the UN Convention to Combat Desertification (CCD) the key areas of focus include, *inter alia:* assessment and evaluation of desertification and land degradation; the collection and dissemination of infor-mation on desertification and land degradation; and emerging social issues of desertification and land degradation such as migration. The outputs of the assess-ment and monitoring activities are direct inputs into awareness-building and promoting action to combat desertification. Therefore, it is imperative to focus on acquiring, providing and disseminating information on desertification and the drylands, in appropriate formats to those who need it. The data generated will promote the development of options, priorities and tools to address the issue of combating desertification and the development of action plans.

One of the fundamental issues remaining is to determine better the nature, extent and socio-economic impact and costs of desertification. This requires agreement on the appropriate indicators of land quality condition and the socio-economic conditions by which changes can be assessed. There is now a concerted effort being made among most of the interested agencies, in coordi-nation with the work of the Commission on Sustainable Development (CSD), on indicators of sustainable development, to establish agreed land-quality indi-cators as soon as possible.

The whole issue of desertification has been blurred by problems of definitions, and by the measurement of a complex issue in the face of fluctuating environ-mental and human circumstances (Berry, 1996). The definition of desertification by the CCD in 1994 as "land degradation in arid, semi-arid, and dry sub-humid areas resulting from various factors including climatic variations and human activities", helps translate these concepts into agreed national-level indicators, and defines the boundaries within which the indicators of desertification in rangelands could be formulated. The implementation of such indicators may require a combination of analytical and subjective assessments, using remote sensing and ground work (Berry, 1996).

This work is a review of literature on desertification assessment and the indi-cators used with a focus on the desertification of dry rangelands.

2. MAIN CAUSES OF RANGELAND DEGRADATION

Total rainfall is by far the most dominant limiting factor in the dry rangelands. Drought diminishes rangeland productivity, but also adversely affects feed quality and species diversity. Drought also affects the composition and size of the herd. Under such conditions, for example, goats suffer least and recover most quickly. If drought continues to the extent of rangeland desiccation, pastoralists abandon the area.

Overgrazing of the rangelands by livestock is believed to be the most widespread cause of degradation in the dry areas. Figure 2.1 gives an example of indicative figures of livestock density per potential carrying capacity in different vegetation zones of the drylands of The Sudan. In the hyper-arid zone, the livestock survives for a period on zerophytic shrubs and ephemeral grasses, and therefore once these plants are grazed the animals have to be moved somewhere else. For this reason, there seems to be a balance between carrying capacity and livestock units in the hyper-arid zones. In the arid and semi-arid zones, livestock density is above the potential carrying capacity most of the year, and these are the areas where most of the desertification takes place. The arid zone, having more than twice as much livestock density than its potential carrying capacity, is very much overgrazed and the soils are severely degraded.

Figure 2.1

Livestock density per potential carrying capacity in different zones of The Sudan

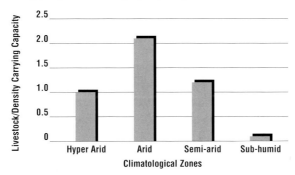

Livestock density in the sub-humid zone is far below the potential carrying capacity. Currently, much of this zone is without livestock, particularly cattle, due to the presence of tsetse fly (Glossina moritans). However, rangeland destruction is not only caused by overgrazing. Fire incidents associated with grazing have equally adverse effects as overgrazing. The dry sub-humid regions are always affected by fire incidents during the dry season, which contribute to degradation. Furthermore, infestation of the area with grasshoppers, rats, and locusts produces a situation similar to that of overgrazing.

Livestock pressure under pastoralism is dynamic and would change mostly with the availability of pastures and drinking water. Warren and Khogali (1992) state that grazing has inflicted much less damage to the Sahelian rangelands than drought and desiccation, and that severe damage is caused more by physical than human factors. The authors added that the exceptions were the limited areas where livestock population was high (e.g., in settlements and around watering centres), which are close enough to influence the carrying capacity.

Overgrazing around settlements is often related to the sedentarization of nomadic herders. The settlement of the former nomads means that their herds would be concentrated onto grazing around their new homes. Under drought conditions, these herders are forced to concentrate their animals in areas where drinking water is available, causing the complete disappearance of the most palatable herbaceous cover in many places, particularly around boreholes which provide drinking water for humans and animals all year round.

The availability of more secure watering centres also induces pastoralists to change their herd composition in favour of sheep, which leads to more pressure around watering centres (Beaumont et al., 1988). While increased water supplies are necessary in the drylands for a proper use of natural resources and to alleviate adverse living conditions, the almost inevitable result is the concentration of population and livestock around these watering points which disturbs the fragile ecological equilibrium. During the period between 1960 and 1991, over 5 500 wells and boreholes were opened in central Sudan. These wells and boreholes have resulted in the degradation – in varying degrees – of about at least 25 million hectares (ha).

A study in western Sudan showed the steady increase of bare soils around boreholes with time, increasing from 20 to 55% in 30 years (Al-Awad et al., 1985). Al-Awad and his co-workers also showed that in the east Kordofan district of western Sudan, with an area of about 29 000 km^2 there were about 150 boreholes, many of which provided overlapping grazing areas. The total livestock population in the area was estimated to be about 500 000 animal units (i.e., about 17 animal units per km^2), which was very high for such a semi-arid area of sandy soils.

3. PRE-UNCED ASSESSMENTS

The United Nations Plan of Action to Combat Desertification, which came out of the 1977 UN Conference on Desertification (UNCOD) called, *inter alia*, for the identification of a complimentary set of indicators of desertification to monitor the status and trends of desertification. In considering the urgent need for action, UNCOD recommended the preparation of detailed maps at national and regional levels, with an emphasis on the assessment at country level and the production of maps of immediate use to the countries concerned. This posed the great challenge of establishing the dimensions of the problem and its growing threat.

After the conference, and in response to its recommendations, UNEP and the Food and Agriculture Organization of the United Nations (FAO) jointly developed a methodology for assessment and mapping of desertification. The conclusions and recommendations arising from the FAO/UNEP consultation formed the basis for the final FAO/UNEP documents published in 1984, the *Provisional methodology for assessment and mapping of desertification* and a *Map of desertification hazards*. The provisional methodology was based on the consideration of natural and human-induced processes leading to desertification.

The following indicators were used: degradation of vegetative covers; water erosion; wind erosion; salinization; soil crusting and compaction; reduction in soil organic matter; and accumulation of substances toxic to plants or animals.

Based on the above quantifiable indicators, the following aspects of desertification were considered and represented on the maps:

- *the Status of Desertification:* the state or conditions existing on a particular piece of land at the time of observation compared to conditions which existed in the past;
- *the Rate of Desertification:* the changes which have occurred per unit of time;
- *the Inherent Risk of Desertification:* the vulnerability of the landscape to desertification processes; and
- *the Hazard of Desertification:* the evaluation of the conditions considering the status, rate and inherited risk of desertification by dominant determinative processes, including human and animal pressures on the environment.

The severity of the desertification was coded as follows: slight, moderate, severe, and very severe. The desert, as the ultimate state of desertification, was taken as the final reference point.

UNEP initiated two pilot projects in Kenya in 1987 to review the FAO/UNEP provisional methodology for use in the assessment and mapping of desertification at local, national and regional levels. The initial evaluation of the provisional methodology by the project showed that most of the indicators and methods proposed could only be used in the assessment and mapping of desertification at local and pilot levels. Five models were developed: water erosion, wind erosion, range-carrying capacity, vegetation degradation and human population.

The aspects of desertification (risk, status, rate and hazard) proposed in the provisional methodology were found adequate and adopted with slight modifications. The ratings of the four aspects of desertification were then expanded to five points: none, slight, moderate, severe and very severe. However, in some cases it was found practical to use only a two or three-point rating.

Another attempt to develop the provisional methodology was undertaken by UNEP in cooperation with the Government of France, on the basis of comparing the aerial photographs taken in 1950 with the SPOT (1987) imageries for a transect from 10°50' to 15°40'N, extending from the northern boundary of Guinea through Mali and Mauritania.

Another attempt to assess the desertification status in six countries of southern Africa, which was sponsored by UNEP, distinguished the following processes indicative of desertification: deterioration of pasture; deterioration of soil fertility in agricultural land; water erosion; wind erosion; sand encroachment; sand dune invasion; sedimentation of dams and rivers; waterlogging and/or salinization; and depletion of forest/woodland.

For the degrees of desertification the following criteria were developed:

- *Very severe:* reduction of land to completely unproductive status as represented by moving sand dunes, widespread large gully systems, or salt-crusted, virtually impervious soils in previously irrigated areas;
- *Severe and moderate:* different degrees of change to less desirable vegetation, the extent of accelerated soil erosion and denudation, or loss of crop yield through reversible salinization of irrigated soils;
- *Slight:* little or no degradation of the plant cover or soil occurred.

The whole assessment process was undertaken by questionnaires in a purely qualitative manner.

All the above efforts of desertification assessment did not lead to reliable and quantitative assessment of the existing situation. However, the above efforts were used by UNEP and its partners, the International Soil Reference and Information Centre (ISRIC) and the International Society of Soil Science (ISSS). Between 1987 and 1990, these organizations developed, within the UNEP/ISRIC project on Global Assessment of Soil Degradation (GLASOD), the methodology for the assessment and mapping of the global status of human-induced soil degradation at a scale of 1:10 000 000, taking into account all previous methodologies, particularly the FAO/UNEP Provisional Methodology.

The following forms of soil degradation relevant to rangeland degradation were distinguished: water erosion (on-site and off-site); wind erosion (on-site and off-site); loss of nutrients; salinization; sealing and crusting of topsoil; and aridification.

The causative factors of soil degradation in rangeland were also considered in the evaluation process, namely: over-grazing of pasture land; deforestation; and domestic overexploitation of vegetation. Five degrees of each of the above-listed processes were also determined. In addition, recent past average rates of soil degradation were recognized. The GLASOD database provided considerable information for the database of the World Atlas of Desertification (1992), which was published by UNEP in time for the United Nations Conference on Environment and Development (UNCED).

4. THE POST-AGENDA 21 AND CCD EFFORTS

4.1 Background

UNEP and the United Nations Development Programme (UNDP) and the United Nations Sudano-Sahchian office (UNSO) are jointly initiating a programme to develop desertification indicators, in response to Agenda 21 and CCD. The new approach has to move from global assessment to national and regional assessments. Integration of key social, economic and demographic factors with the full range of physical factors and indicators, as appropriate to the local situation, is perceived as essential (Berry, 1996).

Past assessments have focused on the global picture and the physical parameters; future assessments will be much more integrated and directed more towards people issues and be linked from local to national levels. The prime purpose of this activity is, therefore, to put the priority assessment at the local level and undertake efforts with the help of local people.

Rangeland desertification indicators are meant to describe the extent and severity of the problem at national and local levels. They could show the status of the problem at a given time, the trend of the severity with time, and could also lead to the prediction of the impacts of desertification. This will help policy makers appreciate the significance of desertification for the livelihood of those who live in the desertification-prone areas, and the consequent impact on the national economy and the social and political stability of the country.

The desertification trend data over time can indicate the success of governments' response mechanisms. The indicators could also provide a means of comparing the severity of the problem from one country to another. However, in defining the indicators a distinction should be made between short-term cyclic episodes of degradation and longer-term trends (Berry, 1996). Bie (1990) states that the two major elements in assessing the existence and extent of land degradation are productivity and resilience factors.

4.2 Useful indicators of rangelands desertification

Mabbut (1986) writes: "The status of desertification is difficult to determine, [and] determination of the trend of desertification is even more difficult to assess." In the case of assessing trends, sequential surveys are needed where environment and practices are changing. Assessment, monitoring, and interpretations of observed variations in interannual vegetative cover proved to be difficult (Lamprey, 1975; El Hag, 1984; Hellden, 1984; Dregne and Tucker, 1988). Rozanov (1990) stated that the only reliable and measurable criterion of desertification is irreversible soil and terrain degradation, or loss. He added that the decline of biological productivity cannot be regarded as an indicator of desertification, because this process might be reversible and connected with climatological cycles.

Ayoub (1996) noted that land degradation and desertification in The Sudan were more linked to soil degradation than vegetation degradation. Vegetation degradation was found to be prevalent in many more areas (i.e., 120 million ha vegetation degradation as opposed to 64 million ha soil degradation). But on the return of rains, the vegetation re-established itself very quickly, at least in areas where soil degradation had not been severe. Natural seed banks in dryland communities are reported to be as high as 500 seeds/m^2 and that helps re-vegetation (Skarpe, 1991). The degradation of soil condition in drylands is more serious than vegetation degradation, because soil degradation is less reversible because of the slow process of soil formation (Sombroek et al., 1993). Even within different soils, some soils are much more resilient to drought and degradation than others.

Figure 2.2 shows the percentage of soil degraded versus soil types in a semi-arid zone of The Sudan. The percentage of degradation varied from a total (moderate + severe + very severe) of 16% in the Vertisols to 58% in the Leptosols and 73% in the Arinosols. Arinosols are mostly depleted of their nutrients and affected by wind and water erosion. They are formed of airborne sands that came from the Sahara Desert thousands of years ago. These soils are low in nutrients and organic matter and have a high sensitivity to erosion. Leptosols are shallow, rocky soils from the Red Sea hills and parts of the Mara mountains that are prone to erosion due to the sloppy terrain and loose structure.

Figure 2.2

Degradation of different soil types in a semi-arid environment

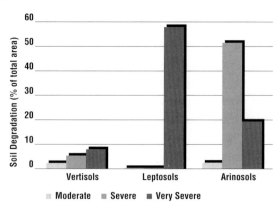

The least degraded soils are the extensive level plains of Vertisols. Their problems lie in their physical characteristic and water management, while their assets are a rather high chemical fertility. Dry Vertisols have a very hard consistency and are very plastic and sticky when wet. These characteristics add to their resilience to erosion by wind and water.

5. SUMMARY

(i)   Rainfall variability in drylands is very high in both time and space. Rainfall, although a major factor in dryland degradation, can not be used as a good indicator of desertification until a clear correlation between rainfall and desertification is demonstrated.

(ii)   Biological and social indicators also provide information on rangeland conditions and should be used in conjunction with physical indicators. The presence, or absence, and the density of particular plant species can be useful indicators of such factors as soil fertility, erosion, and salinization. The presence of soil crust is characteristic of rangelands, and indicates changes in both the soil and landscape characteristics. Crust formation results from extreme erosion and trampling by livestock in cases of overgrazing, and is therefore a good indicator of rangeland degradation.

(iii)   Wind erosion is a serious threat to soils in drylands. Finer soil fractions like silt, clay and organic matter are removed as dust and carried away by the wind, leaving coarser particles like sand and gravel behind. In the case of severe wind erosion and long-term land degradation trends, dust-storms become more frequent. Indeed, the numbers of dust and sand-storms occurring seasonally or annually, are good indicators of changes in soil and landscape characteristics. Figure 2.3 shows that the number of dust-storms (i.e., with visibility of less than 1 000m) in El Fasher has increased from about three incidents per year in the 1960s to about 45 incidents per year in the 1970s and 1980s. Peaks of dust-storms seemed to arise with low rainfall. Air pollution with suspended dust particles can also be a useful indicator of desertification.

(iv)   In the extreme cases of wind erosion, the sands begin to drift and form moving dunes, encroaching on surrounding lands. Sand drifting and dune encroachment is a striking feature, which is easy to demonstrate.

(v)   Because of their ability to migrate, larger mammal species are not good indicators. Birds, vertebrates and some species of small animals, particularly rodents, are identified as key indicators of desertification.

(vi)   Many of the socio-economic indicators applicable to the people living in areas undergoing desertification may not be uniquely related to desertification. However, social indicators may serve as early warning signals that desertification processes are beginning.

(vii)   Much of the rangelands desertification scenario is influenced by vulnerability, marginalization, and overstocking of carrying capacity. Awareness-raising and promoting action through the participation of local people are the best remedies for the problem of desertification.

Figure 2.3

Annual rainfall and dust-storms in El Fasher, The Sudan (1960-80)

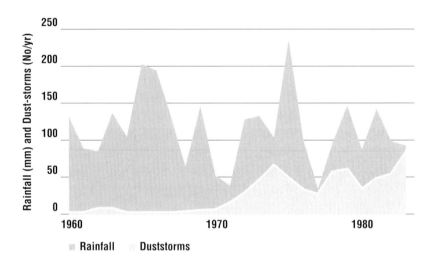

References

Al-Awad, A.A., Mohammed, Y.A. and El-Tayeb, S.A. 1985. *Natural resources and rural development in arid lands: case studies from Sudan* (H.R.J. Davis (ed)). The United Nations University, Tokyo, Japan.

Ayoub, A. 1996. The extent, severity, and causative factors of land degradation in Sudan. UNEP, Nairobi (unpublished).

Beaumont, P., Blake, G.H. and Wagstaff, J.M. 1988. *The Middle East: a geographical study.* David Fulton, London.

Berry, L. 1996. *Dryland assessment and monitoring for sustainable development.* A draft joint UNDP/UNEP proposal. UNSO/UNDP, New York.

Bie, Stein W. 1990. *Dryland degradation measurement techniques.* World Bank, Environment Work Paper No. 26. 42 p.

Dregne, H.E. 1991. Desertification costs; land damage and rehabilitation. International Centre for Arid and Semiarid Land Studies. Texas Tech University, Lubbock, Texas, USA.

Dregne, H.E., Tucker, C.J. 1988. Desert encroachment. *Desertification Control Bulletin* No.16:16-19.

El Hag, M.M. 1984. *Study of desertification based upon Landsat imagery, North Kordofan, Sudan.* (Doctoral thesis). Rijksuniversitiet Gent, Belgium.

Food and Agriculture Organization of the United Nations (FAO)/United Nations Environment Programme (UNEP) 1984. *Provisional methodology for assessment and mapping of desertification.* FAO, Rome.

Hellden, U. 1984. *Drought impact monitoring.* Lund Universitets Naturgeografiska Institution, Rapporter och Notieer 61, Lund, Sweden. 61p.

Lamprey, H.F. 1975. Report on the desert encroachment reconnaissance in northern Sudan, 21 October to 10 November 1975. UNESCO/UNEP, Paris/Nairobi.

Mabbut, J.A. 1984. A new global assessment of the status and trend of desertification. *Environmental Conservation* Vol. II, No. 1. Switzerland.

Mabbut, J.A. 1986. Desertification indicators. *Climate Change 9:* 113-122.

Middleton, N.J. 1985. Effect of drought on dust production in the Sahel. *Nature,* Vol. 316, 431-434.

Rozanov, B.G. 1990. Assessment of global desertification: status and methodologies. DC/PAC, UNEP, Nairobi, Kenya.

Skarpe, C. 1991. Impact of grazing in savanna ecosystems. *Ambio* 20: 351-356.

Sombroek, W., Brinkman, R., and Gommes, R. 1993. Land degradation in arid, semi-arid and dry sub-humid areas: 1. definitions, concepts and databases. FAO, Rome.

United Nations Conference on Desertifaction (UNCOD) 1977. Plan of Action to Combat Desertification. Report on the UN Conference on Desertification. Nairobi.

UNEP 1992a. *World Atlas of Desertification.* Edward Arnold, London.

UNEP 1992b. *Status of desertification and implementation of the United Nations Plan of Action to Combat Desertification.* Report of the Executive Director to UNEP/GCSS. III/3, UNEP, Nairobi.

UNEP/International Soil Reference and Information Centre (ISRIC) 1990. World Map of the Status of Human-Induced Soil Degradation (GLASOD).

Warren, A. and Khogali, M. 1992. *Assessment of Desertification and Drought in the Sudano-Sahelian Region 1985-1991.* United Nations Sudano-Sahelian Office, New York.

Comments on dryland degradation assessment

3

U. Hellden

Synopsis

This paper presents a short review of recently initiated and future desertification research cunducted by Lund University in the Sahel, South-west Africa and central Asia.

Key Points

1. *Desertification has long been considered a serious global environmental problem. The causes of desertification are commonly thought to be the result of long-lasting mismanagement of natural resources that diminishes the potential for a sustainable production of food, fodder and fuelwood.*

2. *The issue was considered an important topic for international consideration on the agenda at the UN Conference on Environment and Development (UNCED) (Rio de Janeiro, 1992). The UNCED reports indicate serious regional and even continental ecological disturbances in Africa and central Asia, possibly leading to a total or partial collapse of the bio-production systems for very large areas in the near future. If so, it would lead to a social unrest, the creation of environmental refugee camps and mass migrations of people of a size never experienced before. The international political implications would be unpredictable.*

3. *Since the end of the 1970s, desertification in The Sudan has been studied at Lund University by a team of geographers, combining remote sensing techniques, extensive field observations, national statistics and spatial modelling. In total, several hundred thousand square kilometres have been repeatedly observed by means of studying historical reports, rainfall observations, old maps, aerial photos and high and low-resolution satellite data combined with repeated field surveys.*

4. *We were not able to verify the commonly-accepted paradigm of desertification and land degradation in Africa. We found that the importance of climatic impact on the productivity of the environment and the resilience of arid and semi-arid ecosystems have been seriously overlooked. The local populations and environmental refugees of the Sahel region in Africa may be facing a climate change rather than the effects of man-made desertification. If so, a new strategy for sustainable development is urgently needed.*

5. *We also found indications that the potential of using NOAA/AVHRR-based NDVI data for green plant biomass monitoring and early warning in the Sahel environment may be limited.*

1. INTRODUCTION: DEFINITION OF DESERTIFICATION

Desertification is defined as "land degradation in arid, semi-arid and dry sub-humid areas resulting from various factors, including climatic variations and human activities" (UNCED, 1992). The concept of "land" includes soil and local water resources, land surface and vegetation or crops.

Degradation implies a reduction of the resource potential by one process or a combination of processes acting on the land. Long-term reduction of the production of biomass (i.e., plants and animals) in the arid lands is often considered to be a serious consequence and symptom of desertification.

2. GENERAL CONCEPT OF DESERTIFICATION

Desertification has long been considered a serious global environmental problem. The causes of desertification are commonly thought to be the result of long-lasting mismanagement of natural resources that diminishes the potential for a sustainable production of food, fodder and fuelwood energy.

The issue was considered an important topic for international consideration on the agenda at UNCED (Rio de Janeiro, 1992). The UNCED reports indicate serious regional and even continental ecological disturbances in Africa and central Asia, possibly leading to a total or partial collapse of the bio-production systems for very large areas in the near future. If so, it would lead to a social unrest, the creation of environmental refugee camps and mass migrations of people of a size never experienced before. The international political implications would be unpredictable.

However, no one has been able so far to monitor and document desertification and the resulting land-cover change through reliable, verifiable and repeated observations on a global, continental, regional or even national scale. We believe the international understanding of the complex processes involved is limited and inadequate to formulate development policies in the name of desertification.

3. THE DESERTIFICATION RESEARCH EXPERIENCE OF LUND UNIVERSITY

3.1 The Sudan

Since the end of the 1970s, land degradation and desertification in East Africa, with special reference to The Sudan, has been studied at Lund University by a team of geographers, combining remote sensing techniques, extensive field observations, national climate, agricultural and population statistics, and spatial modelling.

In total, several hundred thousand square kilometres have been repeatedly observed by means of studying historical reports, rainfall observations, old maps, aerial photos and high and low-resolution satellite data combined with repeated field verification surveys (Hellden 1978, 1984, 1988, 1991; K. Olsson, 1985; L. Olsson, 1985, 1993; Ahlcrona, 1988).

We were not able to verify the commonly accepted paradigm of desertification and land degradation in Africa. We found that the importance of climatic impact on the productivity of the environment and the resilience of the arid and semi-arid ecosystems have been seriously overlooked. The local populations and environmental refugees of the Sahel region in Africa may be facing a climate change rather than the effects of man-made desertification. If so, a new strategy for sustainable development is urgently needed.

It was also indicated that important land productivity-degradation driving forces can be found in the socio-economy and policy sphere on different administrative/political and market levels (local, regional, national and global).
The different methods and technical approaches we used are summarized below.

3.2 Experience of assessment approaches

There is not one single indicator of dryland degradation or an approach to assess and study desertification. Land degradation has many faces (driving forces as well as symptoms) and can only be assessed and understood through a multidisciplinary study of the changing characteristics and integrated trends of a variety of biological, agricultural, physical and socio-economic indicators over a long time period and at a variety of spatial scales. An important indicator is the decreasing biomass productivity and production potential of the land.

Essential components included in our desertification studies including the following:
- *Climate assessment.* Assessment of climate over time, in a historic and modern time perspective, for a comparison with the indicators of degradation desertification.

- *Soil erosion and conservation.* Assessment of desertification rate and trends as indicated by modelled water runoff soil erosion and observed geomorphology and soil conservation measures over historic and modern time.
- *Regional biomass monitoring.* Assessment of regional green biomass distribution as an indicator of desertification in late modern time (1981-1998), through (NOAA/AVHRR) retrospective monitoring.
- *Land-use/land-cover change.* Assessment of the change of land cover, land use and agro-production as indicators, but also possible causes, of desertification over historic and modern time.
- *Land-use policy and socio-economy.* Assessment of changes in land resources policies, population pressure and socio-economic status, over historic and modern time, for a comparative analysis with indicators of desertification.
- *Integration and synthesis.* Comparative studies and a synthesis of the components listed to assess the dryland degradation status, trends and consequences for a formulation of policy implications.

3.3 Remote sensing and GIS

The status and rate of arid land degradation can be assessed through a monitoring (i.e., repeated assessments) approach referring to an established baseline. Availability of data on the spatial distribution of the supply, demand and consumption of natural resources over time is essential for an understanding of the complex drylands and the possible degradation of its production systems.

Technology development during the 1980s has offered new, and to some extent unique, possibilities to collect and analyze interesting environmental data. Remote sensing, when integrated with geographic information system (GIS) techniques and spatial modelling, and complemented with modern field data collection methods based on satellite-aided global positioning systems (GPS), provide important tools to support such a monitoring approach. In the case of national and regional environmental monitoring, there are no practical alternatives to the use of repeated satellite observations.

We have used a variety and combination of remotely sensed data, from high-resolution aerial photos and digital SPOT satellite data via medium resolution data (Landsat MSS and TM data), to low-resolution and high-frequency coverage data from the National Oceanic and Atmospheric Administration (NOAA) series of meteorological satellites for the time series analysis in our studies. Although all the remotely sensed data may have serious limitations, the combination of them all is a useful complement to the analysis of conventional statistics (e.g., demography, climate, agriculture) and other field-collected data of biophysical and socio-economic origin.

Whenever land use and land cover data are needed for retrospective analysis, historical remotely sensed data are often the only available data source. For land-use studies, high or medium-resolution data (e.g., aerial photos, SPOT or Landsat equivalent data) are usually needed for a meaningful categorization of the land. Manual interpretation of computer-processed satellite imagery, followed by a vectorization of category boundaries (i.e., normally five to ten land-use categories), is a useful approach to prepare the data for GIS processing.

We have used data from the Advanced Very High Resolution Radiometer (AVHRR) sensor onboard the NOAA satellite series for vegetation and drought-impact studies in Kenya, Ethiopia and The Sudan (Hellden, 1984; Hellden and Eklundh, 1988; Eklundh, 1996). The idea was to assess land degradation trends, as indicated by possible green biomass negative productivity anomalies, by means of the Normalized Difference Vegetation Index (NDVI). The NDVI is commonly used as an indicator of green plant biomass on global and continental scales.

It was found that there is a good correspondence between the spatial distribution of vegetation and average NDVI at low and medium-rainfall levels. However, analyses of the temporal relationships between AVHRR-NDVI and rainfall data have not been able to prove any strong relationships. This suggests that NOAA-NDVI data can be very useful for drought and vegetation mapping, but may be of limited value for monitoring purposes.

4. ONGOING RESEARCH IN AFRICA AND CENTRAL ASIA

Personnel at the Department of Physical Geography are presently engaged in desertification-related research in the Sahel, in south-west Africa and in northern China.

The Sahelian research focuses on regional ecosystem models and climate interactions. It is based on an European network cooperation (1995-97), coordinated from Lund University and includes laboratories from universities in Copenhagen, London, Wageningen and Louvain (1995-1997).

The research project in South-west Africa has been in preparation since 1994. It aims at a remote sensing-based assessment of land-use and land-cover change related to climate change and observed desertification over the past 40-100 years. It will be carried out between 1997 and 2000 by Lund University in cooperation with governmental agencies and universities in South Africa and Namibia.

The project on desertification in China was initiated during 1993/94 in cooperation with the Chinese Academy of Sciences. It presently focuses on the Horquin

Sandy Lands in Inner Mongolia and the Mu Shu Sandy Lands on the Ordos Plateau in the central part of northern China. Both areas are reported to suffer from severe desertification. The project aims at an understanding and documentation of the interrelationships between land resource policy decisions, land use and management, desertification and climate change in the major drylands of China. Remote sensing and GIS are important technology components.

References

Ahlcrona, E. 1988. The impact of climate and man on land transformation in central Sudan - applications of remote sensing. *Meddelanden Fran Lunds Universitets Geografiska Institutioner. Serie Avhandlingar,* Nr. 103. Lund University Press and Chartwell-Bratt Ltd.

Eklundh, L. 1996. AVHRR-NDVI for monitoring and mapping of vegetation and drought in East African environments. *Lunds Universitets Geografiska Institutioner, Avh. Nr. 126.* Lund University Press and Chartwell-Bratt Ltd.

Hellden, U. l978. Evaluation of Landsat-2 imagery for desertification studies in northern Kordofan, The Sudan. Lunds Universitet Naturgeografiska Institution (LUNI). *Rapporter och Notiser Nr. 38.*

Hellden, U. 1984. Drought impact monitoring- A remote sensing study of desertification in Kordofan, The Sudan. *Rapporter och Notiser Nr 61.* LUNI.

Hellden, U. 1988. Desertification monitoring - is the desert encroaching? *Desertification Control Bulletin,* No. 17, 1988. United Nations Environment Programme, pp. 8-12.

Hellden, U. 1991. Desertification-time for an assessment? *Ambio,* Vol. 20, No. 8, pp. 372-383.

Hellden, U., Eklundh, L. 1988. National drought-impact monitoring – A NOAA-NDVI and precipitation data study of Ethiopia. *Lund Studies in Geography.* Ser. C. No.15, Lund University Press and Chartwell-Bratt Ltd.

Olsson, K. 1985. Remote sensing for fuelwood resources and land degradation studies in Kordofan, Sudan. *Avhandlingar* C., Nr. 103. LUNI. Lund University Press and Chartwell-Bratt Ltd.

Olsson, L. 1985. An integrated study of desertification - applications of remote sensing, GIS and spatial models in semi-arid Sudan. *Lund Studies in Geography Ser. C.,* No. 13. (doctoral thesis).

Olsson, L. 1993. On the causes of famine: drought, desertification and market failure in The Sudan. *Ambio,* Vol 2. pp. 395-404.

Monitoring dryland degradation to define and implement suitable measures towards sustainable rangeland management

4

R. Geerken, M. Ilaiwi, M. Jaja, H. Kauffmann,
H. Roeder, A.M. Sankary and K. Segl

Synopsis

The paper discusses the possibilities and constraints of extracting information from satellite data for the definition of proper strategies to combat and to monitor desertification. It gives prospects for future possibilities with sensor systems of higher spatial resolution (MOMS-02), or covering other spectral ranges (ERS-1). The significance of the human component is considered along with the role of remote sensing in acquiring information. The process of introducing collected information into a decision-finding process, and conflicts created among concerned parties, will be outlined using the steppe region of Syria as an example.

Key points
1. *Basic information for the definition of action plans and for implementing field measures can, in part, be interpreted from satellite data. Specifically, information related to the vegetation cover, sand accumulation, and soil classification is often derived. Depending on the spectral and spatial resolution of the images, this information can be extracted with greater or lesser accuracy. This paper discusses the problems of identifying named categories in semi-arid areas.*
2. *Apart from the physical information about degraded areas, increasing interest is focused on retrieving information about the population of humans and livestock. The traditional way, via the collection of information from field surveys, is a rather time-consuming process. Alternative means are being sought. Discussion centres on the role of satellite remote sensing and the feasibility of using it as a means to obtain some of the information. The processing techniques needed to do this are also examined.*

3. *This paper briefly outlines some steps required to feed the information into a decision-finding process involving all concerned parties: politicians, scientific experts and the affected population.*
4. *Conflicts of interest between concerned parties can influence the successful implementation of measures. Traditional (and modern) constraints of the nomads might also prevent them from cooperating. Many disciplines need to be involved in order to tackle the manifold problems of desertification and land degradation.*

1. INTRODUCTION

The continuous increase of desertification and degradation in semi-arid lands in Third World countries is the result of rapid population growth, the availability of modern techniques and technologies for land cultivation, as well as the loss of traditional habits and changes in traditional land use. These major factors are additionally influenced by political and economic regulations, lack of awareness among concerned parties, and the non-availability of information about the current situation in the affected areas.

In order to combat desertification sustainably, an integrated approach is required that deals with all the above issues. It is a major concern of desertification projects that have been established either on an institutional or on a ministerial level to work on all these aspects, but the issue of population growth is discussed at a higher level. Even if this main causative factor is not considered, there is still a wealth of possible actions to alleviate and improve the impact of land degradation.

In this context, the Arab Centre for the Studies of Arid Zones and Dry Lands (ACSAD), in cooperation with the German Agency for Technical Cooperation (GTZ), is currently carrying out a project for improved desertification combating strategies in the Syrian steppe. During a later stage, this will be transferred to other Arab countries.

2. DEVELOPMENT OF LAND DEGRADATION IN THE BISHRI MOUNTAINS

The Bishri Mountains (Mts) and their adjacent lowlands make up a great part of the Syrian steppe. They receive an average annual rainfall of 160 mm (Colour Plate 1) and can be classified as semi-arid lands. These are traditionally used as grazing areas during the wet season. Except for a few permanent settlers, the Bedouins are used to leaving these areas during summer, moving to grazing areas of moderate temperatures and higher rainfall.

The first known degradation in the area started with the cutting of trees for charcoal production during the first half of this century. Since afforestation was not practised, most parts of the area by the end of the 1940s were completely cut and habitats of various wild animal species (e.g., gazelles, antelopes) had been destroyed.

The situation became even more serious in the 1970s when, as a consequence of the increase in population, cultivable land along the River Euphrates and north of it became scarce and cultivation moved into the marginal lands. Even though barley planting in the drylands was also commonly practised during ancient times, the impacts on soil erosion could be neglected since it was restricted to only small areas. Nowadays, due to the increase of population and the availability of modern machinery, huge parts of the best grazing land, preferably in the higher, central region, are being used for barley planting. In addition, the ploughing activities destroy the thin, fragile soil cover and expose it to wind and water erosion, especially in the periods immediately after sowing (November, December) and after harvesting (May, June). Areas dismantled of their original soil cover now reveal barren, gypsic rocks or gypsiferous soil layers. In the lowlands, the eroded materials are sedimented, forming moving sand sheets, nebkha dunes and barchans. The situation was additionally aggravated by economic regulations at the end of the 1980s, when agricultural productivity was to be increased, which was only possible by further expansion into the marginal lands.

The combination of cutting fuelwood, the use of heavy agricultural machinery, cross-country driving, cultivation, and overgrazing lead to degradation on a tremendous scale (Colour Plate 2). Visible environmental effects are soil erosion, accumulations of eolian sands, decrease of vegetation density, loss of plant diversity and destruction of animal habitats. Between 1985 and 1993, the loss in grazing areas was estimated to be about 350 km^2.

In order to initiate proper measures to arrest these processes, relevant information was collected not only to analyze the current situation and on that basis formulate combating strategies, but also to sensitize the population, decision-makers and politicians.

3. FIELDS OF ACTIVITY

For sustainable success, the project is working on different issues. Apart from analyzing remotely sensed data to be described later in this paper, major concern is focused on the local population.

3.1 Socio-economics

The Bishri Mountain Bedouins can no longer be described as nomads. Most own houses along the Euphrates where they stay during the hot season. However, during the rainy season from November to May/June, the Bedouins move into the Bishri Mountains for grazing sheep and planting barley. Running two households comprises additional costs. To cover expenses people have had to expand or find new sources of income that mainly involve selling sheep, milk, barley (distinct tribes only), and, to a minor extent, selling handicrafts (Figure 4.1) (Roeder, 1995; Pape-Christiansen et al., 1995). Barley is also needed for self-sufficiency, especially for preparing bread and feeding animals.

Figure 4.1

Major income sources (left) and expenditures (right) of Bedouins from the Bishri Mts. area

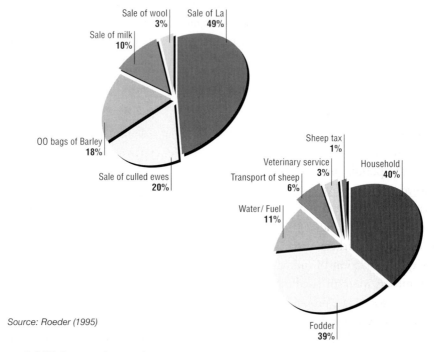

Source: Roeder (1995)

3.2 Water requirements

Since water is scarce, the local population is calling on the Government to provide them with additional wells. The provision of these wells, however, will have negative impacts on rehabilitation measures. Unlimited water provision, in combination with moveable water tanks, allows the population to stay longer than usual and shortens the period for recovery of vegetation. As an alternative, the project is promoting a more efficient use of surface water (e.g., dams, cisterns) that can act as a natural regulative for the Bedouin's residential time in the steppe areas.

3.3 Animals

Increasing flock sizes and their need for fodder puts additional pressure on the steppe areas (Wachholtz et al., 1993). Feeding behaviour, migration patterns, and residential times are analyzed to optimize pastoral land use. Practices like the shredding of spiny plants and others are tested to increase fodder availability in the area and to decrease costs for fodder purchase (Figure 4.1).

3.4 Cutting fuelwood

Cutting fuelwood, mainly done by female family members, causes additional destabilization of the soil, since shrubs are usually uplifted together with their roots. Shrubs are cut with no regard for their nutrient value (e.g., as sheep fodder), or for their protective value for the ground. The introduction of gas stoves, although mostly desired by the female population, is still slight due to costs. Selective cutting of non-palatable shrubs is practised only by a minority, but is continuously spreading among Bedouin families.

3.5 Extension service

A successful implementation of combating measures depends on successful co-operation with the local population. Extension workers have to facilitate and enable the population to act according to an agreed upon combating strategy. However, a proper extension service has not yet been established for the steppe areas. At the present time, the project is carrying out training courses on participatory approaches and communication techniques, in oder to change the role of the extension workers from a controlling function to an advisory one. This activity naturally requires a clear commitment from the Government to support such initiatives.

3.6 Rehabilitation measures

For active rehabilitation, the Syrian Ministry for Agriculture and Agrarian Reform (MAAR) prohibited any cultivation in the drylands and carefully surveys its adherence. Selected areas are being revegetated by using different techniques (e.g., seedlings, seeds), in combination with erosion protection measurements such as setting up sand barriers (e.g., gabions) in wadis in the upper parts of the Bishri Mountains to fix the sand material and stop its downhill transport.

The role of the nomadic population is still a passive one since necessary figures on population densities and their distribution, stocking rates, carrying capacity and grazing potential are either unknown or incomplete. Improved information is expected from satellite data evaluations.

4. REMOTE SENSING TECHNIQUES IN COMBATING DESERTIFICATION

The decision to use one or another information source for basic data collection related to desertification processes is based on such criteria as costs, time and the reliability of information. Some of the major advantages of remotely sensed data are the nearly real-time provision of information, regular updates, the coverage of large areas, low man-power, and the more objective interpretation by using processing routines.

In reality, most processes, relationships, causes, reasons, trends and extent of desertification in the Bishri Mountains can directly be seen from a properly processed TM colour composite, without any additional sophisticated data processing. It also reveals where particular kinds of erosion protection measures can be successfully applied and where combating measures are useless. The image clearly shows the starting point of the sand material in the central Bishri Mountains, its linear transport down to the plains, and where it is being distributed by west to east directed winds after leaving the wind-protected valleys. Physical combating measures appear most promising in the central part where the problem is concentrated in the wadis. In the plains, where sand material is being aerialy distributed, efficient combating measures are no longer realistic.

4.1 Relevant phenomena and their detectability via remotely sensed data

Even though most phenomena are qualitatively visualized by the colour composites, decision-makers expect precise figures and facts about degradation processes that require further data processing.

An attempt was made to classify some desertification relevant targets, according to their detectability and the quality of achieved results. Valued phenomena are listed in Table 4.1. The feasibility column gives a semi-quantitative valuation with which the phenomena can be described from satellite data interpretation.

4.1.1 Vegetation

The mapping of vegetation covers that is generally accepted and usually practised in humid areas, turns out to be rather difficult in semi-arid regions. Limiting factors are the sparse vegetation coverage, the typical low proportion of leaves of steppe plants producing only weak spectral signals, and the insufficient multitemporal comparability. The latter is greatly influenced by the prevailing weather conditions shortly before data acquisition.

In computer simulations, the minimum detectable vegetation coverage was calculated at 20%. The value varies with plant species, water availability, and background reflectance. Common densities in Syrian steppe areas, however, are between 1 and 10%. At given densities, spectral signatures are dominated by the soils, which prevents any realistic estimation of biomass indices (Normalized Difference Vegetation Index, NDVI) for natural vegetation covers from VNIR bands.

Table 4.1

Desertification phenomena and identification possibilities from remotely sensed data evaluated from the Bishri Mountain area

Target	Phenomenon		Spectral VNIR [5]	Spectral SWIR [6]	HR-pan [2]	Mwave [3]	3-D	Rep Cov [4]	Acq.Date	Feasibility [1]
Vegetation	Distribution		x					3	Apr-May	3
	Biomass		x					3	#	2
	Differentiation	Irrig. fields	x		x			6	#	5
		Rainfield	x	x	x			3	#	3
		Natural	x	x		InSAR [6]		3	#	1
		Wadi	x		x			3	#	3
	Species / Type		x	x				3		0
Rocks / Soils	Lithology			x	x				Sept	4
	Outcrops		x		x	SAR		6	#	4
	Soils		x	x					#	3
	Eolian Sands		x	x		InSAR		3	#	4
Topography	Morphology					InSAR	x	1	Sept	5
	Relief					InSAR	x		#	5
	Micro-Catchm.					InSAR	x		#	5
	Drainage P.		x	x	x			6	Apr-May	5
	Catchment A.		x	x	x				#	5
	Dam Sites		x	x	x				#	4
Population	Camp Sites				x			1	Apr-May	4
Flocks	Pop. Density				x				#	Stats.
	Stocking R.				x				#	Stats.
Climate	Rainfall									NA
	Wind	Speed								NA
		Direction	x	x						5
	Temperature								July	1,TM-6
	Evapotransp.									NA

1/ Ranking from 0 (not detectable) to 5 (excellent)
2/ High resolution panchromatic
3/ Micro Wave
4/ Required repitition coverage
5/ Visible and Near infrared, Short wave infrared
6/ SWIR (interferometry, Side-Looking Aperture Radar)
Source: Unpublished

An estimation of degradation degrees from NDVI values is additionally affected by errors introduced due to the non-detectability of plant species. Some kinds of severely degraded areas, in contrast to non-degraded areas, show a much denser vegetation cover. However, these areas are composed of spiny invaders and non-palatable species. Biomass values calculated from these areas imply relatively good conditions for an actually degraded area, an error that can only be avoided by combining its results with evaluations of eolian sand covers and/or field check.

A reliable vegetation signal is produced by the barley fields (the result of illegal rainwater harvesting practices), enabling the monitoring of their development and especially the surveillance of their setting aside. High-resolution panchromatic data can support their identification by enhancing field structures. Less dense barley fields, as well as the few natural vegetation covers of higher densities, could only be separated when implying the SWIR bands in data processing.

Vegetation is a rather sensitive indicator for desertification and degradation processes. However, a sufficiently reliable retrieval of information on vegetation from remote sensing data is impossible unless monitoring intervals for NDVI calculation are narrowed down to intervals of two weeks, as recommended by Tucker et al., (1991).

4.1.2 Rocks/soils (eolian sand)

The background material (i.e., original surface) in the Bishri Mountains area is composed mainly of silty soils with sometimes a little clay and varying gypsum content. In places, the silt is covered by pebbles of chert, limestone or gypsum of different grain size (1 to 2 cm and up to 15 cm) to different extents.

Wind-transported sand is composed of quartz particles of grain sizes between 0.5 and 0.8 mm. They form a distinct spectral signal that allows discrimination of the slightest accumulations of sand that can be visualized best in colour composites, including one of the SWIR bands. Already, extremely thin layers (1 to 2 mm) of sand covering the silt to an extent of around 20% (or even less), produce a pronounced spectral signal. This allows the detection of sand accumulations, its dynamics and trends already in the incipient stages. Furthermore, the multitemporal appearance of eolian sands is less affected by outer conditions (i.e., rainfall, season) than vegetation. It therefore appears to be a more reliable indicator, and a much more suitable target, for satellite-based monitoring of degradation processes in the drylands.

Evaluations for eolian sands based on optical data (e.g., VNIR, SWIR range) allow a good delineation of different stages of sand accumulation. Monitoring of greater changes in time are also feasible once the data are precisely calibrated.

In order to monitor changes within shorter periods (to validate effects of implemented combating measures), subtle variations in accumulation heights (i.e., cm-range) can be detected with interferometric methods from SAR data.

4.1.3 Census data

Data on nomadic populations (e.g., number, whereabouts, migration patterns) are rarely collected, and where available, are rather doubtful. The inaccessibility of their living areas and the lack of sufficient numbers of qualified staff for raising data result in only fragmentary information.

New sensor systems, with spatial resolutions of up to 5 m, for the first time allow a satellite-based collection of census data. Tents of sizes usually used by the nomads can be detected as long as they are in pronounced contrast to their environment. Non-detectable Bedouin homes are those permanent buildings that were constructed from building material found in the area and do not contrast with the environment.

In the example of a township in Zimbabwe, a combined classification scheme was applied making use of spectral and shape features (Segl, 1995). With increasing spatial resolution of satellite systems, many objects can be better separated by their individual shape characteristics than by their spectral information. The extraction of shapes requires firstly an image segmentation and secondly a shape extraction (Segl, 1995). The shape information, together with the information retrieved from common multispectral classifications, are commonly evaluated. For this purpose, a modular classification scheme had been elaborated based on the combination of multispectral (spectral features) and panchromatic data (shape features). The final information fusion is performed by an artificial neural network.

4.2 Information extracted from satellite data: procedures and results

Not all of the following processing techniques may be important or applicable to all kinds of degraded areas in the same way. Evaluation and processing techniques need to be adapted where reflectance of major surface categories differ. However, many surface categories and inherent problems presented in this paper will be encountered in many semi-arid areas that are affected by desertification.

Main surface categories encountered in the Bishri Mountain area can be summarized as aridisols, eolian sand (mainly quartzitic), gypsum and vegetation. With respect to the already mentioned dominating surface categories, interest was focused on the detection of vegetation, eolian sand and gypsiferous surfaces and how their distribution change in time. This activity aimed to derive trends of development and to analyze relationships among them or their interaction with socio-economic data.

4.2.1 Image calibration

For a comparison of the images taken in 1985 and 1993 respectively, images were calibrated with the "empirical line method" to absolute reflectance. This was to eliminate any outer influences or radiometric differences (e.g., atmospheric, sun elevation, sensor specific) that might be responsible for differing conditions during data acquisition. After optimum calibration, changes extracted from the calibrated images can be attributed to true changes in surface conditions.

For the calibration process, various samples from homogeneous surfaces were collected. Suitable surfaces are those that are not submitted to changes in time, especially with respect to their spectral appearance (e.g., rock outcrops). Since the correlation between lab-measured reflectance and satellite-acquired digital numbers (DNs) is not linear, the sampling plots were chosen representing surfaces of different albedo (i.e., light, intermediate, and dark). From the lab-measured spectra and image-extracted spectra (after haze correction), the calibration factors were calculated for each band and for each selected area that were used for calculating the mean calibration factor (Table 4. 2).

Table 4.2

Calibration factors for the haze corrected TM-images 172/36, acquired on 13/6/93 and 25/7/85 (calibraton to absolute reflectance)

TM - image	TM - band					
	#1	#2	#3	#4	#5*	#7
mean calibration factor 93	0.8190	1.3311	1.0040	1.1796	0.7819	1.1559
mean calibration factor 85	0.8550	1.4039	1.0260	1.1968	0.7982	1.1894

Source: Unpublished
* not considered for processing due to data overflow

Problems encountered during calibration were: the non-availability of data from desired acquisition dates; the compared data differing in acquisition date for one month; and the 93-image showing severe striping and haze that could not be removed. These factors negatively influenced calibration and prevented better results.

4.2.2 Calculation of biomass

Agricultural activities within the Bishri Mountains is one factor triggering desertification processes in the area. To visualize this relationship, efforts were focused on the identification of vegetation covers separated into naturally vegetated areas and areas under cultivation, both of which were evaluated for different acquisition dates.

A measure for the biomass is the Normalized Difference Vegetation Index (NDVI), a quotient calculated from the infrared band (TM-4) and the red band

(TM-3). This provides good results for areas of high biomass such as the irrigated fields along the River Euphrates, but does not allow for distinguishing sparsely, naturally-vegetated areas or some rainfed agricultural fields from highly reflecting eolian sand, a constellation commonly encountered in the drylands. Detectable areas of natural vegetation show densities between 15 to 30%. Detectable barley fields planted as rainfed agricultural fields provide similar DNs for the NDVI, despite their higher coverage degree lying between 40 and 60%. This was attributed to the late acquisition date of data where plants, especially barley, were already submitted to considerable water stress and was also due to species-specific reflectance peculiarities.

The wide range of coincidence of sand and vegetation in their NDVI-values required a different approach to separate vegetated areas in the drylands. Distinct differences are visible in the water absorption bands, especially TM-band 7[1] (Figure 4.2). The slight water contents stored in the biomass indices distinguished absorptions. For the final result, a combination of the NDVI and the ratio 4/7 was used. In combination, they provided good results for both densely and sparsely vegetated areas.

Vegetation cover in the Bishri Mountains of less than about 20% density[1] are not to be identified by use of TM-data. This applies to most naturally vegetated areas, not only in the Bishri Mountains, but also in the whole Syrian steppe.

To get a better idea of natural vegetation cover, intensive field checks were carried out and isolines for vegetation densities were constructed. Sample points will be regularly rechecked (i.e., three-years intervals) and the point net will be narrowed down in places.

4.2.3 Sand distribution and sand accumulation

As already mentioned, the multitemporal evaluation of the distribution of eolian sands is less affected by the acquisition dates or the weather conditions (rainfall) prevailing during the days before data recording. Its results (visual interpretation or computer-supported) give a clearer idea about extent distribution and trends of degradation. The colour saturation allows estimatation of the severity of sand accumulation which can be monitored even more accurately with interferometric methods. Potentially endangered areas are also highlighted. Sand encroachment is progressing to the south-east propelled by north-westerly and south-easterly directed winds. In the north-west the sand is blown around the Bishri Mountains which form an obstacle that is being bypassed (Colour Plate 2).

1/   The value might be modified by parameters like plant species, leaf structure, leaf density, water stress and others.

Figure 4.2

A separation of vegetated areas based on the calculation of NDVI values is only possible for the irrigated fields located along the River Euphrates. Reflectance of eolian sand and sparse vegetation, however, are too similar in bands 3 and 4 to allow any separation. The only differences can be seen in band 5 and 7, from which band 7 was used to calculate the ratio 4/7. The final result was calculated from a combination of the two ratios.

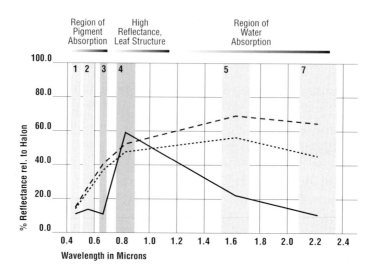

		NDVI = $\dfrac{\#4 - \#3}{\#4 + \#3}$	Ratio = $\dfrac{\#4}{\#7}$
Irrigated Fields	– – – – –	0.647	5.500
Rainfed Agric.	··········	0.134	1.085
Eolian Sand	————	0.120	0.813

During multitemporal classification (i.e., change detection) of eolian sands, the described calibration results negatively influenced the comparability of sand-cover classes. In addition, once areas are covered by a thin layer of eolian sand they provide improved growing conditions for some palatable and especially non-palatable species, which may suggest an improvement of the vegetation cover or a decrease in eolian sands, respectively. Both affect the calculation of sand-covered areas shown in Table 4.3. Errors introduced by vegetation could be better ruled out by choosing images taken at the end of the dry period.

5. CONCLUSIONS AND FURTHER ACTIVITIES

In order to combat desertification processes in the Bishri Mountains more efficiently, more detailed information about its settlers (e.g., the number, distribution and migration) is needed. Necessary information would be retrieved from

Table 4.3

Changes in sand coverage between 1985 and 1993, as visually interpreted from Thematic Mapper satellite data

Sand Coverage / Year	1985	1993	Difference
Moderate (km²)	1084.02	997.95	- 86.07
Severe (km²)	504.51	1024.18	+ 519.67
Very severe (km²)	229.30	170.59	- 58.71
Total area covered by eolian sand (km²)	1817.83	2192.72	+ 374.89
Total monitored area (km²)	9724	9724	0

Source: Unpublished

spatially high-resolving panchromatic data (IRS-1, MoMS-02) acquired during the Bedouin's main residential period in April to May.

The distribution of camp sites (from which a rough estimate of the number of animals can be derived), together with the grazing potential of the area, would allow for the elaboration of grazing plans, with grazing and fallow cycles. Regular animal surveys are targeted to optimize animal feeding and to analyze the possibility of shortening the residential period for Bedouins in the area. This could extend the recovery time of vegetation and prevent further overgrazing. Successful implementation, however, is greatly dependent on an efficient extension service as well as the Bedouin's willingness to cooperate. The local population still sticks firmly to traditional and tribal habits and rules, especially where land use and land ownership are concerned.

Preference should be given to natural rehabilitation practices since the potential is there and because the costs for artificial recultivation are high. Planting of shrubs and throwing of seeds should only be applied to areas where successful implementation can be expected or immediate soil fixation is required. As regards planting shrubs, emphasis should be given to depressions where water availability is higher and growing conditions are most favourable. Identification of these micro-catchments is being undertaken with interferometric methods. In particular, planting of seedlings proved to be too expensive due to the necessary nurseries, machinery and field staff. In addition, seedlings require twice the amount of which irrigation can hardly be implemented by nomads.

There are commitments from several Bedouin families for direct seeding in cases where seeds have been provided by the government. Even though this is as yet untested for feasibility, it does not seem realistic to expect that nomads would play an active role in afforestation or re-greening activities except in some smaller areas. Indeed, a real active participation by nomads is not to be expected unless in range management where people need to be trained in such issues as indicators that signal when an area should be left before it is overgrazed or proper fuel-wood-cutting techniques.

References

Geerken, R., Ilaiwi, M., Sankary, M.N., Askar, M., Geerken, E., Aloul, M., Katlan, B.,

Ibrahim, S., Al Imam, N., (in press) *Remote sensing and GIS as a planning tool for the definition of strategies for combating desertification.* The International Conference on Desert Development in the Arab Gulf Countries, Kuwait, 23-26 March 1996.

Lechtenberger, Ch. and Kaufmann, H., 1995. *The use of MOMS-02 data for population statistics in developing countries: Chitungwlza/Zimbabwe.* Proceedings of the MOMS-02 Symposium, Cologne, Germany, 5-7 July 1995. pp. 347-353.

Roeder, H., 1995. *Socio-economic studies in the Bishri Mountains.* Internal Project Report. (not published).

Segl, K., 1995. *Classification of MOMS-02 image data using spectral and shape features.* Proceedings of the MOMS-02 Symposium. Cologne, Germany, 5-7 July 1995. pp. 315-321.

Sankary, M.N., 1995. (in press) *Rangeland ecology, rehabilitation and improvement in Syria.* International Workshop on intensification and Desertification - Challenges in Marginal and High Potential Areas in Syria. University of Hohenheim, 18-22 September, 1995.

Pape-Christiansen, A., Doppler, W., and Nordblom, T.L., 1995. (in press) *The contribution of women to labour and decision-making processes in Bedouin farming systems in northern Syria.* ICARDA Regional Symposium on Integrated Crop-Livestock Systems in the Dry Areas of West Asia and North Africa. Amman. 6-8 November 1995.

Tucker, C.J., Newcomb, W.W., Los S.O., and Prince, S.D., 1991b. Mean and inter-year variation of growing normalized difference vegetation index for the Sahel 1981-1989. *International Journal of Remote Sensing* 12(6):113-1135.

Wachholtz, R., Nordblom, T.L., and Arab, G., 1993. *Characterization of round-year sheep feeding and grazing calendars of Bedouin flocks in the NW Syrian Steppe:* the Pasture, Forage and Livestock Programme. ICARDA Annual Report 1Q92. Aleppo. pp. 215-233.

Impact of development programmes on deterioration of rangeland resources in some African and Middle Eastern countries

M. A. El-Shorbagy

5

Synopsis

This paper discusses the impact of some "unbalanced" development programmes on the degradation of rangeland resources in Africa, the Middle East and Southwest Asia. Causes of failure in rangelands development are discussed and the lessons learned are outlined. Recommendations for more effective range development policies are included.

Key Points

1. By the end of the twentieth century, the rangelands of most African and Middle Eastern countries have been subjected to extraordinary pressures. This is reflected in an obvious degradation of rangeland resources and increasing desertification hazards. Much current academic and political interest has focused on these problems, and many people are interpreting these problems as the result of over-use and mismanagement of vegetation and livestock by traditional pastoralists.

2. During the last four decades, awareness of the need to develop and restore the rangelands of these countries has increased and has been expressed in many development activities. Various programmes and projects with general and specific objectives were carried out in some rangeland areas located in various ecological zones. Some programmes were simple with only a few components, while others were very ambitious and involved some packages with the following components: establishing regulations and by-laws on rangeland utilization, and protection (grazing rotations); artificial revegetation; digging boreholes for permanent water supply; sedentarizing nomads; veterinary care; constructing water harvesting and water spreading facilities; establishment of feed reserves; creating pastoral and fattening cooperatives; and subsidizing feeds and livestock production.

3. *Reviewing the outputs of many of these development programmes showed largely disappointing results when judged by the criteria of improving forage production, the economic rate of return, the welfare of nomads and the conservation of range-land resources.*

4. *Evaluation of development policies carried out in some African and Middle Eastern countries during the last four decades demonstrated that the policies themselves are the root cause of many difficulties and problems encountered in range-lands and that these policies themselves have contributed to the deterioration of range resources and the acceleration of desertification hazards.*

1. INTRODUCTION

A large portion of the earth's land surface is classified as rangeland. Rangeland ecosystems include deserts, shrublands, grasslands and open forests and only exclude commercial forests, cultivated lands, ice-covered regions and areas covered by solid bare rocks. These rangelands amount to nearly 50% of the earth's land surface and are considered the primary land type of the world. Based on data from the FAO Yearbook of Production (1994), 11% of the land in the world is farmed; 26% is in permanent pasture and 32% is forest and woodland; and deserts, glaciated areas, high mountain peaks and urbanized/industrialized land comprise the other 31% (Tables 5.1 and 5.2). Although exact estimates vary, the total land covered by concrete (e.g., houses, cities, highways) is between 3 and 4% (Holechek et al.,1989). FAO (1994) defines permanent pasture as land used for five years (or more) for herbaceous forage crops, either cultivated or growing wild. However, these data do not include vast areas of land classified as forests, woodland, deserts and tundra that fall into the "other land" category and are, in many cases, grazed by livestock herds. If all the land resources presently grazed by domestic animals and all the uncultivated land with the potential to support livestock is taken into account, rangelands comprise about 70% of the earth's land area, of which a major part lies within the world's dry regions. On a worldwide basis, rangelands contribute to 70% and over 95% of the feed needs of domestic and wildlife ruminants, respectively (ARPAC, 1975).

African and Southwest Asian countries contain a substantial portion of the world's arid and semi-arid rangelands which are highly diverse in climate, land forms and vegetation. These rangelands are characterized by their high spatial and temporal variability in precipitation which directly affect their production. Forage for livestock is their primary contribution, providing between 60 and 85% of the total feed needs of their domestic ruminants. Some rangeland values go far beyond grazing to include water, food, fuel, recreation and antiquities.

Drought is a common feature of the region's rangelands and pastoralists

Table 5.1

Land use of the world, 1994 (1000 ha).

Regions	Land area	Arable perma. crop	Perm. pasture	Forest and woodland	Other land
Africa	2,963,611	187,887	852,595	760,788	1,161,727
N. & C.America	2,178,176	271,447	362,059	855,414	689,256
S. America	1,752,925	102,767	495,251	846,380	308,227
Asia	2,679,013	468,661	800,062	535,493	875,021
Europe	472,625	136,005	79,841	158,448	93,402
Oceania	845,349	51,500	427,894	199,965	165,990
USSR(the former)	2,195,070	231,540	325,200	983,000	650,330
Total	*10,980,243	1,447,509	3,361,733	4,179,808	4,127,014

Source: FAO Yearbook of Production, (1994) vol.48
* The correct value is approximately 13,000,000 (1000ha) = 13 x 10 ha
= 13,000,000,000 ha.

Table 5.2

Land use of the world, 1994 (1000 ha).

Regions	Farm land	Permanent pastuureland	Forestland Woodland	Rangeland (total estimated potentially grazeable land)
Africa	6	26	24	69
Europe	30	18	33	55
N. & C.America	13	17	32	66
Oceania	5	56	18	66
S.America	8	26	53	72
USSR (the former)	10	17	21	62
China	11	31	13	77
India	57	4	23	35
World	11	24	31	70

Source: Holechek et al., 1989

(i.e., nomads, transhumants and settlers) are highly adapted to variable water deficits and shortage of forage supplies. However, for thousands of years these rangelands had traditionally supported some extensive forms of animal production, somewhat in harmony with the indigenous wildlife population and the more intensive cropping systems of adjacent higher potential lands. The functioning and survival of range systems of these countries are dependent on complex interrelationships between people, domestic animals, vegetation, other wild organisms and the physical environment. Similarly, the ability of pastoralists to survive in these marginal lands is attributed to their opportunistic mobility, their large numbers of animals and diversified livestock husbandry, as well as a wide spectrum of adaptive strategies. Some of these strategies are ecologically based, while others depend upon socio-economic relations.

The regions in question are characterized by the predominance of communal rangelands which are equally available to the herds and flocks of all members of the community, and are utilized and managed by nomads and transhumants according to agreed roles and traditions. In drought years, accessibility to communal grazing could be granted to neighbouring tribes or groups and the donors of such a grant receive, in return, an equal treatment when the need arises (Zaroug, 1985).

For centuries, traditional livestock movement from dry to wet season or from low to high-altitude ranges formed a simple but very efficient rotation, in which pastures are utilized for a specific period then livestock are moved to another season's pasture. The availability of water from temporary dugouts, natural ponds and springs, the occurrence of biting insects and the prevalence of low temperature govern the period for which livestock utilize forage in a particular site. Hence rangeland plants in different sites have a rest period that allows them to recover, store carbohydrates needed for regrowth and set seed.

At the turn of the century, rangelands of most African, Middle Eastern and Southwest Asian countries had been subjected to extraordinary pressures due to the obvious increase of human and livestock population, which caused an obvious degradation of range resources (Tables 5.3, 5.4 and 5.5). During the last four decades, many development projects and various activities (based on technology and range management principles developed in the more advanced countries) had been carried out in the regions to solve degradation problems and restore range resources. Unfortunately, most of these projects failed to overcome the problems and failure was attributed to many different reasons.

Table 5.3

Population of the world, 1980 -1994 (thousands)

	Africa	N.& C. America	S. America	Asia	Europe	Oceania	USSR (the former)	World
1980	475664	370870	240029	2586528	483467	22687	265085	4444331
1985	548800	396404	266535	2842584	490521	24457	276662	4845962
1990	632678	424423	293131	3120139	499655	26429	288362	5284808
1992	6699627	436671	303799	3227911	502916	27269	-	5458981
1993	688783	443131	309134	3280493	504179	27696	-	5544612
1994	708285	448973	314465	3333188	505502	28123	-	5630240

Source: FAO Yearbook of Production, 1994. vol. 48.

Table 5.4

Growth and density of the human population in various parts of the world, 1985

Regions	% Net Growth per year	Doubling time years	Population per km²
Africa	2.9	24	19
Europe	0.3	233	101
N. & C. America	0.9	78	12
Oceania	1.5	47	3
S. America	2.4	29	15
USSR (the former)	0.9	78	12
China	1.8	39	108
India	2.2	32	234
World	1.7	41	36

Source: Holechek et al., 1989.

Table 5.5

Livestock numbers of the world and Africa, 1979 - 1994 (thousands)

	1979-81	1992	1993	1994	1979-81	1992	1993	1994
Horses	59499	60738	59592	58158	3671	4688	4763	4758
Mules	13357	15004	15066	14952	1499	1403	1421	1394
Asses	38266	43676	43688	43772	11585	13271	13340	13408
Cattle	1218136	1281376	1281606	1288124	172011	189658	189244	192180
Buffalo	121665	147485	148475	148798	2346	3165	3466	3200
Camels	17042	18625	18632	18831	12667	13580	13632	13815
Pigs	778811	864673	869537	875407	10114	18923	20484	21080
Sheep	1088794	1133372	109604	1086661	180465	206843	205785	208845
Goats	456380	581317	592874	609488	138228	168452	171468	176089

Source: FAO Yearbook of Production, (1994). vol.48

Evaluation of the outputs of these projects showed that the development policy itself is the main root cause of many difficulties and problems encountered in the rangelands of the regions. This development policy brought on many changes and innovations that upset previous ecological constraints on traditional husbandry and further added to the process of overstocking and overgrazing.

This paper will focus on the impact of selected development projects on rangeland resources in some African and Southwest Asian countries. The sometimes depressing results of development projects, as well as recommendations for more effective range development policy, are included.

2. DEVELOPMENT POLICY AND ITS IMPACT ON RANGELANDS DEGRADATION

The ecological degradation of natural resources of some African and Southwest Asian countries can be traced back to the colonial empires of the Romans, Ottomans and European countries. However, when Libya became an Italian colony, the Ancient Romans were often extolled as an ideal example of how humans could make desert regions fertile by a judicious combination of investment and wise government. Recent changes in the way history is viewed in parts of North Africa indicates that the Romans could now be cited as a prime example of how colonial exploitation can destroy the agriculture potential of overseas possessions (Dannell, 1982). In ancient literature, the degraded Mediterranean coastal zone of Egypt (always called "the bread basket of the Roman Empire"), and parts of Syria, provide further historical evidence of Roman exploitation and destruction of natural resources. Similarly, some ancient documents indicate that the Ottoman and European empires exploited forest resources of the region for their military and civil purposes, owned fertile agriculture land and pushed farmers and pastoralists to marginal areas. The political boundaries of most African and Arab countries (mostly imposed by European politicians) that do not correspond to the ecological and/or social boundaries, still cause many conflicts, problems and difficulties in the utilization and management of natural resources, particularly, water, forest and rangeland resources (El-Shorbagy, 1996).

The first awareness of ecological degradation can be traced back to the nineteenth century. The convention that degradation cannot be allowed to continue appeared only in the 1950s, when the international development effort got underway and the limits of the world's capacity to produce food to satisfy anticipated levels of demand became evident (Spooner, 1982). That development effort was based on the very simple assumption that increased production and improved health and well-being could be induced by the injection of investment and the transfer of technology into existing low-growth systems of production (i.e., in the Third World). Implicit in this matter was the related assumption that such degradation was caused by the traditional system that development was designed to transform. The assumption of unlimited growth potential in the Third World became very common during the 1960s and 1970s, even within United Nations' organizations. In 1977, for example, the then Director-General of FAO announced in Moshi, Tanzania that he could see around him abundant resources awaiting exploitation - resources that could make the region self-sufficient in food. At that time, assumptions such as abundant resources and unlimited growth potential in the Third World had been politically attractive because it avoided North - South conflict over the international distribution of food and land (Schulz, 1982). In the same period, other attractive assumptions related to international agricultural development policy (particularly for rangelands) had emerged and were accepted on a worldwide basis. Examples of such assumptions included: (i) industrialization (e.g., mechanization, chemical fertilizers and pesticides) increases agricultural production; (ii) cultivation of crops is a more highly evolved and specialized form of livelihood than pastoralism; (iii) ranching systems of cattle and sheep are more productive and profitable than herding; (iv) goats are the main cause of desertification and camels are less productive than sheep and wildlife; and (v) full bioclimatic potential of any system can be realized only in the absence of all human activity especially herding (El-Shorbagy, 1996).

These previous assumptions demonstrate that the trend of international development effort was led by technology (i.e., formulated in terms of highly-advanced technology), investment and management. Socio-economic factors were not considered, with the implicit assumption that the social relations that constitute the societies in question would re-arrange or reform themselves in adaptation to the new exogenous techno-environmental condition.

During the last four decades, large-scale interventions represented in many development projects had been carried out in African and Asian rangelands to overcome the degradation problems of their resources. Most of these projects were based on technology and range management principles developed in the USA, Europe, Australia, the former Soviet Union and South Africa, and responded to problems by attempting to institute radical management changes. These projects included the following strategies: sedentarizing nomads; digging boreholes for permanent water supply; veterinary care; subsidizing feeds and livestock production; artificial revegetation of depleted ranges; constructing water harvesting and water spreading facilities; establishing feed reserves; creating pastoral and fattening co-operatives; and establishing regulations and by-laws to optimize utilization of rangeland resources. Unfortunately, most of these development projects failed to overcome the degradation problems and the failure was often attributed to one or more of the following reasons: the traditionalism of pastoralists; the inadequacies of administrations; problems of land tenure and rights of rangeland utilization; conflicts between pasture production and other agriculture production systems, as well as between individual and common interests of pastoralists; rural and urban communities; underestimation of environmental constraints of the pastoral areas; and the lack of adequate information for the selection of appropriate technology in the approach to development.

In fact, failure of such projects was due to the development policies themselves which disturbed the traditional utilization and management of these rangelands and caused more degradation of resources. A number of authors argue that the recent drought in East Africa and the Sahel had a disastrous impact on nomad populations, because uninformed manipulation of these societies had produced unpredicted and ramifying changes both in the environment and in the nomads capacity to exploit it (Baker, 1975). A major factor in the social tragedy that followed the Sahelian drought was the recent loss of flexibility in resource use, which is a very important aspect of any land-use system particularly in arid and semi-arid regions. In retrospect, massive interventions based on technology and range management principles developed in advanced countries may not provide optimal solutions to the problems of African and Asian pastoralists because of the significant differences in their ecological and cultural histories. However, it is now generally accepted that technological change does not occur (and cannot be induced) in isolation from economic change and general social change. It has also become clear that, in order to induce change successfully in any social system, it is necessary first to investigate the dynamics of the existing system. It is unscientific to expect to change particular social practices without first ascertaining what generates the social formation underlying those practices.

Therefore, the understanding of the interaction between the technical and socio-economic constraints was mostly inadequate and led to implementation of inappropriate, uniform projects that not only overlooked the goals and strategies of the pastoral communities, but also failed to involve them in planning (Livingstone, 1985; Sidahmed et al., 1986; Sidahmed, 1995b; Hall and Dixon, 1988; Swift, 1988).

3. MECHANIZATION AND CULTIVATION OF MARGINAL LANDS

One of the most important recommendations approved by the 1977 United Nations Conference on Desertification (UNCD) was directed toward land degradation in rainfed farming areas. The recommendation called for the establishment of legal limits to cultivation by tractor ploughing in marginal drylands, which are ecologically more suited for grazing and was based on the assumption that these areas are particularly vulnerable to extensive clearing and excessive mechanical treatment. This recommendation directly challenged the belief of policy-makers and international lending agencies who maintained that mechanization increased productivity and who prefered to invest in mechanized farming projects. They were supported by multinational manufacturers of farm machinery, with the backing of the governments of the exporting countries and by many technical assistants and leaders. As a result, mechanized farming spread dramatically in the marginal lands of many developing countries and covered most of the semi-arid lands in the non-industrialized world.

The destructive effect of mechanization upon land that already is of poor quality was becoming clearer by the end of 1980, particularly in Africa and west Asia (e.g., North African countries, the Sudan, Somalia, Turkey, Iran and Pakistan). The multilateral development banks, other development funding agencies and industrialized countries had supported agriculture with high mechanization requirements, while investment in improving land was considered unattractive (Schulz, 1982).

A good indication of the recent growth of mechanized farming is the increase in numbers of tractors in use. In The Sudan, for example, tractor numbers nearly tripled between 1967 and 1973 (Lees and Brooks, 1977). In Pakistan, tractor imports were doubled between 1968 and 1972; in fact the Government of Pakistan subsidized tractor sales so heavily that they were far cheaper to buy there than in the United States (Herring and Kennedy, 1977). Similarly, the number of tractors imported into Iran increased tenfold between 1962 and 1972 (Aresvik, 1976).

Opportunistic ploughing of rainfed marginal areas may produce a few good harvests in the short term, but will, in the longer term, lead to erosion. The wild vegetation produced by such soils often constitutes the better rangeland of traditional pastoralists. As a result of erosion, the land is lost to both agriculture and pastoralism, and the pastoralists are thereby pushed back on to less productive rangeland which becomes further impoverished as a result.

4. MULTILATERAL DEVELOPMENT BANKS AND RANGELAND DEVELOPMENT

The World Bank was formed to help finance the reconstruction of Europe after World War II. It began operating in 1946 and made its first loan to developing country in 1948. Initially, lending was almost exclusively confined to infrastructure projects and the guiding purpose of the Bank was to promote private foreign investment and gross national product (GNP) growth. Over time, the focus has been broadened to include loans that encourage overall social progress in such areas as health, housing, education, sanitation and low birth rates. The regional development banks (e.g., the Inter-American Development Bank, IDB, the Asian Development bank, ADB, and the African Development Bank, AFDB) were established in the late 1950s and early 1960s, and have evolved in a somewhat parallel manner. From 1950 to 1985, all multilateral development banks (MDBs) did not consider the environmental aspect in their policies. Instead, they have offered more rhetoric than substantive action on the environment. The bulk of MDBs' contribution was directed to development projects; many failed and had disastrous effects on the environments of developing countries. Only very recently have MDBs begun to take the environmental effects of their loans into account. However, most have formed environmental departments with permanent staff specialists, and all recognize an obligation to limit funding to projects that would cause deterioration of the environment (Mikesell and William, 1992).

5. PREFERENCES AND PREJUDICES OF EXOGENOUS GROUPS

The preference and prejudices of groups living outside the dry regions towards particular resources or technologies can be superimposed on dryland development programmes. The goat is a good example in this context. West Europeans and North Americans tend to hold this animal in very low esteem on the basis that it wreaks ecological havoc. When this outlook is combined with that of past generations who believed that the goat had destroyed much of the original agricultural potential of the Near East and North Africa, it is easy to see how the elimination of the animal was often regarded as one of the main remedies for desertification (Dannell, 1982). Yet, the evidence that the goat has browsed its way over the last ten millennia through a lush and fertile "Eden" is far from conclusive, and is certainly open to other interpretations. After all, this animal has been an integral part of subsistence economies in the Near East, the Mediterranean and North Africa for some eight millennia, and it would seem dubious that a resource would persist for so long if it were as much of an ecological vandal as is frequently claimed.

The camel is another example of prejudice; it is viewed by groups living outside dry regions as a very slow-growing animal, consuming bigger amounts of herbs and with a production potential far lower than other animals. Many do-gooders had recommended excluding it from rangelands of the regions and substituting it with cattle in the more favourable rangelands, and by sheep and/or wild animals in the poorer ones. As a result (and for other reasons), camel population in the regions decreased sharply during the 1970s and 1980s. Absence of camels from these ranges resulted in the increasing frequency and cover of spiny plants such as Astragalus sp., Zillaspinose, and Fagonia sp. The common shape of Acacia sp. (i.e., low umbrella shape trees) has changed and become more taller and unavailable for browsing by sheep and goats. In addition, low-palatable species for sheep and goats, such as Haloxylon salicornicum and Anabasis sp. increased drastically and the substituted Panicum turgidum and Rhanerium epapposum are more palatable and nutritious for livestock (El-Shorbagy, 1996).

6. SOME REGIONAL DEVELOPMENT PROJECTS AND THEIR IMPACT ON PASTORALISTS AND RANGELAND RESOURCES

6.1 Settlement of nomads

Pastoralists practise nomadism if seasonal variations of environmental factors (i.e., temperature, water availability, diseases and insects, local flooding and/or feed shortage) make livestock-keeping in one area more or less risky than in another area (based on a regular and predictable seasonal timetable). Government officials (e.g., veterinarians, doctors, administrators) dislike the mobility of nomads because it spreads diseases and re-infects areas once cleared, imposes difficulties in providing them with social services, causes many clashes between them and results in many complications at the international borders which may pose a threat to national security. Therefore, their settlement is desirable because centralized control can be increased, taxes can be levied, a herd's size can be limited in line with some ideal of predetermined carrying capacity, and herders can be encouraged to commercialize their production (Sanford, 1983).

This line of reasoning is justified by the argument that pastoral areas are experiencing a crisis in terms of over population and overgrazing, producers are "backward" because of their apparent failure to respond to price incentives and it is time for people to take individual responsibility for limiting their herd size. Sedenterization is thought to make it easier for governments to provide services such as health care and education. It is, therefore, viewed as a necessary precondition for development.

In cases where settlement has been imposed on nomads compulsorily or by government decree or by other means, the results have been disastrous. Settlement impoverishes pastoralists and it has caused almost massive losses of livestock through starvation and diseases. Furthermore, it has changed the nature of society's structure and organization with some consequent loss of feeling of identify and continuity. Finally, it does not improve social services due to the low density of population per area.

6.2 Water development

Better-distributed water supplies can reduce the distance that livestock travel and, therefore, the amount of energy they expend in obtaining water. Furthermore, when water is provided closer to where livestock are grazing, this enables them either to take water more frequently or to spend more time in grazing which is reflected in increasing herd productivity. In the past, many claims have been made for the benefits of developing water points in areas lacking them. The most important effect of the development of water supplies is to open up previously unused areas to pastoralists, areas only used by certain animal species (e.g., camels) or those used only at certain times of the year.

During the last four decades, many governmental organizations in many countries of the regions (backed by different aid agencies) have actively competed with each other for opportunities to scatter water points around pastoral areas without any clear conceptions of what is there already or why they are adding to them. It seems that many governments in the regions encouraged the programmes of watering-point development, not only to ensure sufficient water supply for more livestock, or more appropriate use of the range, but also often as a way to gain political support from pastoral groups or to secure specific agreement with them for a range management programme or other development projects. This resulted in the development of some thousands of watering points which covered most of all the rangelands in the regions and opened up to pastoral use many areas not previously used at all or only used to a limited extent. For example, between 1965 and 1976 the area of land in Botswana accessible to domestic livestock approximately doubled as a consequence of borehole drilling programmes, financed from both public and private sources (Sanford, 1977). In north-east Kenya, a water development programme has allegedly doubled the area of land now accessible to grazing in the dry season; previously its grazing had been restricted to the wet season. In The Sudan, the number of watering sites was quadrupled between 1957 and 1968 by constructing nearly 1 000 water points equipped with bore-holes, reservoirs and dams (Sudan, Ministry of Agriculture and National Council for Research, 1976). In Saudi Arabia, drilling of boreholes has proceeded to such an extent that it is now reported that there are no ranges considered inaccessible to domestic livestock (except in the Empty Quarter), because almost every rangeland site can be reached by truck from one or more water points (Al-Saleh, 1976).

The development of many new watering points in the rangelands of African and Southwest Asian countries increased the proportion of sacrificed areas around them; it attracted more animals, created the growth of permanent settlements of people (e.g., herders, officials, traders, immigrant cultivators), who gradually increased the area designated as pasture reserves for their animals, carried out cultivation and finally excluded pastoralists.

6.3 Other non-adapted development measures

Despite the fact that there are alarming examples of rangeland degradation in most of Africa and west Asian countries, until now there has been a dearth of ecologically oriented, integrated rural development projects that aim at the active participation of the respective pastoral target groups and take into account the socio-economic status of pastoral societies.

The most important of the many problems besetting the regions is the continuing destruction of the natural rangeland habitats by many activities and inappropriate forms of land use. The responsibility for this environmental damage (e.g., through extension of cultivation into rangelands, subsidizing feeds and animal production, cutting and uprooting of trees and shrubs, overgrazing), cannot be assigned primarily to the pastoralists and their livestock. On the contrary, an equal (or greater) share of the responsibility should be levelled at the urban élite, merchants, businessmen, politicians and, in particular development policy decision-makers (Janzen, 1991).

Other development measures that seem to have made a major contribution to environmental destruction of range ecosystems are the legal changes which occurred in communal (or tribal) pastoral areas through nationalizing rangelands and opening them to free grazing. These actions has created considerable uncertainty for the pastoralists over their grazing rights, since everyone, (whether nomadic or sedentary), can graze his animal when and where he pleases. Private ownership of animals and nationalized, open ranges led to a "free rider" situation with individuals maximizing their own use of the range by increasing individual holdings, which in turn resulted in more degradation of rangeland resources (Livingstone, 1991).

On the other hand, the privatization of range areas of communal pastures, through encouraging the establishment of enclosures of rangelands and the registration of exclusive rights to grazing by individuals or particular groups of the pastoralists (e.g., Somalia and Kenya), or through creating range cooperatives in the most productive areas for particular pastoralist groups, had disturbed patterns of land use and tenure and caused negative impacts on livestock production. However, the majority of the pastoral populations (already economically underprivileged) were thus further weakened in economic terms, since they were forced to move to less productive ranges or to restrict, in some cases even abandon, mobile livestock-keeping. On the other hand, influential town dwellers and wealthy pastoralists have gained considerable economic advantages through appropriating or buying what used to be communal (or tribal) land.

The ecological equilibrium of rangeland ecosystems had been disrupted by: subsidizing consumers and/or secondary producers of rangeland ecosystems (i.e., with feeds, veterinary care, water tankers, tractors and other services); and marginalizing (or neglecting) developmental and conservative measures of the primary producers (i.e., range plants). The result has been disastrous in accelerating degradation of rangeland resources. However, this created artificial conditions that enabled pastoralists to maintain a large number of animals on rangelands for longer periods, which in turn has resulted in the overutilization of resources (i.e., over-grazing, wood-cutting, cultivation).

As artificial revegetation of depleted ranges and water harvesting and water spreading schemes (e.g., contour furrows, pits, earth concrete dams, earth dikes and contour terracing) are known as useful and effective means for improving and conserving the vegetation and water of arid and semi-arid ranges, they were applied widely in some countries of the region (El-Shorbagy, 1995). Unfortunately, the results achieved from such measures were far less successful than expected, due to lack of proper implementation and/or management prac-tices. Furthermore, some of these measures had, in many cases, contributed to further degradation of resources due to a lack of adequate information for selecting ecologically adapted plant species, appropriate technology and the proper approach for implementation.

7. DEPRESSING RESULTS OF SOME NATIONAL DEVELOPMENT PROJECTS

7.1 Egypt

In 1918, the Government of Egypt established a dry-farming station at Burg El-Arab (40 km west of Alexandria) to develop and improve dry farming methods and supply Bedouins with seeds and seedlings, as well as technical advice to enhance their settlement. An oil-rich variety of olive (Olea europea cv Shemlah) was introduced from Tunisia and given free to Bedouins (who already recognized its usefulness for planting). Cultivated areas by olives, figs (Ficus sp), vines (Vitis vinifera) and almonds (Prunus amygdalus) increased gradually, but unfortunately most of the trees were destroyed at the battle of Alamein during World War II. Again, plants were given to the inhabitants and tree plantations expanded from Burg El-Arab to near the western border of Egypt. The estimated number of olives and fig trees carried during the spring of 1975 amounted to about 2.5 million trees (El-Shorbagy, 1996). The expanded development of tree culture showed that inhabitants (originally nomads) are not "natural enemies of trees" as is often alleged (Lowdermilk, as quoted by Draz 1954). During the 1980-1990 period, many areas of the coastal land had been sold to tourism companies and cultivated trees were replaced by tourism villages.

During the 1950s, the Desert Research Institute of Egypt initiated the foun-dation of the Ras El-Hakma Range Research Station (220 km west of Alexandria). It was established in 1954 by a cooperative agreement between Egypt and the United States. The objective was to carry out research and studies to improve the coastal rangelands of Egypt and increase productivity. Over

300 promising plant species, mostly introduced, were planted in 12 out-station plots along a 300 km strip from Burg El-Arab to Sidi Barrani (about 100 km from the Libyan-Egyptian border). Merino sheep were introduced for producing wool of a better quality and for cross-breeding with local sheep. Dams and dikes were constructed for water spreading, Roman wells and cisterns were cleaned and restored, windmills and powerful mechanically-driven pumps were used to lift the well water for domestic and livestock use, and supplementary fodder plants were grown by irrigation with ground water. Many extensive basic studies on soil, vegetation, livestock, climate and water resources were carried out. After the war of June 1967, top priority was given to military efforts and so the budgets of the Desert Research Institute (and most other Egyptian governmental organizations) were greatly cut. In 1972, the Ras El-Hakma Research Station was added to the responsibilities of the General Egyptian Organization for Rehabilitation of Deserts. Two years later, the situation at Ras El-Hakma looked desperate; most of the project's activities and components had stopped, deteriorated or been destroyed, and today very little remains. For example, the introduction of the foreign fodder species was not established and the merino sheep were not accepted by the Bedouins, and so the project ended without achieving substantial success. This was primarily due to hastiness in the implementation of uninformed ideas on a large scale with insufficient knowledge about the structure and function of the ecosystem and the inadequate integration of socio-economic parameters. The real achievements were the base studies carried out in the coastal desert areas and the number of postgraduate students and scholars who are now senior experts in ongoing projects in Egypt, other Arab countries, and in regional and international organizations (Imam, 1978; Ayyad, 1976).

7.2 Libya

In 1973, the Socialist People's Libyan Jamahiria started to implement a wide programme to improve its rangelands, with the objective of reducing range degradation and provide more feed to the increasing number of range ruminants. Seventeen range projects (with an area of approximately 3 million ha) had been established and various improvement techniques were applied. About 60 000 ha of these rangelands were fenced and planted mostly by Atriplex halimus, Atriplex nummularia and Acacia cynophylla (Messaudi, 1985). These three species were the most widely-planted forage shrubs in Libya. Other species such as Priplocal laevigata, Calligonum comosum and Opuntia ficus indicus var. inermis. were also planted at some projects. During the 1980s, it became clear that results were falling considerably short of expectations. Evaluations carried out for some of these projects during 1982, 1985, 1988, and 1990 showed that most of the planted shrubs died before their expected lifespan. The average number of dead trees amounted to 55, 69, 84 and 91%, respectively, for the former respective years (Sidahmed, 1986a; El-Shorbagy, 1996). In spite of the very high financial investments, the Libyans failed to increase range productivity or to restore it. On the contrary, these projects contributed to a large loss of adjacent range resources. This failure was not due to the lack of formal or institutional knowledge because management practices were well-detailed in the technical reports. However, even though the importance of cutting Acacia shrub at three-year intervals was stressed by experts, they failed to elaborate on community-related management methodologies. The workforce in most projects was comprised of a very limited number of untrained technicians and alien herders. Pastoralists were prevented from using these ranges and were never consulted during project initiation and implementation (Sidahmed, 1986a & 1995; El-Shorbagy, 1996).

7.3 The Sudan

Since the 1950s, extensive mechanized rainfed farming of sorghum and sesame had been expanded gradually in the rainfed areas of The Sudan, but it received heightened support in the 1970s with the injection of foreign capital and the promotion of The Sudan as the "breadbasket" of the Middle East. In 1974, the Government Mechanized Farming Corporation (MFC) approved a livestock and cattle project proposed by the Arab-funded Trade Invest Company. Technical assistance for the project was provided by the US-based Arizona - Colorado Land and Cattle Company (Lees and Brooks, 1977). Another project "The Simsim Mechanized Farm Project", was jointly funded by the International Bank for Reconstruction and Development (IBRD) and the Government of The Sudan and implemented by MFC. The cost was divided among land development (clearing and roads), machinery and equipment, and advisor and administration costs. Two-thirds of the costs were for foreign exchange, with the IBRD's share of costs making it an expensive project from the standpoint of Sudanese investment alternatives. The project promoted private mechanized farming on marginal lands where soil fertility had been a perennial problem.

The normal framework is for private investors, usually urban, to obtain from the pastoral Mechanized Farming Corporation a lease on a 1 000 or 1 500 acre plot of rainfed land, upon which they then become eligible for a wide range of soft loans and other services. Land is initially cleared, then disc-ploughed and sown in a single operation each year; weeding and harvesting were done manually by seasonal migratory labour. The structure of profitability encouraged the adoption of highly deleterious farming practices for a few years, after which a new plot could be leased. It also encouraged the extension of cultivation onto marginal lands outside the scheme limits, on which an existing farming operation could make profits. This extension by registered farmers is recognized by the MFC, and there are also cases of farmers cultivating without obtaining any lease from the MFC, but who nonetheless receive MFC services. Mechanized policy is based on the premise that there is empty land available for cultivation. In practice, cultivated lands under the scheme, and (even more so) unofficial and illegal cultivation, have encroached massively on pastoral grazing lands (Schulz, 1982; Morton, 1988).

The political significance of The Sudan's strategic position on the volatile Horn of Africa explains the upsurge of interest in its agricultural development and the interest of western and other conservative governments in gaining access to Sudanese bureaucracy. For them, The Sudan at that time had become a valuable buffer against the pro-Soviet regime in Ethiopia, the radical Libyan regime and the liberation movements active in some adjacent countries. In this connection, it is interesting to note that farm labourers for the Simsim project were drawn from Eritrea and from the Tigre provinces, both of which were in rebellion against the Government of Ethiopia (Schultz, 1982).

7.4 Saudi Arabia

Before the exploration for oil in 1930s, about 70% of Saudi Arabia's population were nomadic pastoralists (Child and Grainger, 1990). Up to that time, stock raising and the traditional form of grazing were regulated by erratic rainfall and the ephemeral nature of vegetation. In years of drought, grazing resources became scarce and livestock population decreased. This strong feedback mechanism linking human, livestock population and vegetation created a dynamic equilibrium to check environmental degradation. For a long time, until about 1953, the pastoralists protected and conserved rangeland resources within the tribal domain. The Hema system (plural Ahmia-i.e., tribal-protected range areas) had emerged in the favourable parts of the western region to safeguard against drought years. Draz (1965; 1969) located 30 Ahmia around Taif and estimated that, at some time in the past, there were about 2 000 Ahmia in the Arabian Peninsula. He classified the Ahmia into five different types, according to the kinds of protection. As well as animal grazing, the various Ahmia regulate the cutting of vegetation and wood from live trees.

Detailed rules establish who can use which resources, where, when and how. Boundaries between tribal areas were reversed in rainy years and abundant vegetation; while during drought years tribal warfare was ignited either to protect range resources or to acquire more grazing land. Protection of rangeland resources through the Hema system and other tribal rules (as well as through the dynamic equilibrium created by natural factors) conserved rangeland resources. Under this traditional grazing system, the rangeland of the peninsula supported 70% of its population (Al-Gain, 1985).

After the unification of the Kingdom of Saudi Arabia in 1932, it was decided to dissipate tribal prejudices and antagonism. To achieve this goal, the tribal realms were assembled into emirates causing the tribal boundaries to fade slowly. Due to conflict in 1953 between three tribes about the ownership of one of the Hemas, a royal decree was issued dissolving public Ahmia. From 1953 until the present, the rangelands of Saudi Arabia have been utilized as open free ranges, as each herder in the Kingdom has the right to graze his herds in any range site and at any particular time and duration he likes. No restrictions had been placed on the size and movement of herds; animal population increased gradually, and rangelands began to suffer from overstocking and continuous over grazing (Tables 5.6 and 5.7). In the 1950s and 1960s, the Government encouraged the settlement of nomads through the establishment of two projects located at Wadi El-Sarhan and at Al-Qainfudhah, but the two projects failed for different reasons.

In the same period, the northern and eastern regions of the Kingdom experienced a prolonged drought; animal losses were from 50 to 90% and the damage caused the destruction of 70 to 80% of the forage species in many areas. In the 1960s, the Government initiated a subsidy programme to encourage pastoralists to rebuild their herds. This programme caused a quick build up of animal numbers mainly from herds crossing from Jordan and Iraq. The vegetation did not have a chance to recover and the deterioration of range resources was accelerated and extended to the central and southern regions (Al Shareef, this volume).

In the early 1970s, petroleum income increased greatly, and the Kingdom was able to adopt the most advanced technologies with both advantageous and disadvantageous effects. A decision was taken to subsidize range animals, either by concentrates (maize and barley grains) or by cash Saudi riyal (SR) (20 per sheep head/year and SR 60/camel/head/year; goats were excluded), to protect livestock against drought hazards (El-Shorbagy, 1996). Similarly, the purchase of agricultural machinery for the farmers and the trucks and water tankers for the nomads were also subsidized. Hundreds of deep wells for permanent water supply had been drilled across the whole rangelands of the Kingdom, to the extent that every range site previously avoided because of a lack of water had become accessible to nomads.

Animal production farms and wheat production had also been highly subsidized. Loans of different national banks for different purposes became easily available for pastoralists, as well as rural and urban dwellers. Vast areas of cultivable land had been distributed to farmers, pastoralists and agricultural companies for increasing agricultural production. Moreover, job opportunities became available to nomads who looked for a more secure source of income (El-Shorbagy, 1996).

All these decisions had a profound impact on the renewable natural resources, particularly forests and rangeland resources. However, the nomads acquired trucks and water tankers which increased mobility by transporting their livestock and haul water from as far as 120 km. No area in the vast rangelands of the Kingdom was immune from over exploitation (Al-Eisa, this volume).

Among the luxuries acquired by the nomads were electric generators and television sets. The weather forecast shown on the TV news gives hints to the nomads as to the whereabouts of rain showers. Sometimes they reach these areas a few days after the rain showers, at a time when most of the plant species are either germinating or emerging from their dormancy. This practice has aggravated the problem of overgrazing. The nomads can bridge any scarcity in grazing resources by feeding barley which is subsidized by the Government.

Moreover, there was a shift in herd composition in favour of sheep and goats rather than camels which are more difficult to transport. Old people and young

Table 5.6

Land use in Saudi Arabia, 1978 - 1993 (thousands ha)

Landuse	1978	1983	1988	1993
Land area	214,969	214,969	214,969	214,969
Arable crops and perm. crops	1856	2770	3130	3740
Perm pastures	85000	85000	110000	120000 *
Forest & Woodland	1360	1360	1600	1800 *
Other land	126753	126349	100239	89429

Source: FAO Yearbook of Production, (1994) vol. 48
* Saudi Arabian estimation for rangelands and forest areas are 270 and 2.7 millions ha, respectively.

Table 5.7

Livestock numbers in Saudi Arabia, 1979 - 1994 (thousands)

	1979-81	1992	1993	1994
Sheep	4040	6890	6973	7257
Goats	2770	3899	4103	4150
Camels	284	410	413	415
Cattle	374	202	202	203
Horses	3	3	3	3

Source: FAO Yearbook of Production, (1994) vol.48

women became responsible for shepherding herds while young men were engaged in permanent jobs in nearby towns and villages. Later, herders on the ranges became mostly foreign labourers, and growing numbers of livestock are owned by absentees (Al-Eisa, this volume).

By 1990, the nomadic proportion of the population in the Kingdom was estimated at only as 3% (Child and Grainger, 1990). The sheep and goat population raised on rangelands increased continuously and herding remains widespread, but 60% of stock owners are settled, semi-settled or short-range nomads. Even the low numbers of the truly nomadic herdsmen now tend to stay for a longer time in one range site. This settlement has been made possible by infrastructure development and the provision of social services (e.g., schools, hospitals, electricity, waters), developed by the Government in various districts of the Kingdom. The camps of the herdsmen are found within a commutable distance from town, village or asphalt road.

The result has been a disastrous breakdown in the self-regulatory process as overgrazing and the degradation of range resources are spreading concentrically around these areas. The loss of natural vegetation cover reduces the amounts of moisture the soil can retain. This increased soil aridity, which in turn increases the rate of vegetation loss in a process of negative feedback until the land is stressed, is beyond the point of recovery.

7.5 Kenya

Herding as a traditional subsistence activity is often cited as among the more prominent causes of environmental degradation and eventual desertification. At the same time, either by inference or by reference to actual experiments in "exclosures", the clear impression is given that only in the absence of all human activity (especially herding), can the full bioclimatic potential of an area be realized. With reference to the Pokot of north-western Kenya, positive features of traditional herding systems and the negative aspects of biological recovery had been identified. However, the Pokot people have exploited Masol and the Simbol area for many generations by managing large herds of cattle, goats, sheep and sometimes camels. They were forced to withdraw from the Masol plains in 1974 because of a state of near warfare and the plains were unused until late in 1978. Preliminary analysis of data from the Landsat satellite system was used to demonstrate a new kind of desertification that could be called "green desertification" i.e., the explosive growth of Acacia sp and the retreat of the grassy cover which is very important for livestock feeding in the area (Table 5.8).

Table 5.8 shows that the major change took place in the bushland and grassland categories. From the last year of regular use of the Masol/Simbol area in

Table 5.8

Preliminary estimates via Landstat of plant cover changes in the Simbol area of the Masol Plains, Kenya

Vegetation type	Pixels	% of Area	Pixels	% of area	Pixel change 1973 to 1978
Bushland	3919	23.92	8191	49.99	+ 4272
Bush-grassland	6161	37.60	2136	13.04	− 4025
Riverine forest	3787	23.11	3885	23.71	+ 26
Black cotton soil bush grassland	1212	7.40	1151	7.07	− 61
Total	15079	92.03	15363	93.81	

Source: Conant, (1982)

1973 to five years later, when the first Pokot began to return to the plains, the bushland category increased from 24 to about 50%, while the grassland category decreased from 38 to 13% in the same years, respectively. Thus, in the absence of the Pokot, the *Acacia millifera*, *Acacia nilotica* and *Commiphora* species doubled its distribution on the expense of grasses (mainly *Digitaria* sp., *Chloris* sp. and *Dactyloctenium* sp.). In fact, so few grasses remained in the Simbol area in 1978 that the few Pokot who began returning avoided the area completely. This avoidance was due to both the decrease in grasses and the increase in tsetse fly that accompanied the proliferation of dense bush (Conant, 1982).

8. LESSONS LEARNED AND RECOMMENDATIONS

(i)   Application of advanced technology and range management principles developed in rich western countries are not necessarily appropriate or feasible for developing countries. Most of the developing countries of Africa and West Asia have different environments and different socio-economic infrastructures with varying levels of total wealth and resources, and even although the ecological principles behind the technology remain constant, the actual application may involve different aspects of those principles in the rangeland systems of these countries. In general, overcoming technical constraints (e.g., control of the tsetse fly) has proven to be more difficult than anticipated. This is at least partly due to the tendency to implement management systems as practiced in the donor countries (Child et al., 1980).

(ii)   Due to social and ecological conditions involved in the rangeland production systems of African and Asian countries and the general lack of understanding of them, projects need to be long-term (i.e., 10-20 years). Changes within these systems occur slowly and projects that end after three to five years tend to confound the development process. One example of this occurred in Kenya. In 1969, under an FAO programme, major inputs were made into the Kiboko and Backoma research stations to initiate research that would generate information and technology appropriate for Kenya. FAO support was terminated in 1973 and, although research priorities had been established and some structures and equipment were left in place, there was a critical deficiency of trained and motivated staff and of resources required to continue the established research programme. In 1979, the realization of the need for a solid research base for rangelands in East Africa prompted the Government of Kenya and United States Agency for International Development (USAID) to begin another six-year range research development project. This kind of "up-and-down" cycle of development should be avoided if long-term goals are to be met.

(iii)   Projects are often established that require a significant level of funding to support the recurrent costs after donor support ends. The ability for the host country to continue to support (or find support) for the recurrent costs of any implementation activities beyond the anticipated funding period should be considered.

(iv)   Many development projects have been designed using the past belief in which one product is isolated and a solution sought. Other development projects for the poorer countries often only look at the short-term alleviation of hunger and political/military objectives. As a result, many development projects for poorer countries have not been designed to include the long-term needs of the total environment. A more holistic approach should be taken during project planning phases, through project implementation to evaluation. Only in recent years have social scientists been involved in the so-called biological research areas. In the past, the social scientists were often "brought in after the fact" instead of being involved in the planning and early implementation phases. This was in part due to the academic training programmes most social and biological scientists received in the past. They have therefore had very little common background to allow for mutual communication. Fortunately, this problem seems to be diminishing but continued efforts must occur, especially in universities, to ensure that interdisciplinary teams work together in all phases of rangeland development projects. This approach is not easy and requires more time during the planning phase, but the long-term success of development in these highly diverse systems requires the broader prospective that is obtained only by using this approach.

(v) The management programmes designed by most range experts and ecologists to address the balance in the relationship between animals and carrying capacity in the arid and semi-arid rangelands are primarily concerned with the long-term production of the resources. On the other hand, the pastoralists are primarily concerned with survival, first in the short term and then in the long term. Survival for the pastoralist means not only his own personal survival but also the survival of his socio-cultural unit which relies upon the productivity of the herds. It is obvious that the two concerns overlap but they are centred on different priorities which are, in turn, based on different values. This conflict between technical experts and pastoralists will not be solved as both of them are not able to provide alternatives to overcome it, but it could be solved in the larger political process.

(vi) A higher portion of training programmes for native staff members of projects (particularly counterparts) should be organized under local prevailing conditions. In countries where the education system has not been developed to the level where the training is possible, training programmes should be selected that will offer trainees the backgrounds and skills that can be related to the ecological and social environment in which they will be working. This can be accomplished by providing projects with the flexibility to have the research portions of advanced degree training programmes conducted within the home country. Major advisors in the universities should be encouraged to visit the research sites and assist in the development of the research. Project staff could serve on the graduate committees for the field work and other in-country degree work (Child et al., 1980).

(vii) Efforts undertaken to solve rangeland problems, in isolation of other favourable areas, have failed. However, as rangelands provide meat and dairy products and other services to both the urban and rural population, it is unfair and unrealistic (both politically and ecologically), to try to implement improvements within the range eco-systems themselves and only at the expense of pastoralists (i.e., re-arrange pastoral activity there). Central governments are responsible for the formulation and implementation of policy, and also for the measures that influence the distribution of economic activity that develop some areas and marginalize others. It is at this level of organization and planning that rangelands could be improved and restored.

(viii) One of the most depressing results of development has been the rinderpest control programme in Africa that led to indiscriminate borehole water development with no plan for grazing management or animal control. The only concern in the programme appeared to be the creation of dipping and vaccination centres that would attract and contain the animals. As a result, hundreds of thousands of hectares across Africa have been turned into a dust-bowl. Generations to come will pay the price of this programme in terms of loss of resource productivity and animal and human starvation.

(ix)   As the effect of most projects are often seen long after the initial projects are completed, a long-term monitoring programme prior, as well as during and after, implementation must be carried out regularly. In addition, many of both plant and animal species had been introduced and tested under normal or optimal conditions, while most rangeland areas experience frequent drought periods, so it is important to monitor management strategies through such periods of stresses. Some failures in range development projects could have been avoided if sufficient testing had been done prior to implementation or if improved monitoring procedures had provided documentation of past mistakes.

(x)   MDBs should refuse to finance activities, such as large-scale irrigation or open-pit mining that deplete the net resource base. However, MDBs should actively support such projects as fish farming, small-scale irrigation, rehabilitation of existing roads, small dams and dikes, artificial water ponds and small-scale hydro-electric power, whose negative environmental effects can be readily mitigated. It is time for MDBs to incorporate sustainable development goals into their lending policies, including: the timeliness and relative import once of conducting environmental impact assessment; performing social benefit cost analyses for every proposal; delegating a more active and independent role to official environmental departments within the institutions themselves; and incorporating non-governmental organizations (NGOs) more fully in the evaluation process.

References

Al-Gain, A. 1985. Integrated resource survey in support of nomads in Saudi Arabia. In: Whitehead, E. Hutchinson, C. Timmerman, B. and Varady, R. (eds). *Arid lands today and tomorrow.* Proc. Int'l Res. and Develop. Conf., Tucson.

Al-Saleh, N. 1976. Some problems and development possibilities of the livestock sector in Saudi Arabia, (Ph.D. thesis). University of Durham.

Agriculture Resource Policy Advisory Committee (ARPAC) 1975. *Research to meet USA and world food needs.* Report of Working Conference, Kansas City. 108.

Aresvik, O. 1976. *The new agriculture development in Iran.* Preager, New York.

Ayyad, M.A. 1976. System analysis of of Mediterranean desert ecosystem of northern Egypt. Progress Report, No.2. Part I: 11-17.

Baker, R. 1975. Development and the pasture people of Karamogo, north eastern Uganda. An example of the treatment of symptoms. In: Monod, T. 1975. *Pastoralism of Tropical Africa.* Oxford University Press, London.

Child, C. and Grainger, J. 1990. A system plan for protected areas for wildlife conservation and sustainable rural development in Saudi Arabia. NCWCD, Riyadh, and IUCN, Switzerland.

Dannell, R.W. 1982. Archaeology and the study of vegetation. In: Spooner, B. and Conant, F.P. 1982. Thorns paired, sharply recurved: cultural controls and rangeland quality in East Africa. In: Spooner, B. and Mann, H.S. (eds) *Desertification and development: drylands ecology in social perspective.* Academic Press, London and New York.

Mann, H.S. (eds.) Desertification and development, dryland ecology in social perspective. Academic Press, London and New York.

Draz, O. 1969. The *Hema* System of range resources in the Arabian Peninsula. Its possibilities in range improvement and conservation projects in the Near East. FAO, Rome.

Draz, O. 1965. Rangelands and methods of their improvement in Saudi Arabia. Riyadh Printery First Edition (in Arabic).

Draz, O. 1954. *Some desert plants and their uses in animal breeding.* Publications de d'Institute du Desert d'Egypte No.2. 95.

Child, D., Heady, H.F. Peterson, R.A. and Pieper, R.D. 1980 Ecological use and management of rangeland resources in developing countries. Review paper.

El-Shorbagy, M.A. 1996. Rangeland resources of Arab countries: their situation and potential. Working review paper (unpublished).

El-Shorbagy, M.A. and Suliman, I.S. 1995. Improvement of some depleted ranges in Syria and Jordan through the application of some technological agricultural practices. In: Omar, S.A.S. Razzaque M.A. and Al-Sdirawi, F. (eds) pp. 251-270. *Range management in arid zones. Proceedings of the Second International Conference on Range Management in the Arabian Gulf.* Keagan Paul, London and New York.

Food and Agriculture Organization of the United Nations (FAO) 1994. Yearbook of Production, 1999. Vol. 48. Rome.

Hall, M. and Dixon, J. 1988. *Transformation and application of technology knowledge to dryland farming.* FAO/Agricultural Services Division. The International Conference on dryland farming, Amarillo, Texas, USA, August 1989.

Herring, R.J. and. Kennedy, C. Jr. 1979. The political economy of farm mechanization policy. Tractors in Pakistan. In: Hopkins, R.F. Puchala D.J. and Talbot, R.B. (eds.), *Food, political and agriculture development.* Westview Press. Boulder, Colorado.

Holechek, J.L., Pieper R.D. and Herbel, C.H 1989. *Range management principles and practices.* Prentice Hall Inc; Englewood Cliffs, New Jersey, USA.

Imam, M. 1978. *Potentialities for improving range management in the Mediterranean coastal desert of Egypt.* Proceedings of the First International Rangeland Congress, Denver, Colorado.

Janzen, J. 1991. *The revival of traditional pastoral systems in the Near East. A survival strategy for pasture lands and mobile livestock-keeping.* Keynote address presented at the FAO/CARDNE Workshop on Pastoral Communities in the Near East: Traditional Systems in Evolution, Amman, Jordan, 1-5 December 1991.

Livingstone, I. 1985. Pastoralism: an overview of practice process and policy. FAO Human Resources Institution and Agrarian Resources Division. Rome.

Lees, F.A., and Brooks. H.C., 1977. *The economic and political development of The Sudan.* Westview Press, Boulder, Colorado.

Livingstone, I. 1991. Livestock management and overgrazing among pastoralists. *Ambio*, XX: 80-85.

Messaudi, M.B. 1985. *The use of fodder shrubs: the Libyan experience.* FAO Expert Consultation on Rangeland Rehabilitation and Development in the Near East. Rome, 22-25 October 1985.

Mikesell, R.F. and William, L.F. 1992. *International banks and the environment: from growth to sustainability: An unfinished agenda.* Sierra Club Books. San Francisco.

Morton, J. 1988. The decline of Lahawin pastoralism (Kassala Province, East Sudan). Pastoral Development network, Agriculture Administration Unit. Overseas development net work.

Sanford, S. 1983. *Management of pastoral development in the Third World.* John Wiley & Sons, New York, Brisbane, Toronto, Singapore.

Schulz, A. 1982. Reorganizing deserts: mechanization and marginal lands in South West Asia. In: Spooner, B. and Mann, H. S. (eds.) pp. 27-41. *Desertification and development: dryland ecology in social perspective.* Academic Press, London.

Sidahmed, A.E. 1995. Towards sustainable development of rangelands/livestock in dryland areas of the Near East and North Africa. In: Omar, S.A.S. Razzaque, M.A. and Al-Sdirawi, F. (eds) pp. 53-69, *Range management in arid zones. Proceeding of the second International Conference on Range Management in the Arabian Gulf.* Kegan Paul International. London and New York.

Sidahmed, A.E., Doghais, A.H., Ibrahim, A. and Mulatim, S. 1986a. *Crown production and survival rate of Acacia cyanophylla in the pilot projects (unit k4) of Bir Kuka grazing perimeter.* FAO Range and Livestock Development Project. Tripoli, Libya.

Sidahmed, A.E., Morton, R.H., Timon, V. and Norse, D. 1986b. *Improving livestock productivity in dryland area.* A FAO Committee on Agriculture (COAG) resource paper. FAO, Rome Italy.

Spooner, B. 1982. Rethinking desertification: the social dimension. In: Spooner, B. and Mann, H.S. 1982. pp. 1-24, *Desertification and development; dryland ecology in social perspective.* Academic Press, London. First Edition.

Sudan Ministry of Agriculture and National Council for Research. 1976. Desert encroachment control rehabilitation programme.

Swift, J. 1988. Major issues in pastoral development with special emphasis on selected African countries. FAO, Rome.

Zaroug, M.C. 1985. *FAO regional programme on range management and fodder production.* FAO Expert Consultation on Rangeland Rehabilitation and Development in the Near East. Rome, 22-25 October 1985.

A policy shift toward sustainable resource development

T. Ngaido, T. Nordblom,
G. Gintzburger and A. Osman

6

Synopsis

This paper is a comprehensive review of nomadic pastoral systems in the West Asia and North Africa (WANA) region. It considers philosophical, economic and social issues. The debate about sustainability of resource use and economic efficiency receives attention, as does the impact of sedentarization policies.

Key Points

1. *Pastoral production systems and societies of the WANA region have been at the forefront of the debate on efficiency and sustainable resource use for more than forty years. In the 1950s, the debate concentrated on whether the nomadic mode of production was efficient. The general view was that pastoralism and, consequently, nomadic systems were both inefficient resource users and a main cause of environmental degradation. Thus, from the 1950s to the 1970s, the governments of WANA introduced policy reforms and implemented rural development projects to sedentarize nomadic people and transform them into agricultural producers by granting them pieces of land. Besides the economic efficiency criteria, control of the nomads was often a political objective.*

2. *In recent years, concerns shifted from people and institutions to resources. This shift has a wider scope because the question is no longer merely about efficiency but also sustainability. Under this policy shift, nomadic production systems are now perceived as examples of efficient indigenous sustainable resource management systems and risk aversion strategies. However, this recognition does not mean that nomadism is the solution to rangeland degradation. National and international rangelands are shrinking.*

1. INTRODUCTION

Pastoral production systems and societies of the WANA region have been at the forefront of the debate on efficiency and sustainable resource use for more than forty years. In the 1950s, the debate concentrated on whether the nomadic mode of production was an efficient resource use. The general view was that pastoralism and, consequently, nomadic systems were not efficient resource users and were the main causes of environmental degradation (Livingstone, 1985). Thus, from the 1950s to the 1970s, most governments of WANA introduced policy reforms and implemented rural development projects to settle nomadic people and transform them into agricultural producers (Bocco, 1990; Leybourne, et al., 1993). A turning point of the settlement policy was the Baghdad meeting in 1954 that recommended settling nomads by granting them pieces of land (Bocco, 1990). Institutional and land tenure reform policies were implemented without taking into consideration the positive features of local resource management systems. Besides the economic efficiency criteria, there were political objectives behind the desire to control movements of the nomads (Livingstone, 1985).

In recent years there has been a shift of concern from people and institutions to resources. This shift has a wider scope because the question is no longer merely one of efficiency but also sustainability. Sayegh (1992) argues that the inappropriate management of land, water and other national resources, "*has been the result of an over-optimistic wish to maximize short-term gains, without taking into account long-term productivity, thereby threatening long-term survival*". Under this mind-shift, nomadic production systems are now perceived as examples of efficient indigenous sustainable resource management systems and risk-aversion strategies (Masri, 1991; Behnke et al., 1993).

This recognition does not mean nomadism is the solution to rangeland degradation: national and international pastures are shrinking as livestock numbers are increasing. Moreover, areas identified as rangelands during the 1940s in the WANA region are actually quite differentiated now, reflecting both environmental variability and the outcomes of forty years of state policy interventions to change local land tenure systems and institutions. Large areas of former rangelands are now farmlands. For example, in Syria, the boundary of the rangelands in the 1940s (i.e., roughly, areas receiving less than 300 mm rainfall) now includes two land-use zones of distinct agricultural vocation and land tenure, the rangelands and a barley zone.

Therefore, any study dealing with sustainable use of rangelands should consider the rangelands and the areas of spontaneous and induced settlement. These considerations are important when we consider that most of the semi-nomads now rely heavily on crop residues and concentrates for feeding their flocks in summer, autumn and winter, and that settled nomads in need of land encroach on the range (Wachholtz, 1996).

This paper is aimed towards elucidating the local community, resource, and state relationships, in order to evaluate the relevance of ongoing rangeland policies. The paper is articulated around three themes: (i) the definition and importance of rangelands; (ii) the pressures affecting rangelands; and (iii) the policy options. The conclusion identifies needs for policy and property rights research.

2. RANGELANDS

2.1 Definition

Defining rangelands seems to be a difficult undertaking due to the confusion that exists between physical factors (soils and rainfall) and the primary use of resources.

2.1.1 Land-use definition

Stoddard et al., (1975) define rangelands as, "*those areas of the world, which by reason of physical limitations...are a source of forage for free-ranging native and domestic animals, as well as a source of wood products, water and wildlife.*" The International Centre for Agricultural Research in Dry Areas (ICARDA) (1979) defined rangelands as "*most categories of land not under forest or cultivation and especially those that sustain grazing or browsing animals on an extensive basis.*" The World Bank (1995) defines rangelands in North Africa and Iran as, "*lands which in general receive annual rainfall of less than 600 mm, whose fragile soil is unsuitable for agriculture but whose vegetative cover is used for extensive raising of ruminants.*" Each of these definitions of rangelands emphasizes unsuitability for agriculture as a key attribute.

2.1.2 Ecosystem definition

The Forage and Grazing Terminology Committee (1991) define rangelands as "*lands on which the indigenous vegetation (climax or natural potential) is predominantly grasses, grasslike plants, forbs, or shrubs and is managed as a natural ecosystem.*" In Jordan, the 1973 Agricultural Law (No. 20) defines rangelands as areas that receive 200 mm or less rainfall. These definitions emphasize the climatic and biophysical factors and suggest that the boundaries of these areas are very well-defined.

Taking the definitions together we can say that rangelands are lands that are marginal for crop production but suitable for livestock production. In recent years, however, the expansion of barley and wheat production in areas previously defined as rangelands, and the extension of the grazing pressure to fragile arid zones, clouds the definition of rangelands.

2.2 Ecosystem vs. land use-definitions for rangeland policy

The recent interest of governments and donor communities in sustainable resource management has rekindled the issue of rangeland development. A challenge for policy intervention in both West Asia (Mashreq) and North Africa (Maghreb) is the confused use of ecosystem and land-use definitions. Since the 1950s, with settlement policies and the urbanization of rural areas, these two meanings of rangelands define different boundaries. Such limits no longer represent the boundaries of native pastures. For example, the Jordanian definition of rangelands below 200 mm, includes up to 90% of the country; in reality only around 40% of these lands are effective pastures. In Syria, where rangeland boundaries are also defined by the 200-mm isohyet, the expansion of agriculture has at times confined native pastures below the 175-150 mm rainfall zone. The question that continues to be debated by government officials, researchers and the donor community is whether to employ the ecosystem definition or the land-use definition for rangeland development.

The land-use definition equates rangelands to native pastures and, therefore, confines the level of intervention. It has the merit of limiting the scope of interventions to those with short-term results. The intervention becomes a sectorial development with an emphasis on technical solutions focused on particular sites. This has been the approach in previous years and is perceived as a contributing cause of the failure of range development efforts (FAO, 1994; Gintzburger, unpublished). There is a need to formulate a broader approach that takes into consideration the experiences and strategies of the different actors and intervening parties in rangelands.

An integrated-land-use system definition has a wider scope, taking into account the seasonal use of crop residues and other feeds from sources outside the rangelands, and may require a higher level of intervention. Choosing this option is more costly, but has greater long-term payoffs than the land-use option. Nowadays, in Jordan for example, the Agricultural Policy Charter opts for the integrated land-use definition of rangelands. The intention is to: (i) integrate the different strategies developed by the different actors in rangelands (i.e. government, donor agencies, private entrepreneurs and rural communities); (ii) coordinate these actions; and (iii) elaborate a sustainable development strategy of the rangeland.

Any definition of rangelands has socio-economic and political implications. In the past forty to fifty years, most WANA countries implemented agricultural policies that favoured the expansion of agriculture on large areas of the former rangelands. These policies have fostered the development of pasture/crop residue-based livestock production systems. In most of the WANA countries, settlement policies have reduced native pastures and changed settled areas from grazing to crop production. The remaining areas that are purely considered native pastures are so dry in some cases, with rainfall of less than 100 mm, that it becomes difficult to justify any investment (Barghouti and Hayward, 1992). Policies aiming for sustainable resource management must not fail to take into consideration the complementarity between what is left as native pastures, and the higher potential agricultural areas that are important sources of crop-residue feed for livestock production.

2.3 Importance of rangelands

Rangelands play an important role in the livelihood of local communities and wildlife. In this paper, however, the three main roles of rangelands in low rainfall areas will be discussed in the following section: (i) as a feed source for livestock production; (ii) a base of survival for local communities, their institutions, and management practices they developed to overcome environmental variability; and (iii) as a means of avoiding conflicts between herders and farmers.

In earlier times, livestock production in the WANA countries relied mainly on native pastures for grazing. In past decades, rangelands provided up to 60-80% of small ruminant diets (Gintzburger, unpublished). This share of small ruminant diets has decreased in recent years due both to increasing animal populations and the shrinking areas of the native pastures, in addition to the degradation of rangelands which is difficult to measure (Nordblom et al., 1995). This trend is promoting an increasing dependency on feed grains, crop residues and other feed sources. Bedrani (1993) noted that pastures at one site in Algeria provide only 19% (compared with 27% from barley) toward the nutrient needs of sheep in the region. Shideed (1995) explained that in Iraq, "overgrazing and loss of valuable grazing areas to cereal production, forced the nomadic people to depend more and more on supplementary feeding".

Much of the development thrust towards resource improvement and conservation has been technically oriented. This approach has been one of the shortcomings of rangeland research and policy-making; economic efficiency of rangeland resources continues to be the guiding principle of government intervention in rangelands. Rangeland users, nomads and transhumants often continue to be perceived as the causes of rangeland problems.

The human dimension of rangelands (i.e., indigenous communities, local institutions, and resource management systems) often unfortunately continues to be disregarded in policy formulation (Sidahmed, 1991). The human dimension is a key factor for sustainable development policies on rangelands. It is timely that policy-makers and researchers start to talk about the interaction between people and resources, not only in terms of efficiency but also in terms of equity and sustainability. The role and rights of local communities on rangeland resources need to be well-defined as these are necessary to their livelihood. As primary beneficiaries of these rangeland resources, local communities ought to be made responsible for their management and long-term conservation (Bruce, 1986; Lawry, 1990).

Such a policy will not be a complete innovation, only a restitution of many traditional rights and management roles that pastoral communities, the Bedouins, used to exercise on rangelands. These local communities went through many years of disturbance, however, which necessitated an assessment of their capacity to reclaim and reassert their management roles. The strength of local communities is indicated by community members' continued adherence to customary rules and institutions. The capacity of local institutions depends on: (i) the existence of their former territory; (ii) their social legitimacy to enforce customary rules; and (iii) their recognition by the state as viable management institutions (Ngaido, 1994, 1996a, 1996b).

An important role of rangelands that is generally missed is in conflict avoidance between farmers and herders. The use of rangelands during the cropping season enhanced the relations between herders and farmers by securing the welfare of each party. Masri (1991) argues that before the 1940s and 1950s in Syria, the sedentarization of nomads took place only "when there was enough rain or water for sustained crop production". The shrinking of the rangelands, the expansion of cropping, and the erosion of traditional resource management systems and social networks have strained the relations between herders and farmers. Some governments (e.g., those of Iraq, Libya, Syria) tried to institutionalize this role of rangelands by obliging herders to stay in the range during the whole cropping season. In Syria, the 1966 Decree (No. 20) obligated all animals to be moved out of cropped areas by late winter and stay out until harvest when they can use crop residues. Such policies had their merits, but have very limited effectiveness due to the lack of local enforcement. Consequently, the number of conflicts between herders and farmers have increased over time in the cropping seasons.

3. PRESSURES AFFECTING RANGELANDS

Pastoralists, policy-makers and researchers have been talking alarmingly about the reduction and degradation of native pastures. The World Bank (1995) found that rangeland areas decreased by 13.2% in Tunisia from 1971 to 1992, by 14.7% in Algeria from 1975 to 1992, and by 9.6% in Morocco from 1977 to 1992. The recent debate around rangeland problems has shifted rangeland development from economic efficiency, which for many years concentrated on settling and transforming the pastoral population into farmers (regardless of the long-term environmental impacts), to the sustainable use of rangeland resources. Several factors are identified as being causes of resource misuse and impediments to sustainable management of rangelands. Some of these causes will be highlighted to provide background and explore the solutions that are being promoted.

3.1 Lack of state commitment

The lack of commitment towards traditional range management and production systems precluded government investments in rangeland areas (Gintzburger, unpublisjed). Barghouti and Hayward (1992) argue that "poor land productivity and high risk caused by variable rainfall have attracted meager investments in these marginal areas because of the near certainty of low economic return". In general, WANA governments perceived local traditional production and management systems as backward, inefficient and unequitable. As such, invest-ments in the rangelands were directed towards promoting new organizations and land reforms for the modernization of livestock production. Range development projects failed because of "top-down" technical approaches to rangeland prob-lems from remote centralized administrations (Sidahmed, 1991; Oram, 1995; World Bank, 1995; Gintzburger, unpublished).

The main problem is not the WANA governments' lack of commitment to rangelands in terms of investment, but the lack of commitment to indigenous rangeland production systems. Such a distinction is important because, since the 1960s, many projects have been implemented on rangelands geared towards changing the indigenous production systems. This attitude could be considered the most negative because it impedes communities' capabilities to control their own resources and to ensure their survival. The nature of state intervention has long-term implications on people as well as on the environment. The promotion of settlement was a clear example, where many WANA states invested a lot of resources to upgrade rural areas by distributing land and by providing education and health services. Consequently, pastoral communities lost their well-adapted responses to environmental crises and climatic hazards.

The debate around rangeland development should focus now, not only on the areas that are considered as native pastures, but also on the settled areas. It is only through such an integrated land-use approach that rangelands could be tackled adequately for sustainable resource use. These areas are a continuum used by the same rural communities who developed different coping strategies in response to nature and to government development policies. Thus, the new interest in rangelands should be oriented towards understanding present communities and their resource-management systems. Any approach that seeks sustainable resource use but does not integrate local communities and management systems in the design process is doomed to failure. There is an ongoing debate around community participation but, in general, commitment to developing local production systems is still missing. This does not mean that local production systems should be used blindly, but they should be studied with respect to their changes and the remaining resource management practices and rules that could be beneficial to future rangeland development (Ngaido, 1996a, 1996b).

3.2 Land tenure confusion

The tenure situation in rangelands is the most confusing. Two systems continue to claim legitimate ownership of rangelands: state and local communities. In all the WANA countries except Morocco, legislation that makes the state the owner of rangelands was enacted. The rights of local communities were reduced to use rights. This appropriation of rangelands by the state has many implications regarding rangeland management because it reduces the capabilities of local communities to control and manage the use of resources. The scope in this paper is not to deal with the different reform paths taken by the WANA countries, which will be addressed within the ICARDA/International Food Policy Research Institute (IFPRI) (Mashreq and Maghreb Technology Transfer and Policy and Property Rights Project, but to highlight existing issues.

The main issue regarding the question of appropriation is to determine the trade-off between efficiency and sustainability. The state, claiming that local communities are not efficient resource users, takes the responsibility to set up new rules of access and create resource control mechanisms. With rare exceptions, WANA countries have generally not been efficient controllers of rangeland management. Bedrani (1993) argued that "any policy based solely on state absolute property regardless of prior claims risks failing partially or even totally". The failure of state control mechanisms is due to the high cost of patrolling a very rough and large area and the lack of community participation. The main question that emerges under state control is how to get local participation for sustainable resource use.

Local communities often continue to view rangelands as their territory and continue to control access on an informal basis. Customary management rules are often no longer being enforced; this is one of the major impediments caused by state appropriation. Neighbouring groups (local institutions) will otherwise continue to use their social networks to demand reciprocal access for grazing from one another. They grant each other access as a means of confirming their claims and strengthening their traditional social relations with other communities. Importantly, these arrangements enhanced their risk management strategies during drought years (Oram, 1995; Behnke et al., 1993).

Pastoral communities have maintained some of their customary claims by adapting their strategies to state development policies. For example, local communities were the major beneficiaries of land allocation in settlement schemes. The only difference has been the change from common to individual resource control. As a result, community members claim two types of rights: (i) individual rights of ownership they derive from their community membership and that are confirmed by the state; and (ii) common ownership rights not recognized by the state, which they continue to claim on unsettled rangelands.

This dichotomy is found in all the WANA countries with the exception of Morocco and Tunisia, where tribal rights were recognized on collective lands. In these two countries, however, land allocation to community members has favoured land fragmentation and reduced common community pastures. In the remaining countries, we find different degrees of this duality. It is important, however, to note that regardless of government land policies, local institutions continue to view their rights over rangelands as superior to state claims. Such claims are even asserted on improved state rangeland reserves. For example, the two surveys conducted by ICARDA in 1995 and 1996 in the Maragha state reserve in Syria showed that all the groups that rented grazing rights in the reserve had traditional claims on the area (Nordblom et al., 1995; Rae, unpublished).

These opposing claims between state and local communities have resulted in poorly defined tenure rights on rangeland resources. The confusion between who manages and enforces rules of use and who grants access to rangelands has fostered a situation of no-control which FAO (1994) calls "open-access". Masri (1991) argues that "instability of life and lack of property rights are the real causes of overgrazing and misuse". In addition, such tenure confusion raises many equity issues because wealthy community members, who have the political means to defend those holdings despite their questionable legal status, enclose large grazing areas at the expense of poor community members (Behnke 1988, quoted in FAO, 1994). Bedrani (1993) reported that enclosing large areas with three rows of cereal crops is becoming a generalized practice in Algeria. These practices negatively affect small producers' access to community-controlled resources.

3.3 Collapse of traditional institutions and management systems

The establishment of national borders, the appropriation of rangelands by the state, and the confinement of herding communities into smaller grazing areas narrowed their traditional grazing access-options. Redjel (1995) argues that "the legal assault on property rights seems to share one common objective by over-throwing the customary rights and breaking the traditional organization of the pastoral society". The collapse of traditional migration patterns has put great pressure on community pastures and increased the use of purchased feeds and stubble. Traditional practices and management systems in rangelands, which were developed by local communities in response to their different constraints, have broken down (IFAD, 1995). In Tunisia, FAO (1988) found that "the north-south transhumance was generally accompanied by movement, in the same direction, of nomads from the steppe going to offer their labor to crop producers in the north. As a result, an interregional complementarity with several advan-tages permitted the preservation of an ecological and socio-economic balance that was obvious, though certainly fragile. These balances that prevailed at the beginning of this century, were broken during the 1920s with the adoption of dry-farming".

Customary institutions lost implicit control over their tribal lands. However, many differences exist within, and between, Mashreq and Maghreb countries. Tadros and Salem (1993) argue that in 1946 in Jordan, tribes lost their unregis-tered lands (i.e. steppes and desert rangelands) following the modern establish-ment of the Kingdom of Jordan. Nordblom et al. (1995) argue that "tribal control of rangelands, virtually 'states-within-states', was revoked in many coun-tries. The unintended result of this was to take rangelands out of traditional common property management and move them to open-access and subsequent uncontrolled use and heavy degradation". In addition, the power loss of tribal institutions fosters the individualization of many common resources.

3.4 Competition between pastoralism and farming

Expansion of agricultural production has shifted the boundaries of rangelands. In a desperate pursuit of food self-sufficiency, the governments of the Mashreq and Maghreb countries have encouraged the production of staple food crops and small ruminants even in high-risk areas, regardless of environmental damage (Gintzburger and Bayoumi, 1977; Oram and Hayward, 1992; Barghouti and Hayward, 1992; Bedrani, 1993). FAO (1988) found that in Tunisia, the state tended to favour privatization for the intensification of agriculture. Nomadic communities are settling and getting involved in agricultural production (Metral, 1993). Tadros and Salem (1993) found that in the Lajjoun area in Jordan, 48% of livestock holders owned land. Bedrani (1993) found that among the Ouled Beida residing in the El Guedid area in Algeria, 41% of the active population are involved in both agricultural and livestock production.

The data presented in Figures 6.1 and 6.2 show the evolution of barley areas and sheep stocks in the eight countries of the Mashreq and Maghreb regions from 1961 to 1994. Maghreb countries had around 3 million hectares (ha) devoted to barley production in 1961; this grew to 4.5 million in the late 1980s, an increase of 60% over the past thirty years (Figure 6.1).

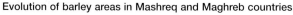

Figure 6.1

Evolution of barley areas in Mashreq and Maghreb countries

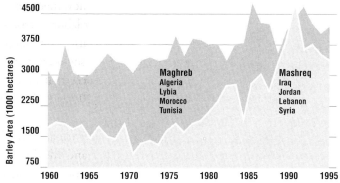

Source: FAOSTAT (1995)

Figure 6.2

Evolution of sheep stocks in Mashreq and Maghreb countries

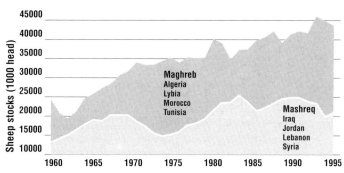

Source: FAOSTAT (1995)

In the Mashreq, however, the increase in lands devoted to barley was spectacular, increasing 300% from 1961 to 1990, but then decreasing somewhat. The expansion of this cropping was largely done at the expense of rangelands. In the Mashreq, Syria witnessed the largest increase in barley cultivation. Leybourne (1996) found a strong correlation (i.e., Spearman's Correlation Coefficient=0.84) between the years and the area planted to barley between 1960 and 1990. The evolution of sheep stocks in these two regions also stand in contrast (Figure 6.2).

The data show a steady growth of sheep stocks in both regions, with the Maghreb countries very much in the lead.

The two phenomena, the increases in barley production and animal population, have multiplied the grazing pressures on rangelands. These processes are the result of many factors that need to be assessed and distinguished between the Maghreb and Mashreq countries.

Nelson (1990) argues that "the extensive opening up of new land, which is increasingly competing with the needs of small farmers and pastoralists, has given higher returns to the mechanized farmer than more intensive use of existing land, in spite of considerable costs to society in terms of lost fuelwood and forage". Tadros and Salem (1993) found that a shift in the cereal production-dominated areas towards fruit trees and vegetables led to the movement of cereal-growing farmers, (especially those with tractors) towards the east to plough the steppe areas to produce cereals. FAO (1988) argues that the extension of cereal and fruit tree production in Tunisia was done at the expense of the best pasture lands and, consequently, reduced the availability of feed resources for livestock production. Jaubert (1993) argues that the 1950s were marked by rapid agrarian development and land concentration in the hands of Bedouin sheikhs; the majority of pastures located in the arid zones (i.e., 200-350 mm rainfall) were converted to crop production.

3.5 Enhanced mobility

The development of the transport system and cheap petrol allow greater mobility of herds, feeds and water (box 6.1). This new access to and availability of water have permitted livestock herders to stay much longer on the range (Tadros and

| **Box 6.1**

The effects of transport development in the rangelands | Transportation by cars and tractors has facilitated the quick movement of flocks in the steppe. Sheep owners are now able to search for good pastures and to move their livestock quickly to take advantage of them. Water is also transported to the grazing sites in tanks pulled behind tractors or mounted on cars. Early grazing and overgrazing are common and are considerably accelerating the decline of the steppe. Moreover, transportation has made water available all the year round; some Bedouins remain in the steppe during the summer and increase the number of their flocks. All these changes have disturbed the long-standing transhumance and, consequently, have disturbed the plant ecology. Undesirable plants such as Noaea mucronota, Alhagi maurorum, Peganum harmala, Anabasis spp., have replaced the palatable species. In addition, considerable damage to the ecosystem is caused by trucks and tractors, which compact the soil and create dust wherever they are used.

Source: Bahhady (1980) |

Salem, 1993; Nordblom et al., 1995). A survey conducted by Tadros (1992) in Jordan found that among 85 sheep farmers, 75% owned tractors, 15.3% owned a water tank, and 7% owned water-tank trailers. Nesheiwat (1991) commented that "modern transport of animals and water has disturbed the traditional flock movements and caused overgrazing".

3.6 Inappropriate price and support policies

Feed subsidies have been one of the major policy tools of WANA governments to support the development of livestock production. These policies, often implemented as part of a drought relief package to sheep owners, have become part of the production base of large and medium-sheep feeders and have created many economic distortions. FAO (1988) found these economic distortions were translated into: (i) stagnation of prices for livestock products; (ii) slow evolution of the livestock sector and the emergence of non-viable production systems; (iii) stagnation of forage production; (iv) increase of imports of animal products; and (v) substitution of beef production for sheep production, following the liberalization of the price of sheep meat when the prices of cattle milk and meat remained controlled. Blench (1995) argues that in Jordan "the system of allocating feeds on per-head basis has created a major incentive to increase herd sizes". These inefficiencies have prompted policy makers to suggest the removal of feed subsidies. They have now been removed in Jordan.

4. POLICY OPTIONS OR THE QUICK-FIX SOLUTIONS TO RANGELANDS PROBLEMS

4.1 Cooperatives and other organizations

In Algeria, the modernization of livestock production was based on the cooperative model (Bedrani, 1993; Redjel, 1995). In Syria, Masri (1991) argues that the state understanding of the importance of the hema system promulgated the 1970 Act (No 140) to: (i) stop the appropriation and ploughing of rangeland; and (ii) require that, "all steppe grazing land was to be managed under Range Improvement and Sheep Husbandry Cooperatives, or under state range reserves for the establishment of Range and Sheep Centers". These cooperatives, which were part of the agricultural modernization agenda, were a means to break the tribal system, as well as to extend collective decision-making to all cooperative members.

Bedrani (1993) attributes the failure of livestock cooperatives, which benefited from state support and the best pastures of the steppe, to the following four factors: (i) only a few cooperatives were beneficiaries; (ii) these cooperatives neither introduced innovations nor improved the range by respecting management practices, such as rotational grazing; (iii) cooperatives were disliked because they excluded non-members on large areas of land that were occupied arbitrarily; and (iv) this form of cooperative could not be generalized because it was expensive and disregarded the welfare of traditional pastoral communities. These findings also apply to many cooperative experiences elsewhere in the WANA countries.

4.2 Rangeland reserves

Since the mid-1980s, rangeland reserves have been the major strategy to reverse the degradation of rangelands and provide fodder to livestock (El Asa'ad et al., 1991; Osman et al., 1994; Leybourne et al., 1993; Nordblom et al., 1995). The rationale to establish reserves for environmental protection and conservation is well-justified (Osman et al., 1994); however, the main approach for the development of rangeland reserves in the WANA countries has been through exclusion of local communities and the complete control of the management by the state. In the case of Syria, Osman et al., (1994) noted that, "shrub plantations have not been put to systematic use for livestock production, as they have mainly been used for seed production". The non-use of shrub plantations in the 1990-1993 period was confirmed in surveys by Wachholtz (1996). In central Tunisia, the development of rangeland reserves with cactus was accompanied by the exclusion of local communities. The main questions that come to mind are: "Why are we spending so much money? Is it for the people or is it for the cosmetic beauty of a green environment?"

The main impediments to existing rangeland reserves are: (i) the lack of a defined and practical strategy regarding the role of local communities in the use and management of these resources; and (ii) the land tenure confusion. These two problems prompted strong local communities to offer new strategies for the use of these reserves. Such practice results in inequities in the use of the resources and is a source of potential conflict between groups. Without naming the people or places involved, we present two recent examples from Rae (unpublished) of how government range rehabilitation programmes were used to bypass traditional tenure arrangements.

Both case studies (Boxes 6.2 and 6.3) show the result of a lack of a well-defined strategy for defining the rights of local people to these reserves. Access to reserves has, so far, been subject only to the purchase of grazing contracts on a "first-come, first-served" basis, regardless of the previous rights of local communities. Both of the examples show the effectiveness of strong local groups in imposing control on rangelands without a legal basis. Groups A and C were capable of using the system of government contracts to prevent other communities with traditional grazing rights from benefiting from government-controlled reserves.

| Box 6.2 | In this first example, range territories of two tribal Groups A and B were taken by the government for establishment of a fodder shrub plantation. Eight years later, parcels of the reserve were made available for low-cost spring grazing contracts. Members of Group A moved quickly to secure contracts along the two sides of the reserve nearest the neighbouring grazing lands of Group B, and to establish their camps along the two other sides. Danger of violence in the event of straying animals during daily transit through the camps or reserve areas of Group A effectively blocked Group B from access to the remaining parts of the reserve. |

Spring grazing blocked

| Box 6.3 | The second example has Group C grabbing all the grazing contracts for another government reserve. Group D, which had prior-use claims on parts of the same land, appeared to be excluded when they returned a few days later. They took their complaint to higher authorities who quickly granted them free access to an unimproved area of the reserve. On urgent appeal to the local authorities, Group C was allowed unlimited access to the remaining part and were relieved of their contract terms which specified the maximum numbers of grazing animals allowed. |

Confounded grazing contracts

These inefficiencies in the contract system are a clear result of the exclusion of local communities from the conceptualization and implementation of reserves. If such groups were allowed legal backing for their traditional claims, there is little doubt of their abilities to protect and sustain rangeland rehabilitation efforts. Without their direct participation, on the other hand, it is difficult to imagine sustainable large-scale success in range rehabilitation.

4.3 Privatization of rangelands

The persistence of rangeland degradation in WANA countries prompted several approaches for better resource use. Generally, poor or destructive resource use is perceived as a consequence of a lack of well-defined rights (Bromley, 1991). In order to promote sustainable resource management, it therefore becomes necessary to grant secure access rights to resource users. Provision of tenure security to resource users promotes better resource use and encourages investment in resources (Feder and Noronha, 1987). This is because holders of such rights can reasonably hope to enjoy the benefits of their investments in good stewardship. Ellis and Swift (1988) noted that "the assumption is that some form of privatization will alleviate the imbalances supposedly induced by communal grazing". As such, privatization of common resources is thought to be one of the most practical solutions to environmental degradation. In this case it is very important to depart from the narrow view of private property, confined solely to the individual (Ngaido, 1994).

The main feature of private property is that it is legally respected by the state and is easily marketable. As such, three types of private property rights are distinguished: (i) community private rights under collective management (i.e., cooperative); (ii) community private rights under individual management (i.e. tribal system); and (iii) private rights under individual management. The first two types are forms of corporate ownership of private property.

(i)   *Community private rights under collective management* occur when the state recognizes the traditional claims of the communities in a developed area and organizes (or allows a spontaneous organization of) community members in a cooperative or users-group. Members of the community have co-owner rights and agree among themselves how to control access and use of the resources, often designating a management committee. The main question is whether community members have the same incentive for resource use and conservation, because in the short-term the gains in the utilization of the resources are superior to costs (required time) of resource rehabilitation and conservation. Such a management system is sustainable in the long-term, only if the members are allowed to transfer their rights to other community members. This could be an important solution to land fragmentation and consolidation in low rainfall areas.

(ii) *Private property rights granted to a community under individual management* could apply to a tribe, to a fraction or an extended family. Contrary to the previous community private property, management continues to be carried out by the individual who traditionally was in charge of resource management. Under this tenure situation, it is not necessary to create new institutions, though provisions should be made to secure the rights of weak community members as well as to enhance awareness of sustainable practices in range use.

(iii) Individual private property occurs when the individual has a total control and decision-making power over his property. This type of property is often thought by the developed world to be the most desirable because it encourages investment and resource conservation. It also offers more security because the owner has total freedom to decide on how to use his resources. Studies on the impacts of such tenure regimes on investment, however, are not very conclusive (Bromley, 1989, 1991; Bruce, 1989).

As a strategy against rangeland degradation, private property could be part of the answer in any of the three forms wherever they are viable. There are still some communities, for example, with strong local leaders who continue to use efficient traditional resource management systems. For such communities, the best strategy may not be individual private property but, through recognizing and strengthening traditional rights, to allow them access to credit.

4.4 Revitalization of traditional management systems

During the late 1980s and early 1990s, the failure of rangeland development projects prompted a new interest in traditional resource management systems. FAO commissioned twelve working papers on pastoral and agro-pastoral societies (Masri, 1991). This was a step towards understanding customary rules and resource management practices. It resulted in a new view of rangeland communities and their livestock production systems. Masri (1991) argues that "nomadism is a sound form of grazing management that ensures the revegetation processes". According to Masri (1991), the efficiency of the nomadic production system was due to groups' common understanding that they were "utilizing a productive resource which had to be maintained". The key element of traditional management systems is the homogeneity of their production system, because all the groups are using the same strategies to feed their animals. Two major impediments to the revitalization of traditional management systems are the reduction of the grazing areas (national and international) and the opportunistic behaviour of community members.

Nomadism depends on social networks that were spread at the national and regional level. The reduction of grazing areas has squeezed herding communities and pushed them to settle and reorient some of their activities. Bedrani (1993) found that "herders and agro-herders of Ouled Beida faction exclusively use pastures around their agricultural fields without doing any transhumance or even using pastures often used by tribal members". As a result, local institutions broke down and the strategies for livestock production are being individualized.

The individualization of production strategies (each sheep owner has his own way to feed his animals in contrast to when they all depended mainly on native pastures) has prompted opportunistic behaviour among community members. Each owner follows his own economic interest. With the transformation of the herding population, more entrepreneurs and the market demand for livestock produce (e.g., meat, milk) have prompted new interest by merchants, urban dwellers, government agents, and migrant workers to invest in livestock production. To carry out their activities, most of these categories of people tend to rely on government institutions and on hired herders. FAO (1994) argues that "many animals are bought by wealthy people who commonly have access to non-pastoral resources such as government jobs, or trading assets which could be reinvested in reproductive capital, labor, or supplementary feed". Sidahmed (1991) concluded that "as livestock owners become less involved in animal rearing (absentee stock owners), their traditional concern for the welfare of the grazing domain diminishes, giving way to the opportunistic practices which intensify the degradation process". This is especially true on open-access rangelands.

Communal tribal pastures are no longer always perceived as a common resource that is important to preserve for the benefit of the whole community, but rather as a resource available for appropriation. Many members are asking for their private shares of tribal collective lands. The National Institute for Agricultural Research (INRA)-Settat in Morocco found that all former collective rangelands of the rural commune of Oulad Bouali were distributed and cropped. This trend is also being generalized in the El Brouj area, where collective lands are being individualized at the expense of livestock production. The trend of individualization and limited access do not allow revitalization of traditional grazing systems. While this does not rule out the possibilities of using traditional grazing systems, such as hema, it highlights the fact that the reduction of range resources, and the changes in community members' behaviour towards grazing land offer a real challenge.

4.5 Market liberalization: the removal of feed subsidies

The removal of feed subsidies is often regarded as an approach to correct some of the economic distortions in the livestock production sector. The negative consequences for medium and small herdowners who depend on these feeds to carry out their activities should be considered. During a Rapid Rural Appraisal of the Mashreq & Maghreb Projects in the village of Mhiiy in Jordan in 1996, a farmer with 100 sheep expressed his difficulties in maintaining his herd because the 1991 census only registered fifty of his sheep as the basis for his feed subsidies. An issue that needs to be well-studied is the importance of feed subsidies in small sheepbreeders' production strategies; for example, to what extent do they depend on imported feeds, and how vulnerable are they to price change, as their financial resources are limited. Blench (1995), in his study on rangelands of Jordan, argues that large herdowners will survive the removal of feed subsidies, while small holders are most vulnerable.

In general, the removal of feed subsidies is an issue that needs to be addressed carefully because of its many socio-economic implications. The country-by-country differences in the degree of dependence on imported feeds preclude blanket statements on this policy. Table 6.1 illustrates that the evolution of feed composition of livestock diets in the Mashreq and Maghreb project countries has several important features: (i) no two countries are alike in their feed endowments and purchases; (ii) all eight countries, however, do show declining proportions of total feed from pastures over the twenty-year period, due mainly to the rising livestock population; (iii) with the exception of Jordan, all countries have increasingly depended on crop residues as a feed source; (iv) the greatest dependency on imported feed grains and other concentrates has developed in Jordan and Lebanon; and (v) the greatest users of domestic feed grains and other concentrates have been Morocco and Syria.

Table 6.1

Compositions of livestock diets by feed categories

Countries	Periods	Feed Grains and other concentrates (%)		Pastures (%)	Residues (%)	Total (%)
		Imported	Domestic			
Algeria	1970-74	1	4	78	17	100
	1980-84	5	5	74	16	100
	1990-94	9	8	63	20	100
Iraq	1970-74	1	9	48	52	100
	1980-84	7	11	49	33	100
	1990-94	2	16	38	44	100
Jordan	1970-74	4	2	69	25	100
	1980-84	22	2	62	14	100
	1990-94	47	3	40	10	100
Lebanon	1970-74	23	2	60	15	100
	1980-84	29	1	62	8	100
	1990-94	29	3	50	18	100
Libya	1970-74	3	2	91	4	100
	1980-84	5	2	85	8	100
	1990-94	15	2	76	7	100
Morocco	1970-74	1	16	38	45	100
	1980-84	2	14	43	41	100
	1990-94	3	14	33	50	100
Syria	1970-74	1	15	30	56	100
	1980-84	3	18	20	59	100
	1990-94	3	17	14	66	100
Tunisia	1970-74	0	5	64	31	100
	1980-84	0	7	59	34	100
	1990-94	0	9	49	42	100

Source: Compiled by Farouk Shomo after methods of Nordblom and Shomo (1995)

In the case of Lebanon, there have been no feed subsidies to support the imports for its growing livestock and poultry industries. In contrast, substantial feed subsidies in Jordan encouraged the highest level of use among the eight countries. Recent policy changes to remove these subsidies are expected to have considerable impacts on some modes of production, particularly that of importing live lambs and feeds and exporting the fattened lambs.

In Syria, 66% of livestock production depends on crop residues and only 17% on home-grown feed grains. For Iraq, Morocco and Tunisia, pastures continue to play an important role in livestock diets. This is being complemented with crop residues rather than imports. The survey conducted in June 1996 by INRA-Settat and the International Centre for Advanced Mediterranean Agronomic Studies (CIHEAM)-Montpellier showed that, in the Khourigba area of Morocco, large sheep owners depended chiefly on their own production to feed their animals. In another example, under the ICARDA/IFPRI Mashreq and Maghreb Project, Iraq is developing a small feed-block industry. Such technologies may play an important role in adding value to agricultural production and reducing import dependency.

5. CONCLUSION

The "top-down", remote, centrally-planned approaches to pastoral people and resources in the WANA region have had several unexpected negative consequences, due largely to a lack of consideration for the short and long-run incentives and interests of the rangeland users.

It is necessary to have an integrated land-use management approach, which takes full account of the larger economic and social contexts of pastoral people, particularly their needs for the security of tenure and authority to form reciprocal resource-use agreements with neighbouring groups who are similarly secure. This permits economic, social and ecological stability beyond what is possible under the western ranching model of set-stocking and carrying capacities.

The past exclusion and denial of pastoral social institutions, justified on the grounds of modernity and the establishment of national unity, have had terrible consequences in terms of rangeland degradation. Economically viable range rehabilitation on a large scale requires direct participation, protection and investments by pastoral people. This requires care and sensitive handling to meet the needs both of the state and of the pastoral people. Much of the research under the ICARDA/IFPRI Mashreq & Maghreb Project creates a partnership of scientists and policy-makers in eight countries of the region, aimed at investigating the methodological, institutional and organizational sides of such development needs.

Acknowledgments

The authors would like to acknowledge the support of the Joint ICARDA/IFPRI Mashreq/Maghreb Project coordinators, Peter Hazell (IFPRI) and Nasri Haddad (ICARDA). The policy and property rights research programme with IFPRI was funded by IFAD/the Arab Fund for Economic and Social Development (AFESD) for the 1995-1997 period, as a third of a larger project "The Development of Integrated Crop-Livestock Production in West Asia and North Africa (Mashreq/Maghreb/M&M)", which supports research on dryland agronomy and livestock technology with the National Agricultural Research Services (NARS) of eight countries (Algeria, Iraq, Jordan, Lebanon, Libya, Morocco, Syria, and Tunisia). The achievements, interdisciplinary research teams, methodologies and goodwill contacts with policy-makers made in the first phase (1995-1997) will provide the foundation for sound and fruitful synthesis and larger positive impacts in the second phase (1998-2000). We also acknowledge the valuable insights and criticisms of Scott Christiansen, Euan Thomson, Farouk Shomo and Jonathan Rae.

References

Awad, M. 1962. The problems of the arid zones. Proceedings of the Paris Symposium by UNESCO.

Bahhady, F. A. 1980. Recent changes in Bedouin systems of livestock production in the Syrian steppe.

Galay, J.G., Aronson, D., Balzman, P.C., and Chouinard, A. (Eds.). *The future of pastoral people* Proceedings of Nairobi Conference, 4-8 August 1980.

Barghouti, S. and Hayward, J. 1992. *Land and water resources in the Middle East and North Africa: issues and challenges.* Paper Presented at the EDI/WB/ICARDA/AOAD Seminar on Natural Resources and Environmental Management in the Dry Areas, Aleppo, Syria. 16-27 February 1992.

Bedrani, S. 1987. *Les pasteurs et agropasteurs au Maghreb.* (631-585 FAO/87).

Bedrani, S. 1993. Les systems agro-pastoraux maghrebins: une etude de cas a El-Guedid (Wilaya de Djelfa-Algerie). *Revue des Regions Arides* no 5/93. pp. 3-34.

Behnke, R.H. 1988. Range enclosure in Central Somalia. *Pastoral Development Network Paper* 25b.

Behnke, R.H., Scoones, I. and Kerven, C. 1993. (Eds.). *Range ecology at disequilibrium: new models of natural variability and pastoral adaptation in African savannas.* Overseas Development Institute. London.

Bernus, E. and Pouillon, F. 1990. Société pastorales et dévélopment. *Cahier des Sciences Humaines* Vol 26, No. 1-2. Editions de L'ORSTOM. Paris.

Blench, R. 1995. *The Hashemite Kingdom of Jordan: National Program for Range Rehabilitation and Development. Baseline survey of socio-economic and animal production data.* IFAD, Rome.

Bocco, R. 1990. La sedentarisation des pasteurs nomades: les experts internationaux face a la question bedouine dans le Moyen-Orient Arabe (1950-1970). *Cahier des Sciences Humaines.* Vol. 26, No 1-2.

Bourbouze, A. and Donadieu, P. 1987. *L'elevage sur parcours en regions mediterraneennes. Options mediterraneennes.* CIHEAM. (636-084.22 ELE/87).

Bromley, D.W. 1991. *Environment and economy: property rights and public policy.* Blackford Oxford, UK; Cambridge, USA.

Bromley, D.W. 1989. Property relations and economic development: the other land reform. *World Development.* Vol. 17, no. 6 (June 1989). pp. 867-877.

Bruce, J. W. 1986. *Land tenure issues in project design and strategies for agricultural development in Sub-Saharan Africa.* Land Tenure Center, University of Wisconsin, Madison. LTC paper N° 128.

Bruce, J.W. 1989. *The variety of reforms: A review of recent experience with land reform and the reform of land tenure, with particular reference to the African Experience.* Paper prepared for conference on Human Rights in a Post-Apartheid South African Constitution, University. September 1989.

El Asa'ad, H., Osman, A.E. and Bahady. 1991. Seeding edible shrubs on degraded marginal lands. *Pasture Forage and Livestock Program Annual Report* 1990/1991. ICARDA, Aleppo.

Ellis, J.E. and Swift, D. 1988. *Stability of pastoral ecosystems: alternate paradigms and implication for development.*

Food and Agriculture Organization of the United Nations (FAO). 1988. *Tunisie: Programme de developpement des productions fourageres et de l'elevage.* Rapport de synthese.

FAO. 1994. *A systems perspective for sustainable dryland development in the Near East region.* FAO Near East Office, Cairo.

Feder, G. and Noronha, R. 1987. Land rights systems and agricultural development in sub-Saharan Africa. *World Bank Research Observer 2*, N° 2, July.

Forage and Grazing Terminology Committee. 1991. *Terminology for grazing land and grazing animals.* Pocahantas Press. Blacksburg, Virginia, USA.

Gintzburger, G. and Bayoumi, M. 1977. Survey of the present situation and production of the Libyan rangelands. FAO-ARC No. 117/77, Tripoli, Libya.

Gintzburger, G. (*in press*). A rangeland strategy for ICARDA.

Hogg, R. 1990. An institutional approach to pastoral development: an example from Ethiopia. *ODI Pastoral Development Network Paper* 30d. (631.585 ODI/90).

International Centre for Agricultural Research in Dry Areas (ICARDA). 1979. *Introduction to range management.* Forage training course 1979. (Reprinted in March 1987). ICARDA, Aleppo.

ICARDA. 1991. Pasture and Forage Livestock Program. *Annual Report for 1990/91.* ICARDA, Aleppo.

ICARDA. 1993. Pasture and Forage Livestock Program. *Annual Report for 1993.* ICARDA, Aleppo.

ICARDA. 1996. Pasture and Forage Livestock Program. *Annual Report for 1994.* ICARDA, Aleppo.

Jaubert, R. 1993. Evolution des systems agro-pastoraux et politiques de developpement des regions seches de Syrie. In: Bocco, R., Jaubert, R. et Metral, F. (Eds.) *Steppes d'arabies: Etats, pasteurs, agriculteurs et commercants: le devenir des zones seches.* Presses Universitaires de France Paris. pp. 161-194.

Kassam, A. 1992. *An overview of land and water resources in the WANA region.* Paper presented at the EDI/WB/ICARDA/ADAD Seminar on Natural Resources and Environmental Management in the Dry Areas. 16-29 February 1992, Aleppo, Syria.

Kruger, A.S. and Kressirer, R.F. 1995. Towards sustainable rangeland management and livestock production in Namibia. *Vieh & Fisch. Abteilung* 422. GTZ. pp. 163-179.

Lawry, S.W. 1990. Tenure policy toward common property natural resources in sub-Saharan Africa. *Natural Resources Journal.* Vol. 30 (spring), pp. 403-422. University of New Mexico School of Law.

Le Houerou, H.N. 1989. An assessment of the economic feasibility of fodder shrubs plantation (with particular reference to Africa). *Biology and Utilization of Shrubs,* Academic Press Inc., pp. 603-30.

Leybourne, M., Ghassali, F., Osman, A.S., Nordblom, T. and Gintzburger, G. 1993. The utilization of fodder shrubs (*Atriplex spp., Salsola vermicula*) by agro-pastoralists in the northern Syrian steppe. *Pasture Forage and Livestock Program Annual Report 1993.* ICARDA, Aleppo.

Leybourne, M. 1996. The Extension of Barley Cultivation in the Arid Zones of Northern Syria. *Pasture Forage and Livestock Program Annual Report 1994*. ICARDA, Aleppo.

Livingstone, I. 1985. *Pastoralism: an overview of practice, process and policy*. FAO, Rome.

Masri, A. 1991. The tradition of hema as a land tenure institution in arid land management: the Syrian Arab Republic. 1995, 61:1-8.

Metral, F. 1993. Elevage et agriculture dans l'oasis de Sukhne (Syrie): gestion des risques par les commercants-entrepreneurs. In: Bocco, R., Jaubert, R. and Metral, F. (Eds.) *Steppes d'arabies: Etats, pasteurs, agriculteurs et commercants: le devenir des zones seches*. Presses Universitaires de France Paris. pp. 194-246.

Nelson, R. 1990. Dryland management: the "desertification" problem. *World Bank Technical Paper*, no. 116.

Nesheiwat, K. 1991. Socio-economic aspects of the traditional hema system of arid land management in Jordan. FAO, Rome.

Ngaido, T. 1994. *Le Foncier dans le processus de la desertification: cause ou remede*. Paper prepared for the IDRC-Senegal workshop on tenure and desertification. 7-9 March 1994.

Ngaido, T. 1996a. *"Accounting for customary land rights": Land and Institutional Policies in Niger*. Paper prepared for the FAO/University of Godollo, Hungary Workshop "Post-Cold War agrarian reform and rural development strategies." 9-13 April 1996.

Ngaido, T. 1996b. Redefining the boundaries of control: post-colonial tenure policies and dynamics of social and tenure change in western Niger. Ph.d. dissertation. University of Wisconsin, Madison.

Nordblom, T., Arab, G., Gintzburger, G. and Osman, A. 1995. *April 1995 survey of Bedouin groups with contracts to graze the government rangeland plantation at Maragha, Aleppo Province, Syria*. Paper prepared for the Regional Symposium on Integrated Crop-Livestock systems in the Dry Areas of the West Asia and North Africa Region. Amman. 6-8 November, 1995.

Nordblom, T., Goodchild, A., Shomo, F. and Gintzburger, G. 1996. *Dynamics of feed resources in mixed farming systems of the North Africa, West Asia and Central Asia regions*. What can Research do? Paper prepared for the International Workshop, "Crop Residues in Sustainable Mixed Crop/Livestock Farming Systems", ICRISAT, Patancheru, India. 22-16 April 1996.

Nordblom, T. and Shomo, F. 1995. Food and Feed prospects to 2020 in the West Asia/North Africa Region. ICARDA Social Science Papers No. 2. ICARDA, Aleppo.

Oram, P. 1995. *Issues for research on the role of agriculture policy and property rights in sustainable development of low rainfall areas of West Asia and North Africa: a position paper*. Paper prepared for the ICARDA/IFPRI Policy Workshop, Tunis, 8-10 October 1995.

Oram, P. and Hayward, J. 1992. *Research and extension services for land and water resources in the Near East and North Africa*. Presented at the EDI/WB/ICARDA/ADAD Seminar on National Resources and Environmental Management in the Dry Areas., Aleppo. Syria. 16-29 February 1992.

Osman, A., Bahhady, F., Hassan, N. and Murad, N. 1994. Use of fodder shrubs in the rehabilitation of degraded rangelands in Syria. *Pasture Forage and Livestock Program Annual Report 1994*. ICARDA, Aleppo.

Rae, J. (unpublished). Custom, pragmatism, and opportunity in steppe administration: an analysis of formal and informal institutions and organizations on the Syrian steppe. Ph.d. Dissertation. Department of Geography, Oxford University, Oxford, England.

Redjel, N. 1995. Property rights and institutions in Algerian steppe rangeland. Paper prepared for the ICARDA/IFPRI Policy Workshop, Tunis, 8-10 October 1995.

Sayegh, A. 1992. *Land resource surveys and land use and development.* Paper presented at the EDI/WB/ICARDA/AOAD Seminar on Natural Resources and Environmental Management in the Dry areas, Aleppo, Syria. 16-27 February 1992.

Seve, J., Ross-Sheriff, B.A., Impara, P.C. and de Treville, D. 1990. *World Bank drylands management study: Lessons of experience.* World Bank Environment Department.

Shideed, K.H. 1995. *Crop/Livestock integration, technology adoption, agricultural policies and property rights under rainfed conditions in Iraq.* Paper prepared for the ICARDA/IFPRI Policy Workshop, Tunis. 8-10 October 1995.

Sidahmed, A.E. 1991. *Towards strengthening the range/livestock research and extension capabilities of the national institutions in the Near East and North Africa.* Paper prepared for the IV Congres des terres de parcours, Montpellier, France.

Sidahmed, A.E. 1992. Sustainable rangelands in the Near East and North Africa. *Rangelands* 14(4). August.

Sidahmed, A.E. 1993. *Towards strengthening the range/livestock research and extension capabilities of the national institutions in the Near East and North Africa.* Staff Working Paper No. 11. April 1993. IFAD, Rome.

Somel, K. 1991. Agricultural diversification in the Middle East and North Africa. Paper presented at the EDI/WB/ICARDA/AOAD Seminar on Natural Resources and Environmental Management in the Dry areas, Aleppo, Syria. 16-27 February 1992.

Spedding, C.R.W. 1995. Sustainability in animal production systems. *Animal Science,* 61:1-8.

Stoddard, L. A., Smith, A.D. and Box, T.W. 1975. *Range management.* McGraw-Hill Publishing Company, New York, USA.

Swift, J. 1988. *Major issues in pastoral development with special emphasis on selected African countries.* FAO, Rome.

Tadros, K.I. 1992. *Current situation and future potentials of dry rangelands in Jordan.* Mimeograph. ICARDA, Aleppo.

Tadros, K.I. and Salem, M.A. 1993. *Rangeland resource management at Lajjoun area.* Final Report of Dryland Resource Management Project. ICARDA, Aleppo.

Wachholtz, R. 1996. Socio-economics of bedouin farming systems in dry areas of northern Syria. In: Doppler, W. (Ed.). *Farming systems and resource economics in the Tropics.* Vol 24. Wissenschaftsverlag Vauk, Kiel.

World Bank, 1995. *Rangelands development in arid and semi-arid areas: strategies and policies.* Natural Resources and Environment Division. November 9, 1995.

part II

*Modelling and other aids
to rangeland management*

The management of the complex dryland grazing systems
is difficult. A suite of tools has been developed to establish
a baseline (inventory) and measure change (monitor).
These have been combined with computer-based decision-
support systems to aid in management. The seven chapters
in this section explore some applications of modelling and
other predictive approaches to decision-making.

The SAVANNA integrated modelling system: an integrated remote sensing, GIS and spatial simulation modelling approach

J. Ellis and M. B. Coughenour

7

Synopsis

This paper describes the modelling approach which was originally developed to describe and analyze the pastoral nomad system of the Turkana in Kenya. The SAVANNA modelling system was designed to address spatio-temporal variability by joining remote-sensed and Geographic Information System (GIS) databases with spatial simulations, in order to compute rates of plant production, forage intake by ungulates, and ecosystem function under varying climatic conditions. SAVANNA has subsequently been used elsewhere to model ecosystems dominated by wide-ranging grazer/browser populations.

Key points

1. *The spatially extensive nature of arid and semi-arid rangelands, coupled with the temporal variability of rainfall, complicate analysis and planning for economically sustainable management and development. There is need for a tool to address this spatio-temporal variability.*

2. *The SAVANNA model system uses Normalized Difference Vegetation Index (NDVI) data based on the National Oceanic and Atmospheric Administration (NOAA) Advanced and Very High Resolution Radiometer (AVHRR) to test model predictions of spatio-temporal patterns of plant production. NVDI data may alternatively be used to drive the plant growth submodel. Weather data serve as a primary driver for the model through the creation of monthly rainfall maps. GIS data layers include maps of topography, vegetation, soils, water distribution and land-use patterns.*

3. *The SAVANNA model has been used to simulate such diverse dynamics as the effects of winter snowfall on elk population fluctuations in Yellowstone National Park in the USA, and the implications of alterations in land-use rights among Turkana pastoralists in Kenya.*

1. INTRODUCTION

Temporal change in climate and vegetation is a fundamental property of arid and semi-arid grazing systems. Seasonal cycles between the wet and dry season or between summer and winter occur each year. Thus, adaptations and behaviours for coping with seasonality are among the most basic strategies of herbivores and humans living in arid and semi-arid lands. Longer-term inter-annual cycles, such as the El Nino-Southern Oscillation, cause intermittent extremes in rainfall, snowfall or temperature, and are the origin of some devastating natural disasters. Because inter-annual climate variability increases as ecosystems become drier (Nicholls and Wong, 1990), dry grazing lands are among the earth's most temporally variable and unstable ecosystems (Caughley et al. 1987; Ellis and Swift; 1988; Westoby et al., 1989). Both ecological models and laboratory experiments have established that spatial heterogeneity can theoretically compensate for temporal instability (Huffacker, 1958; DeAngelis and Waterhouse, 1987). And in nature, spatial heterogeneity acts as an important stabilizing property in highly-dynamic, temporally unstable grazing systems (Coughenour, 1992). Thus, changes over time and heterogeneity in space are, in some ways, compensatory forces balancing the dynamics of variable ecosystems.

The SAVANNA simulation model was developed to investigate the dynamics of a highly variable ecosystem in northern Kenya, inhabited by Turkana pastoral nomads. Because the ecosystem is both strongly seasonal and drought-prone, the Ngisonyoka Turkana nomads are among Africa's most mobile people (McCabe 1985; Ellis et al., 1987). At the same time, this region is characterized by landscape and vegetation heterogeneity, the result of strong elevational and climatic gradients (Coughenour and Ellis, 1993). In order to replicate the time-space dynamics of this ecosystem and the coping strategies of the nomads, SAVANNA needed to represent accurately both the spatial heterogeneity and the temporal instability inherent in the Turkana grazing system. The model was therefore constructed to simulate long-term dynamics of grazing system processes within the spatial framework of a GIS. Since the initial development of the Turkana version of SAVANNA, the model has been modified and adapted to several different grazing systems. It now exists in versions which are all spatially-explicit, process-oriented models of grassland, shrubland, savanna and forested ecosystems. The model has been implemented to simulate processes at local to regional scales, operating over years to multi-decadenal time periods (Coughenour, 1993).

SAVANNA is unusual, or possibly unique, among grazing system models in that it:

(i)   couples an ecosystem/grazing system simulation with remote-sensed and other spatial data-bases within a GIS format;

(ii)   simulates at each time step, changes in vegetation quantity, quality and distribution in response to climate and other drivers (i.e. fire), as well as removal by herbivores;

(iii) simulates the spatial redistribution of herbivores in response to changes in vegetation quality and availability; and

(iv)   simulates the production and demographic responses of herbivores to changes in vegetation.

Every simulation model has a certain level of trade-off between mechanistic detail and model simplicity. While highly aggregated or simplified models are easier to use, these are less realistic, less generalizable and less explanatory. On the other hand, highly mechanistic models are more difficult to implement and the marginal costs of added complexity are high.

Highly resolved models are more computationally demanding, which may prohibit their implementation at (very) large spatial or long temporal scales. Therefore, SAVANNA treats ecological processes at an intermediate level of resolution. The time step of the SAVANNA model is a week, which allows simulations over longer time scales and larger spatial scales (Coughenour, 1993). As computer technology has advanced, the scale and time frame of SAVANNA has expanded. Currently, the model simulates landscapes composed of 100-10 000 grid cells of any size and operates over timeframes of years to several decades, in reasonable computation time on a personal computer (PC) with the current generation of microprocessors.

2. MODEL STRUCTURE

SAVANNA was designed to operate at a landscape or local level, i.e., it was envisioned to be applied to landscapes incorporating the entire spatial domain of a selected grazing system. In the Turkana case, the local grazing system covered a sub-tribal territory of approximately 10 000 km². Today, this grazing system could be simulated at a scale of one grid cell per square kilometre (km²); when the model was first constructed, grid cells had to be considerably larger due to computational limitations. The spatial component of the model has a hierarchial structure. Grid cells may be of any size; each cell is simulated and changes in cell characteristics or redistribution of herbivores among cells is updated at selected time steps. Each cell has a subarea corresponding to the configuration of physical factors like topography and soils. For each subarea the model simulates vegetation patch cover (i.e. herbaceous, shrub, and tree cover) but this "within cell" patch structure is modelled as a proportion of the grid cell, rather than in terms of explicit patch structure.

The model is composed of several interacting submodels (Figure 7.1). It is driven by monthly weather data, although NDVI values can be used to drive the model if climate data are not available. Monthly precipitation and temperature drivers may be entered as spatially explicit values or, if not available in that form, as mean values for the ecosystem. A snow submodel simulates snow depth and water content; snow crusting is related to temperature. The water submodel simulates soil moisture dynamics for each patch type within each grid cell. The model includes precipitation, interception, runoff, runon, infiltration, deep drainage, bare soil evaporation and transpiration. The light submodel simulates shading within and among plant canopies and provides information for competitive interaction among plant types and resulting change in vegetation structure.

Figure 7.1

SAVANNA model structure

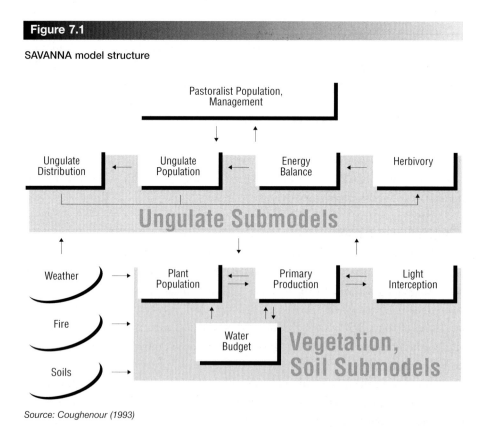

Source: Coughenour (1993)

Plants are simulated in the net primary production (NPP) and plant population submodels. The NPP submodel is affected by light, water, temperature, soil properties and herbivory. Plant biomass is generated or lost in response to these drivers. The plant population submodel simulates establishment, size class and mortality of specific functional groups. The population submodel is linked directly to the NPP submodel.

Herbivore dynamics and impact are the outcome of several interacting submodels. The herbivory submodel simulates forage intake which is determined by species dietary patterns (i.e., diet selection) and by forage availability and quality. An energy balance submodel uses patterns of energy intake and expenditure to simulate the mean body weight of each sex and age class for each animal species. Body weight is used to develop a condition index which affects herbivore population dynamics. Birth rates and death rates are simulated in the population dynamics submodel, for each of five sex/age classes. Animals may also be removed from the population by sales, culling or other managerial means in a rule-based routine. A predator model interacts directly with the herbivore population dynamics submodel. Predation rate is density-dependent and predator dynamics are regulated by prey-intake rates. The herbivore spatial distribution submodel dynamically distributes animals among grid cells over the simulated region, on a monthly basis, in relation to habitat suitability. Suitability is determined by changing forage distributions as well as by the basic characteristics of the ecosystem and managerial inputs, such as herding and water distribution. For a more detailed description of SAVANNA, see Coughenour (1993).

3. SAVANNA OPERATIONS

Utilization of the SAVANNA integrated system generally involves a series of linked GIS operations and model simulation runs (Figure 7.2). In order to run the system in such a way as to take advantage of the precision inherent in SAVANNA, the physical and dynamical characteristics of the selected ecosystem must be specified at a commensurate level of resolution. Spatial databases needed to meet research or management objectives are entered into a GIS system (SAVANNA interfaces with ARC-INFO, GRASS and IDRISI).

Regional soils, climate patterns and vegetation are generally required; vegetation structure can be entered from aerial photos, T-M or other R/S imagery, or from other sorts of maps. When basic information (e.g., vegetation, climate, soils), is accumulated in the GIS, SAVANNA is parameterized to fit the local conditions. The model can then be run to replicate the vegetation dynamics of the selected region, based on extant seasonal and long-term climate patterns. At this stage, it is useful to compare model output to observed NDVI dynamics.

Figure 7.2

SAVANNA operations and output files

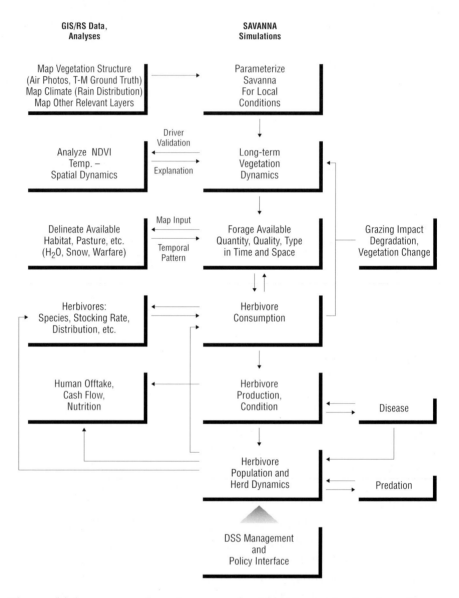

The model demonstrates how the system should behave under the given climate regime, and it explains at the process-level why system dynamics followed the simulated pattern.

Comparison with observed NDVI dynamics provides a validation test for the model; if results match, the ecosystem and the model are in synchrony. If results differ, the ecosystem is not reacting to climate dynamics as expected, indicating that there is a mismatch between real ecosystem characteristics and those used to parameterize the model. For example, an undiscovered shift in plant species composition or overgrazing might cause a mismatch between simulated and observed NDVI trends.

Simulation of vegetation dynamics provides the information needed to specify the spatial distribution and temporal dynamics of forage for herbivores, within the region of interest. If some of this forage is unavailable to herbivores for reasons such as poor water distribution, unsuitable terrain, and warfare zones, these areas can be eliminated within the GIS. Information on herbivore species, sex and age classes, stocking rate and distribution are then entered in GIS format. SAVANNA then simulates herbivore consumption based on the forage and herbivore inputs, and updates forage conditions and herbivore condition for simulation at the next time step.

These SAVANNA operations provide, (among other things), numerical values for, and spatial distribution of:

(i)   grazing impact on vegetation and resulting changes in vegetation;
(ii)   herbivore production and condition;
(iii)   herbivore production translated into human offtake; and
(iv)   herbivore population and herd dynamics.

4. SAVANNA APPLICATIONS

The exact operation of the SAVANNA integrated system depends upon the objectives at hand and the characteristics of the ecosystem/grazing system under investigation. SAVANNA has been used in a research context to evaluate the long-term dynamics of the Turkana grazing system mentioned above. The model has also been used to assess management options for several North American national parks, where questions of ungulate carrying capacity, grazing impact and appropriate management techniques have been addressed. Currently, the modelling system is being adapted to evaluate climate and land-use interactions and their joint effects on the production characteristics, stability and resilience of a very large grazing region encompassed by the Mongolian Steppe in east Central Asia. An early prototype of the integrated system was first developed to evaluate patterns of energy flow from plants, through livestock to Turkana pastoralists in northern Kenya. In this study, we used a primitive GIS application and a static ecosystem model to trace the seasonal and spatial dynamics of energy in this large (10 000 km^2), unstable and highly seasonal ecosystem (Coughenour et al., 1985). Through this analysis, we were able to identify critical paths of energy flow, the relative importance to pastoralists of various plant types and herbivore species, and we identified that livestock removed an extremely small portion of the total forage produced over the ecosystem as a whole. From this beginning, we developed a dynamic ecosystem model (SAVANNA) and, among other objectives, coupled it with NDVI data to evaluate ecosystem recovery rates following a severe drought (Coughenour, 1992). In addition, we used the SAVANNA system to conduct a retrospective analysis of drought dynamics and livestock production over a 67-year period (1923-1990) covered by historical climate data (Ellis et al., 1993).

SAVANNA has recently been used to assist in research and management of ungulate populations in several national parks and conservation areas in North America. A general concern in parks and conservation areas is the question of natural regulation of ungulates versus intense management, in order to keep populations within levels perceived to be compatible with ecosystem vegetation and other properties. In this context, SAVANNA has been used to provide park biologists and managers with simulation studies of winter-range carrying capacity, ungulate impact on forage plants and riparian zones, and ungulate population responses to fire and climate change.

Yellowstone National Park is one of the largest parks in the US (i.e., about 8 900 km^2) and supports a high diversity of native ungulates and high densities of some species. Since the early years of the park, elk were culled in the belief that they would otherwise become too abundant, as they were protected from both human hunting and natural predation. In the late 1960s, the culling policy became a point of public controversy and since 1968 the northern Yellowstone elk herd has been managed under the concept of natural regulation. SAVANNA was used to test the concept of natural regulation in northern Yellowstone and to evaluate the potential effects of a massive 1988 fire on winter-range carrying capacity and elk population dynamics (Coughenour and Singer, 1996a,1997b). Using climate data from 1968 to 1990 and the Yellowstone GIS habitat and vegetation map, SAVANNA simulations closely matched the numbers of elk observed over that time period. It correctly simulated four die-offs occurring between 1968 and 1989, both in terms of the year of occurrence and the magnitude of elk mortality. SAVANNA predicted that if conditions were to remain generally the same over the period 1992-2011, elk populations would rise to the levels achieved before the 1989 die off, then fluctuate with climate conditions around a long-term mean of about 25 000 animals. The model suggested that the 1988 fire would have only limited effects on range forage; would result in slightly depressed elk numbers in the first decade after the fire, and would lead to slightly (10%) higher numbers for the second decade after the fire.

At present, GIS data are being organized and SAVANNA is being adapted to address questions of climate and land use interactions on the Mongolian steppe. Throughout central and east Asia, there is concern about degradation of grazing lands resulting from socio-economic changes, land tenure changes, expansion of livestock numbers and alterations in spatial patterns of grazing exploitation (Kerven et al., 1996). In this research programme SAVANNA, simulations will be linked with NDVI analyses at broad regional scales to identify subregions and/or locations (i.e., sums or small aimags in Mongolia) which appear to be performing poorly, given extant climate regimes. The model will then be adapted to selected 'suspect' degradation locations and finer scale information on land use intensity, livestock numbers, plant cover, etc. will be entered. Model simulations will explore: (i) whether extant land use practices are compatible with the current climate regime; (ii) how land use might be altered to achieve better ecosystem performance; and (iii) potential degradation trajectories if improper land use continues (Ellis et al., 1995).

5. NEW FEATURES

Over the next several months we hope to make several improvements and additions to the modelling system. The current socio-economic submodel will be revised to better represent monetary flows resulting from sales of animals or other activities undertaken at the firm or enterprise level. A disease interaction submodel will be developed to address the effects of disease on ungulate production. We are particularly concerned about disease transmission and its implications where livestock and wild ungulates utilize a common environment. A decision support system was developed for one version of SAVANNA, aimed at making the modelling system more user-friendly for biologists and managers at one national park (Buckley et al., 1993). We plan to develop a more general user-friendly interface which will serve as a shell, amenable to modification to suit the objectives and conditions at any location.

References

Buckley, D.J., Coughenour, M.B., Blyth, C.B., O'Leary, D.J., and Bentz, J.A. 1993. Ecosystem management model - Elk Island National Park: A case study of integrating environmental models with GIS. Proceedings of the Second International Conference on Integrating GIS and Environmental Modelling. Breckenridge, Colorado. National Center for Geographic Information and Analysis, University of California, Santa Barbara.

Caughley, G., Shepherd, N. and Short, J. 1987. *Kangaroos - Their ecology and management on the sheep rangelands of Australia*. Cambridge University Press, Cambridge.

Coughenour, M.B. 1991. Spatial components of plant-herbivore interactions in pastoral, ranching, and native ungulate ecosystems. *J. Range Manage.* 44: 530-542.

Coughenour, M.B. 1992. Spatial modelling and landscape characterization of an African pastoral ecosystem: a prototype model and its potential use for monitoring drought. Pp 787-810 In: McKenzie, D.H. Hyatt, D.E. and McDonald, V.J. (eds.), *Ecological Indicators*. Vol. I. Elsevier Applied Science, London and New York.

Coughenour, M.B. 1993. *The SAVANNA Landscape Model - Documentation and Users Guide*. Natural Resource Ecology Laboratory, Colorado State University, Fort Collins, CO.

Coughenour, M.B., Ellis, J.E., Swift, D.M., Coppock, D.L., Galvin, K., McCabe, J.T. and Hart, T.C. 1985. Energy extraction and use in a nomadic pastoral population. *Science* 230:619-625.

Coughenour, M.B. and Ellis, J.E. 1993. Climate and landscape control of woody vegetation in a dry tropical ecosystem, Turkana District, Kenya. *J. Biogeography* 20:383-398.

Coughenour, M.B. and Singer, F.J. 1996a. Elk population processes in Yellowstone National Park under the policy of natural regulation. *Ecol. Appl.* 6:573-593.

Coughenour, M.B. and Singer, F.J. 1996b. Yellowstone elk population responses to fire – A comparison of landscape carrying capacity and spatial-dynamic ecosystem modeling approaches. p 169-179, In: Greenlee, J. (ed.). *The Ecological Implications of Fire in Greater Yellowstone. Proceedings of the Second Biennial Conference on the Greater Yellowstone Ecosystem*, IAWF, Fairfield, West Virgina.

DeAngelis, D.L. and Waterhouse, J.C. 1987. Equilibrium and nonequilibrium concepts in ecological models. *Ecol. Monogr.* 57:1-21.

Ellis, J.E. and Swift, D.M. 1988. Stability of African pastoral ecosystems: Alternate paradigms and implications for development. *J. Range Manage.* 41:450-459.

Ellis, J.E., Galvin, K., McCabe, J.T. and Swift, D.M. 1987. Pastoralism and drought in Turkana District, Kenya. A Report to NORAD, Nairobi.

Ellis, J.E., Coughenour, M.B. and Swift, D.M. 1993. Climate variability, ecosystem stability and the implications for range and livestock development. pp 31-41 In: Behnke, R., Scoones, I. and Kerven, C. (eds.) *Range ecology at disequilibrium*. Overseas Development Institute, London.

Ellis, J.E., Coughenour, M.B., Galvin, K.A. and Tucker, C.J. 1995. *Integrated assessment of the effects of climate and land use change on ecosystem dynamics, stability and resilience on the Mongolian steppe*. NSF proposal -MMIA-OPP.I, No. 95-9.

Huffacker, C.B. 1958. Experimental studies on predation: dispersal factors and predator-prey oscillations. *Hilgardia* 27:343-383.

Kerven, C., Channon, J., Behnke, R. and Channon, S. 1996. *Planning and policies on extensive livestock development in Central Asia*. Working Paper 91, Overseas Development Institute, London.

McCabe, J.T. 1985. Livestock management among the Turkana: a social and ecological analysis of herding in an East African pastoral population. Ph.D. Diss., State University of New York-Binghamton.

Nicholls, N. and Wong, K.K. 1990. Dependence of rainfall variability on mean rainfall, latitude, and the southern oscillation. *J. Climate* 3:163-170.

Templar, G., Swift, J. and Payne, P. 1993. The changing significance of risk in the Mongolian pastoral economy. *Nomadic Peoples* 33:105-122.

Westoby, M., Walker, B.H. and Noy-Meir, I. 1989. Opportunistic management for rangelands not at equilibrium. *J. Range Manage.* 42: 266-274.

A GIS-modelling approach to monitoring rangeland degradation and desertification

A. Grainger and D. Bradley

Synopsis

This paper describes a new Geographic Information System(GIS)-based planning technique that is appropriate to the planning of complex land use systems and that involves participation by local peoples. To overcome the general lack of data on the extent and rate of spread of desertification, this paper suggests that data on vegetation distribution acquired by remote sensing techniques should be more intensively processed using GIS models, to correct for climatic variations which can convey confusing signals. To identify the human causes of degradation patterns apparent in the resulting corrected maps, the latter can be compared with modelling scenarios. The paper focuses on rangeland degradation but views this as part of broader changes in national land-use morphology. The raster-based modelling approach suggested here for large area monitoring is illustrated with a simple, mathematical simulation model. But its limitations are identified and the potential for using a more sophisticated vector-based approach is discussed. This appraoch involves a model which can simulate likely spatial patterns in rangeland growth and exploitation in a given rangeland area.

Key Points

1. *Nomadic and semi-nomadic pastoralism has long been a sustainable way of exploiting the biological productivity of arid and semi-arid rangelands, characterized by rainfall that is low and of high spatial and temporal variability. But over the last 30 years, rising herd sizes and shrinking rangeland areas have put increasing pressure on this sustainability, and led to more state intervention that has substituted for traditional cultural control mechanisms.*

2. *The failure of successive attempts to introduce rational management schemes left governments with no option but to try to replicate traditional forms of management with modern analogues, e.g., pastoral associations, which are part of a broader move to decentralize state control of resource management in developing countries.*

3. *In spite of this, governments cannot renounce their overall strategic responsibilities for management at a national level. Economic development will doubtless lead to further changes in national land-use patterns that are likely to mean a further reduction in rangeland area and a greater risk of degradation. The variability of precipitation is likely to increase as an expected consequence of global climate change.*

4. *GIS-based planning techniques might satisfy these criteria. The one described here involves a model that can simulate likely spatial patterns in rangeland growth and exploitation in a given rangeland area. Comparison of these with up-to-date satellite imagery then shows areas likely to be suffering from overstocking and degradation trends. The feasibility of two possible planning techniques that use these maps as inputs is then evaluated. The first technique is a conventional raster-based model, which is simple to execute but must reinstate the block management approach that has failed in most countries where it has been attempted. The second technique is an expert systems model that is vectorbased, takes account of the expertise of pastoralists and involves their participation in producing a technique that is better suited to the new ethos of dispersed and decentralized management.*

1. INTRODUCTION

Desertification, which is the degradation of vegetation and soil in dry areas, is a major component of global environmental change and a serious threat to the sustainability of agriculture in the world's drylands. But it is difficult to monitor over large areas. The resulting lack of reliable data has even caused questions to be raised about the existence of desertification (Thomas and Middleton, 1994), though the world community reaffirmed its support for the concept by agreeing to an international Convention on Desertification (UNEP, 1992). However, as Dregne (1983) argued, without convincing data the level of commitment to programmes to combat desertification will remain low.

There are good reasons for the lack of reliable data. Firstly, sensors on remote sensing satellites may have insufficient spatial and spectral resolution to fully monitor changes in areas (Tueller, 1987). Secondly, the changes that are most immediately detectable may be misleading. Thus, the high climatic variability of drylands can make it appear as though there is significant expansion of desertification. Such findings for the Sahel were presented to the UN Conference on Desertification in 1977. But as Tucker and Choudhury (1987) have shown, this could be explained by a natural oscillation in biomass production over time, related to the corresponding variation in precipitation.

It is entirely possible that in many areas desertification is not occurring and that the lack of data reflects that situation. However, it is also possible that desertification is occurring but has not been detected since present monitoring techniques are inadequate.

This paper argues that desertification cannot be monitored in the same straightforward way as, for example, tropical deforestation. Instead, monitoring data must be processed more intensively, by combining image analysis with (GIS) models that take account of both environmental and human impacts (Burrough, 1986). This will extend our ability to monitor change, though it will not overcome all technical obstacles and remove all uncertainty. This paper reports on work in progress at the University of Leeds and focuses on the vegetation degradation component of desertification.

Using models in this way will not only have applications in desertification monitoring. Rangelands have so far been rather neglected by those devising models of terrestrial global environmental change and surface-atmosphere interactions that can be included as part of comprehensive global climate models. Vegetation degradation also takes place in other areas, such as the humid tropics. At the same time, as large areas of tropical rain forests are cleared, significant areas of forest are degraded. Forest also regenerates naturally elsewhere, but the regeneration is only partial in many instances, (e.g., in shifting cultivation areas), so the result is yet more degraded forest. Our current inability to monitor the degradation of closed forests contributes to the great uncertainty about the actual rate of tropical deforestation (Grainger, 1996a) and even more uncertainty is attached to rates of deforestation and degradation in the open forests found in the world's drylands. Devising new hybrid model-enhanced monitoring techniques could therefore improve the monitoring of vegetation degradation throughout the world and so improve our ability to monitor global environmental change as a whole, and not just desertification.

This paper is divided into three main parts. Part I reviews the main types of spatio-temporal variability that influence the biomass status of rangelands. It is based on a simplified modelling perspective and so does not claim to be definitive or comprehensive. Part II suggests how desertification monitoring could be improved by using a raster-based approach to model these phenomena. Part III outlines a more elaborate vector-based approach which could also be used by governments to provide information to pastoralists.

2. TYPES OF SPATIO-TEMPORAL VARIABILITY

2.1 Desertification as a long-term trend

Desertification has been traditionally defined as a long-term trend in vegetation and soil degradation, in contrast to more short-term variations in biomass growth due to drought and other types of climatic variation (Grainger, 1990). Reliable desertification monitoring demands that any short-term fluctuations disguising long-term trends be removed from the overall temporal sequence of vegetation maps. The task is made even more difficult by the fact that the fluctuations are spatial as well as temporal. So, it is not just a question of designing suitable temporal filtering algorithms. The algorithms must be spatio-temporal and applied to image data using GIS techniques.

2.2 Environmental variations

A variety of environmental influences lead to spatio-temporal variation in pasture growth. These can be corrected for by incorporating them in rangeland simulation models. Such models should also take account of lagged resilience following periods of low biomass growth, and perhaps also consider simultaneous degradation caused by overgrazing.

2.2.1 Latitudinal oscillation

The first kind of variation can be termed latitudinal oscillation, and corresponds to the north-south oscillation in biomass production identified in the Sahel by Tucker and Choudhury (1987). This should be removed, either by careful choice of the monitoring period or by modelling, if real spatio-temporal trends are to be identified.

2.2.2 Temporal variation

Drylands also experience a great temporal variability in precipitation, which can be concentrated in a very short period of the year and vary considerably from year to year. Both phenomena will influence apparent changes in vegetation. The first can be accommodated by the current practice of estimating average Normalized Difference Vegetation Index (NVDI) values from a number of Advanced Very High Resolution Radiometer (AVHRR) images. The second is partly linked to latitudinal oscillation.

2.2.3 Altitudinal variation

Considerable spatial variation in precipitation takes place in a given year. Thus, rain may fall in one place but not a few kilometers away. The resulting longitudinal variation in biomass density must also be taken into account. Such variation is not solely longitudinal, but an orthogonal modelling correction will complement latitudinal corrections. If low resolution AVHRR images are used, some of the variation is removed by aggregation in large pixels. Longitudinal variation will be more evident in images from higher resolution sensors.

2.2.4 Global climate change impacts

There is still no consensus on the likely impact of future global climate change on the climate of dry areas. Some models predict that the Sahel, for example, will get wetter, and other models predict that it will get drier. If the impact of global climate change is linear, it will be easy to simulate scenarios reflecting alternative trend directions, for example, a southward shift in isohyets if there is a net drying trend.

It will be more difficult to simulate another proposed impact of global climate change: increased variability. It has been suggested that the prolonged drought in the Sahel from 1970 onwards - a very extreme example of increased variability - was connected with global climate change, but this could not be proven (Grainger, 1990). Our ignorance of such large-scale processes limits our ability to model all possible environmental impacts.

3. HUMAN IMPACT VARIATIONS

Rangeland biomass stocks are also influenced by spatio-temporal variations in human and animal impacts.

3.1 Spatial variation in grazing pressure

The impact of herds on rangelands exhibits considerable spatial variation. Nomadic herds do not graze rangelands homogeneously, leading to neat spatial patterns like those produced by mowing lawns. Instead, their exploitation involves a complex mixture of opportunism, and place-based grazing centred on boreholes and herding routes between boreholes. Models of the overall impact of herds on rangelands need to take account of such exploitation, as well as those of transhumant and sedentary herds.

3.2 Temporal variation in grazing pressure

It is well known that the grazing pressure of a given herd fluctuates over time because the pastoralist varies the size of the herd according to the prevailing climate. A series of wet years will therefore be accompanied by an increase in the size of the herd, to take advantage of improved vegetation growth. But when the rains decline again, there is a delay in the speed at which herd size is reduced, which may lead to overgrazing.

3.3 Fire impacts

The condition of vegetation in dry areas is also affected by large-scale range-land fires, which are not necessarily as advantageous to pastoralists as has traditionally been claimed. Fires are an important form of vegetation degradation which become apparent in the surface albedo for a limited time, but then add to the overall variability of reflectance. To account for the impact of fires requires frequent infra-red monitoring, building a cumulative log of fires and their timing, and then modelling the likely temporal change in reflectance, making certain assumptions about subsequent regeneration and grazing.

3.4 Changes in land-use patterns

Models of human impacts must also take account of changes in overall grazing territories. These are best explained through the four desertification processes proposed by Grainger (1992): expansion, confinement, displacement and commons' failures.

3.4.1 Expansion

Rising demand for food production in the poorest developing countries is often met by increasing farmland area rather than yield per hectare (ha) because of an inability to invest in more productive agricultural practices. Much of the expansion tends to occur on marginal land which can soon become degraded. Expansion is particularly evident in Africa, where farm productivity has risen much more slowly than in other tropical regions.

3.4.2 Confinement

Sometimes, however, expansion is impossible, and land use has to be intensified within a limited area, resulting in the process of confinement. This is evident for example, in the degradation of pastures around villages and near boreholes along nomadic herd movement routes, caused by overgrazing; and the overgrazing of marginal rangelands when nomadic pastoralists are excluded from moister areas by the expansion of other land uses, or the imposition of management schemes.

3.4.3 Displacement

As national land use changes, land is often re-allocated to more productive uses. For example, export cash crop cultivation expands in wetter areas where it is more productive and profitable. This can result in subsistence or commercial rainfed cropping being displaced onto lands that are marginally suitable for it, and nomadic pastoralism being displaced in turn onto even more marginal lands. Over cultivation on marginal croplands and overgrazing on marginal rangelands leads to desertification, the latter often being the most noticeable, but it may not be immediately apparent that the overgrazing was originally caused by a change in land use, far away, in more humid areas.

3.4.4 Commons' failures

In the first three processes, overgrazing is more a consequence of outside pressures than poor management by pastoralists. This final process, in which herd pressure on a common property rangeland exceeds its sustainable carrying capacity, seems to be an exception to this rule. But that is not necessarily the case. For millennia, nomadic pastoralists managed common property rangeland resources sustainably by using various "social control" mechanisms. Today, however, these traditional mechanisms have disintegrated with the encroachment of the market economy, the decline of nomad cultures and attempts by governments to introduce more "rational" range management schemes in the Sahel. The real "tragedy of the commons", as too many herders exploit limited grass resources, is more a cultural tragedy than a failure of management techniques, since management mechanisms and cultures were previously closely linked together.

3.4.5 Economic and political considerations

Rangelands are usually found not only at a country's climatic margin, but also at its economic, political and cultural margin. This exacerbates the spatial shifts described in the previous section, in which rangelands accommodated the residual of national trends since herders had too little power and influence to resist them. Most governments of developing countries are still unable to properly control marginal areas and also exhibit a general lack of interest in them. So they have little incentive to monitor rangeland environments or provide support for herders to make grazing more sustainable.

3.5 Human-environment interactions

Modelling human impacts on the environment is made difficult by the complex, and often unpredictable, feedbacks that can occur between human societies and the environment. Ideally, these should also be included in models but this may not always be possible.

A good example is the bio-geophysical feedback theory, suggested as the reason for the prolonged Sahel drought in the 1970s and 1980s. In this theory, drought leads to lower biomass production, prompting a rise in grazing intensity which reduces vegetation cover even more. This changes the albedo of the land, and hence the surface-atmosphere heat balance, which leads to reduced rainfall, and the cycle continues.

This is a classic example of a "vicious circle" theory, but it neglects a major human characteristic: the ability to choose. The reactions of farmers and pastoralists to adverse environmental conditions are not predetermined. They can choose to reduce their pressure on the environment, for example, by diversifying their livelihoods to include activities other than livestock raising. If they do so, this can reduce the risk of rangeland degradation.

4. RASTER-BASED MODELLING APPLICATIONS

If desertification is to be effectively monitored, the raw data emerging from satellite remote sensing and other monitoring techniques must be corrected for, or interpreted in the light of, the phenomena described in the previous section. This section suggests how this could be accomplished using a raster-based modelling approach.

4.1 Correcting for environmental variation

A straightforward approach to monitoring degradation over a given period would involve comparing two satellite images collected at the beginning and end of that period, to test for a discernible trend in biomass density. However, the results obtained will be misleading if no correction is made for the different types of environmental variation described above.

4.1.1 Correcting for latitudinal oscillation

If the monitoring period chosen is relatively short, then a degradation trend might be apparent. But this may simply be the result of latitudinal oscillation, and not reflect actual degradation. It is therefore important to correct for this, for example, by choosing the monitoring period carefully so that the two years involved are at similar phases of the latitudinal oscillation, or by using a modelling correction, such as averaging biomass over the mean oscillation period. The possible effects of global climate change will be modelled below using a scenario approach.

4.1.2 Correcting for longitudinal variation

The aggregation of reflectance within a 4 km (or larger) AVHRR pixel should remove much longitudinal variation, although if higher resolution sensors are used it might be more difficult to remove this variability. Correcting for this may therefore require mathematically simulating the distribution of biomass resulting from a random distribution of rainfall.

4.2 Simulating the effects of longitudinal variation

A simple model was developed by the authors to estimate the variation in biomass resulting from a random distribution of rainfall within a series of grid cells in five homogeneous mean rainfall bands that represent a section through a country's drylands: (A) 0-200 mm; (B) 200-300 mm; (C) 300-400 mm; (D) 400-500 mm; and (E) 500-600 mm (Figure 8.1). The mean annual rainfall in each grid cell was generated using random number tables. It was assumed that the productivity of tropical grassland is limited by water availability, since Walter (1984) and Jones et al., showed this relationship to hold up to threshold of 600-800mm mean annual rainfall. The mean above-ground biomass density Y (kg/ha) in each grid cell was estimated, based on mean annual rainfall X (mm) and using the following equation devised by Le Houérou and Hoste (1977):

$$\text{(Equation 1)} \quad Y = 2.643X^{1.001}$$

Figure 8.1

Degree of rangeland degradation for three grazing pressure scenarios. (A) Uniform livestock density plus displacement; (B) Variable livestock density plus displacement; (C) Variable livestock density plus drought and displacement;

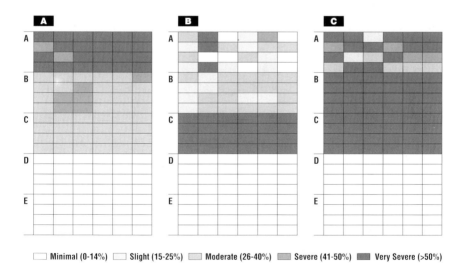

☐ Minimal (0-14%) ☐ Slight (15-25%) ▨ Moderate (26-40%) ▧ Severe (41-50%) ■ Very Severe (>50%)

5. MODELLING DEGRADATION CAUSED BY LAND-USE CHANGE

Once raw image data have been corrected to take account of environmental variation, the degradation of biomass can be assessed in a more reliable way. In order to try to identify the human origins of this degradation, the resulting maps could be compared with various modelling scenarios designed to simulate degradation resulting from human causes. A series of computer-based experiments could be run to compare the actual state of rangelands with hypothesized states resulting from different types of human impacts.

5.1 Basic principles

The basic principles of a national land-use model for a country with a heterogeneous precipitation distribution can be seen from Figures 8.2 and 8.3, based on Grainger (1996b). The model refers to a typical country in West Africa, in which rainfall declines from south to north, (Figure 8.2A) and there is a corresponding sequence of biomass, from moist forest to desert (Figure 8.2B). National land-use morphology has evolved into four zones: (i) intensive food crop and export cash crop cultivation and forest; (ii) rainfed food crop cultivation; (iii) pastoralism; and (iv) desert (Figure 8.2C). It is assumed that urban settlements are concentrated in the south. Open forests (savanna woodlands) are often used for multiple purposes and so are assumed to be part of the rainfed cultivation and pastoral zones.

Figure 8.2

Changes in national land-use change morphology in heterogeneous climatic conditions: (A) climatic zones; (B) vegetation zones; (C) initial land use and (D) land use after expansion and displacement

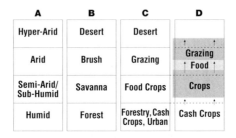

5.2 Modelling Land-use change

For convenience, suppose that the national land-use morphology of the country portrayed in Figure 8.2 is identical to its ideal land suitability classification, i.e., each area of land is used in an optimum, non-degrading way. But suppose that the following sequence of land-use change then occurs (Figure 8.2D):

(i)   Economic development and government policy lead to the expansion of export cash crop cultivation and the growth of urban areas. Rainfed food crop cultivation is displaced northward towards drier areas;

Figure 8.3

Degradation following changes in national land-use morphology and global climate change: (A) national land suitability classification; (B) land use after expansion and displacement; (C) degradation eventually associated with scenario B; and (D) potential degradation associated with scenario B and aridification caused by global climate change

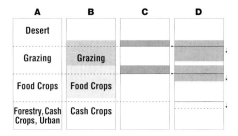

(ii)   Population growth leads to more demand for food, satisfied principally by an expansion of rainfed food crop cultivation. (The rise in demand may be reduced by using some of the revenue from cash crop exports to pay for food imports); and

(iii)   The combined expansion and displacement of rainfed food crop cultivation displaces pastoralism onto more marginal lands.

These changes could be simulated by a GIS model of land use, interfaced with a mathematical model that generates changes in land use in response to changes in demand for food and other farm products that are driven by the underlying driving forces of population growth, economic growth, government policy and the external demand for cash crops.

An actual model would be more complex than this scenario. It would have separate demand functions for export cash crops and domestic food crops. The need for additional land for each type of farming would be simulated, using alternative assumptions about the annual rise in farm productivity. The ability of each of the four main zones of national territory to supply demand for extra land would be assessed, in terms of: (i) the availability of spare land (e.g., land still forested in the humid zone); and (ii) the willingness of farmers in the humid and semi-arid/sub-humid zones to convert from food cropping to cash cropping, reflecting the inertia of land uses to displacement.

Since in practice the division between food crop cultivation and export cash crop cultivation is not as strict as implied above, this will increase the difficulty of modelling displacement. The same would be true for livestock raising, which has traditionally depended on grazing fallow areas on farms in the dry season. The balance between the need for new land and its availability would determine the extent to which land uses that would otherwise expand or be displaced are instead confined to limited areas. The model could also take account of possible increases in the productivity of food crop cultivation obtained by investing some of the income from cash crop exports, and changes in demand for domestic food production as export crop prices vary.

5.3 Modelling degradation

5.3.1 Comparing land use and land suitability

Land becomes degraded when it is under a type of land use and intensity of use that it does not have the capacity to support. So, in theory, the land degradation likely to result from the above land-use changes could be predicted by comparing the actual land-use distribution with a national land suitability classification (Carpenter, 1981). This shows the boundaries within which each land use can be practised sustainably at a given intensity, and the physical and economic margins beyond which it is not sustainable and likely to degrade soil and vegetation.

The land capability classification could be generated by applying a rule-based model to a similar set of GIS environmental data layers to those used above to estimate suitability such as precipitation, temperature, length of growing season, soil type, soil texture, soil quality, elevation and slope. Alternative scenarios could be produced to take account of varying technical inputs, such as fertilizer and irrigation (Higgins et al., 1983).

Figure 8.3A shows a country's ideal land suitability classification and Figure 8.3B its national land-use morphology after the change in land use in Figure 8.2D. A GIS-comparison of the two maps would show that both rainfed food crop cultivation and pastoralism exceed their margins and so super-marginal areas would be very susceptible to degradation (Figure 8.3C).

Land degradation is already extensive in many countries, and comparing a current land-use map with a land-suitability map should show those areas likely to be degraded. These predictions could be checked by ground truthing. Alternative scenarios for future trends in degradation could then be simulated mathematically to assist ongoing monitoring.

5.3.2 Simulating the effects of global climate change

The model could also be used to simulate the possible impact of global climate change. Suppose that the country suffers a net decline in rainfall and a southward linear shift in isohyets occurs. The northerly boundaries of land uses would prob-ably follow, but social pressures might still cause them to exceed the capability margins (Figure 8.2C). This would result in degradation between the former margin and the new one, adding to that which previously occurred above the former margin (Figure 8.2D). Of course, any such impact of long-term climate change would need to be tested against data that had already been corrected for short-term variations of the kind mentioned above.

Qualifications

The land-use zonation employed here is based, for simplicity, on the physical margin for the viability of a given land use. This will differ from its economic margin, but seems a reasonable approximation given the scale and aggregation of our modelling approach.

Caution is needed when using land-suitability classifications in dry areas, as they are subject to highly variable rainfall. Rainfall is only one of the factors determining the suitability of an area for different land uses, but it is a vital one. Because of variable rainfall the physical and economic margins within which each land use is sustainable at a given intensity will vary from year to year, and this needs to be incorporated in the model. Moreover, the use of "scientifically determined" carrying capacities for arid rangelands has been shown to be highly misleading (Grainger, 1990a).

The model should also take account of the general intensity and sustainability of land uses in different areas. In some areas that are clearly marginal for a displaced land use, over-intensive land use leads very quickly to degradation. In areas where land uses are confined by external circumstances and forced to become more intensive, land managers may follow the Boserup (1965) route and ensure that greater intensity is sustainable in the long term, or the alternative Blaikie and Brookfield (1987) route and accept degradation as long as they produce enough food to feed themselves in the short term. If land managers do take the first course and respond to the threat of degradation by either reducing the intensity of their land use or increasing the use of artificial inputs, then this may lead to no degradation at all, which is one of the scenarios that must be included.

There is a danger that this kind of modelling might be seen as environmentally deterministic. That is not the intention. Indeed, the whole aim of the model is to show how the expansion of land use in response to socio-economic driving forces can lead to degradation when the expansion encounters environmental constraints. These constraints are still very important in areas where farmers are too poor to invest in fertilizers and other artificial inputs, but alternative scenarios could be simulated to show what might happen if more fertilizer and irrigation were used.

A quantitative modelling experiment

To show the potential for this kind of approach, the quantitative model of biomass production described above was extended to model grazing pressure and estimate degradation in a series of grid cells within the five main rainfall bands (Figure 8.4).

Figure 8.4

Predicted mean above-ground biomass density (tonnes/km²) for grid cells in five homogeneous rainfall bands

A	12	3	46	20	10	48
0–200 mm	28	8	16	26	14	18
	17	52	40	13	27	42
	36	7	22	38	38	33
	15	23	4	15	21	13
B	68	75	67	66	69	61
201–300 mm	76	80	59	61	69	64
	74	64	57	79	76	67
	77	54	60	68	62	65
	77	68	74	55	74	56
C	84	106	105	10	84	81
301–400 mm	85	88	90	106	84	102
	96	83	99	106	94	87
	88	81	104	85	93	89
	91	86	84	102	84	95
D	123	113	110	128	115	110
401–500 mm	112	119	130	114	128	121
	124	122	109	111	112	128
	121	117	131	109	130	119
	121	130	1166	118	127	110
E	146	138	136	156	155	141
501–600 mm	138	133	147	133	150	153
	158	157	144	156	152	145
	146	159	152	146	153	145
	149	150	151	157	158	152

Grazing Pressure Scenarios

Grazing pressure was simulated using various alternative scenarios:

1. *Uniform Livestock Density.* A mean density of 6.53 Total Livestock Units (TLUs)/ km² where I TLU = a 250 kg zebu cow, was assumed.

2. *Displacement.* Livestock are restricted to Bands A-C by the displacement process and their mean density is 10.88 TLU/ km2.

3. *Variable Livestock Density* Plus Drought. Rainfall and biomass production are reduced by drought. Herds are free to distribute themselves in better

rainfall areas and livestock density is proportional to biomass density (ranging from 0.5 TLU/ km² in Band A to 12.15 TLU/ km² in Band E).

4. *Variable Livestock Density Plus Drought and Displacement.* This is equivalent to Scenario 3 plus a northward displacement by cropping.

In Scenarios 3 and 4, the biomass dependent livestock density values are based on ILCA (1981) and Le Houérou (1989).

Degradation Scenarios

The degree of degradation per grid cell was estimated for the six scenarios, based on the percentage of biomass removed by grazing, and then converted into degrees of desertification using the classification of Dregne (1985), which is based on the following values of percent reduction in biomass: (i) slight (15-25%); (ii) moderate (26-40%); (iii) severe (41-50%); and (iv) very severe (>50%).

With an even herd distribution (Scenario 1), the degree of degradation is determined by moving from the high rainfall bands to the low ones. If herds were also displaced toward low rainfall areas, this caused severe degradation in the lowest rainfall bands (Scenario 2). In a drought situation with variable herd density (Scenario 3), there were peaks of degradation in the lowest rainfall bands but most degradation was in higher rainfall areas where herds had moved in search of forage. When there was both drought and herd displacement (Scenario 4), rangeland resources were heavily depleted in the lower rainfall bands where climatic stress significantly reduced sustainable carrying capacity.

6. DISCUSSION

The model presented here is very simple and still under development. It probably overestimates forage removal, and hence degradation, and exaggerates the impact of drought on rangeland. It has no capacity to direct herds to the wettest areas or take account of vegetation regrowth and the differences in palatability of different species. However, it could show: the lower carrying capacity of the low rainfall areas; the effectiveness of displacement in increasing degradation; the triggering of further degradation by drought; the strong possibility of overgrazing in moister areas as well; and the potential for conflict as herds move into moister areas where forage is plentiful but farming is intensive.

7. THE POTENTIAL FOR A VECTOR-BASED MODELLING APPROACH

The raster-based modelling approach has the advantage of simplicity and ease of use for monitoring large areas. On the other hand, its very simplicity may mean that its scenarios do not correspond well with observed patterns of use and degradation. It could be applied in practice to support block management techniques, but these have been discredited after having failed in most countries where they have been attempted (Grainger, 1990).

A better representation of grazing pressure and degradation may be obtained by a vector-based approach, that can encompass discrete borehole distributions and herding routes. This will require a much more elaborate model, and may only be feasible in the first instance if applied to much smaller areas. But the model could have important practical applications to support rangeland management.

This is because there has been a shift in emphasis in recent years to more community-based, or place-based techniques, following the failure of "scientific" or large-area management methods to ensure sustainable rangeland management especially in Africa. The new methods encourage the development of pastoral associations to take responsibility for individual boreholes and pasture in the surrounding area.

Such changes have major consequences for rangeland monitoring. Firstly, monitoring programmes should be place-based, as well as block-based, and vector-based monitoring approaches are appropriate for these programmes. Secondly, monitoring programmes should be able to deliver reliable and up-to-date information to a large number of resource managers dispersed throughout remote areas, if they are to enhance sustainability. Whether this is feasible is open to question, though it is technically possible by the use of radio or telephone communications. Thirdly, to match the new ethos of participatory management, the monitoring programme should emphasize participation in data collection as well and utilize the expertise of pastoralists wherever possible.

8. CONCLUSIONS

- Desertification monitoring could be improved by correcting raw data on vegetation degradation acquired by remote sensing techniques for environmental variability.
- The underlying causes of degradation patterns apparent in the resulting corrected maps could be identified by comparing with scenarios that simulate spatio-temporal changes in human impacts.
- A raster-based modelling approach would be simplest to use for this purpose, but a vector-based approach might eventually prove to be more accurate.

Acknowledgements

The authors wish to acknowledge the support given to Daniel Bradley by the Economic and Social Research Council (UK), and the generous hospitality of the Centre de Suivi Ecologique (Dakar, Senegal).

References

Boserop, E. 1965. *The conditions of agricultural growth: the economics of agrarian change under population pressure*. Aldine, Chicago.

Blaikie, P. and Brookfield H. 1987. Approaches to the study of land degradation. In: Blaikie, P. and Brookfield, H. (eds). *Land Degradation and Society*. 27-48. Methuen, London.

Burrough, P.A. 1986. *Principles of geographic information systems for land resources*. Clarendon Press, Oxford.

Carpenter, R.A. (ed.) 1981. *Assessing tropical forest lands: their suitability for sustainable uses*. Proceedings of the Conference on Forest Land Assessment and Management for Sustainable Uses, 19-28 June 1979, Honolulu, Hawaii. Tycooly International Publishers, Dublin.

Dregne, H.E. 1983. *Desertification of arid lands*. Harwood Academic Publishers, Chur, Switzerland.

Dregne, HE. 1985. Aridity and land degradation. *Environment* 27(8): 16, 18-20, 28-33. Grainger, A. 1990. *The threatening desert: controlling desertification*. Earthscan Publications, London.

Grainger, A. 1992. Characterization and assessment of desertification processes. In: Chapman, G.P. (ed.) *Proceedings of Conference on Grasses of Arid and Semi-Arid Regions*:17-33, 27 February-1 March 1991. Linnean Society, London. John Wiley, Chichester.

Grainger, A. 1994. Review of the United Nations Environment Programme, World Atlas of Desertification (1992). *Progress in Physical Geography* 18: 621.

Grainger, A. 1996a. An evaluation of FAO's Tropical Forest Resource Assessment 1990. *Geographical Journal* 162: 73-9.

Grainger, A. 1996b. Modelling anthropogenic degradation of drylands and the potential to mitigate global climate change. In: Squires, V. Glenn, E. and Ayoub, A. (eds.) *Proceedings of the International Workshop on Combating Global Warming by Combating Land Degradation*, UNEP, 2-7 September 1995, Nairobi.

Higgins, G.M. et al., 1983. *Potential population supporting capacities of lands in the developing world*. Technical Report of Project, FPA/INT/5 13. FAO/UNFPA/IIASA.

Le Houérou, H.N. and Hoste, C.H. 1977. Rangeland production and annual rainfall relations in the Mediterranean Basin and in the African Sahelian and Sudanian zones. *J. Range Management* 30: 181-189.

Thomas, D. and Middleton, N. 1994. *Desertification: exploding the myth*. John Wiley, Chichester.

Tucker, C.J. and Choudhury, B.J. 1987. Satellite remote sensing of drought conditions. *Remote Sensing of Environment* 23: 243-51.

Tueller, D.T 1987. Remote sensing and scientific applications in arid environments. *Remote sensing of Environment* 143-154.

United Nations Environment Programme (UNEP). 1992. *World Atlas of Desertification*. Edward Arnold, London.

UNEP. 1995. *United Nations Convention to Combat Desertification*. United Nations, Geneva.

Expert systems and other computer-based decision support systems for managing marginal rangelands

9

V. R. Squires

Synopsis

This paper reviews the application of Decision Support Systems (DSS) in the context of rangeland management. It outlines the processes involved in developing a DSS which can involve the use of quantitative, qualitative and numerical data. It argues the case for developing DSS which incorporate local knowledge. Examples are given of several expert systems which have been developed as management aids for semi-arid rangelands. These illustrate the strengths and weaknesses of DSS.

Key Points

1. *DSS software has evolved in a number of disciplines to facilitate efficient allocation of resources. Such computer-based decision tools are especially useful for resources derived from complex systems, such as rangelands, whose response to human intervention may be difficult to predict. Due to computational powers of computers, DSS empowers land managers to readily estimate the ecological and economic implications of a wide range of alternative management strategies, including least-risk production and short-term profit maximization.*

2. *Expert systems are decision support systems that offer advice based on capturing the "rules" lurking behind the intuitive judgements of experienced decision-makers. They attempt to mimic the thinking processes used by a human expert on the topic(s): their reasoning is based on an "if...then" logic .*

3. *Expert systems have advantages over mathematical programmes which frequently suffer from an inability to represent the often non-linear nature of biological processes and the marked variations in seasons, particularly those that carry over into subsequent years. Unlike conventional simulation models, expert systems have an ability to deal with imprecise information, as well as rigorously defined*

data. This is clearly an advantage in the pastoral management context, where precise empirical data is frequently unavailable. The principal value of expert systems is in providing a user-friendly interface between model users and the models themselves.

4. *Increasingly, the Geographic Information System (GIS) is being linked to decision-support systems which do more than just selectively regurgitate the information they contain. These hybrid systems allow the user to make inferences about places which are not immediately obvious from looking at the previously stored data. But not all expert systems are geographically oriented. Many are designed to help managers with choice-selection problems, such as choosing between candidate technologies or treatment options. Furthermore, decision-support information has a spatial dimension: landforms, management decisions, and the socio-economic context all have a spatial dimension.*

1. INTRODUCTION

There is growing concern about land degradation, global climate change, loss of biodiversity and other environmental issues that threaten the sustainability of the world's agricultural and pastoral production systems. This has led to action by many nations to sign and ratify the International Conventions on Drought and Desertification, Biodiversity and Global Climate Change. At the same time many international agencies and non-governmental organizations (NGOs) working in pastoral lands, especially in the Middle East, the West Asia and North Africa (WANA) regions, and in the Sahel, have come to realize the failure of the conventional approaches to rangeland management (Sidahmed,1995).

A new paradigm, based on disequilibrium assumptions, has now come to the fore (Behnke and Scoones, 1993; Sidahmed, 1995). It is recognized that complex social, cultural, technical and political matters interact in quite a complex way with the long-term climatic variability to produce outcomes that are difficult to predict. Pastoral societies have developed coping mechanisms that help them to survive. Increasingly, more reliance is placed on capturing this local knowledge and incorporating it into the management system. Some of this knowledge is qualitative, but nonetheless sound. Conventional models, which rely on quantitative data, find it difficult to cope with this traditional knowledge.

New methods have been sought which can combine qualitative, semi-quantitative, quantitative and multi-state "yes/no" information into decision-support systems. But we need more than data, we need expertise; data may be accurate, but valueless. Expert systems and DSS are aids to help managers make decisions. The power of the computer now allows the synthesis of information in a way which was impossible a few years ago. But we need to ask how this technology helps to solve problems. The most important part of the DSS paradigm is the focus on the end-user (Stuth and Stafford Smith, 1993).

2. DECISION-SUPPORT SYSTEMS: WHAT ARE THEY? HOW CAN THEY BE USED?

The term "decision-support system" (DSS) is contemporary jargon for an integrated approach to the age-old problem of helping people make better decisions (Stuth and Stafford Smith, 1993). The broad concept of a DSS was born as a tool which helps problem-solving by using and integrating whatever approaches are appropriate to the problem. They offer a mechanism for improving the objectivity of decision-making, especially where complex interactions are involved. DSS use heuristic approaches to problem-solving that blend hard data with semi-structured procedures and common sense expertise, to allow an appropriate level of detail to be considered for the problem at hand. There is a need for such a mechanism for the reasons described below.

- Problem-solving and decision-making for environmental resource managers have become increasingly complex tasks. For this reason, the response has been to develop computer-aided decision-support tools that may alleviate the problem. DSS technologies are being developed as decision-making aids to cope with the difficulties faced by the resource manager.

- Research continues to demonstrate that both natural and disturbed eco systems are inherently complex, with respect to both their structural organization and their functional activity. The complexity (e.g., biophysical, socio-economic and cultural) is overlain by this spatial dimension. Equally complex are the ecological processes that govern ecosystem structure and function. It is essential for resource managers to understand the operation of these processes, since they directly determine ecosystem productivity, stability and resilience to disturbance (Conway, 1985).

- Decision-making for environmental resource managers now occurs within a broader context than was the case only a decade ago. Popular notions of "sustainable development" and "environmental conservation" have markedly modified the desirable goals and outcomes for environmental resource management (Squires, this volume). In addition to dealing with the complexity of environmental resource management at the biophysical (or ecological) level, the manager must give due consideration to the prevailing economic, social cultural, legal and political factors that may be relevant when making the "appropriate" management decision.

- Resource managers are frequently required to make immediate decisions, whereby the time restrictions are likely to deny them the opportunity to adequately research relevant background data and information that they would normally use in informed decision-making. Even if the available information is readily accessible, there may frequently be gaps in the database which hinder the decision-making process.

Management decisions involve evaluating the interactions between adjacent areas. All rangeland management decisions are made in a spatial context (e.g., where to graze, when to graze). The spatial context is therefore the key. This calls for creating a linkage between GIS and DSS.

3. EXPERT SYSTEMS: DEFINITION AND PURPOSE

Expert systems are decision-support systems which offer advice based on capturing the "rules" lurking behind the intuitive judgements of experienced decision-makers. They attempt to mimic the thinking processes used by a human expert on the topic(s); their reasoning is based on an "if...then" logic. DSS use heuristic approaches to problem-solving.

Expert systems have advantages over mathematical programmes that frequently suffer from an inability to represent the often non-linear nature of biological processes and the marked variations in seasons, particularly those that carry over into subsequent years. Unlike conventional simulation models, expert systems have an ability to deal with imprecise information, as well as rigorously defined data. This is clearly an advantage in the pastoral management context where precise, empirical data is frequently not available. The principal value of expert systems is in providing a user-friendly interface between model users and the models themselves.

There is considerable interest in using specialized, well-focused expert systems, embedded in DSS, to help users with parameterizing simulation models and to match technological development options with management systems.

Increasingly, GIS is being linked to decision-support systems which do more than just selectively regurgitate the information they contain. These hybrid systems allow the user to make inferences about places which are not immediately obvious from looking at the previously stored data. But not all expert systems are geographically oriented. Many are designed to help managers with choice-selection problems, such as choosing between candidate technologies or treatment options.

4. PROCESSES INVOLVED IN DEVELOPING AN EXPERT SYSTEM

The key players are one or more domain experts and a knowledge engineer. The former are specialists in one or more disciplines relevant to the region or land use involved. They develop a body of knowledge which is encapsulated and encoded by the knowledge engineer into a software package. The approach is to develop a series of "what if...? questions. Decision rules (i.e., a kind of manual) are prepared which give justification to every decision rule.

There are several distinct stages in the development of an expert system including:

(i)   asking the questions: "Who might be the users and what are the problems they are trying to solve?" "What do we want DSS to do and is it amenable to a DSS?";

(ii)   determining functional specifications and the basic design of the software package from advice provided by local domain experts;

(iii)   expanding the prototype using commercially available knowledge engineering methodology (i.e., the "shell");

(iv)   constructing a prototype of the expert system from this information;

(v)   seeking advice from other domain experts to evaluate the software and recommending improvements in the final version of the software; and

(vi)   establishing field sites for testing and validation.

4.1 Developing the relevant questions

Decision-support systems rely on a series of "if...then" and "what if...?" questions. These are developed by the domain experts from their accumulated experience and from scientific literature. Many expert systems are based on a set of about 200-250 questions. The greater the number of questions, the greater the scope of the expert system. However, this makes it more difficult and time consuming to develop.

Each question must be supported by an explanation/justification. This is so that non-expert users can learn. The nature of this process varies with the type of decision-support system being put in place.

Coding and programming is the role of the knowledge engineer. It is a key process in converting the information (i.e., expert knowledge) into computer language and writing the appropriate programmes to run it.

4.2 Capturing existing knowledge

Years of experimentation with different management strategies to achieve different goals have provided us with much knowledge about local land-use systems. Unfortunately, this knowledge is not available to the community on a collective basis. Similarly, much of the valuable knowledge that scientists have accumulated is fragmented, held in different databases and, consequently, not always readily available, even to other scientists or land users. The challenge is to bring local and scientific knowledge systems together into a single accessible and structured database. This would provide both land users and scientists with more opportunities to inform and stimulate each other.

4.3 Placing knowledge in context

Given the complexity and different social perceptions of many agricultural and environmental situations, an essential component of the process focuses on placing contributed information in context. As Ison (1993) points out, sharing understanding of how different groups of people see the world and what they do in it involves participation by all those who might be affected by the outcome (i.e., the stakeholders).

Ongoing community dialogue reduces conflict and clarifies issues by defining more clearly the context within which any piece of information is provided. Accordingly, contradictory management strategies are not displaced without the approval of those who practised them. This process encourages a learning environment which helps constructive and voluntary behavioural change. In a manner similar to the sharing of local knowledge, scientific knowledge is not used to displace that of land managers, but to complement local knowledge.

Involving the community in participatory research is essential if we are to resolve sustainable land management issues in a constantly changing environment (Andrew and Fargher, this volume). In turn, involving the community enhances our ability to learn from the experiences gained within local land-use systems.

If land managers and land users are to be encouraged to become formally involved in the monitoring and adaptive management process, they also require access to user-friendly tools. The DSS framework provides for the inclusion of software to support land managers in assessing and interpreting the condition of their land.

5. EXAMPLES OF SOME AUSTRALIAN DECISION SUPPORT-SYSTEMS

The Environmental Resources Assessment and Management System (ERAMS) is a decision-support system developed in Australia (Squires and Thomas, 1995). It is an aid to land-use planning and allocation. ERAMS was developed to obtain information on the present and potential productivity of grazing lands in arid and semi-arid regions.

ERAMS has become incorporated into DRYPLAN, an expert system which aims to provide assistance in making decisions about the planning and operational management of rangeland production systems (Figure 9.1). Specifically, it provides users with an intelligent land map of the area delineating land units of different levels of capability with respect to pastoral production. A major outcome is a description of the possible land uses, based upon the land's ecological capabilities, as well a weighted consideration of the landholder's objectives, and environmental, political, economic, cultural and logistic constraints (Figure 9.2a).

Figure 9.1

Land-use planning flowchart: ERAMS expert system

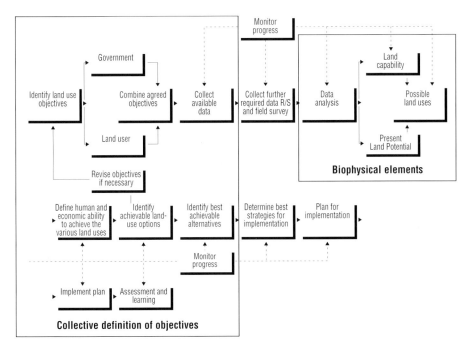

Source: Squires and Thomas 1995

Identification of the "best alternatives" for land-use allocation and land-management practices follows (Figure 9.2b).

Cost-benefit analyses of the effectiveness of different land-use and land-management strategies upon sustained and optimal production levels are also incorporated. There is an opportunity to monitor the outcomes of specific strategies to provide feedback for ongoing management and planning.

Other Australian DSS include RANGEPACK, developed by the Commonwealth Scientific and Industrial Research Organization (CSIRO) in Central Australia (Stafford Smith and Foran, 1991). This is a suite of packages which enable the manager to make decisions, from those at the level of the individual fenced paddock to the whole enterprise. GRAZPLAN is another DSS which helps to decide on stocking rates (Moore et al., 1991), while SHRUBKILL assists in decisions about woody weed control (Ludwig, 1990). There are numerous other examples (Squires and Tow, 1991; and Stuth and Stafford Smith, 1993). A recent paper by Bellamy et al. (1997) reviews the use of DSS for sustainable grazing on spatially heterogeneous rangeland in Australia.

Figure 9.2a

Rangeland inventory flowchart: the creation of an intelligent land map

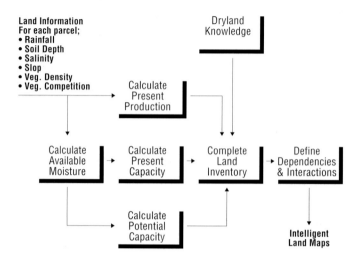

Source: Unpublished

Figure 9.2b

Rangeland planning flowchart: the identification of the best alternatives for land allocation

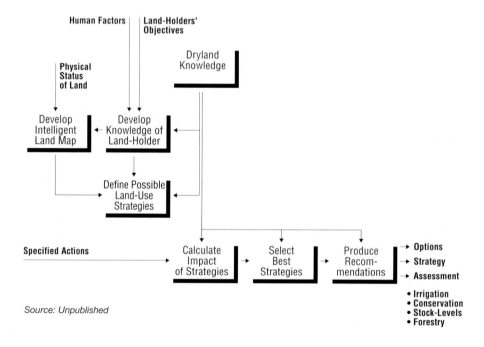

Source: Unpublished

6. EXPERIENCE FROM THE TEXAS A & M UNIVERSITY

The Ranching Systems Group, within the Department of Rangeland Ecology and Management at Texas A & M University, is currently using a decision-support system to develop a management planning system for grazed ecosystems. It was developed in response to the need for managers to utilize the large amounts of complex information characteristic of natural resource systems. The decision-support system is called Grazing Land Applications and was developed to facilitate area management planning for sustainable use of grazing lands (Stuth et al., 1990). Grazing Land Applications provides resource managers with a system that can:

(i)   facilitate collection of and access to resource information;

(ii)   act as conduit to channel the flow of traditional knowledge to the resource manager;

(iii)   serve as a tool for educating resource managers about the requirements for sustainable use of natural resources;

(iv)   be a focus for systematic, rationally planned use of natural resources; and

(v)   facilitate selection of appropriate management and development alternatives.

7. MANAGEMENT IMPLICATIONS

Decision-support systems are more than just expert systems and can act as an aid to resource management planning and for selecting development alternatives that promote sustainable use of grazing land resources. Furthermore, decision-support systems provide a format for integrating the ecological, economic and sociological information characterizing the environment of the grazing animal development project.

There is a risk that large and seemingly complex computerized decision-support systems will inhibit users. Conversely, they may accept a system as a means to reduce difficult resource management problems to cookbook solutions, making it unnecessary to know more about the system and how it works (i.e., the "black box" syndrome). User involvement (see above) provides feedback and ensures that the system is updated (Hamilton and Sheehy, 1993).

Users' understanding of the principles and the logic used in the system is essential, not only for correct use of the software, but also to build confidence by users that outputs are rational and revelant to their specific requirements. Without this degree of familiarity (achieved through training), it is likely that it will become a form of window dressing with little real application. Involvement of the end-user is vital (Figure 9.3) (Bosch, et al., 1996).

Introduction of decision-support systems is best done by teaching the principles used in the system, and by using data sources and local knowledge that show the system can work with the information and conditions from the specific local region (Hamilton and Sheehy, 1993).

Figure 9.3

Maximizing land management knowledge: the first step is to share existing knowledge and the next step is to enable the sharing and evaluation of collated information through community dialogue.

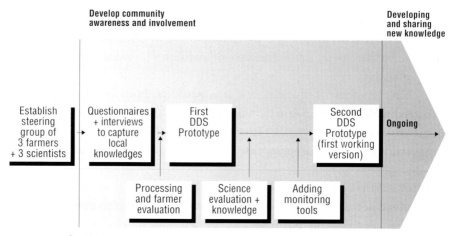

Combining existing local and scientific knowledge into a single decision-making system

Source: Bosch et al., 1996.

8. CONCLUSIONS

There has been a marked growth in the application of expert system technologies as decision-support aids within the realm of natural resource management. Since 1987, there has been a journal dedicated to the subject, "AI Applications in Natural Resource Management". The vast majority of DSS development for grazing lands is occurring in technologically advanced countries of the world, especially in North America, Europe, Australia and New Zealand. Yet most of the world's grazing lands lie elsewhere. The development of DSS in technological countries provides good opportunities for the approaches to be thoroughly tested, but ultimately it is important that ways be found to transfer the same improved decision-making processes to all other relevant countries (Stuth and Stafford Smith, 1993).

Decision-support systems, including expert systems, have considerable potential. They allow the resource manager to critically compare and evaluate, in real time, a range of possible land-use policies and/or land-management practices, by asking a series of "what if....?" questions.

Clearly, DSS can offer managers of rangelands a valuable tool for guiding them through the maze of problems they face, giving them sound advice on what experts would do when faced with a particular situation. Based on this premise, DSS developers must ensure that the tool suits the task. Above all, developers must meet the needs of DSS users. Not only must the land management problem be important, both ecologically and economically, but the solution to the problem must be non-trivial (Ludwig, et al., 1993).

Despite the substantial progress that has been made in the application of expert systems to environmental resource management, there remains several areas requiring further research and development.

• Most of the work on applying expert systems to "agriculture and land management" has been focused at the farm or paddock level. It is primarily concerned with farming practices. More effort is required to expand the application to a broad-scale regional level, where land-use policy can be evaluated. Several DSS already do this but more effort is required, especially to integrate GIS.

• It is widely acknowledged that most land management problems have a spatial dimension. This has been reflected in the increased interest in remote sensing and GIS. However, most of this effort has been data-driven and is uncoordinated. Consequently, the utility of GIS has been limited to serving as sophisticated device for storing spatial data in a digitized form, as well as being capable of generating maps. They are not widely used as analytical tools. The challenge is therefore to link GIS with expert systems, with the latter operating as an intelligent interface that will enable the GIS to be used as an analytical tool. In addition, there is a need to link those two with remote sensing and image processing devices.

The ability of expert systems to capture and use the traditional knowledge of the local population in almost any form (e.g., hard data, qualitative information or multi-state), and combine it with data from other sources, is the biggest single advantage. DSS have considerable relevance to marginal pastoral lands. Efforts should be made to develop them.

The future challenge is to integrate more effectively GIS and DSS into a system that recognizes the importance of the spatial dimension. The technological development of GIS and remote sensing began years ago as separate endeavours, but now the two meet at a time when their unification is an important objective for development of DSS for natural resource management agencies (Grainger and Bailey, this volume).

References

Andrew, M.H. and Fargher, J. (*in press*). Meeting the needs of nomads: the usefulness of the Farming Systems Research (FSR) approach. (this volume).

Bellamy, J.A., Lowes, D., Ash, A.J., McIvor, J.G. and Mc Leod, N.D. 1997. A decision support approach to sustainable grazing management for spatially heterogeneous rangeland. *Rangel. J.* (Special Issue: Grazing Management).

Behnke, R.H. and Scoones, I. 1993. Rethinking range ecology: implications for rangeland management in Africa. In: Behnke, R.H., Scoones, I. and Kerven, C. (eds.). *Range ecology at disequilibrium: new models of natural variability and pastoral adaptation in african savannas.* Overseas Development Institute, London. pp. 1-30.

Bosch, O.J.H., Allen, W.J., Williams, J.M. and Ensor, A.H. 1996. An integrated approach for maximizing local and scientific knowledge for land management decision-making in the New Zealand high country. *Rangel, J.* 18(1): 23-32.

Conway, G.R. 1985. Agricultural ecology and farming systems research. In: J.V. Remenyi (ed.). *Agricultural systems research for developing countries.* ACIAR Proceedings (No.11). Australian Centre for International Agricultural Research, Canberra. pp. 43-59.

Ellis, J. and Coughenour, M. 1997. The SAVANNA modelling system: an integrated remote sensing, GIS and spatial simulation modelling approach (this volume).

Grainger, A. and Bailey, D.(*in press*). A GIS-modelling approach to monitoring rangeland degradation and desertification (this volume).

Hamilton, W.T. and Sheehy, D.P. 1993. Introducing a decision support system to agriculturally developing countries: an example from North China. In: Stuth, J.W. and Lyons, B.G.(eds.). *Decision support systems for the management of grazing lands.* UNESCO\Parthenon Press, Paris. pp. 221-254.

Ison, R. L. 1993. Changing community attitudes. *Rangel.* J. 15: 154-166.

Ludwig, J.A. 1990. SHRUBKILL: a decision support system for management burns in Australian savannas. *J. Biogeography* 17: 547-550.

Ludwig, J.A., Clewett, J.F. and Foran, B.D.1993. Meeting the needs of decision support system users. In: Stuth, J.W. and Lyons, B.G.(eds) *Decision support systems for the management of grazing lands.* UNESCO/Parthenon Press, Paris. pp. 209-220.

Moore, A.D., Donnelly, J.R. and Freer, M. 1991. Grazplan: an Australian DSS for enterprises based on grazed pastures In: Stuth, J.W. and Lyons, B.G. (eds) *Decision support systems for resource management,* Texas A & M University, College Station, Texas USA. pp. 19-22.

Sidahmed, A. 1995. Towards sustainable development of rangeland/livestock in dryland areas of the Near East and North Africa. In: Omar, S.A. Razzaque, M.A. and Alsdirawi, F.(eds) *Range management in arid zones.* Keegan Paul, London. pp. 53-69.

Squires,V.R. (*in press*) Sustainable development: a dream or an economic and environmental imperative? (this volume).

Squires, V.R. and Thomas, D.A. 1995. ERAMS - a decision support system for rangeland inventory and management. In: Omar, S.A. Razzaque, M.A. and Alsdirawi, F.(eds). *Range management in arid zones.* Keegan Paul, London. pp. 113-125.

Squires, V.R. and Tow, P.G. (eds.). 1991. *Dryland farming: a systems approach.* Oxford University Press, Melbourne.

Stafford Smith, D.M. and Foran, B.D. 1990. RANGEPACK: the philosophy underlying the development of a microcomputer-based decision support system for pastoral land management. *J. Biogeography* 17: 541-546.

Stuth, J.W. and Stafford Smith, M. 1993. Decision support for grazing lands: an overview. In: Stuth, J.W. and Lyons, B.G. (eds.). *Decision support systems for the management of grazing lands.* UNESCO/Parthenon Press, Paris. pp. 1-36.

Stuth, J.W., Conner, J.R., Hamilton, W.T., Reigel, D.A., Lyons, B.G., Myrick, B.R. and Couch, M.J. 1990. A resource systems planning model for integrated resource management. *J. Biogeography* 17: 531-540.

A simulation model for evaluating long-term impacts of grazing practices

E. Al-Haratani and M. Fogel

Synopsis

The simulation model has been developed to predict future conditions of the range-lands and thereby assist the pastoralist. The basis of the model and the expected outcomes are outlined. The model is applicable to both short and long-term periods. However, as the short-term prediction relies heavily on seasonal or medium-range weather forecasting which is almost, but not yet, operational, this paper will discuss the long-term situation for assessing the impacts of a particular grazing practice.

Key Points

1. To describe the grazing management scheme in a precise manner, a discrete state-system model is defined formally. The major elements of the model are: an input set consisting of weather and decisions variables; a state set representing the range potential; and a state transition function that calculates the elements of the state at a future time, as a function of the input and the current state.

2. For simplification purposes, the weather input is seasonal precipitation and the decision input is rainfall intensity. Using available data, a frequency distribution of seasonal rainfall is obtained. Then, a Monte Carlo simulation technique is used to develop a time series of seasonal rainfall. For a particular management strategy or range condition, a time series of range conditions can now be generated using the aforementioned state transition function. The long-term impact of grazing can be evaluated.

1. INTRODUCTION

For centuries, nomads have roamed the Arabian rangelands, a delicately balanced marginal natural resource, in search of feed for their camels, sheep and goats. Precipitation and sun, water and energy were the natural variables that brought life to the grasslands. While energy was distributed on more or less a uniform basis, water was not. Precipitation varied from year to year and from place to place. Water was the prime motivation that kept nomads on the move; water for livestock to drink and water to make the grasses grow year after year. Through drought, windstorms and other natural disasters, the rangeland kept on producing forage for livestock without too much change over the long run.

Then, with the discovery of oil in Saudi Arabia in the 1930s and the end of World War II, came a seemingly endless gushing of consumer products. One such product greatly increased the mobility of the nomad. Trucks were used to carry livestock to areas where feed was available and to haul water to livestock. Trucks were also used to distribute feed grains at relatively low cost, subsidizing the raising of sheep, a Saudi-preferred livestock. No longer did the animal population fluctuate with natural conditions as it had for centuries. No longer was there a balance between animal numbers and available rangeland forage.

At the onset of each rainy season, usually in October, the nomad starts his migration in pursuit of feed for his livestock. The problem centres around nomad-controlled herds being at the right place at the right time to benefit from the ephemeral annual vegetation that results from widely scattered and very localized rainfall. The complexity of the problem, as presented by Al-Gain (1985), is illustrated by not only the low annual rainfall but also by the great variability from year to year.

During low rainfall years, which occurred all too frequently, there was often not enough forage to feed the number of animals grazing on an unchanging rangeland area. Overgrazing would have been the result in the past had the nomad not recognized this problem. He compensated for this reduced feed by opening up grazing reserve areas, hema, and by reducing the number of livestock on the range.

Today, however, there are pressures on the pastoralist to raise more and more locally grown livestock, as they are preferred to meet the increasing demand. This has resulted in overgrazing the range, a major cause of desertification.

This paper presents a smaller part of a pilot project of the Meteorology and Environment Protection Administration (MEPA). The Environmental Support of Nomads (ESON) addresses the problem of providing information to livestock growers, whether nomads or not, that will assist them in utilizing the rangeland in a sustainable and economically viable manner. A systems approach is presented, whereby the rangelands converts inputs, both natural and human actions, into outputs, livestock and environmental indicators.

2. A GENERAL RANGE SYSTEM MODEL

2.1 Purpose of modelling

Range yield forecasts are seen as being beneficial in helping determine annual carrying capacities for more efficient grazing management. This is especially important during drought years when advanced warnings enable grazing adjustments to accommodate livestock needs and protect range resources from damage due to overgrazing.

In the past, advanced warnings to indicate the onset of a period of drought were beyond the scope of meteorologists. Nowadays, however, with the use of dynamic modelling the extended-range: prediction of climate (in terms of monthly forecasts and seasonal outlooks) is nearly operational.

Simulation presents another benefit of modelling. These models, which attempt to represent the real-time occurrence of events in a time series, can be used to test the sustainability of a given practice over the long term. The impacts of an action should be noted not only in "average" years or seasons but in abnormal seasons, i.e. those that are "wet" or "dry" which occur in a frequency similar to the real-time occurrence of such events.

2.2 Defining the Model

In order to describe a grazing management scheme in a precise manner, a discrete state-system model is defined formally (Figure 10.1). The elements of the model are:

(i)   A time scale, t=0, 1, 2, ..., in appropriate units such as month, season or year;

(ii)   An input set X which includes:

Xc - climatic variables (e.g., rainfall, temperature, wind, etc.)

Xd - action or decision variables (which range to graze or rest, when and duration of grazing, herd size and composition);

(iii)   The state set S which represents the state of health of the range, commonly called range condition. It should not be confused with immediate availability of forage, which may be a reflection of past weather conditions, and is considered to be part of the output. The term is used to relate the current condition of the range to the potential of which the particular area is capable (Stoddart et al., 1975). Indicators of range conditions are vegetal composition (i.e., dominance of desirable species),

       plant production, ground cover (both living vegetation and litter) and a
       soil erosion index;

(iv)   The state transition function F which calculates the elements of the state
       at time (t +1) as a function of input and the state at time t:

$$S(t+1)=F[X(t)xS(t)]$$

       The function F is actually a vector set of functions, which relates the
       future range condition to that of the past and both the decision and
       climatic variables. In range management terms, the current range condi-
       tion is a function of the previous range condition, plus the grazing use
       (management actions) and the precipitation, temperature, humidity and
       other climatic factors that affect vegetative growth. It is not necessary for
       the transition function to be given in quantifiable terms. For example, as
       a hypothetical case, assume the climatic variables are denoted by either
       favourable, average or unfavorable conditions, and that the decision vari-
       able is classified as either high or low-grazing intensity. Then, if the range
       condition classes are either excellent (EX), good (GD), fair (FA) or poor
       (PR), a table (such as shown in Table 10.1) can be developed, as the state
       transition function F (Fogel and Duckstein, 1978); and

(v)   The output set includes elements of interest to the decision-maker and
       may include outputs from simulation models, such as an indicator of
       range condition, forage production, vegetal composition, ground cover,
       soil erosion and vegetation species.

Figure 10.1

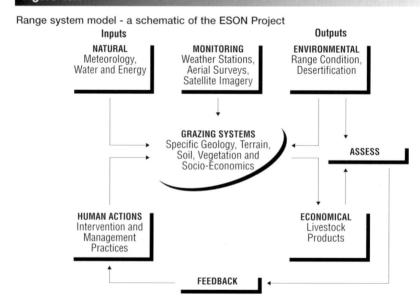

Range system model - a schematic of the ESON Project

Table 10.1

State transition for determining expected range condition as a function of past range condition and climatic conditions

Range condition at time t, s (t)	Climatic Conditions					
	Favourable		Average		Good	
	Grazing Intensity					
	High	Low	High	Low	High	Low
EX	GD	EX	GD	EX	FA	GD
GD	GD	EX	FA	GD	FA	GD
FA	FA	GD	FA	FA	GD	FA
PR	PR	FA	PR	PR	PR	PR

Source: ESON Project

EX - Excellent   GD - Good   FA - Fair   PR - Poor

3. SIMULATION MODEL

3.1 General approach

An overview of the simulation model being proposed by the ESON study is shown in Figure 10. 2. The model is based on two relationships: (1) the relation of future range condition to the present state of the range and to the present meteorological variables, principally rainfall; and (ii) the prediction of forage yield from meteorologic variables and range condition.

Figure 10.2

An overview of the simulation model being proposed by the ESON study

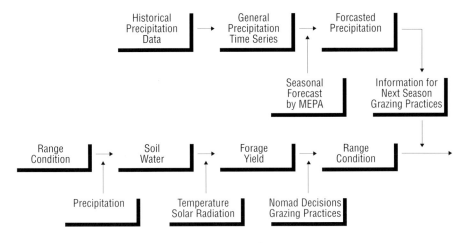

3.2 Time series of rainfall events

The basic input to the simulation model is the time series of daily rainfall events. The event-based approach is used rather than continuous modelling, as the null event (i.e., no precipitation) dominates the data. This requires that an event be defined; for example, an event is considered to occur when precipitation is recorded as being above a specified threshold value; such as 1 or 5 millimetres.

Meteorological conditions will dictate whether the event-based data can be lumped together on a monthly, seasonal or annual basis. For most situations in Saudi Arabia, three seasons, (each with different synoptic meteorology) are sufficient to characterize the occurrence of rainfall events.

To develop a time series of rainfall events, two probability distributions obtained from historical rainfall data are needed (Fogel and Duckstein, 1982). One is the amount of precipitation per event, and the other is the inter-arrival time or time between such events. Then, using Monte Carlo simulation techniques, a time series of rainfall events is readily developed for each season which can be combined to produce a time series for the entire year. Figures 10.3 and 10.4 are examples of these two probability distributions of data from the ESON Project.

Figure 10.3

Probability distribution of daily rainfall amounts over 1mm in north central Saudi Arabia

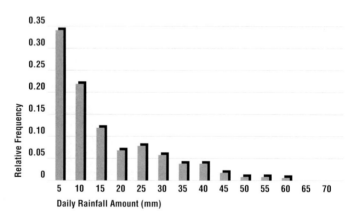

Source: ESON Project

Figure 10.4

Probable distribution of inter-arrival times between daily rainfall events of over 1mm in north central Saudi Arabia

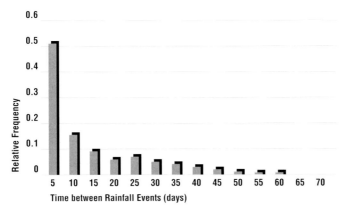

Source: ESON Project

3.3 Seasonal forecasting

A time series of rainfall events will not predict what will happen next season or next year. When run for an extended time, say a 100-year period, it can be used to estimate the probability of a normal or abnormal season with respect to rainfall. While this is useful in long-term planning, it is more critical to forecast what will happen during the next season. As previously mentioned, such forecasts are nearly operational. MEPA is currently conducting meteorological studies for the purpose of being able to make seasonal forecasts three to six months in advance.

3.4 Herbage yield prediction by USDA model

A rather sophisticated model has been developed by the US Department of Agriculture (USDA) Agricultural Research Service, based on data obtained in the western United States (Wight, 1987). ERHYM-II is a climate/water balance rangeland model which simulates soil water routing, from which it computes herbage yield. It can use real-time climate data, principally precipitation and temperature and/or radiation, to simulate ongoing processes or long-term actual or synthetic weather records in order to simulate herbage yields under a range of climatic conditions. This latter process allows for the calculation of probabilities of the forecast yield and associated confidence intervals.

The principal limitation of ERHYM-II to be used in Saudi Arabia is the data requirement, much of which is not readily available.

3.5 Simplified herbage yield model

Predicting herbage yield is an important rangeland management variable for nomads. Pastoralists, be they the traditional nomad or the more sedentary type, are always in need of information on where to bring their animals for grazing, when to graze and the number of animals to graze. Thus, some estimate of carrying capacity is needed. In 1990, MEPA presented information on carrying capacities of ESON Project rangelands based on information it had gathered from several sources, primarily Le Houerou (1977, 1984) (Table 10. 2).

Table 10.2

Carrying capacities of ESON Project rangelands

Annual rainfall mm	Range condition G - good F - fair P - poor	Hectares required or one ILU[1]	
		All-season range	Seasonal range[2]
50	P	82	328
	F	36.5	146
	G	20.8	83
75	P	54.4	218
	F	24.3	97
	G	13.5	54
100	P	40.9	163.6
	F	18.2	72.8
	G	10.1	40.4
150	P	27.2	108.8
	F	12.2	48.8
	G	6.8	27.2
200	P	20.4	81.6
	F	9.1	36.8
	G	5.1	20.4

[1] The average animal (0.2 ILU) consumes 1.5 kg dry weight per day.
[2] Carrying capacity of seasonal range roughly estimated at one-fourth that of all-season range.

Sources: Livestock consumption; Barret and Larkin (1974); rainfall-use efficiency (RUE) and the value of 0.67 for overgrazed arid steppes in Saudi Arabia, le Houerou (1977, 1984)

With the information from Table 10.2, a relationship was developed to estimate herbage yield as a function of annual precipitation and range condition, is as follows:

$$\left(1 - \frac{Y}{S*Ymax}\right) = \left(1 - \frac{P}{Pmax}\right)$$

where Y   = herbage yield estimate, kg/ha
    Ymax = maximum herbage yield, kg/ha
    S   = range condition (good, fair or poor)
    P   = seasonal precipitation, mm
    Pmax = maximum seasonal precipitation, mm

Then, using maximum values for seasonal precipitation (300 mm) and herbage yield (800 kg/ha) and estimates of range condition, estimates of herbage yield are shown in Table 10. 3.

Table 10.3

Herbage yield estimates

Annual Precipitation mm	Range Condition S*	Estimated Yield, kg/ha
100	P	80
	F	160
	G	270
150	P	120
	F	240
	G	400
200	P	160
	F	320
	G	530
250	P	200
	F	400
	G	660
300 (max)	G	800 (max)

*S =   1.0 for good condition   0.6 for fair condition   for poor condition
Source: ESON Project

4. CONDITION AND TREND OF GRAZING LANDS

The concept of range condition serves to integrate the responses of grazing land to management into one measure. It is an "index" of whether the principles of good range management and improvement have been applied properly. As defined above, range condition is the state of health of the rangeland, based largely upon what that grazing land is capable of producing naturally. Condition is expressed, somewhat arbitrarily, from excellent to poor. Range trend, on the other hand, is the direction of the change in rangeland condition. Trend is described as improving, stable, or deteriorating. Both of these definitions imply that an assessment of the rangeland is made at a specific point-in-time and in relation to a predetermined standard.

A judgment of range condition is an appraisal of the difference between current plant cover and the plant cover required for the highest sustained level of productivity attainable under the prevailing ecological site conditions and the best range management practices. In applying the concept of range condition, it is assumed that there is an "optimum" plant cover for the site.

Criteria to consider in the assessment of grazing land condition and trend include:

(i)   Ground cover: herbaceous plant density, species composition, vigour and litter accumulation;
(ii)   Shrub cover: the above factors, and relative height and age measures;
(iii)   Forage value: nutritive value, bulk, seasonal variations, potential level of productivity and palatability; and
(iv)   Soil features: depth of soil, texture and structure, extent of erosion, nutrient status, microbial activity and infiltrative properties.

Additionally, criteria should also reflect the health and performance of livestock, degree of grazing and browsing, and the presence of pests. All of these criteria should be evaluated together, as they all can affect the productivity of a rangeland ecosystem.

5. SIMULATION OF RANGE CONDITION

For a particular management strategy or range practice, a time series of seasonal range conditions can now be generated (Khalili et. al., 1988). A time series of seasonal precipitation (rather than daily precipitation) and the transition between past and future range condition (Table 10.1) was used to generate future range condition.

As an example of this approach, two diverse range practices were evaluated over a 100-year period. One practice was high-intensity grazing, the other low-intensity grazing (or fewer animals per grazing area). Figures 10.5 and 10.6 illustrate the results of this simulation. It should bbe noted that for high-intensity grazing, the ultimate range condition will be poor regardless of whether the initial condition was excellent or poor. On the other hand, for low-intensity grazing, future range condition varies between good and excellent depending on the amount of seasonal precipitation. This will be the case, regardless of whether the initial condition is poor or excellent.

It should also be noted also that a range in good condition will deteriorate in about 10 years, while it takes much longer to recover from a poor condition with light or no grazing.

6. CONCLUSIONS

An effort is being made to quantify the rangeland system so that managers can make decisions that will result in an economically viable and sustainable system. A major key to the process is being able to determine the potential of the rangeland to produce forage, a term commonly called range condition.

Figure 10.5

Range condition index under low-intensity grazing

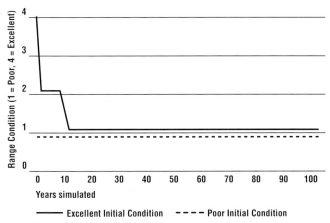

Source: ESON project

Figure 10.6

Range condition index under low-intensity grazing

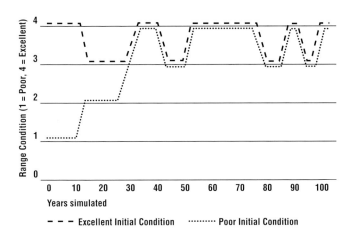

References

Al-Gain, Abdulbar. 1985. *Integrated resource study in support of nomads in Saudi Arabia: A proposal.* Proceedings of the International Research and Development Conference, Arid Lands: Today and Tomorrow, Tucson, USA. pp. 1213-1221.

Barret, M.A. and Larkin, P.J. 1974. *Milk and beef production in the Tropics.* Oxford University Press, Oxford.

Fogel, M.M. and Duckstein, L. 1978. *Desertification under natural uncertainties and man's activities: a decision model.* Presented at Bilateral US-Argentinian Workshop on Droughts, Mar del Plata, Argentina.

Fogel, M.M. and Duckstein, L. 1982. *Stochastic precipitation modelling for evaluating non-point source pollution.* Proceedings of the International Symposium on Rainfall-Runoff Modelling. Mississippi State University. pp.119-136.

Khalili, D., Duckstein, L. and Fogel, M. 1988. A multiobjective, discrete system representation of rangeland watersheds. *Water Resources Bulletin* 24 (5): 1035-1040.

Le Houerou, H.N. 1977. *The grasslands of Africa: classification, production, evaluation and development outlook.* Proceedings of XIIIth International Grassland Congress. Akademik Verlag, Berlin.

Le Houerou, H.N. 1984. Rain use efficiency: A unifying concept in arid-land ecology. *J. Arid Environments.* 7 : 213-247.

Stoddart, W.C., Smith, A.D. and Box, T.W. 1975. *Range management.* McGraw-Hill, Inc., New York.

Wight, I. R. 1987. ERHYM-II: Model description and user guide for the BASIC version. USDA/ARS. ARS-59.

A multiple-resource computer simulation system

11

P.F. Ffolliott

Synopsis

This paper describes a multiple-resource computer simulation system, which can be an alternative means of predicting the consequences of any proposed rangeland management practice. This system has been structured to assist land managers and decsion-makers in predicting the impacts of proposed management practices. Impacts can be evaluated in the framework of selecting the best management practice for implementation to meet established objectives and existing constraints.

Key Points

1. *Marginal rangelands throughout the world are being subjected to many changes as a consequence of their intensified use, both planned and unplanned. These changes generally affect the natural resources found on them and, therefore, can have a beneficial or adverse impact on people that live on the rangelands or reside in nearby villages and towns. It is important, therefore, that predictions of the impacts of these changes become available before comprehensive management practices are implemented on these marginal rangelands in order to sustain the existing use or the changes allowed to occur.*

2. *A large number of field studies have been made on the effects of alternative management on the rangelands. Information from these studies is valuable and, therefore, should be continued. However, results obtained from one location can seldom be applied directly to estimate the impacts at other locations. An alternative means of predicting the consequences of proposed management practices is needed in many instances. One means can be the application of a multiple-resource computer simulation system similar to that described in this paper.*

3. *The system contains simulators to describe the key parameters. These are: the production and composition of forage plants; the growth and yield of woodland tree and shrub species; the carrying capacity of an area; and the dynamics of livestock and wildlife animals within the ecosystem. In addition, they simulate the largely intermittent streamflow regimes in the area, and the physical, chemical, and bacteriological quality of the streamflow. Timing and sequencing of these simulators is controlled through a command system, which also outputs summary displays for interpretation by land managers and decision-makers.*

1. INTRODUCTION

Marginal rangelands throughout the world are being subjected to many changes as a consequence of their increasing use, both planned and unplanned. These changes generally affect the natural resources found on them and, as a consequence, have both beneficial and adverse impacts on people that live on these rangelands or reside in nearby villages and towns. It is important, therefore, that predictions of the impacts of these changes be available before comprehensive management practices are implemented on these marginal rangelands in order to sustain the existing use or the changes allowed to occur.

A large number of field studies have been made on the effects of alternative management practices on marginal rangelands. Information from these studies is valuable and should be continued. However, results obtained from one location can seldom be applied directly to estimate the impacts at other locations. An alternative way of predicting the consequences of management practices is needed in many instances. One alternative is the application of a multiple-resource computer simulation system similar to that presented in this paper.

2. THE COMPLETION SIMULATION SYSTEM

The computer simulation system presented is represented by a group of multiple-resource simulation models, originally developed for application on rangelands in the southwestern United States (Larson et al., 1978; Rasmussen and Ffoliott, 1981). The system is structured to assist decision-makers and managers in predicting the impacts of management practices on these rangelands. The most appropriate management practice to meet established objectives and existing constraints is then selected from the simulations of these future impacts.

The simulation models in the system possess input-output interfaces so that they can be included, modified, or deleted as needed in a simulation problem. This structure allows the models to be linked together to estimate the impacts of management practices. The basic structure of the system is flexible and, therefore, adapted to applications in ecosystems elsewhere, if the required developmental information is available or can be obtained (Ffolliott et al., 1984). The models in the system are contained in three modules:

(i)   FLORA - to simulate herbaceous rangeland understories tree overstories and organic material on the soil surface;

(ii)   FAUNA - to estimate carrying capacities, wildlife habitat conditions and dynamics of animal population; and

(iii) WATER - to predict intermittent streamflow regimes, suspended sediment concentrations, and chemical quality of water.

A command module allows a user to operate the system through a common language written in straightforward terminology. Appropriate databases are accessed when required. This design provides flexibility in simulating the impacts of management practices by operating the selected models interactively. Other models can also be incorporated into the command module as required.

2.1 The FLORA module

The FLORA module consists of simulators that predict the production and composition of herbaceous rangeland understories, the growth and yield of tree overstories, and the accumulations of organic material on the soil surface.

2.1.1 Herbaceous rangeland understories

A simulator has been structured to estimate herbage production from knowledge of tree overstory parameters, precipitation, and (when part of the simulation problem) the time since implementation of a management practice. A user can operate this model, called UNDER, either individually or coupled with other models in the system, depending upon the simulation objective. In the latter case, outputs from other models in FLORA and other modules in the system are utilized as inputs.

Computer simulation models that estimate herbage production are largely dependent upon input variables depicting tree overstory density conditions. While this approach is used in several routines in this simulator, UNDER can also utilize knowledge of tree overstory growth rates. Estimates of herbage production that are based on this latter variable are consistently higher in accuracy than those based on knowledge of tree overstory densities alone.

UNDER partitions simulated herbage production into grasses and grass-like plants, forbs and half-shrubs, and shrubs in order to estimate the composition of forage vegetation.

2.1.2 Tree overstories

Three models are available to estimate the growth and yield of tree overstories. TREE simulates the growth of an individual tree from knowledge of the diameter, height and volume. A user can also determine how individual tree growth is influenced by tree size and age.

STAND predicts the growth and yield of: stands; a community of trees possessing uniformity in composition; age; spatial arrangement; and condition. Inputs to this model include a listing of trees by species, associated diameter growth rates and volume expressions. When management (i.e., treatment) specifies a change in these inputs, estimates of post-treatment growth and yield are generated. Management practices that can be simulated within STAND represent a range of options for the different tree overstory compositions and structures.

ENTIRE is an interactive version of a large-scale model structured to simulate the growth and yield of vegetative communities, comprised of single or mixed tree species, and even-aged or uneven-aged structures. This model also provides estimates of seed production, dispersal and germination, competition and mortality.

2.1.3 Organic material

Three models describe the development, accumulation, and distribution of organic material on a soil surface. One component, referred to as FLOOR, estimates the accumulation of tree leaves, twigs, and other plant biomass (by layer of decomposition) at a point-in-time; the rate of accumulation with respect to time; and spatial distribution of organic material. FLOOR outputs parameters in relation to the tree overstory density levels for different management practices. Litter, fermentation and humus layers are considered in terms of accumulation at a point-in-time. The rate of litter accumulation is the only simulation output that provides a time dimension. The spatial distribution of only the total accumulation of organic material is represented.

Other models, named CROWN and BOLE, predict the magnitude of tree crown and branch-wood accumulations, respectively, associated with the management practices being simulated.

2.2 The FAUNA module

The FAUNA module includes computer simulation models that describe the carrying capacities of an area, habitat qualities for a variety of wildlife species and dynamics of animal populations within specified ecosystem conditions.

2.2.1 Carrying capacities

In a model structured to predict livestock carrying capacities on a rangeland, termed CARRY, herbage production is either entered directly by a user or obtained from UNDER, the herbage production simulator. Herbage production is then partitioned into usable forage for livestock types (e.g., sheep or goats). Plant species in each forage component are determined from knowledge of the preferred foods for these animals.

Desired levels of forage consumption by livestock types are introduced to the simulation problem by a user to meet a specific management objective. For example, it often becomes necessary to reduce a proper use factor on a rangeland that has been subjected to prolonged grazing pressures. The amount of usable forage required per animal unit month (AUM) for the species being considered is also input by the user. An AUM is defined as a mature animal grazing for a one-month period on a rangeland. The number of months that livestock consume forage on an area is frequently variable, depending largely upon the weather factors that characterize the rangeland ecosystem. Only estimates based on knowledge of average situations are made.

The effects of management practices on livestock-carrying capacities are evaluated largely through predictions of changes in herbage production. Changes in production of herbage are then converted into AUM values that are distributed over the rangeland ecosystem.

2.2.2 Wildlife habitat qualities

HABRAN (HABitat RANking) is a model that synthesizes ranked response predictions of changes in wildlife habitat qualities, which are then summarized in a pattern recognition format. Habitat qualities are assigned numerical values ranging from 0 to 10, with habitat quality within a specific ecosystem increasing with numerical value. Assignment of these values is achieved through analyses of functions that relate habitat preference to available parameters, the magnitude of which are altered by alternative management practices.

An increase (+), a decrease (-) or no change (0) in habitat qualities is determined by comparing numerical habitat quality values for existing conditions with those predicted for habitats modified by management. A matrix of pluses, minuses, and zeros is displayed for all of the wildlife habitats and management practices, to provide estimates of alternative management impacts in a pattern recognition model.

2.2.3 Animal population dynamics

A population dynamics model, called DYNAMO, simulates the impacts of management practices on the reproduction, growth, mortality and structure of selected animal populations. This model is designed to predict the manner by which a given population of animals will respond to changes in food, cover and diversity that are attributed to the management practices being considered. Emphasis is placed on simulating the dynamics of large herbivores in the model.

2.3 The WATER module

The WATER module contains models to simulate intermittent streamflow regimes, suspended sediment concentrations and the chemical quality of stream-flow water. These models can be operated individually or interfaced together to operate as a package.

2.3.1 Intermittent streamflow regimes

The need for a model with simple data requirements to represent intermittent streamflow regimes led to the development of a simulator called YIELD, in which there are optional simulation routines. One routine predicts a water balance on a daily basis. Required data inputs to this routine are few and commonly available. Another routine is a water balance model developed to include varying textures and depths of soil, and a range of vegetative types.

The initialization variable is precipitation, while the driving variable is a measure of the tree overstory density conditions. Outputs are values representing the simulated streamflow regime, and changes in soil moisture, evapotranspiration and deep seepage. Linkages to other models are used to obtain estimates of tree overstory density, while outputs of streamflow are inputs to models used to simulate suspended sediment concentrations, and the chemical quality of the streamflow water.

2.3.2 Suspended sediment concentrations

Another simulator, named SED, predicts the concentrations of suspended sediment in streamflow water. This model is structured to offer a choice between two sets of input data. Input data, representing either the tree overstory density conditions or spatial distributions of organic material on the soil surface, are entered directly by a user or generated by other models in the computer simulation system. The other input needed, the streamflow regime, can be obtained from YIELD. The core of the model is a set of mathematical relationships between suspended sediment concentrations and streamflow discharge rates.

Outputs include the maximum concentrations of suspended sediment on a daily basis; maximum streamflow discharge; and the total weight of suspended sediment produced in streamflow regimes, representing the alternative management practices simulated.

2.3.3 Chemical quality

A simulator is included to estimate the concentrations of selected, dissolved chemical constituents in intermittent streamflows. The driving variable in the model, called CHEM, is the streamflow regime, the magnitude of which will generally vary with alternative management practices. This variable can be entered directly by a user or obtained from outputs of YIELD. Concentrations of 13 chemical constituents are estimated within the CHEM framework, including: calcium; magnesium; sodium; chloride; sulfate; carbonate; bicarbonate; fluoride; nitrate; phosphate; total soluble salts; the hydrogen ion (pH); and conductivity.

A routine is also available to simulate the impacts of management practices on heavy metal and the nutrient transport capacities of suspended sediment.

3. COMMAND SYSTEM

The command module for this system is largely dispersed into the respective models. Initial selection of the modules and models within the modules, and the assignment of default values needed in the operation are handled by the module. Timing and sequencing in the operation of the individual models are also executed. Summary displays (tables, graphs, and maps) of the simulation results are achieved through the command module.

All the computer simulation models in the system are structured to have three modes of operation:

(i)   Initialization;
(ii)   Cycling through time; and
(iii)   Summarization.

The necessary input data are introduced directly by the user or entered from stored data files in the initialization mode. While the computer simulation system is designed to operate with minimal input data, default values are offered so that simulation can proceed whether or not a user has the required input data. The second mode of operation is a cycling in-time, with the processes being simulated (e.g., daily streamflow yields, monthly carrying capacities and annual growth and yield of tree species.) The third mode of operation is the summary, and other activities at the end of a simulation problem.

4. SUMMARY

Multiple-resource simulation models must be formulated from accepted relationships and be practical, if they are to be useful to decision-makers and managers. The computer simulation system presented in this paper is representative of a group of such models. Because the basic structure of this system is flexible, it can be adapted for application in ecosystems elsewhere if the required developmental information is available or can be obtained.

The advantage of this system is that individual models can be updated as needed without disrupting the operation of other models in the system (Larson et al., 1978). Furthermore, a user can add or delete models to suit particular informational requirements. The mix of models is easily adjusted from one situation to another, facilitating application of the system to location conditions. Besides being more flexible to use, the simulation approach offered by this system is less expensive to operate, easier to use and requires less data than larger, all-purpose ecosystem models.

References

Ffolliott, P.F., Brooks, K.N. and Guertin, D.P. 1984. Multiple-resource modeling - Lake States application. *Northern Journal of Applied Forestry* 1:80-84.

Larson, F.R., Ffolliott, P.F., Rasmussen, W.O. and Carder, D.R. 1978. Estimating impacts of silvicultural management practices on forest ecosystems. In: *Best Management Practices for Agriculture and Silviculture*. Proceedings of the 1978 Cornell Agricultural Waste Management Conference. pp. 281-294.

Rasmussen, W.O., and Ffolliott, P.F. 1981. Simulation of consequences of implementing alternative natural resources policies. In: Ffolliott, P.F., and Halffter, G.F., (technical coordinators). *Social and environmental consequences of natural resources policies, with special emphasis on biosphere reserves*. USDA Forest Service, General Technical Report RM-88. pp. 41-43.

A probabilistic approach to assessing arid rangelands' productivity, carrying capacity and stocking rates

12

H. N. Le Houérou

Synopsis

This paper reviews the concept of Rain-Use Efficiency (RUE) in the context of arid rangeland management. It outlines the possibilities of deriving other useful formulae which have a capacity for predicting carrying capacity.

Key points

1. *One of the major difficulties in arid rangeland management and development planning is the very large and unpredictable inter-annual production variability, which, in turn, is tied to rainfall vagaries. The difficulty may, however, be overcome to some degree using rainfall statistics, together with two productivity concepts and parameters: the RUE and the Production to Rain Variability Ratio (PRVR) factors.*

2. *RUE is the amount of plant dry matter (DM) produced on one hectare (ha) over one year (yr) for each millimetre (mm) of rain fallen (kg DM/ha/yr/mm). It tends to decrease with aridity, but it is above all tied to range status, i.e., it sharply decreases with range degradation. The mean worldwide value is 4.0 ± 0.5.*

3. *PRVR is the quotient of the coefficient of variation of annual production by the coefficient of variation of annual rainfall (CVP/CVR). It tends to increase with aridity and with range depletion, but it is also linked to soil characteristics increasing with texture fineness and decreasing with soil depth. PRVR is inversely related to ecosystem productivity and to RUE. The mean worldwide value is 1.5 ± 0.07.*

4. *The two concepts and parameters may be combined in an empirical mathematical equation that provides a model for predicting annual primary above ground production for a given ecosystem or range type from annual rainfall statistics and*

productivity data. Thus it allows for predicting carrying capacity and adjusting stocking rates, according to production probabilities. It is an improvement on traditional trial and error empiricism. The method has been validated in large-scale live situations over extended geographic areas. The predicting equation reads:

(Equation 1) $\qquad$ P = (1 + B.r - r /r) r. RUE

Where: P $\quad=\quad$ Production in a given year

$\qquad$ r $\quad=\quad$ Rainfall in a given year

$\qquad$ r $\quad=\quad$ Mean annual rainfall

$\qquad$ B $\quad=\quad$ CVP/CVR

$\qquad$ RUE $\quad=\quad$ Rain-Use Efficiency (kg DM/Ha/Yr/mm)

$\qquad$ CVP $\quad=\quad$ Coefficient of variation of annual production

$\qquad$ CVR $\quad=\quad$ Coefficient of variation of annual rainfall

1. PRIMARY PRODUCTION

1.1 General

Primary production is herein understood as the concrete amount of net total plant matter produced per unit of surface (NPP) over a unit of time. In practical terms, it is often expressed in kg DM ha^{-1} yr^{-1} (or any other unit such as: g.m^{-2} month^{-1}, or lbs acre^{-1} year^{-1} etc.).

Primary production should not be confused with primary productivity, which is a relativity concept (i.e., the ability to produce), nor with plant biomass or phytomass which is the amount of plant matter actually present over a given surface at a given moment, without any reference to a time frame.

NPP is, in theory, concerned with both below and above ground production (roots and shoots). However, due to the difficulty of assessing below ground production, we shall consider here only the above ground (or aerial) production (ANPP).

ANPP is approximately represented by the Maximum Standing Crop (MSC) (i.e., the yield). On a practical basis, actual ANPP is tedious, time-consuming and costly to evaluate in an accurate manner; but as a matter of fact, ANPP and MSC are closely related; MSC is approximately equal to 75% of ANPP (Le Houérou 1982, 1984, 1989; Le Houérou et al., 1988 ; Le Houérou and Hoste, 1977).

1.2 Rain-Use Efficiency (RUE)

Many authors have related primary production to rainfall in arid and semi-arid rangelands, either on a seasonal or annual basis; many local predictive equations and models have been worked out over the past 30 years (Le Houérou, 1982, 1984; Le Houérou et al., 1988).

Rain-Use Efficiency (RUE) is the amount of plant DM produced on a hectare (ha) over one year for each millimetre (mm) of rain actually fallen; it is often expressed in kg DM ha^{-1} yr^{-1} mm^{-1}.

On a world basis, the average RUE is 4.0, with a Standard Error of 0.5 (Le Houérou, 1984). But the RUE factor may vary greatly from one range type to the next, depending on the nature and functioning of the ecosystems considered, particularly the vegetation structure, range condition, perennial plant cover, perennial phytomass, soil fertility and water budget. Most figures, stemming from the analysis of 2000 pairs of data from various arid and semi-arid rangelands of the world, lie within the 1-10 kg DM ha^{-1} yr^{-1} mm^{-1} bracket; 80% of the data are actually concentrated in the 1-6 RUE limits (Figure 12.1). Typical figures for arid rangelands from the West Asia and North Africa (WANA) region are presented in Table 12.1, which shows that the overall RUE figure for the WANA region (4.1) is similar to the worldwide value (4.0). It also shows that exclosure and control grazing allow for a nearly three-fold increase of RUE, as compared to adjacent areas grazed in the usual manner, i.e., overgrazed and overstocked. In many cases, the increase factor is considerably greater (four to five-fold) (Mirreh and Al Diran (1995); El Shorbagy and Suliman (1995)). This is perfectly coherent and fully consistent with other specialists' experience in the region (Le Houérou, 1962, 1969 a and b, 1992, 1995 ; Le Houérou et al., 1983).

Table 12.1 also shows a poor correlation between RUE and rainfall. Rangelands in low rainfall areas may have a high RUE and vice-versa; conversely relatively high rainfall rangelands may exhibit a low RUE, since RUE depends more than anything on the ecosystems' dynamics and functioning (as mentioned above) and is shown by data from exclosures vs adjacent grazed areas.

Figure 12.1

Statistical distribution of the RUE factor in 1 500 pairs of data on annual production and annual rainfall, from world arid and semi-arid lands

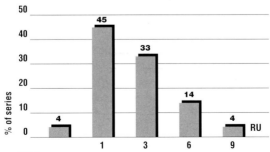

Source: Le Houérou, (1984).

1.3 Production to Rain Variability Ratio (PRVR)

It has been shown that annual primary production is globally more variable than annual rainfall; the comparison between these two parameters may be established by the ratio between the coefficient of the variation of annual production and that of annual rainfall ($\frac{CVP}{CVR}$ = PRVR), or their deciles. The overall worldwide value of PRVR, based on 80 series with 1 000 pairs of annual data on either parameter, is 1.5. In other words, the variability of annual production is 50% larger than the variability of annual rainfall (Le Houérou et al., 1988) (Figure 12.2). Data from the WANA Region are globally similar to worldwide figures (Table 12.2). Again, the regional overall PRVR figure is similar to the world mean (1.5 0,17 vs 1,5 0,07).

Although it does not seem obvious from the small number of series (19) above, PRVR and RUE tend to be inversely related. Depleted rangelands tend to exhibit a low RUE and a high PRVR and the opposite tends to be true for rangelands in good condition, with a high perennial plant cover and phytomas. The overall worldwide relationship between PRVR and RUE is shown in Figure 12.3. (Le Houérou, 1988).

Figure 12.2

Statistical distribution of the PRVR factor in 1 000 pairs of data on annual production and annual rainfall, from 80 series from world arid and semi-arid lands

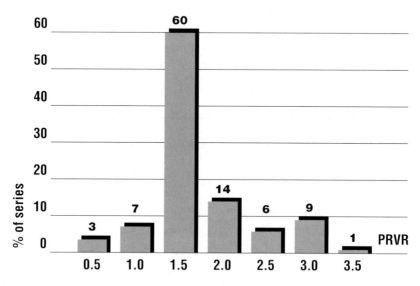

Source: Le Houérou et al.,1988).

Table 12.1

Examples of RUE in WANA arid and semi-arid rangelands

Mean Annual Rainfall mm	RUE	Area, Reference, Remarks, Grazing Status
54	0.5	Al Jouf, S. Arabia, Mirreh & Al Diran, 1995, 12 sites, grazed, 4 yrs
54	2.1	Al Jouf, S. Arabia, Mirreh & Al Diran, 1995, 12 sites, exclosure, 4 yrs
63	3.0	Kuwait, Kernick, 1966, *Rhanterium epapposum,* exclosure, 6 yrs
68	14.2	Al Jouf, S. Arabia, Mirreh & Al Diran, 1995, exclosure, Wadi Tamirat, *Haloxylon persicum* communities
75	0.7	Saudi Arabia, Heady, 1963, calculated from stocking rates
81	1.5	Kuwait, Zaman & Taha, 1995, *Halox. salicornicum,* exclosure 5 yrs
95	2.6	Kuwait, Zaman & Taha, 1995, *Rhant. epapposum,* exclosure 9 yrs
100	1.2	Iraq, Thalen, 1979, Depleted *Rhant. epapposum* steppe
131	3.3	Algeria, Nedjraoui & Touffet, 1994, Alfa grass steppe on sand
140	10.0	Syria, El Shorbagy & Suliman, 1995, Deir Attia, exclosure
140	4.0	Syria, El Shorbagy & Suliman, 1995, Deir Attia, grazed
142	2.2	Cyrenaica, Libya, Shishov & Kharin, 1980, fair condition rangelands
150	2.7	Egypt, Ayyad, 1977/88, exclosure, Ommayed
150	0.9	Tripolitania, Libya, Le Houérou, 1965, depleted rglds
150	1.8	N. Syria, Van der Veen, 1967, depleted rglds, Wadi el Azib
154	4.8	Tunisia, Novikoff & Skouri, 1981, control grazing, *Rhant. suaveolens*
187	0.6	Iraq, Thalen, 1979, depleted steppe
206	2.3	Algeria, Aïdoud, 1987, fair condition *Artemisia herba alba* steppe
206	3.4	Syria, Van der Veen, 1967, exclosure, Wadi el Azib
208	2.3	Algeria, Aïdoud, 1992, Alfa grass rangeland
214	4.7	Tunisia, Floret & Pontanier, 1982, control grazing
220	2.9	Algeria, Le Houérou, 1974, control grazing, Hodna
214	6.3	Jordan, El Shorbagy & Suliman, 1995, Bala'ma, exclosure
214	4.6	Jordan, El Shorbagy & Suliman, 1995, Bala'ma, grazed
225	4.0	Libya, Le Houérou & Dumancic, 1981, control grazing
227	1.2	Tunisia, Floret & Pontanier, 1982, depleted rangeland
231	3.6	Tunisia, Floret & Pontanier, 1982, control grazing
250	2.8	Tunisia, Le Houérou, 1969, mean of 130 plant communities
250	2.8	Algeria, Rodin, Vinogradov & al, 1970, mean of 80 plant communities
250	1.9	Algeria, Nedjraoui, 1981, Alfa grass steppe
250	2.1	Algeria, Nedjraoui & Touffet, 1994, Alfa grass steppe
258	9.6	Israel, Benjamin & al, 1982, weed communities, fertilized
262	9.6	Israel, Tadmor & al, 1974, weed communities, fertilized
317	5.0	Tunisia, Floret & Pontanier, 1982, exclosure, sandy steppe
392	1.2	Algeria, Nedjraoui & Touffet, 1994, Alfa grass steppe
529	4.6	Israel, Naveh, 1982, Medit. shrubs communities
600	5.5	Israel, Gutman, 1978, Medit. shrubs communities
621	8.7	Israel, Gutman & Seligman, 1979, Medit. shrubs communities
734	5.0	Israel, Katznelson & Putievsky, 1972, non-fertilized
734	10.6	Israel, Katznelson & Putievsky, 1972, fertilized

	Means Overall		Enclosures		Grazed		RUE
	R	RUE	R	RUE	R	RUE	Excl./Graz.
X	239	4.1	281	5.4	195	1.9	2.8
SD	184	3.2	217	3.4	116	1.3	2.6
CV%	77	71	77	63.0	59.6	66.1	0.95

Source: Unpublished

Table 12.2

PRVR in WANA arid rangelands

R	PRVR	RUE	Nr of yrs	Area	Reference	Remarks
68	2.1	14.2	6	Al Jouf, S. Arabia, Mirreh et al., Diran; 1995, Wadi Tamirat		
81	1.4	2.6	9	Kuwait, Zaman & Taha, 1995, *Rhant. epapp.* excl.		
95	2.1	1.5	5	Kuwait, Zaman & Taha, 1995, *Halox, salic,* excl.		
131	0.6	3.3	3	Algeria, Nedjraoui & Touffet, 1994, Alfa grass		
206	1.8	2.3	10	Algeria, Aïdoud, 1987, *Artemisia herba alba*		
208	1.6	2.3	12	Algeria, Aïdoud, 1992, Alfa grass range		
214	1.1	4.7	6	Tunisia, Floret & Pontanier, 1982, *Rhant. suaveolens*		
214	2.1	4.6	3	Jordan, El Shorbagy & Suliman, grazed, Bala'ma		
214	3.4	6.3	3	Jordan, El Shorbagy & Suliman, excl.		
227	1.5	1.2	3	Tunisia, Floret & Pontanier, 1982, gypsic soil		
231	1.5	3.1	5	Tunisia, Floret & Pontanier, 1982, fair range sandy silt		
237	1.0	2.8	3	Tunisia, Floret & Pontanier, 1982, poor cond., coarse sand		
250	1.3	2.1	3	Algeria, Nedjraoui & Touffet, 1994, Alfa grass steppe		
258	1.1	18.1	10	Israel, Benjamin et al., 1982 loess, weed com., fertilized		
259	1.2	9.6	10	Israel, Benjamin et al., 1982, non-fertilized		
392	1.0	1.2	3	Algeria, Nedjraoui & Touffet, 1994, alfa grass		
529	1.9	4.6	6	Israel, Naveh, 1982		
600	0.6	5.5	9	Israel, Gutman, 1978		
621	0.5	8.7	10	Israel, Gutman & Seligman, 1979		

overall

	R	PRVR	RUE
X	270	1.5	6.2
SD	168	0.7	4.7
CV%	62.2	46.5	70.4
SE	–	0.17	1.17

Source: Unpublished

1.4 Predicting annual primary production

An empiric mathematical equation combining the RUE and PRVR concepts has been worked out to predict annual production from rainfall and production data (Le Houérou, 1988; Le Houérou and Skerbek, 1983; Le Houérou et al., 1988).

The equation was validated under the conditions of Libya (Le Houérou and Skerbek, 1983; Le Houérou et al., 1988); the conditions of the Sahel (Le Houérou, 1989, 1993b), and the subtropical rangelands of Argentina (Le Houérou, 1995b; Guevara et al., 1996a and b; Guevara et al., 1997). In all three cases, the equation was found to produce realistic data, consistent with the empirical experience of ranchers and stockmen (Guevara et al., 1996a and b) (Tables 12.3, 12. 4 and 12.5).

Figure 12.3

Statistical relationship between RUE and PRVR from 80 series of data from world arid and semi-arid lands

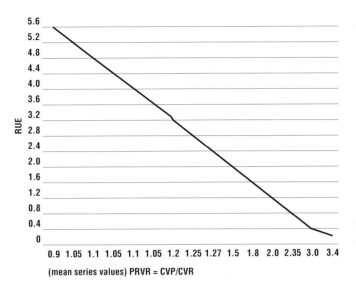

(mean series values) PRVR = CVP/CVR

Source: Le Houérou (1988)

The equation reads :

(Equation 2) $y\alpha = \left[\beta\,\frac{\alpha r}{\overline{x}} + (1\beta)\right]\alpha r.$ RU (Le Houérou and Skerbek, 1983)

Where :

$y\alpha$ = yield under probability α

αr = Rainfall under probability α

RUE   = Rain-Use Efficiency

$\overline{x}$ = Mean annual rainfall

$\beta = \dfrac{CV\ Production}{CV\ Rainfall} = PRVR$

This equation may be simplified in the following way (Le Houérou et al., 1988):

(Equation 3) $P = (1 + \dfrac{\beta.r\text{-}r}{\overline{r}})\ rRUE$

Where :

P = Production in a given year RUE = Rain-Use Efficiency (kg DM ha^{-1} yr^{-1} mm^{-1})

r = Rainfall in a given year CVP = Coefficient of variation of annual production

r = Mean annual rainfall CVR = Coefficient of variation of annual rainfall

β = CVP/CVR

Table 12.3

Case Study no.1 in the Mendoza plain rangelands, Argentina

Site 1: El Divisadero Range Research Station: *Coarse sandy soils*

	Rainfall Probability %	Annual Rainfall mm	Annual R Mean R	Primary Edible Production kgDM ha^{-1} yr^{-1}	RUE	Carrying Capac. Ha/LSU
	90	137	0.47	334	2.4	36
DR	80	190	0.65	526	2.8	23
	70	229	0.78	688	3.0	18
	60	262	0.89	841	3.2	14
Mean	50	293=R	1.00	996	3.4	12
	40	324	1.11	1163	3.6	10
	30	357	1.22	1354	3.8	9
	20	396	1.35	1597	4.0	8
	10	449	1.53	1957	4.4	6

RUE = 3.4; PRVR = 0.5

Site 2: Nacuñan, Range Research Station: *Silty alluvial soils, 50 km away from site 1*

	Rainfall Probability %	Annual Rainfall mm	Annual R Mean R	Primary Edible Production kgDM ha^{-1} yr^{-1}	RUE	Carrying Capac. ha/LSU
	90	152	0.52	0.0	0.0	0.0
DR	80	200	0.68	124	0.6	98
	70	235	0.80	363	1.5	34
	60	265	0.90	619	2.3	20
Mean	50	294=R	1.00	911	3.1	13
	40	321	1.09	1224	3.8	10
	30	350	1.19	1602	4.6	8
	20	386	1.31	2133	5.5	6
	10	434	1.48	2947	6.8	4

RUE = 3.1; PRVR = 2.5

DR = Dependable rainfall, i. e., occurring 4 years in 5.

RUE and PRVR were established over a 10-year clipping experiment in both stations.

Source: Le Houérou (1995b); Guevara et al., (1996a and b, 1997).

For similar RUE and mean rainfall, silty soils show a much larger production variability than sandy soils, with PRVRs of 2.5 and 0.5 respectively. The production variability of silty soils is thus five-fold larger than on sandy soils; a fact well-known to arid-land ecologists (Le Houérou, 1959; Floret and Pontanier, 1982).

1.5 Predicting Grazeable Production (GP)

Predicting Grazeable Production (GP) is a fairly simple operation, knowing the size of two further parameters: (i) the proportion of edible material (EM) (i.e., forage) in the overall primary production; and (ii) the Proper Use Factor (PUF), the amount of forage that can be safely levied by grazing animals without jeopardizing the long-term future productivity for subsequent years. The proportion of edible material present may vary largely, from less than 10% in rangelands invaded by unpalatable range weeds, to over 90% in good grassland, such as those dominated by *Cynodon* spp. It appears that PUF in arid rangelands is much less than was assumed for decades (Le Houérou, 1989, 1992; Holecheck, 1988; Kothmann, 1992). Many specialists now think that PUF should not exceed 25 to 35% of the grazeable material, instead of the 40 to 80% traditionally assumed on the basis of data from non-arid lands. But, again, this depends to a large extent on range type and condition. Rangelands dominated by ephemerals (e.g., Aacheb, Ghizzu) may be more heavily grazed in good years than those based on shrubs, on perennial grasses and/or legumes, up to the point where seed production is seriously hampered. Grazeable production may thus be expressed by the following empiric equation:

(Equation 4) $\qquad$ GP = MSC.EM.PUF

Where :
GP is grazeable production in kg DM ha-1
MSC $\quad$ Maximum Standing Crop in kg DM ha-1
EM $\qquad$ Edible material in % of MSC
PUF $\qquad$ Proper Use Factor in % of EM

2. CARRYING CAPACITY AND STOCKING RATES

Carrying capacity, expressed in hectares per animal unit per annum, stems from Annual Animal Feed Requirements minus Supplementary Feed, divided by the Grazeable Production :

(Equation 5) $\qquad \dfrac{\text{AAFR-SF}}{\text{GP}} = \text{CC (ha/Anim Unit)}$

Where:
AAFR = Annual Animal Feed Requirement, SF = Supplementary Feed,
GP = Grazeable Production and CC = Carrying Capacity.

Equations 2 (or 3) and 4 predict the amount of forage available under a given rainfall probability, and therefore, the carrying capacity under the same probability.

The stocking rate to be applied will then depend on this prediction, but also on some other considerations such as the trade-off between the cost of supplementary feeding and the market value of the animal product output. Such a trade-off will determine the frequency at which supplementary feeding will be economically feasible.

If the cost of supplementary feed is low compared to the animal product sold, supplementary feeding will be more frequently affordable than in the opposite situation and the stockmen could then elect a rather high stocking rate, corresponding to a rainfall probability of, for instance, 35 or 40%, In the opposite situation, the producer would elect a lower stocking rate corresponding, for example, with a rainfall probability of 65-75%. In the first case, he will have to supplement one year in two or three whilst in the second case he will have to supplement one year in three or four.

But supplementary feed may be economically prohibitive. In such a case, the farmer will elect a very low stocking rate corresponding with a range production probability of 80 or 90%, according to which he will supplement one year in five or one year in ten. In many instances, a 100% rainfall probability strategy is not actually feasible because production may then be zero in some years. The zero production intercept is approximately 50 mm yr-1 (Le Houérou, 1959, 1969, 1984; Le Houérou and Hoste, 1977; Noy-Meir, 1973, 1979; Webb et al., 1978). The probability of having a rainfall of 50 mm one year in ten roughly corresponds with a mean annual rainfall of 150 mm (Le Houérou, et al., 1993; Le Houérou, 1995). This is the reason why settled, fully rainfed animal production systems are scarcely in existence below that isohyet of 150 mm of mean annual rainfall.

Other considerations may also interfere with decision-making, e.g., the need for range regeneration or rehabilitation that would set a low stocking target for a given period of time until the desired level of regeneration is reached, such as after a severe drought.

3. CONCLUSION

A probabilistic approach to evaluating primary production, carrying capacity and stocking rates is progress compared to the traditional trial-and-error method. But the probabilistic approach described here also has its limitations; the lack of data on RUE and on PRVR (rainfall data are usually appropriate). The missing data may, to some extent, be extrapolated from research findings on ecosystems having similar characteristics under similar climates, for example, the *Artemisia herba alba* rangelands that extend throughout the WANA region from Morocco to Afghanistan and Baluchistan, the vicarious plant communities such as those of *Rhanterium epapposum* in West Asia and *Rhanterium suaveolens* in North Africa (both locally called Arfaj), or those of *Haloxylon elegans* throughout WANA. Determining stocking rates requires additional economic information, in particular the trade-off between the cost of supplementary feeding and the monetary value of the animal goods produced.

This probabilistic approach has been validated in large rangeland areas and the model was found to be a realistic predictor of range potentialities, as long as other information could complement it, notably data on the proportion of Edible Material (EM) within the Maximum Standing Crop (MSC) and on the Proper Use Factor (PUF) to be applied.

References

Aïdoud, A, 1992. Production des écosystèmes steppiques à Armoise blanche (Artemisia herba alba Asso). *Variations inter-annuelles et implications pastorales.* Proceed. XVI Intern. Grassld Congr., vol. II, INRA, Nice. pp.1595-1596.

Aïdoud, A., 1992. Les parcours à alfa des hautes plaines algériennes. Variation interannuelle et productivité. In: Gaston, A., Kernick, M.D. and Le Houérou, H.N. (edits). Proceedings *IVth Internat. Rangelds Congress*, vol. 1, CIRAD-UCIST, publ. Montpellier. pp. 198-199.

Benjamin, R. W., Eyal, E., Noy-Meir, I and Seligman, N.G., 1982. Intensive Agro-pastoral system in the Migda experimental farm, Northern Negev. *Hassadeh*, 62: 2022-2026 (in Hebrew, with English summary).

El Shorbagy, M.A. and Suliman I.S., 1995. Improvement of some depleted ranges in Syria and Jordan through the application of some technological agricultural practices. In: Omar, S.A.S., Razzaque, M.A. and Alsdirawi, F. (edts). *Range management in arid zones*, pp. 251-270, Keagan Paul, London.

Floret, C. and Pontanier, R. 1982. L'aridité en Tunisie présaharienne. *Trav. et Docum.*, n° 150, ORSTOM, Paris.

Guevara, J.C., Cavagnaro, J.B., Estevez, O.R., Le Houérou, H.N. and Stasi C.R., 1997. (in press) Productivity, management and development problems in the arid rangelands of the central Mendoza Plains (Argentina) *Journ. of Arid Environm.*

Guevara, J.C., Estevez, O.R., Stasi, C.R. and Monge, A.S. 1996b. Botanical composition of the seasonal diet of cattle in the rangelands of the Monte Desert of Mendoza (Argentina). *Journ. of Arid Environm.*, 32: 387-394.

Guevara, J.C., Estevez, O.R. and Torres, E.R. 1996a. Utilization of the Rain-Use Efficiency factor for determining potential cattle production in the Mendoza Plains. *Journ. of Arid Environm.* 33, 3 : 347-354.

Gutman, M. 1978. Primary production of transitional Mediterranean steppe. *Proceed. 1st Internat. Rglds Congr.*, Denver, Colorado. pp. 225-228.

Gutman, M. and Seligman, N.G. 1979. Grazing management of Mediterranean foothill range in the Upper Jordan River Valley. *Journ. of Range Mgt*, 32: 86-92.

Heady, H.F. 1963. Grazing resources and problems: report to the Government of Saudi Arabia. *EPTA Report* nr 1614, FAO, Rome.

Holecheck, J.L. 1988. An approach for setting the stocking rate. *Rangelands*, 10: 10-14.

Katznelson, J. and Putievsky, E., 1972. Range fertilizing trials in the Upper Galilee and in the Golan. *Hassadeh,* 52: 1040-1044 (in Hebrew with English Summary).

Kernick, M.D. 1966. Plant resources, range ecology and fodder plant introduction: report to the Government of Kuwait. *EPTA Report.* nr. TA 218, FAO, Rome.

Kothmann, M.M. 1992. Nutrition for livestock grazing rangelands and pasturelands. In: Howard, J.L. (ed.) *Current Veterinary Therapy, 3: Food Animal Practice,* WB Saunders, Publ., Philadelphia. pp. 285-293.

Le Houérou, H.N. 1959. Ecologie, phytosociologie et productivité de l'olivier en Tunisie méridionale. *Bull. Serv. Carte Phytogéogr.,* B, IV, 1 : 7-72, CNRS, Paris.

Le Houérou, H.N. 1962. *Les paturages naturels de la Tunisie aride et désertique.* 110 p., XII pl., 4 cartes. Instit. Sces Econom. Appliquées, Paris-Tunis.

Le Houérou, H.N. 1965. Improvement of natural pastures and fodder resources: report to the Government of Libya, *EPTA Report* nr 1979, FAO, Rome.

Le Houérou, H.N. 1969a La végétation de la Tunisie steppique, avec références aux végétations analogues de l'Algérie, de la Libye et du Maroc; *Ann. Inst Nat. Rech. Agron. de Tunisie,* 42,5.

Le Houérou, H.N. 1969b Principes méthodes et techniques d'amélioration pastorale et fourragère en Tunisie. *Etude Paturages,* n° 2. Divis. Prod. Végétale, FAO, Rome.

Le Houérou, H.N. 1980. The rangelands of the Sahel. *Journ. of Range Mgt,* 33: 41-46.

Le Houérou, H.N. 1982. Prediction of range production from weather records in Africa. *Proceed. Tech. Confer on Climate in Africa.* WMO, Geneva. pp. 286-298.

Le Houérou, H.N. 1984. Rain-Use Efficiency: a unifying concept in arid-land ecology. *Journ of Arid Environm.,* 7: 213-247.

Le Houérou, H.N. 1988. Interannual variability of rainfall and its ecological and managerial consequences on natural vegetation, crops and livestock. In: di Castri, F., Floret, C., Rambal, S. and Roy, J. (eds.) Time cales and water stress, *Proceed. 5th Medecos Confer.,* IUBS, Paris. pp. 323-346.

Le Houérou, H.N. 1989. The grazing land ecosystems of the African Sahel. *Ecological Studies,* nr 75, Springer Verlag, Heidelberg.

Le Houérou, H.N. 1992. Rangeland management in Northern Africa and the Near East : Evolution, Trends and Development Outlook. In: Gaston, A., Kernick, M.D. and Le Houérou, H.N. (eds.) *Proceed. IVth Internat. Rangelds Congr.* vol. I, , CIRAD-UCIST publ., Montpellier. pp. 543-552.

Le Houérou, H.N. 1993a. The grazing lands of the Mediterranean Basin. In: Coupland, R.T. (ed.) *Natural Grasslands,* ch. 7, Ecosystems of the world, vol. 8B, Elsevier Science Publ., Amsterdam, pp. 171-196.

Le Houérou, H.N., 1993b. The grasslands of the Sahel. In: Coupland, R.T. (ed.), *Natural Grasslands,* ch. 8, *Ecosystems of the world,* vol. 8 B, Elsevier Science Publ. Amsterdam, pp. 197-220.

Le Houérou, H.N. 1995a. Bioclimatologie et biogéographie des steppes arides du Nord de l'Afrique, *Options Méditerranéennes,* B, 10: 1-396.

Le Houérou, H.N. 1995b. *Informe de las visitas a la Argentina, octobre-noviembre 1992 y settiembre a noviembre de 1995.* multig r., IADIZA, Mendoza.

Le Houérou, H.N. 1996. Contraintes environnementales pour l'élevage en zone aride *In:* Bourbouze, A. and Hardouin, J. (eds) *Zootechnie Comparée,* Aupelf-Hatier, Paris, ch. 5-6 pp. 481-495.

Le Houérou, H.N., Bingham, R.L. and Skerbek, W. 1988. Relationship between the variability of primary production and the variability of annual precipitation in world arid lands. *Journ. of Arid Environm.* 15 : 1-18.

Le Houérou, H.N., Claudin, J., Haywood, M. and Donadieu, P. 1974. *Etude phytoécologique du Hodna.*, (carte: 3 feuilles coul. 1/200 000) FAO, Rome.

Le Houérou, H.N., Claudin, J. and Pouget, M. 1981. Etude bioclimatique des steppes algériennes (3 cartes 1/1 000 000). *Bull. Soc. Sces Nat. de l'Afr. du Nord*, 68 : 33-74.

Le Houérou, H.N., and Dumancic, D. 1981. *Acacia cyanophylla* Lindl. as supplementary feed for small stock in Libya. *Journ. of Arid Environm.* 4: 161-167.

Le Houérou, H.N. and Hoste C.H. 1977. Rangeland production and annual rainfall relations in the Mediterranean Basin and the African Sahelian and Sudanian Zones. *Journ. of Range Mgt,* 30 : 181-189.

Le Houérou, H.N., Popov, G.F. and See, L. 1993. Agro-Bioclimatic classification of Africa. *Agrometeorology study* n° 6. FAO, Rome.

Le Houérou, H.N., Servoz, H., Shawesh, O. and Telahique, T. 1983. *Evaluation of development potentials of existing range projects in Western Libya. (Jefara Plain and Jebel Nefousa)* UTF-Lib O11, FAO (Rome) and Agric. Res. Centre Tripoli. 130 p. mimeo.

Le Houérou, H.N. and Skerbek, W. 1983. *A probabilistic methodology for assessing the productivity and carrying capacity of Libyan rangelands.* UTF Lib 018, Technical Paper n° 47, FAO (Rome) and Agric. Res. Centre (Tripoli) 18p. mimeo. Also Key-Note Plenary Address, 2nd Internat. Rangeland Congress, Adelaïde, Australia, *Towards a Probabilistic Approach to Rangeland Development Planning.*

Mirreh, M.M. and Al-Diran, M.S. 1995. Effect of protection and grazing pressure in the desert rangelands of Al Jouf region, Saudi Arabia. In: Omar, S.A.S., Razzaque, M.A. and Alsdirawi, F. (edits) pp. 189-194, Range management in arid zones, Keagan Paul London.

Naveh, Z. 1982. The dependence of the productivity of semi-arid Mediterranean hill pasture ecosystems on climatic fluctuation. *Agriculture and Environment,* 7: 47-61.

Nedjraoui, D. 1981. *Evolution des éléments biogènes et valeurs nutritives dans trois principaux faciès: Artemisia herba alba, Lygeum spartum et Stipa tenacissima de végétation dans les hautes plaines steppiques de la Wilaya de Saïda.* Fac. Sces, Alger. mimeo.

Nedjraoui, D. and Touffet, J. 1994. Influence des conditions stationnelles sur la production de l'Alfa (*Stipa tenacissima* L.). *Ecologia Mediterranea,* XX (1-2): 67-75.

Nedjaroui-Driss, D. 1990. Adaptation de l'alfa (*Stipa tenacissima* L.) aux conditions stationnelles. Contribution à l'étude de l'écosystème steppique. 256 p. *Thèse Doct. Sces,* USTHB, Alger.

Novikoff, G. and Skouri, M. 1981. Balancing development and conservation in presaharan Tunisia. *Ambio,* X: 135-141.

Noy-Meir, I. 1973. Desert ecosystems: environment and producers. *Annual Review of Ecology and Systematics.* 4 : 25-51.

Noy-Meir, I. 1979. Structure and function of desert ecosystems. *Israel Journ. of Botany,* 28: 1-19.

Rodin, L.E. and Vinogradov, B. (eds.) 1970. *Etude géobotanique des pâturages du secteur ouest du Departement de Médéa, Algérie,* (2 cartes coul. 1/200 000) Nauka, Leningrad.

Shishov, L.L. and Kharin, N.G. (eds.) 1980. Soil and geobotanical studies in the pasture zone of the Socialist Peoples Libyan Arab Jamahiriya, (Vol. 2: Vegetation and Ecology, 208 pp., 4 col. maps; Vol. 3: Pastures, 246 pp., 2 col. maps) Selkopromexport, Moscou.

Thalen, D.C.P. 1979. *Ecology and utilization of desert shrub rangelands in Iraq.* Junk publ., The Hague.

Tadmor, N.H., Eyal, E. and Benjamin, R.W. 1974. Plant and sheep production on semi-arid annual grassland in Israel. *Journ. of Range Mgt,* 27: 427-432.

Vander Veen, I.P.H. 1967. Preliminary results of grazing trials in the Syrian steppe. *Netherland Journ. of Agric. Sces,* 15: 198-206.

Webb, W., Szarek, S., Lauenroth, W., Kinerson, R. and Smith, M. 1978. Primary productivity and water-use in native forest, grassland and desert ecosystems. *Ecology,* 59: 239-247.

Zaman, S. and Taha, F.K. 1995. Quantitative evaluation of vegetation in two main steppes of Kuwait's rangelands. In: Omar, S.A.S., Razzaque., M.A. and Alsdirawi, F. (eds.) *Range management in arid zones,* Keagan Paul, London, pp. 163-170.

Meeting the needs of nomads: the usefulness of the Farming Systems Research (FSR) approach

13

M. H. Andrew and J. D. Fargher

Synopsis

This paper outlines the Farming Systems Research (FSR) approach as a way of incorporating modern technology, such as the Geographic Information System (GIS), into practical outcomes. It draws on experience of developed and developing-world projects to illustrate principles which, if followed, will assist in meeting the real needs of nomads.

Key Points

1. *The Farming Systems Research (FSR) approach has proved a useful model for solving real-world land management and rangeland development problems in both the developed and developing-world contexts. This FRS approach embodies the following:*
   - *working with various stakeholders to identify their real needs;*
   - *identifying the possible solutions available to solve these problems, including technology;*
   - *where solutions are not available, working with stakeholders to develop possible alternatives;*
   - *working with stakeholders to implement these solutions; and*
   - *monitoring the outcomes to ensure their continuing effectiveness.*
2. *A key feature of the FSR approach is that appropriate technology is utilized to solve identified problems. It is a process led by client needs and is not driven by a "technology push".*
3. *GIS technology has considerable promise in large-scale rangeland projects. Examples from the Mauritania Second Livestock Project and the Kuwait Soil Survey demonstrate how the FSR approach can have relevance for meeting the needs of nomads, and in rangeland planning at the national or sub-national level.*

1. INTRODUCTION

This workshop focuses on the role of technology in achieving the sustainable use of rangelands.

The point we wish to make in this paper is that while technology itself is important, it is not the most important thing. The most important thing is to know what outcome is really desired. The key is then to determine what particular technology, or combination of technologies, is most appropriate to achieve the desired outcome. Thus, technology is only a means to the end, not the end itself; it is a great servant but a poor master. Determining the desired outcome, and the best way to achieve it, is the most difficult part of the research and development (R&D) process.

Technology alone does not solve problems, but a partnership between people and technology often does solve them. Research planning needs to consider both elements of this partnership. The FSR approach is an effective framework for achieving this as it regards farmers as partners in the R&D process.

We will draw on examples from our Australian experience to illustrate where good technology has been applied inappropriately, and to show how the FSR approach has been developed as a process to reduce failures by incorporating technology in appropriate ways.

Our thinking is consistent with IFAD's approach in addressing the issues of rural poverty, as presented by Jazairy et al., (1992). They advocate empowering those who manage the land (i.e., the "farmers"), to develop their human potential, to take control of their circumstances and to be effective participants in their societies. This is best achieved by working with farmers in a genuine partnership that values them as individual people; this is the "bottom up" approach to development. From a research, development and evaluation (R,D&E) perspective, farmers should occupy the centre of R,D&E activities, not the periphery. This is in contrast with the traditional "top down" approach to development, in which the "growth of the overall economy is believed to lead automatically to wealth 'trickling down' to the poor" (Jazairy et al., 1992). In that approach, the rural poor were considered as an homogenous group and not as individuals, and programmes were often poorly tailored to their particular needs.

2. EFFICIENCY VS EFFECTIVENESS

Edward de Bono characterized efficiency as doing the thing right and effectiveness as doing the right thing. The former focuses on analyzing what has been done (i.e., it is looking backwards). Effectiveness focuses on the future, the direction towards which one is headed. While effectiveness is about the end result, efficiency is about the means to achieve it.

Scientists and technologists trained in a reductionist environment tend to focus on efficiency, for example, to perform accurate and precise calculations, to minimize error, to design experiments which have statistical efficiency and to develop processes which are efficient in minimizing the use of resources. Scientists and technologists are focused on the details, on how to do things. However, a focus on efficiency can lead to us doing things very well which are inappropriate, and this is a waste of resources.

Our mission is to use research and development to meet the needs of our clients (i.e., the nomads, in the present context of this workshop). Thus, we must be concerned primarily with the concept of effectiveness, i.e., doing those "right things" which will meet the real needs of nomadic rangeland users. Any technology, no matter how elegant, is only important in so far as it is needed to bring about these improvements.

To use an extreme analogy: a lawn-mower, no matter how elegantly designed and expertly manufactured and inexpensively priced, is of little use to someone who lives in a high-rise apartment building. Sometimes, our single-minded focus on the technology we know leads us to recommend lawn-mowers for apartment dwellers. Finding out what these "right things" are is the hardest part of the R&D process.

The business world provides a good analogy. In the 1960s, the emphasis was on using "efficiency experts" to improve the performance of businesses. The end result was that some businesses became very efficient at doing what they did, and were thus very successful for a while. Over time, however, what they were doing became less relevant in a changing world, and they ended up doing things that were inappropriate, indeed "wrong"; they failed as a business. Thus, the emphasis in business today is on mission statements, goals, in other words, a focus on effectiveness. So it must also be our focus as we consider the needs of nomads.

Our focus must be *problem solving* which leads to a partnership between technologists and owners of the problem. In order to identify the "right things", these partners need to distinguish between *symptoms* and *causes*. These ideas are illustrated in Figure 13.1.

A key point is that the "right things" needed to bring about a particular improvement may not necessarily include more R&D, and if R&D is needed, it may not be in your field of study, or mine.

Figure 13.1

The problem solving/investment cycle

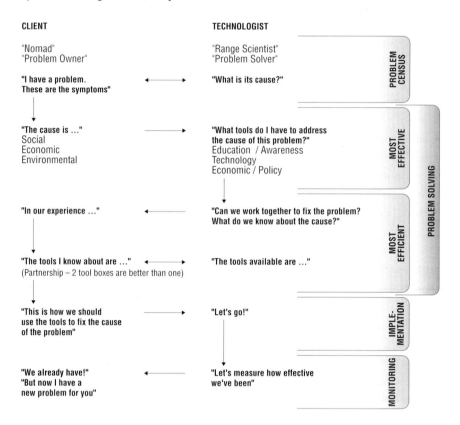

2.1 An example of good technology applied inappropriately: the improved forage legume Stylosanthes in northern Australia

In a keynote paper to the 3rd International Rangelands Congress (Andrew, 1989; Squires et al., 1992), the senior author put forward some of the ideas included this present paper, and detailed the example of pasture improvement in northern Australia.

Briefly, the tropical and sub-tropical rangelands of northern Australia, which have a wet-dry annual climate cycle, are very nutrient poor. The forage is dominated by tall, rank tropical grasses of low forage value (except for a brief period at the start of the growing season), and few legumes. Thus, cattle productivity was very low and the traditional cattle enterprise (i.e., extensive properties of hundreds of square kilometres) was managed on a low-input, "cattle-hunting" basis.

To improve cattle production, scientists imported forage legumes from South America, especially the *Stylosanthes* species, and successfully selected and bred cultivars which were productive when fertilized with superphosphate, thus mimicking the legume-based pasture systems (i.e., subterranean clover and super-phosphate), which had been so successful in southern Australia. The scientists' vision was to have improved legume pastures covering most of northern Australia.

These pastures were not widely adopted by the pastoral industry, despite extensive promotion by R&D organizations. Subsequent insights showed that the pastoralists' conservatism was well-placed.

The *Stylosanthes*-based pastures were expensive to establish, and required regular applications of fertilizer. Despite the good cattle production that could be obtained from them, computer models showed that it would take about 20 years to pay back the costs incurred in establishing them.

Indeed, other research showed that a better way to overcome the nutritional deficiencies of the native grass pasture was to feed the nutrients directly to the cattle as a mineral supplement, rather than indirectly via fertilizer. Supplemented cattle grew as well on native pasture as on improved pasture (although at much lower stocking rates), and the native pasture would sustain that grazing pressure if fire was used to break up the pattern of area-selective grazing. This approach was low-cost, low-risk, relatively easy to implement by the ranchers and returned a profit quickly.

Stylosanthes pastures do have an important role today, but as part of a total property management system, integrated with extensive areas of native pasture. They are confined to the pockets of better soils, and are used strategically for high-value purposes (e.g., for weaner calves, for finishing animals for slaughter).

2.2 The Farming Systems Research (FSR) approach

The traditional approach to R&D was a "top-down", "technology-push" model of reductionist, discipline-based research. Research findings were translated into technology that was then extended to the producers for them to adopt, in a linear way: R,D&E. The only problem was this: producers often failed to adopt the technology.

The Farming Systems Research (FSR) approach developed out of experiences with this failure of farmers to adopt new technology. This failure occurred both in developed countries, including Australia, and in developing countries. Indeed, this failure is highlighted in the objectives of this workshop as a feature of the West Asia and North Africa (WANA) region which the workshop aims to overcome.

A major developer of FSR ideas noted that:

> *"... the search for explanations [for the failure of farmers to adopt technology] revealed that the well-known conservatism of farmers was not the main problem. Rather, agricultural scientists too often ignored or misunderstood the needs and constraints of the farming system and in consequence conducted inappropriate research. This realization and the enormous importance of the problem has resulted in the development of a philosophy and a procedure for making research more efficient [i.e. effective] in terms of benefiting producers ..."* (i.e., the FSR approach) (McCown, 1990).

In other words, researchers have too often answered questions that their clients were not asking and which had little relevance for them. In part, this has been due to barriers between the researchers and the farmers, who were frustrated communicating directly with each other, namely by the extension agents who came between them.

McCown (1990) also noted that some technological interventions that aimed to increase yield had caused serious land degradation, and there was a need to view farming within an ecological systems framework, in order to achieve both productivity and sustainability goals.

Figure 13.2 illustrates the way the FSR approach links producers and their on-farm contexts (where the priorities are identified), uses conventional R&D to solve those problems and utilizes modern information technology to provide decision-support tools for the producers to use. Properly conducted, this is an interactive partnership between producers (i.e., the nomads, in the context of this workshop) and the R&D community.

When the producers' own questions are answered in a co-learning partnership with researchers, the resulting technology is readily adopted by them.

FSR requires a different way of thinking to the one provided in conventional, discipline-based university courses which tend to assume the R,D&E model. Since nothing changes without a change in thinking, this represents a particular challenge for agricultural education (Andrew, 1991). As Roe (1989) noted, after studying rangeland livestock development south of the Sahara:

> *"Thus the good news for project designers is that livestock rangeland projects are still needed in Africa (or everywhere else). The bad news is that the real need is for a new type of project that most livestock rangelands specialists have not been trained to undertake".*

Figure 13.2

A schematic view of a FSR methodology for targeted agricultural research

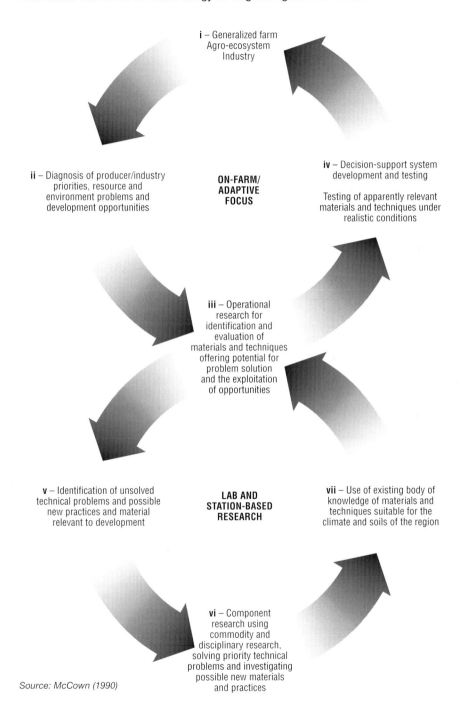

i – Generalized farm Agro-ecosystem Industry

ii – Diagnosis of producer/industry priorities, resource and environment problems and development opportunities

ON-FARM/ ADAPTIVE FOCUS

iv – Decision-support system development and testing

Testing of apparently relevant materials and techniques under realistic conditions

iii – Operational research for identification and evaluation of materials and techniques offering potential for problem solution and the exploitation of opportunities

v – Identification of unsolved technical problems and possible new practices and material relevant to development

LAB AND STATION-BASED RESEARCH

vii – Use of existing body of knowledge of materials and techniques suitable for the climate and soils of the region

vi – Component research using commodity and disciplinary research, solving priority technical problems and investigating possible new materials and practices

Source: McCown (1990)

3. CASE STUDIES

We present three case studies with which we are (or have been) involved, and which variously illustrate the principles above.

3.1 The Mauritania Second Livestock Project

The Mauritania Second Livestock Project, funded by the World Bank, ran from 1986 to 1990 and aimed to help Tuareg and Hassanyah pastoralists develop rules of thumb for managing rangelands in the three rangeland zones of Mauritania (Sahara, grass savanna, tree savanna). The intention was to raise the overall quality of rangeland management, so that cattle numbers could be reduced whilst maintaining the overall production from the rangeland. John Fargher worked with the pastoralists and government scientists to develop and implement a monitoring system.

It was an exercise in problem-solving and resource monitoring with nomads, and applying GIS and monitoring techniques to develop the best management practice at the family, regional and national levels.

A key feature was that the indigenous knowledge of the nomads was tapped to provide information to link range condition with animal production and management. For example, how did the nomads recognize good-quality range and how did they match range condition to animals' needs? This was done by providing data books to the herders which they filled in each day and summarized each month. The data, which was gathered separately for camels, cattle, goats and sheep, and for adults and juveniles, included:

on a daily basis
- condition of pasture on which animals are grazing;
- watering (watering point used, distance from water at which the animals were grazing, who watered the animals (woman, man, child), and time taken to water);
- supplementary food (numbers supplemented; how much grain or minerals fed);
- veterinary care (numbers of animals treated; kind of care; what illnesses);
- herd dynamics (numbers mated; births (live, still born); abortions; deaths before weaning; adult deaths before slaughter; lost; found); and
- production (numbers slaughtered (hallal, other); sold; given away).

on a weekly basis
- animal condition (very poor, bad, fairly good, very good);
- numbers weaned;
- numbers in transhumance and numbers retuning from transhumance;

- numbers bought; given; loaned;
- time spent between grazing and encampment;
- milking (numbers milked; quantity obtained);
- number castrated; and
- breeding (numbers on heat for the first time; numbers who returned to service; number mated by herd males born in the herd; numbers mated by herd males born outside the herd; numbers mated by outside males).

The data books were collected monthly by trained data recorders who replaced them.

The data books were written in the local language, Hasseniya, and since the books were filled in by the children, the exercise fulfilled the pastoralists' wish to have their children learn to write in their native tongue. The language is rich for range management; over 100 words are used to describe unique variations in range condition. One outcome was a lexicon relating Hasseniya terms to botanical and technical descriptions in Arabic, French and English.

Data recorded by pastoralists and collected by recorders were entered into a database which was spatially referenced and interpreted with the help of imagery from the National Oceanic and Atmospheric Administration (NOAA) to integrate range management data with range condition information for the whole country.

One finding was that not all nomads had an equally sophisticated knowledge of range management. The wealthier nomads were generally that way because their knowledge of the landscape, and their understanding of range condition and its relationship with animal production, was superior.

The outcome was the identification of the best management practices for each agro-ecological zone and the development of extension packages to promote these practices among all pastoralists in Mauritania. This has resulted in lower stocking rates, better marketing systems and has encouraged ecologically sustainable management.

A feature of the project was the use of high-quality camels for transport, rather than the top-of-the-range, four-wheel drive vehicles for which the project had budgeted. The latter were inappropriate because of the lack of roads, fuel and spare parts in the target regions; the former were both practical, and, being much admired by the nomads, gave credibility to the project team.

3.2 The Kuwait Soil Survey

Australian Agricultural Consulting and Management (AACM) International is working with the Kuwait Institute of Scientific Research (KISR) to implement the soil survey for the State of Kuwait. The objectives of the Kuwait Soil Survey are to:

- carry out a comprehensive soil survey of the entire State of Kuwait, including the islands but excluding urban, industrial and restricted areas;
- design and implement a soil information system, comprising a database management system and a GIS, to store, process, retrieve and manage soil-related information;
- select up to 200 000 ha of land with potential for irrigation; and
- train Kuwait scientists in soil survey, GIS/Database Managerment System (DBMS) management and laboratory analysis.

At the completion of the national survey in early 1997, Kuwait will become the first country to have a complete and consistent soil database and GIS.

The survey is being carried out systematically using innovative and modern soil survey procedures, with an emphasis on landscape-scale features and practical application of taxonomy and survey outcomes. Site locations are precisely located with Global Positioning System (GPS) technology, and with GIS/DBMS technology being used to store, retrieve and manipulate the data. The project is a good example of the use of modern technology to meet practical needs in a powerful way.

The project also illustrates a partnership between the parties involved, namely the Australian experts and local scientists and technicians. It is a co-learning experience for both; for the Australians, working in a new context; and for the Kuwaitis, learning new techniques by working with the Australians. The formal training component is needs-driven so as to optimize the skills of the AACM [Australian] consultants and to build on the strengths of the Kuwaiti trainees. The AACM and KISR teams are using this survey to review the taxonomy of Aridisols in the system of the United States Department of Agriculture (USDA).

3.3 The Sustainable Grazing Systems Key Programme of the Australian Meat Research Corporation: a model for partnership research

The principles underlying successful economic development based on the use of natural resources apply equally well to countries like Australia. Because many programmes have failed to meet expectations, or have caused undesirable environmental impacts, a great deal of attention is being given to finding ways of conducting R&D more effectively.

The Australian Meat Research Corporation (MRC) invests money from producers' levies and matching Government funds into R&D, in order to improve the Australian meat industry. Its research portfolio includes several large "key programmes" of R&D projects, each programme aimed at a major issue facing the meat industry.

In the past, MRC's programmes have been perceived by producers as having been developed with too little input from them, and perceived by researchers as being too rigidly prescribed in a "top-down" manner. The MRC took notice of these criticisms.

The Sustainable Grazing Systems Key Programme (SGSKP) commenced in July 1996 to address the problem that the pastures on many high rainfall temperate zone farms were unable to meet producers' needs for farm profits and were not sustainable. The senior officer is the research facilitator. SGSKP is planning to bring about a real improvement in both productivity and sustainability, by addressing past criticisms to maximize its likely effectiveness.

There are three guiding principles:

(i)   partnerships between the various stakeholders, including producers, researchers, extension agents, and other R&D corporations (e.g., for wool);

(ii)   a "bottom-up" vs a "top-down" approach to planning; and

(iii) co-learning between the producers and the researchers.

These principles have achieved the following results:

- systematic input from all stakeholders in the planning phase, which extended over some 18 months;
- a business plan prepared by a group of producers. The MRC funded them to visit New Zealand to study how the R&D process occurs in that country. The recommendations of their business plan were adopted into SGSKP;
- R&E occurring in parallel, with information flowing between the two. Enough is known that "best bet" management ideas can be trialed from the start;
- a Steering Group being formed, comprising producers, staff of other relevant R&D corporations, and senior officers from the R&D delivery agencies (e.g., government agriculture departments), to oversee the direction of the programme;
- closely linking production research with research into sustainability issues. The actual research programme has been developed, in collaboration with the researchers and key producers, to be nationally coherent and locally relevant. The result is an interactive matrix of national sustainability themes, local experimental sites, and modelling;
- the majority of the budget being allocated for "extension" activities; and
- regional delivery of the programme so that local relevance is ensured. Each of the 11 regions has a producer committee elected by producers, which will determine which extension activities occur in their region, and how their budget will be allocated.

Early indications are that the SGSKP is seen by the stakeholders as a refreshing change, and is being enthusiastically embraced. This augurs well for the effectiveness of the SGSKP Programme.

4. CONCLUSIONS

The relevance of the FSR approach for the sustainable use of rangelands and desertification control in West Asia and North Africa:

The objective of this workshop was to produce development strategies that bring to bear modern technology to meet the needs of the nomads in ways which recognize their socio-economic context, and thus avoid the failures of the past in which technological interventions were not adopted by the nomads. It is this very context which the FSR approach is designed to help.

Furthermore, the focus of this workshop is the application of modern satellite and information technology to solve the problems of nomads. Much of this technology is very clever, and state-of-the-art. It will be very easy for us to let the technology drive the agenda. However, experience tells us that this is a recipe for failure. We must be vigilant to ensure that it is the nomads' problems we solve, and that their needs drive the adoption of technology in a partnership with them.

References

Andrew, M.H., 1989. Rangeland ecology and research in the tropics in relation to intensifying management of the beef cattle industry. In: Singh, P., Shankar, V. and Srivastava, A. (eds) *Proc. 3rd Intl Rangel. Congress,* New Delhi, India. pp. 197-213.

Andrew, M.H., 1991. Education and training: north-south relationship. Co-Rapporteur's paper for session G16. *Proc. 4th Intl Rangel. Congress,* Montpellier, 22-26 April 1991. pp. 1195-1199.

Jazairy, I., Alamgir, M. and Panuccio, T. 1992. *The state of world rural poverty. An inquiry into its causes and consequences.* IFAD/New York University Press.

McCown, R.L., 1990. Adapting farming systems research concepts to Australian research needs. In: *Proc. 5th Australian Agron. Conf.* Perth, Western Australia, September 1989, pp. 221-233.

Roe, E.M., 1989. Six myths about livestock rangeland development south of the Sahara rangelands. *Rangelands* 11(5): 217-221.

Squires, V.R., Mann, T. and Andrew, M.H. 1992. Problems in implementing improved range management on common grazing lands in Africa - an Australian perspective. *J. Grassld Soc. South. Afr.* 9(1): 1-7.

part III

Processing multitemporal imagery for natural resources estimation and monitoring

The advent of satellites and the ready access to a succession of imagery at one site over a period of months or years (multitemporal imagery) has created an opportunity for land managers to make more timely interventions. Advances in technology and in software development mean that multitemporal imagery is now more reliable, especially if certain safeguards are put in place.

The ten chapters in this section explore the potential and limitations involved in using multitemporal imagery for monitoring drylands. The experience of NASA and ESA is based on the analysis of data collected over more than twenty years.

The European Space Agency's Earth Observation Programme (ERS) and its possible use for rangeland and desertification monitoring

14

J. Lichtenegger

Synopsis

This paper reviews the potential use of ERS-1, the European Space's Agency remote sensing satellite, for rangeland and desertification monitoring. Examples are presented to demonstrate the use for geomorphic mapping and possible detection of subsurface drainage patterns.

Key Points

1. *With the launch of the European Space Agency's remote sensing satellite ERS-1 in July 1991, a considerable amount of microwave remote sensing data became available on a continuous basis. By now they have been used and evaluated by researchers and application scientists worldwide.*

2. *Spatial resolution of the ERS-1 satellite is comparable to conventional spaceborne sensors and, therefore, allows mapping in the mid-scale region.*

3. *The complementarity of microwave data, in combination with optical/infrared sensors, is a special feature. The specific characteristics of backscatter-from-ground features has particular value in relation to surface penetration, soil moisture and soil roughness.*

4. *The evidence so far is that data from the ERS-1 satellite will add to the complement of tools in the fight against desertification.*

1. INTRODUCTION

The main requirement for environmental monitoring from space is a high reliability of data and rapid access. While optical sensors may provide the necessary information due to high spatial, spectral and temporal resolution, bad weather limits their use, often in a considerable way. Only sensors based on microwave can provide images independent of cloud-cover and sunlight.

The European Space Agency (ESA), in response to the need of the scientific community, has developed and launched two remote sensing satellites; ERS-1 on 17 July 1991 and ERS-2 on 21 April 1995. The main instruments carried on board include: the Active Microwave Instrument (AMI), consisting of a Synthetic Aperture Radar (SAR), for high-resolution imaging on land and on sea and for sampling of information related to ocean waves; a scatterometer for wind speed and wind direction estimation; and an altimeter to measure wind speed, wave height and surface topography, all on ocean areas. Further instruments aboard the ERS are the Along-Track Scanning Radiometer to measure the ocean surface temperature, the Microwave Radiometer for atmospheric correction support and the PRARE for precise orbit-determinations. In addition, ERS-2 carries the Global Ozone Monitoring Experiment, to measure the chemical composition of the atmosphere.

The ERS series of satellites are sun-synchronous polar-orbiting spacecraft, with a repetition frequency of 35 days. Since adjacent orbits are overlapping, and ascending and descending passes can be acquired, the revisit frequency of a unique site is four times within 35 days for mid-latitude locations. ERS SAR data can be received only in the coverage zone of a station, but with few exceptions all land masses can be observed by a (to-date) existing ERS receiving station. However, data access from stations outside Europe is unreliable. The ERS Help Desk in European Space Research (ESRIN), (Frascati/Italy) provides all related information. The data distributor for Europe is EURIMAGE (with an office also in ESRIN). For most other areas it is Spotimage, (Toulouse/France).

In the framework of pursuing an active promotional policy, the European Space Agency has issued a number of announcement opportunities. Four of those are aimed at research, the last one specific to ERS-2 data. A further two were issued to develop data applications for future operational services. In four symposia, investigators had to report on their results (ESA 1992, 1993, 1994 and 1995).

For some of the data application reported, the SAR of ERS represents a unique source of information. This is the case when surface penetration and soil moisture detection is required. The same is true for the newly evolving interferometric technique, with its extraordinary application for Digital Elevation Model (DEM) generation and small terrain movement monitoring, as well as for coherence measurements for change detection.

This paper discusses the potential use of SAR images for mapping of natural surfaces, such as desert or semi-desert areas, of rangeland and the gradual transition to dense forest, and in particular:

(i)   SAR image geometry and radiometry that is characteristic, especially in mountainous terrain;

(ii)   the representation of the geomorphology in SAR images and its potential to basic mapping;

(iii)   SAR stereo-viewing;

(iv)   the penetration capability of microwave into very dry soil; and

(v)   some promising findings for an improved data product for thematic mapping using interferometric techniques.

2. SOME BASIC REMARKS ON SAR IMAGE GEOMETRY AND RADIOMETRY

The radar "sees" the ground according to a perspective line that corresponds to the antenna/target distance or slant range so that in a flat terrain the image geometry can be easily corrected. However, in mountainous terrain this is different; since the echoes of the emitted pulses are registered in a time sequence the part of a mountain facing the sensor will be shortened. This is also the basic difference of a projection resulting from an oblique viewing, where the facing slope is stretched. A slope opposite the radar illumination with an angle steeper than the sensor depression angle provokes a radar shadow. The distance measurements, as described above, provide the cross-track component of the image. The along-track component is the result of repeated transmissions during the sensor motion along the flight line.

The displacement of an object in a radar image with respect to its real position on the ground depends on its height (positive or negative) with respect to the reference height assumed for the image generation processing. As a rule of thumb the displacement for ERS is 2.35 times the height difference, e.g., objects 100 m above the reference height are displaced for 235 m in slant range towards the sub-satellite track (Schreier, 1993). Even a height difference of merely 10 m will shift an object almost 2 pixels.

Figure 14.1 demonstrates the limitations, especially of steep-looking spaceborne sensors like ERS. In fact, Figure 14.1 represents somewhat the worst case. A slope facing the sensor always appears compressed in an image. If the slope angle is well below the incidence angle, foreshortening occurs and the real geometry and radiometry can be reconstructed. If the slope angle is equal or higher than the incidence angle layover occurs and the data is ambiguous and irrecoverable.

Figure 14.1

Geometric and radiometric characterization of SAR data in mountainous terrain. (For a full expalanation see text).

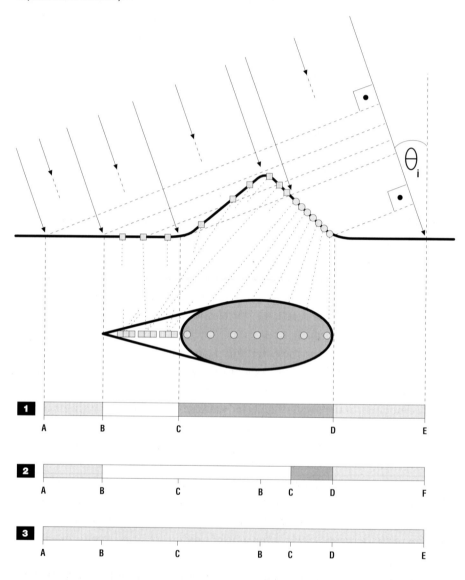

The upper part of Figure 14.1 shows the transect through a mountain illuminated by a radar. The dotted lines in the upper part represent lines of equal time-distance with respect to the SAR antenna. Below the transect, the mountain is shown in a ground-range display, with small squares representing the layover part and circles representing the stretched dark part of the opposite slope. In the lower part of the figure, the range-lines across the mountain are sketched as: (i) original SAR geometry; and (ii) corrected for the geometry of the terrain.

At point A, the pulse hits the ground in just one place. Between points A and B the backscatter produced is of medium strength, as marked in Bar I. In B, the irradiated energy from the SAR antenna hits the flat area and the mountain top simultaneously, thus marking the summit in the SAR geometry in the extreme of the layover position (B').

Between points B and Cc, a radar pulse always hits the terrain simultaneously in three different positions. The backscattered signal is therefore of a different origin; it is ambiguous and therefore useless data. On the ground-range image this area is represented by a very bright zone, mainly due to the small local incidence angle and the spatial squeezing.

Between Cc and D, the lower opposite slope is stretched in its geometry. Less energy is received per surface unit and therefore it appears very dark.

In Bar II, a terrain corrected rangeline is presented. By means of a DEM, all picture elements are shifted along the relevant range-line in their correct position. Of course, the ambiguous bright part remains and still no meaningful information can be extracted. The back-slope part is now correctly represented. This type of correction corresponds to the GTC-products of ERS-SAR data, and is the highest level of standard products distributed by ESA.

2.1 SAR image products and visual interpretation

Thematic mapping with SAR images in rough topography is rather limited but there is large potential in flat or gentle hilly areas. In high-relief terrain, the slopes facing the SAR sensor might cover the valley and the opposite slope might be hidden. For less steep slopes, foreshortening might still reduce a slant to a narrow bright band. Opposite slopes are often very dark and in extreme cases they fall into the radar shadow. For better image interpretation, it is recommended to use the negative display of a scene, rendering the opposite slope bright. In general, the use of multitemporal sets helps to discern features. Better perception can also be achieved when observing a scene in the opposite way as the SAR illumination and by tilting the image.

2.1.1 The representation of the geomorphology and its potential to basic mapping

For the representation of the relief in a map in gently hilly terrain, spaceborne SAR imagery from ERS has proved to be very useful since an oblique viewing allows a very distinctive display of local topography in a much better way than with vertically acquired optical satellite data. Multitemporal images that are colour composite from data acquired at different seasons of the same area are especially well-suited for visual interpretation of land-cover types, such as forest, agricultural areas, rangeland, desert areas and associated elements (e.g., dunes), waterbodies and urban areas.

Spatial resolution depends on the type of object but, in general, it is similar to Landsat Thematic Mapper and it can be much better for so-called strong scatterers, such as man-made features especially of the metallic type (e.g., single houses, highpower line masts, railways etc.). Multitemporal ERS-SAR imagery has proven useful in The Sudan to accurately map the round agriculture fields which show different colours due to irrigation in action, sand areas, and higher, rocky plateaux. Linear features such as car-tracks show up quite clearly.

2.1.2 The penetration capability of microwave into very dry soil

This potential of the penetration capability of microwave has already been observed during the US radar shuttle missions and could be confirmed for the C-band of ERS. Data has been used experimentally to detect and quantify soil moisture in irrigated plantations, not only on the surface, but also down to several centimetres in depth. A deeper penetration into very dry sand revealed on SAR images subsurface structures interesting to geologists, not only for a better analysis, but also for buried drainage systems, which are an important as indication for prospecting of wells.

A data merge of optical and SAR demonstrates the complementary of the two data sources.

2.1.3 SAR stereo-viewing of SAR

Stereo-viewing of SAR scenes was reported to be of particular interest, especially for geologic and geomorphologic mapping, (ESA, 1993; Chorowicz, et al.).

Scenes from parallel orbits (i.e., a pair from ascending or a pair from descending orbits), with an appropriate overlap, are needed. During the 35-day mission phases, the frame overlap depends on the latitude and is minimal at the Equator. With respect to the 168-day repeat orbit (April 1994 - March 1995), different degrees of overlapping can be found anywhere in the acquisition areas.

2.1.4 Thematic mapping using interferometric techniques

Interferometric techniques use a SAR data pair taken from parallel orbits that are not more than a few hundred metres apart. The phase difference for equivalent pixels in the corresponding scenes is used to determine contours of fringes, which after a further computation are converted into real contour lines. Limitations observed and the accuracy achieved are very much discussed in the relevant literature. It has been observed that in extreme atmospheric conditions irregularities may appear. However, in optimal conditions where DEM is generated with SAR, interferometry are superior to products derived with traditional methods from all other spaceborne data available to date.

As an additional tool for the assessment of suitable land use and related decisions in planning for sustainable development, a remote sensing product shall be presented which is based on interferometric techniques. It, therefore, not only contains the traditional two-dimensional information on land cover but also contains a quantitative indication about the relief. Together with soil maps, such information represents a prerequisite to assess erosion processes.

The input to the interferometric process is a pair of ERS scenes acquired from the same orbital track. The resulting colour composite combines in one display the coherence and the phaseshift between the two data acquisitions as well as the intensity of the backscattered signal. (Copies of such imagery are available from the author on request).

3. CONCLUSIONS

The prerequisite for a reliable monitoring of large areas such as rangeland and semi-desert areas are spaceborne sensors. The radar known as the Synthetic Aperture Radar (SAR) aboard the European Space Agency's ERS-1 and ERS-2 satellite was found to have a good capacity for general mapping tasks and is fully complementary to optical sensors. Moreover, new techniques have evolved using the interferometry which allows a three-dimensional analysis of an area. Used especially in countries where smaller-scale maps are the only available products derived from high resolution, this interferometric analysis could represent a major contribution to sustainable development.

References

European Space Agency (ESA) 1992. Proceedings on the First ERS-1 Symposium, Cannes, 4-6 November 1992. ESA SP-359, Volume I and Volume II.

ESA. 1993. Proceedings on the Second ERS-1 Symposium, Hamburg, 11-14 October 1993. ESA SP-361, Volume I and Volume II.

ESA. 1994. First Workshop on ERS-1 Pilot Projects, Toledo, 22-24 June 1994. ESA SP-365.

ESA. 1995. Second ERS Applications Workshop, London, 6-8 December 1995. ESA SP-383.

Schreier, G.(ed.) 1993. *SAR geocoding*. Wichmann Verlag GmbH, Karlsruhe.

Digital airborne multi-spectral videography for monitoring and managing natural resources

15

P. T. Tueller

Synopsis

This paper considers questions of land degradation and ways of monitoring land that can provide timely information necessary for the wise use and management of arid landscapes. It is proposed that large-scale, near-earth sampling of range sites with either low-level aerial photography or airborne multi-spectral videography constitutes a potential source of monitoring and management information that can be useful to managers of arid lands.

Key Points

1. *The world's arid rangelands provide forage and fodder for burgeoning populations in many parts of the world. These resources are extensive and fragile. They must be managed carefully for their products. The goal is to have these lands provide their products in perpetuity. Utilization will need to be based on sustained yield basis. Tools are required to monitor impact; the potential utility of some of these is reviewed.*

2. *Newer, more cost-effective techniques can provide this help. Airborne video imagery captured directly onto the hard drive of an on-board aircraft computer constitutes a relatively new technology with many advantages over conventional aerial photography and high potential for use on arid rangelands.*

3. *The limitations are that videography is more suitable for linear features and subsampling of landscapes rather than total area coverage. A further limitation is the lack of trained professional range conservationists who have ecological and remote sensing understanding to accomplish the interpretations that are required.*

4. *It is concluded that airborne multi-spectral videography has excellent potential to provide timely remote sensing information. Large scale imagery is now becoming*

Chapter 15 • Digital airborne multi-spectral videography   **195** *available. The cost, portability, near-real-time availability and the ease of digital analysis and interpretation of airborne videography make such a technology useful in any part of the world where film processing may not be readily available.*

1. INTRODUCTION

The landsat Thematic Mapper (30 m pixels) and the Landsat MSS (80 m pixels) data have been quite valuable for many uses, while the SPOT Image 20 m likewise pixels have had many uses. The Advanced Very High Resolution Radiometer (AVHRR) data with its very low resolution (1 km pixels) have been used for many studies because of their high temporal resolution (i.e., daily). However, for many activities in natural resources, these good data sets have not been sufficient. For this reason, many range ecologists have turned to large-scale aerial colour and colour infrared photography. In addition, new developments with multi-spectral airborne videography with high resolution (0.3 - 1.0 m pixels) will be very important in the future for the monitoring of rangeland vegetation and soils. There is also potential to couple the small-scale satellite imagery to these near-earth large-scale images for overall analysis and interpretation, or range condition and trend.

Research into spectral unmixing (i.e., a quantitative assessment of the proportion of rock, soil, litter, microphytes, plant species or species groups inherent in individual pixels) (Kruse, 1996) offers the opportunity to routinely assess rangeland characteristics, such as erosion and livestock and wildlife use with remotely-sensed data. Arid land management concerns, such as forage and browse productivity, suitability for class of grazer or browser, carrying capacity, forage utilization and the monitoring of vegetation and soil surface changes can be evaluated. Successional changes related to the desertification process can also be measured. Remote sensing gives the opportunity for repetitive, annual or seasonal multispectral examination (Tueller, 1989).

For a number of years, a few investigators have been working with airborne video as an alternative to aerial photography and Landsat satellite data. For the most part, these systems have been constrained by VHS recorders which have not had the capability of high resolution. A few years ago, super-VHS recorders became available but these only had about 400 lines of resolution or considerably less than a home TV set with about 500 lines. The imagery was not of high quality and was far from the quality of aerial photography based on film emulsions and their processing. In the last few years, there has been a move to use digital videography wherein the signals from several charge-coupled device (CCD) video cameras are captured directly to the hard drive of an on-board computer. This technology allows a much higher resolution product that approaches aerial photography in quality (King, 1995). A common level of resolution now being used has pixel sizes from about 0.3 m to 1.0 m, giving images that have representative fraction scales of 1: 800 down to 1: 2 000. With airborne videography, it is normal to talk about "swath width" and "pixel size" rather than "RF scale".

Rangeland degradation is often difficult to measure successfully over extensive land areas. Ground-based vegetation sampling techniques must be sensitive to changes in parameters capable of defining this degradation or lack thereof. These parameters include species cover, frequency, density and composition, along with various surface soil characteristics. Since arid lands are extensive and management is not intensive, remote sensing has a role to play. The permanent record provided by the remote sensing products becomes an important element in land condition studies (Tueller, 1977). Pickup et al. (1994) have developed a model for forecasting large-scale patterns of soil erosion and deposition from Landsat MSS data in arid grazing lands. This paper therefore discusses how we can use remote sensing to measure rangeland condition and monitor range trend, especially on arid, shrub-dominated rangelands.

2. RANGELAND CONDITION

Rangeland condition refers to a set of characteristics defined by the ecological site, which includes soil type, topography, hydrology and a specific plant species composition. Range condition is a measure of how the vegetation relates to some standard. These standards are usually related to site quality. The term "ecological site", coined and used by the Natural Resources Conservation Service (US) (formerly the Soil Conservation Service), refers to vegetation/soil complexes with roughly equivalent ecological site potential. The extent of severely impacted areas of vegetation, such as "sacrifice areas" around stock watering facilities, or perhaps the level of forage use on nomadic grazing sites, are indicative of sites in poor condition.

Range trend is a measure of vegetation change measured in both the short term and long term. In the short-term range, conservationists measure utilization in relation to weather, fencing, water, and availability of feed. Long-term monitoring is the successive question and is reflected as changes in species composition, soil stability and other factors that occur over decades rather than annually.

Range management in arid regions is complicated by characteristics, such as low biomass, low leaf-area indices, low ecosystem productivity, wind, high evaporation rates, high temperatures, drought and slow successional responses to management and, often, very few funds for management. Mapping and analysis of desert ecosystems from either aerial photography or digital images is complicated by the sparsity of the vegetation, the diversity of geomorphic surfaces, water erosion patterns and soil and rock colour variations common to desert landscapes (Tueller, 1987).

Plants serve as indicators where precipitation is scarce and irregular, indicating such factors as moisture, soil type and salinity. Some plants may indicate different conditions in different areas. Changes in environmental conditions can potentially change dominant patterns and species composition, effectively changing the habitat (Tausch et al., 1993). Land use on fragile arid ecosystems can potentially be measured with remote sensing techniques, which allow managers to maintain biological productivity, soil stability, species diversity and the vigour of native plant communities (Tueller, 1993).

The natural processes are governed by a balance between incoming and outgoing energy and between water received and lost. Vegetation is the result of this process: precipitation is taken in by plants stored and later transpired; the rest is stored in the soil, runs off, or evaporates. Thus, the vegetation adapts to the available precipitation and soil characteristics. Deserts can occur without drought, but drought can trigger desert-like conditions that may or may not be reversible. When left alone, arid ecosystems undisturbed by drought return to normal. Former water and energy balances are restored and the original vegetation cover recovers (Barrow, 1991).

Desertification occurs when land uses persist at the same levels throughout a drought which can lead to irreversible change (Thomas, 1992). When the balance between precipitation and energy patterns is impacted due to land management practices, vegetation decreases and bare ground increases. Rain falls on bareground and breaks it down. The sun causes a thin crust to form which increases run-off and topsoil is washed away, soils becomes less fertile, vegetation decreases in vigour and produces less biomass and becomes more susceptible to drought (Barrow, 1991; Milton et al., 1994; Walton, 1969).

Dry rangeland vegetation grows near the limits of the ecosystem to sustain vegetation. Vegetative patterns form where the topography concentrates run-off, collects precipitation, or where plants are able to reach moisture. For example, the floristics of bajadas, and the arroyos dissecting them, are quite different from each other and from the intervening upland ecosystems in most deserts.

Under drought conditions, the plants themselves have a growth form leading to circular or strip patterns with patches of bare ground in between. Vegetation that exists so close to these limits is susceptible to slight changes in the environment and responds with more bare ground, loss of species, and a change in species composition leading to increased erosion (Barrow, 1991). These patterns, species changes and related vegetation and soil characteristics - especially the changes in plant cover and increases in erosion - are those we wish to measure with remote sensing.

3. LARGE-SCALE IMAGERY

Over a number of years large-scale near-earth remote sensing has been developed for evaluating natural resources. One important objective has been to identify plant species and evaluate surface soil features, including soil erosion. These features are of considerable importance for the monitoring of vegetation and assessing the success of grazing management. Such requirements led to the development of technology for acquisition of large-scale imagery with useful scales and resolution.

With higher resolution and measurement of these features, it was suggested that procedures for assessing vegetation and soil changes could be developed into an efficient remote sensing trend analysis tool for use on rangelands. Several researchers began to develop applications to provide the kind of remotely sensed data that would truly prove useful for rangelands. Some managers are also starting to realize the importance of multiple scales. Small-scale Landsat data is important for studying landscape matrices and patch dynamics but there is still a need to know what is going on at the site (large-scale) level (Tueller, 1996).

Near-earth remote sensing is done with scales generally larger than 1:10 000, with an optimum scale near 1:1 000. In the case of airborne videography, the anticipated pixel sizes are sub-meter or even sub-decimeter. The concept can be further defined, in a rangeland use context, as remote sensing techniques that will provide resolution high enough that one can identify and interpret rangeland parameters, such as individual species and characteristics of the surface soil, which can be related to range condition and trend.

Since areas covered by large-scale, near-earth images are small (a 1: 600 scale aerial photograph has a physical "on-the-ground size" of about 3.0 m on the side of a 70 mm frame), the user must be very precise in locating photographs or images on the ground. Subsampling must be exact and air-photo transects carefully selected, so that data can faithfully represent rangeland plant communities or range condition situations of interest.

If only a small proportion of the area of interest is imaged, it is critical that the data faithfully describe range condition over larger areas, i.e., a key area sampling concept must be used. The data from the study area (or where the images are acquired) must represent range condition or trend over the entire allotment or management unit, whatever it might be. It then remains for aerial photography (flown from light fixed-wing aircraft or helicopters) to allow photographic sampling over large areas in short periods of time, and on random sites far removed from easy ground access (Tueller, 1996).

Tueller (1996) has provided a review of the technology and uses of large-scale aerial photography for rangeland applications. High levels of accuracy have been obtained in detecting vegetative characteristics (e.g., species density, cover, community types) with these films. For example, large-scale imagery of range resources has allowed for more detailed analyses of plant communities and habitat-type variation in semi-arid environments (Tueller and Lorain, 1972; Everitt et al., 1980).

This has, in turn, contributed to an expansion of applications within the realm of "rangeland management requirements", as outlined by Tueller (1982) and Poulton (1974). For example, specific delineation of erosion in the Great Basin (Tueller and Booth, 1975; Tueller, 1977) serves to promote better monitoring of surface characteristics for grazing status, recovery potential, watershed protection and habitat condition and trends. By far, the primary use of large-scale remote sensing in range management has continued to be that of vegetation monitoring (Tueller et al., 1988; Everitt and Escobar, 1992; Pickup et al., 1994).

Multi-spectral videography data is but a very small subset of the larger field of hyperspectral-imaging technology. Spencer (1992) suggests that, "the Holy Grail of remote sensing is the ability to determine all the properties of points on the ground. Central to the quest is the ability to identify correctly the materials returning electromagnetic energy back to the observation platform. For many remote sensing observations the spectral resolution has been too course. Can we filter video cameras to acquire adequate spectral resolution to inventory and monitor many of the vegetation and soil parameters that we are interested in? Also, how do we compare the different kinds of digitized data acquisition devices now available?"

The requirement is to provide data in a raster format that can be used with image processing software, to identify, classify and monitor changes in natural resource features. We can observe, as have many others, that remote sensing of natural resources often requires timely availability of data. The data are often required in a multi-spectral format and, finally, the data must be easily manipulated and managed via the computer. These requirements suggest the use of video data because of the relatively easy transition to image processing for identification, interpretation and analysis.

The capabilities of image processing are expanding very rapidly. Inexpensive images can be quickly gathered by airborne videography and analyzed with an image processing system. The need is to develop and/or procure a highly interactive system that will allow capture of video frames directly into computer memory and be followed by expedient analysis of the information content of the captured scenes. One objective of this paper is to describe such a system that we are using and testing for several natural resources' remote sensing applications.

4. AIBORNE VIDEOGRAPHY

In the early 1980s, large-scale imaging began a move toward the use of airborne videography and new applications were developed. Several review articles were written on videography between 1989 and 1995 (Everitt and Escobar, 1989 and 1992; Mausel et al., 1992; Wright, 1993; and King, 1995). The term "videography" includes digital cameras as well as video cameras. Digital cameras are those with solid-state arrays that produce a digital two-dimensional frame image (King, 1995). To date, no pure digital cameras with a binary output signal form each photo-site (pixel) exists; the analog signal must be converted to digital, either within the cameras or by using a frame-grabbing device exterior to the camera.

Current video sensors with approximately 780 x 512 photo-sites on the chips are usually coupled to frame grabbers with the same sampling frequency. Digital cameras typically with more than 1 024 x 1 024 photo-sites, utilize an in-camera analog to digital converter, but the signal must still be formatted into a raster grid for subsequent computer display. Frame-grabbing in the same format as the imaging chip does not mean, however, that spatial resolution is not degraded in the digitization process, as all signal processing steps contribute to spatial resolution degradation (King, 1995). Unlike video, there are no current standards for spatial formatting of true digital camera sensors. Recently, a format of approximately 1 500 x 1 024 has become common. Others are being worked on. A 3 k x 2 k sensor is becoming common as an alternative to 35 mm film. The most significant milestone of these increases in the number of photo-sites will probably be the development of a sensor with enough photo-sites and angle of view to match the resolution of standard large-format (i.e., 23 cm x 23 cm) aerial photography. Sensors with this capability are still very costly (King, 1995).

Future developments will involve firstly radiometric and then geometric, calibration procedures. The multi-spectral nature of digital video systems allows the analysis of several spectral bands. Using such multi-spectral imagery research on the evaluations of first-and-second-order texture measures, fractal dimension, and image semi-variance in video and digital camera imagery, is being conducted in forestry applications by King (1995).

Further statistical image processing approaches for rangeland applications should be researched. King (1995) suggests that, with the development of stereo viewing capability, videography will eventually replace photgraphy in most visual analysis applications. Photographic interpretation depends heavily on three-dimensional perspectives of plant and soil features. As workstation capabilities for stereo display of digital camera and video imagery continue to develop and decrease in cost, the need for hardcopy photographs will diminish. Digitized data can be easily incorporated into a Geographic Information System (GIS), providing further opportunities for interpretation. The Global Positioning System (GPS) can potentially add another dimension to the capability of videography, providing a rapid means for georeferencing imagery for use by others and locating exactly where the data derives in relation to the surface of the earth (Everitt and Escobar, 1996). However, at the present, most systems record only the position of the aircraft and fail to precisely provide the elevation of the nadir point on the image. Georeferencing of entire images must await further development of procedures to integrate GPS data with various points on each image, perhaps with the use of laser altimetry.

Video has many attributes that are attractive for remote sensing of natural resources' investigations. The most prominent advantage is the near real-time availability of imagery (Everitt and Escobar, 1989). Video data is relatively inexpensive to acquire and the time between acquisition, availability and utilization can be hours instead of weeks, or even days as is often the case with other multispectral remote sensing systems. Another advantage of video data is its potential for immediate digital processing of the electronic signal (Vlcek and King, 1985; Richardson et al., 1985; Lulla et al., 1987). The ability to obtain imagery in very narrow spectral bands (i.e., 0.05-0.10 microns) is another advantage.

Everitt and Nixon (1985) found that false colour video imagery was a useful substitute for more costly colour infrared aerial photography. The use of video image data in digital form can be used in a GIS system to allow rapid, interactive map updating and the integration of any spatially related databases (Ehlers and Hintz, 1989). Meisner (1986) suggested that an important application for video is air-transect sampling, where lull-area coverage is not required, such as utility rights-of-way or narrow stream courses.

Other applications of videography include: distinguishing plant species (Everitt and Nixon, 1985); assessing grass production, evaluating plant succession, making fence-line comparisons (Nowling and Tueller, 1989); and measuring weed infestations (Everitt and Escobar, 1992; Everitt and Escobar, 1996). Everitt and Escobar (1992) were able to show significant differentiation of vegetation and soil types, according to the digital values under each separate wave band. These authors suggest that employing this kind of pixel analysis to large-scale images will achieve close to 100% accuracy in the interpretation of many of the target species. The problem of "critical resolution" within pixels -

essentially an image-motion or blur problem – has been shown to increase substantially as image-scale increases (Hinkley and Walker, 1993). The great advantage of large-scale in providing detailed surface feature assessments will no doubt enhance the use and applications of videographic images for near-earth monitoring in the future.

5. A GENERAL APPROACH TO THE USE OF AIRBORNE MULTI-SPECTRAL VIDEOGRAPHY

A typical system is totally controlled by an on-board computer. When instructed by the control computer, the digitizer card locks onto the standard video signal from the cameras. From this signal the card derives synchronization signals and timing. Using the aforementioned signals, the digitizer digitizes the incoming video signal as a complete video frame. The digitizer uses a flash analog to digital converter to digitize each pixel into eight bits of resolution. The data is stored in a set of frame buffers until read by the computer. The computer can start reading data almost immediately after issuing the capture command. The data is transferred from the frame buffer directly to the disk drive. Each frame is stored as an individual file. These files can be concatenated or combined into any format for use in GIS or image-processing software.

The system we are using is comprised of three Charge Coupled Device (CCD) digital cameras, a Pentium-based computer equipped with an image digitizing board, a colour encoder and a VHS recorder. The VHS recorder and encoder allow simultaneous capture of the scenes on both video tape as an analog colour-infrared (CIR) composite and on the hard drive of the computer as a three-band image. The cameras are visible/near-infrared (NIR) (0.4 - 1.1 um) light-sensitive. Visible yellow-green, red and near-infrared wavebands are captured and the data are displayed as infrared images. The computer is a Pentium 100 with a 1 Gb hard drive, allowing the capture of up to 1 000 images in a single flight. The image grabbing board gives 640 x 480 pixels.

Images are captured almost instantaneously (1/30 second), and downloaded as three-band images to the hard drive in approximately 2 seconds. Each image is stored as a raster file in TIF format and uses a bit less than 1 Mb of hard drive storage. The important point is that these images are captured directly onto the hard-drive of the on-board computer, with pixel size dependent upon flying height, and the data can be immediately analyzed with image processing software. Hard copy can be printed when necessary.

We have calculated that the capture of each frame requires 256 K/scene (frame or image). These are 512 x 512 pixel full frames. For a four-band multi-spectral system this would then require 1 Mb for each frame. We use a 200 Mb hard disk for our on-board computer. This allows approximately 180 frames per flight and, depending upon the scale, would allow for considerable coverage of sampling sites or for total coverage of given landscape areas.

An intervalometer algorithm has been included within the software and uses flying altitude, airspeed and focal length to determine the intervals for frame capture. At the same time a database is recorded along with the even pulse, including such things as air speed, date, time of day, altitude and GPS coordinates. A camera mount, to be used with a light high-wing aircraft, is being manufactured. Image motion can be controlled with the use of ferro-fluidic dampening mounts.

There are three important aspects to the development of the system. These are: (i) the synchronization or the cameras to give absolute registration of band upon band for this multi-spectral system; (ii) the design and building of the high-speed flash digitizer; and (iii) the writing of the software necessary to run the system. A camera mount appropriate for an 18" camera hatch in a Cessna aircraft has been designed and used. It will also be possible to use a mount in the door of a Cessna that can be changed when imagery is to be obtained.

GPS tags indicating the nadir of the captured image can be added to each video frame or image, in order to fix the data points to known points on the ground. This will require the use of two GPS units for locating field sites. During video data acquisition, one GPS unit will be carried on board the aircraft to tag the frames and will have its internal location data updated by comparison with the other unit on the ground. Our initial specifications called for 1 metre (m) accuracy, but this may prove too costly for the low cost unit with which we are working. Possibly a lower positional accuracy of 10-15 m may be adequate, especially if the data points can be located with respect to ground features observable in the frames when displayed on the image processing monitor; or related to known points on the ground, depicted on topographic maps.

The video imagery can be acquired at a relatively large scale (1: 500 - 1:1 000) with high resolution (sub-metre) expected. Our data is analyzed using Map and Image Processing System (MIPS) software. Other image-processing software is also appropriate. Commonly used GIS formats (e.g., ARC INFO) can be used with the image-processing software. The digital data will be in raster format but can be transformed to vector data format to use with the Digital Elevation Models (DEMs) and other information layers. The idea is to provide for the capture of high-quality video scenes at times and places specified by the user with short "turn around" times.

Digitized data can be easily incorporated into a GIS, providing further opportunities for interpretation. A GPS can potentially add another dimension to the capability of the videography, providing a rapid means for georeferencing imagery for use by others and locating exactly where the data comes from with respect to the surface of the earth (Everitt and Escobar, 1996). However, at the present most systems record only the position of the aircraft and fail to provide precisely the elevation of the nadir point on the image. Georeferencing of entire images must await further development of procedures to integrate GPS data with various points on each image, perhaps with the use of laser altimetry.

We have also used digital orthophotoquads (DOQs) with 1 m pixels and a scale of 1: 24 000 to georeference. These are available for many parts of the United States from the US Geological Survey, but such digitized orthophotquads are not likely to be commonly available in many other parts of the world.

With a 12.5 mm lens the swath widths vary with the flying altitude. At 304.8 m (1 000 feet) above terrain the swath width is 210.3 m (690 feet) giving 0.33 m pixels; at 609.6 m (2 000 feet) above terrain the swath width is 420.6 m (1 380 feet) giving 0.66 m pixels; and at 2 500 feet the swath is 914.4 m (2 070 feet) with 0.8 m pixels. These parameters generally make videography more useful for linear features and subsampling of landscapes rather than total area coverage.

This digital airborne video system offers several advantages, particularly: (i) near-real-time availability (data can be viewed and analyzed only minutes after the images are captured; (ii) the data is already computerized and lends itself to immediate image processing (images can be mosaicked, georeferenced, classified and manipulated by other procedures, rapidly performed via the computer); (iii) after the system is acquired and tested the acquisition of new images is routine and low in cost; (iv) the procedure is useful where high resolution is required; and (v) the images are very useful for analyzing natural resource features, such as fire scars, range condition, range utilization, fire fuel, the quality and quantity of vegetation along narrow linear corridors (e.g., riparian zones, pipelines, power lines), forest succession, desert plant succession and many other variables.

In this paper, consideration is given to desert plant succession. It is possible to have the data flown for use by natural resource scientists and managers who then analyze and interpret the image data. This consideration is not a trivial one. In my opinion, it is absolutely necessary to have practitioners that have the proper education and experience to really do justice to the reading and interpretation of the imagery. Just what kind of training and experience are we talking about?

The most important requirement is that the interpreters have a good working knowledge of range ecology, including the vegetation and soils of the area being studied. The minimum needs are to be able to recognize and judge the significance of the species growing on the site and how these species, based on soil classification and plant synecology, are combined into useful plant communities depicted as polygons on aerial maps or within a GIS. Only then can the remotely sensed data become an important and definitive dataset. Without this education, experience and background the interpretations tend to be general, inapplicable and, in many cases, almost useless.

6. SUMMARY AND CONCLUSIONS

In many areas of the world rangelands have been degraded or are being degraded. Degradation is a result of improper grazing procedures, drought and other factors, and is especially insidious in the most arid areas. Both the vegetation and the soil must be examined in a monitoring programme to determine if grazing practices are successful in maintaining the health of the range landscape.

Rangeland monitoring is often done using costly ground techniques. There is a continuing need to develop useful remote sensing techniques for inventory and monitoring of the extensive rangeland resources throughout the world.

Small-scale satellite imagery has been promoted for rangeland monitoring but problems with pixel size and resolution have tended to preclude success. However, there is a potential to couple the small-scale satellite imagery to near-earth large-scale system data for overall analysis and interpretation.

Large-scale photography has been studied for monitoring landscapes on both forest and range for over 30 years, but there are few instances where large-scale photographic procedures have been routinely used for overall analysis and interpretation.

Large-scale imagery is now becoming available using a new technology, airborne multi-spectral video. The cost, portability, near real-time availability, and the ease of digital analysis and interpretation of airborne videography make such a technology very useful in any part of the world where film processing may not be readily available. These systems can be complete and "stand alone" when the hardware and software are in place. Use can be immediate, and the analysis, interpretation and training can be carried on simultaneously.

The technology of airborne multi-spectral videography is rapidly growing. The capabilities, pixel size, computer requirements, input and output devices and software are continually being improved and upgraded. Description of this technology and the procedures for adaptation and use for rangeland applications are now evolving. This includes the integration of airborne multi-spectral videography with aerial photography, satellite imagery and hyperspectral remote sensing. The best of the new technologies must be publicized, continually updated and detailed prescriptions of their use developed for the benefit of rangeland managers. Possibly the one stumbling block is the lack of trained professional range conservationists who have the ecological and remote sensing understanding to accomplish the interpretations required.

A digital video system bypasses the need for film emulsions and processing and the need for capturing data on VHS recorders; it provides imagery that is getting closer to aerial photography in quality and has much higher resolution than satellite imagery. The one-time costs for complete systems that are currently available vary from USD 60 000 to USD 250 000. A reasonable system can be put together for under USD 50 000. Digital video imagery is then easily repeatable. The initial data can be used to identify, measure and analyze many features of interest to resource managers and repeat imagery can be used to successfully monitor many phenomena of interest on arid landscapes.

Other specific applications will follow as the uses of airborne video become more common and the data becomes readily available to resource managers. Airborne multi-spectral videography has excellent potential to provide timely remote sensing information. The ease of data analysis and digitization give it great potential value to natural resource managers for mapping and monitoring vegetation, soils and other features of arid landscape. A system with the video data stream going directly from the camera to the hard disk of a computer, and then to the image processor, has the greatest potential. Recent experience in both hot and cold desert ecosystems in western North America provide good evidence of the possibilities.

Finally, one important word of caution. The image data and the information derived from it will only be as good as those who have the training and experience to do justice to the interpretation of the datasets.

References

Barrow, C.J. 1991. *Land degradation: development and breakdown of terrestrial environments.* Harvard University Press. Cambridge, Mass.

Ehlers, M. and Hintz, R.J. 1989. *High resolution airborne video system for mapping and GIS applications.* 12th Biennial Workshop on Color Aerial Photography and Videography in the Plant Sciences and Related Fields. American Society of Photogrammetry and Remote Sensing. pp. 171-177.

Everitt, J.H., Gerberman, A.H., Alaniz, M.A., and Bowen, R.L. 1980. Using 70 mm aerial photography to identify rangeland sites. *Photo. Eng. and Remote Sens.* 47:1357-1362.

Everitt, J.H. and Nixon, P.R. 1985. False Color Video Imagery: A potential remote sensing tool for range management. *Photo. Eng. & Remote Sens.* 51:675-679.

Everitt, J.H. and Escobar, D.E. 1989. *The status of video systems for remote sensing applications.* 12th Biennial Workshop on Color Aerial Photography and Videography in the Plant Sciences and Related Fields. American Society of Photogrammetry and Remote Sensing. pp. 6-29.

Everitt, J.H. and Escobar, D.E. 1992. Airborne video systems for real-time assessment of rangelands. *Geocarto Int.* 7: 19-26.

Everitt, J.H. and Escobar, D.E. 1996. Use of spatial information technologies for noxious plant detection and distribution on rangelands. *Geocarto 1* 1(3):63-80.

Hinkley, T.K. and Walker, J.W. 1993. Obtaining and using low-altitude large scale imagery. *Photo. Eng. and Remote Sens.* 59(3): 310-318.

King, D.J. 1995. Airborne multi-spectral digital cameras and video sensors: A critical review of system designs and applications. *Canadian Jour. of Remote Sens.* 21(3):245-73.

Lulla, K., Mausel, P., Skeleton, D. and Kramber, W. 1987. *An evaluation of videoband based vegetation indices.* Proceedings 11th Biennial Workshop on Color Aerial Photography and Videography in the Plant Sciences and Related Fields. Amer. Soc. Photogrammetry and Remote Sensing. pp. 270-279.

Mausel, P.W., Everitt, J.H., Escobar, D.E. and King, D.J. 1992. Airborne videography: current status and future perspectives. *Photogramm. Eng. And Remote Sens.* Special Issue: U.S. National Report. 58:1189-1195.

Meisner, D.E. 1986. Fundamentals of airborne video remote sensing. *Remote Sensing of Environment.* 19:63-79.

Milton, S.W., Dean, J., Pleiss, M. A. and Siegfried, R. W. 1994. Land degradation land management practices. *Bioscience* Feb. 94: pp. 74-76.

Nowling, S. and Tueller, P.T. 1989. *A low-cost multi-spectral airborne video image system for vegetation monitoring on range and forest lands.* Proceedings 14th Biennial Workshop on color Photography and Videography in Resource Monitoring. Logan, Utah May 25-28 1989.

Pickup, G., Bastin, G.N. and Chewings, V.H. 1994. Remote-sensing-based condition assessment for nonequilibrium rangelands under large-scale commercial grazing. *Ecol. App.* 4(3):497-507.

Poulton, C.E. 1974. Range resources: inventory, evaluation and monitoring. In: L.W. Bowden (ed.) *Manual of Remote Sensing,* Vol. 2. American Society of Photogrammery, Falls Church, Virginia.

Spencer, C. 1992. Remote sensing with hyperspectral-imaging technology. *Earth Observation Magazine.* December. pp. 53-55.

Tausch, R.J. and Tueller, P.T. 1988. Comparison of regression methods for predicting single leaf pinyon phytomass. *Great Basin Naturalist* 48 (1): 39-45.

Tausch, R.J., Wigand, P.E. and Burkhardt, J.W. 1993. Viewpoint: plant community thresholds, multiple steady states, and multiple successional pathways: legacy of the Quaternary? *J. Range Man.* 46:439-447.

Thomas, G. 1992. *Desertification: position.* A paper presented at the Earth Summitt. Rio de Janero, Brazil.

Tueller, P.T. and Lorain, G. 1972. Application of remote sensing techniques for analysis of desert biome validation studies. *Desert Biome IBP.* RM 73-6.

Tueller, P.T. and Booth, D.T. 1975. Photographic remote sensing techniques for erosion evaluation on wildlands. Nev. Agr. Exp. Sta. Proj. *Final Rep. to Bureau of Land Management.*

Tueller, P.T. 1977. *Large scale 70 mm photography for range resources analysis in the western United States.* Proceedings 11th Int. Sym. on Remote Sensing of Environment. Ann Arbor, Mich. pp.1507-1514.

Tueller, P.T. 1982. Remote sensing for range management. In: Johannsen and Sanders (eds) *Remote sensing for resource management.* Soil Conservation Society of America. pp. 125-140.

Tueller, P.T. 1987. Remote sensing science applications in arid environments. *Remote Sensing of Environment.* 20:143-154.

Tueller, P.T. 1989. Remote sensing technology for rangeland management applications. *Journal of Range Management* 42: 442-453.

Tueller, P.T. 1993. *Satellite remote sensing for desertification analysis and monitoring.* Proceedings Fourth International Conference on Desert Development: "Sustainable Development For Our Common Future". Mexico City. July.

Tueller, P.T. 1996. Near-earth monitoring of range condition and trend. *Geocarto* 11(3):53-62.

Vlcek, W.A. and King, D. 1985. *Development and use of a 4-camera video system.* Proc. 19th Symp. on Remote Sensing of Environment. pp.483-489.

Walton, K. 1969. *The arid zones.* Aldine Publishing Company. Chicago, IL. ION World Bank 1986.

Wright, R. 1993. Airborne videography: principles and practice. *Photogrammetric Record.* 14:447-457.

Use of remotely sensed data for estimating precipitation

S. Amer and S. Miller

16

Synopsis

This study was conducted to investigate the use of satellite-based optical and microwave data for estimating rainfall, relate greenness to climatological rainfall over large scales and evaluate the pattern of rainfall in a semi-arid environment. Monthly total rainfall estimates were obtained using the Special Sensor Microwave Imager (SSM/I) F10 platform; bi-weekly Normalized Vegetation Index (NDVI) were derived from red and near-infrared (NIR) reflectance factors obtained from a satellite-based sensor; and rain-gauge data were used. Data were collected between August and October of 1992. The results reported here demonstrate that remotely sensed data can be used to estimate rainfall on the large scale in semi-arid regions. The paper discusses the possible application of high-technology methods of remote sensing and in situ measurements to study the problems currently facing countries of the Cooperation Council for the Arab States of the Gulf (GCC) and those in the West Asia and North Africa (WANA) region.

Key Points

1. *Arid and semi-arid rangeland ecosystems cover over 40% of the earth's land surface and are one of the more sensitive land types to climate anomalies and land-use practices.*
2. *Precipitation plays a significant role in the global climate, not only in the exchange of water between atmosphere and ocean or land, but also in the exchange of heat.*
3. *Remotely sensed spectral and microwave measurements can provide indirect means of deriving the spatial distribution of geophysical parameters, such as soil wetness or moisture, land cover, precipitation and vegetation status.*

4. *The results reported for this study cover the North American (NA) summer monsoon region, which is characterized as a semi-arid region, and demonstrate that remotely sensed measurements can be used, similarly, over the GCC countries and those in the WANA region to estimate vegetation status and precipitation.*

1. INTRODUCTION

Arid and semi-arid ecosystems cover more than one-third of the earth's land surface and are often characterized by extremes of various hydrologic components, such as low and variable rainfall, high evapotranspiration and low water yield (Gifford, 1996). About 630 million people inhabit slightly over half of that area; the remainder of the area is climatically so arid and unproductive that it cannot support human life. The heavy pressure on the limited land and water resources by human activities is turning potentially productive drylands into unproductive deserts in Asia, Africa and America. Any attempts to adopt technical solutions for the natural resources in any area must involve the people occupying that area as an integral part of the solution (Brooks et al., 1991).

Precipitation plays a significant role in the global climate, not only in the exchange of water between atmosphere and ocean or land, but also in the exchange of heat. Flood and summer monsoons provide an immediate need to learn more about precipitation, as do the drought regions in the world. Recent events in the midwestern United States (US), and other parts of the world, such as the northern shores of the Indian Ocean are an indication of the impact precipitation can have on people's lives. Such questions as "Why does it always rain here and never over there?" and "How does rainfall vary seasonally and annually in this region?" have prompted many scientific studies of the entire precipitation process and its relationship to local, regional and global meteorological conditions.

The NA summer monsoon phenomenon affects the entire southwestern US and northern Mexico. It is a major player in the climate of the continental US and a major producer of rainfall over the southwestern US and northern Mexico. Each summer, the global circulation drives a tremendous amount of warm moist air inland over the NA monsoon, leading to a dramatic increase in precipitation. In many areas of the NA monsoon, at least half of the total annual rainfall falls during the three months of the summer monsoon, almost entirely in the form of afternoon thundershowers. These storms, typically, form first over nearby mountains and, in late afternoon, either move over the valley areas or simply develop there. Disturbances that originate over the southwestern US and northern Mexico often result in major rainfall events in the US midwest, or farther east. Storms are probable almost every afternoon, although they affect a particular location once out of every four or five days on average. The intensity and duration of this system may vary from year to year in response to changes in other global systems, differences in sea surface temperatures, internal variability and feedback between regional soil moisture and precipitation systems.

To characterize the NA monsoon rainfall as part of the global climate system for an input for surface hydrology, we need not only the monthly mean patterns but also more accurate statistical information, i.e., data on the fractional areas covered by precipitation and distribution functions for rainfall intensity and how these statistics vary from the beginning to the end of the monsoon, with the diurnal cycle and with the terrain.

On the other hand, precipitation in the tropics is especially important. Two-thirds of global precipitation occurs between 30S and 30N latitude. The latent heat released by tropical precipitation is a major driver of the Hadley Circulation, which transfers heat and moisture from the tropics to the mid-latitudes.

The importance of the spatial distribution and the temporal variability of the global rainfall on the biological, ecological and economical status of the planet has led to the proposed Tropical Rainfall Measuring Mission (TRMM), to be flown in November, 1997. TRMM is a joint space project with Japan. It consists of precipitation radar (provided by Japan), a multi-frequency microwave radiometer and a visible and infrared radiometer. Precipitation data obtained from TRMM will be of great significance for studies of the global hydrological cycle and for testing the realism of climate models and their ability to simulate and predict climate accurately on the seasonal timescale. TRMM combines a suite of sensors to overcome many of the limitations of remote sensors previously used for such measurements from space.

The overall goal of this project is to prepare to utilize TRMM and ancillary data to: (i) better understand the NA summer monsoon on large temporal and spatial scales, as part of the global climate system, including its interaction with terrestrial vegetation and other hydrological and biophysical processes; and (ii) develop rain-rate algorithms which most efficiently use the data available from TRMM (Dickinson and Emery, 1991; Emery and Miller, 1993).

This report presents a preliminary examination and analysis of the microwave and spectral remotely sensed data and ancillary data, to estimate rainfall.

2. EXPERIMENT

The experiment was designed to acquire ground data and remotely sensed data in the visible, NIR and multi-frequency microwave wavelengths from satellite platforms over the southwestern US and northern Mexico. Data analyzed were from the 1992 wet or "monsoon" and drying or "post-monsoon" seasons (August and October). In the monsoon season (August), the vegetation is usually near the peak of green leaf area and soil moisture is highly variable. The post-monsoon season (October) is characterized by less green vegetation and lower soil moisture content than during the monsoon period.

3. GROUND DATA

Monthly rain-gauge values (mm/month) over the southwestern US for the months of August and October 1992 were obtained from the National Climatic Data Center, (Figure 16.1). There were no rain-gauge data available for Mexico. The rain-gauge values were spatially averaged using a mixed log normal distribution into 2 degree square bins.

Figure 16.1

Rain-gauge distribution as reported by the National Climatic Data Center

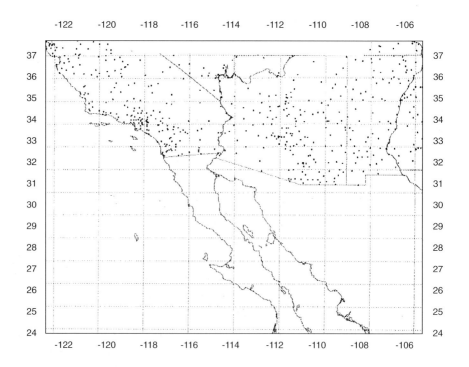

4. REMOTELY SENSED DATA

The Special Sensor Microwave Imager (SSM/I) F10 platform multi-frequency data (Table 16.1) were used. The data covers the entire globe from which data covered in the study area were extracted.

Table 16.1

Summary of SSM/1 channels and footprints

Freq.(GHz)	Polarization	Integration Period	Along track	Across track
19.35	vertical	7.95 ms	69 km	43 km
19.35	horizontal	7.95 ms	69 km	43 km
22.235	vertical	7.95 ms	50 km	40 km
37.0	vertical	7.95 ms	37 km	28 km
37.0	horizontal	7.95 ms	37 km	29 km
85.5	vertical	3.89 ms	15 km	13 km
85.5	horizontal	3.89 ms	15 km	13 km

Source: Wentz (1992)

There are two different regimes of passive microwave remote sensing where precipitation is concerned. At lower frequencies, emission is the dominant process. The higher the signal in these frequencies, the higher the estimated precipitation. This method has been the one chosen for oceans. Application of this method to SSM/I data means usage of the 19 GHz channels and the 22 GHz horizontally polarized channel. The other regime of microwave remote sensing of precipitation involves scattering. At higher microwave frequencies, it is a lower signal which suggests higher rainrates. The bigger the drops, however, the more radiation is scattered away as opposed to reflected. This method works better at higher rainrates, however, and it is independent of the background; hence it works over land, where high and changing emissivities make the emission method practically useless in many instances. The two 85 GHz channels on SSM/I can then be used for the scattering method of rainrate estimation.

The monthly total rainfall estimates (mm/month) from the F10 for the months of August and October 1992 were obtained (Figures 16.2, C and D) using James Ferriday's precipitation algorithm over the land background (Ferriday, unpublished). Ferriday's algorithm differs, depending upon the background (ocean and land). It is applicable between 60N and 60S latitude, with estimates over the coastlines presumed to be indeterminant. Thus, the contours on the coastlines are most likely in error and should not be considered valid. The same is true for any contours seen over the ocean surface or over the Gulf of

California (Figures 16.2, A-D). The point estimates for the SSM/I data were spatially averaged for each orbit using a mixed-log normal distribution. These spatially averaged values were generated for 2 degree square bins, and then temporally averaged over a month, again using a mixed-log normal distribution (rainfall has been seen in several studies to follow this distribution in both space and time).

The biweekly maximum NDVI was calculated over the study area using the National Oceanic and Atmospheric Administration (NOAA-11) Advanced Very High Resolution Radiometer (AVHRR) 1-km data. The bi-weekly NDVI covered the period of late July/August and October 1992. The data were acquired, archived, processed and made available by the United States Geological Survey, EROS Data Center. The Land Analysis System software package was used to generate the bi-weekly NDVI images. The data from NOAA-11 were received in High Resolution Picture Transmission (HRPT) format with Local Area Coverage (LAC) resolution, meaning it uses the full resolution of AVHRR (1.1-km at nadir). The NDVI is simply the difference of near-infrared (NIR, 0.72-1.1μm) and red (0.55-0.68μm) reflectance values, normalized over their sum $((\rho NIR-(red)/(\rho NIR+\rho red))$.

5. RESULTS AND CONCLUSIONS

Based on preliminary examination of the data collected, the results are summarized below:

(i)   The correlation of the binned values for the rain-gauges and the SSM/1 calculations were 0.72 and 0.53 for August and October, respectively (Figures 16.2, A-2D). These are rather typical; the decline in correlation in October does not necessarily mean either method is more "wrong" as much as it indicates that there was a great deal less precipitation (smaller signal —> lower SNR, signal-to-noise ratio). The NA monsoon collapses near the end of September/early October. The SSM/I F10 platform passes over the NA monsoon once in the morning and once at night. Thus it might completely miss the active afternoon rainfall during and post monsoon. In our experience of looking at particular areas of the NA monsoon, we witnessed situations where the substantial amount of rainfall for a particular month occurred on one or two days at a particular time of the day.

(ii) The NDVI values calculated here are in the range of -1.0 to 1.0, where increasing positive values indicate increasing green vegetation and negative values indicate non-vegetated surface features such as water, barren, ice, and snow or clouds. Visual comparison of the bi-weekly maximum NDVI (Colour Plate 3, A-C) and monthly rainfall (Figures 16.2, A-D)

Figure 16.2

Relation between rain-guage rainfall monthly totals (mm/month) 1992, (A) August (B) October and rain SSM/1 monthly totals (mm/month), (C) August, (D) October

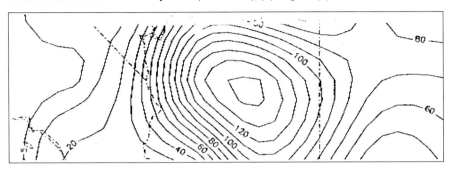

A

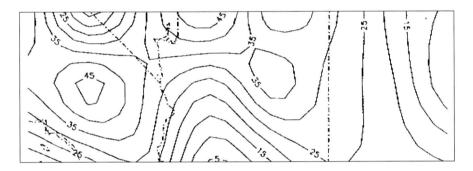

B

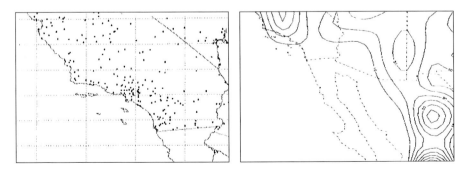

C   **D**

reveals strong correlation in some parts, and weak or no correlation in other parts of the study area. Examining the NDVI (Colour Plate 3, B and C) plots showed a strong correlation between NDVI and total in the New Mexico-Colorado border area and in the lower Texas-Mexico area (Figures 16.2, A-D). Both rain-gauge values and SSM/I estimates indicated higher rainfall rates in August than in October and, hence, more green is seen in August than in October on the NDVI plots in the above areas. On the other hand, NDVI values for the California area showed no correlation with rain measurements (Colour Plate 3, B and C and Figures 16.2, A-D). Therefore, we interpret variations in the NDVI to be related to the differences in the phenology primarily associated with rainfall distribution and amount. Quantitative information on these phenological aspects of vegetation has heretofore been unavailable in such a spatially comprehensive manner. In addition, other factors might contribute to variations in the NDVI, such as soil background, water vapour, and clouds.

(iii)   In summary, the results presented here are encouraging, considering the spatial aspects and the wide range of variations (i.e., soil background, soil moisture, atmospheric conditions, vegetation) in the study area. The availability of a wide range of remotely sensed and ancillary data acquired on a routine basis by the US and foreign ground stations suggests that rainfall estimation and vegetation monitoring experiments can be conducted over selected regions, or even on a global scale. However, the availability of TRMM data in the near future and the ongoing development of algorithms (or a combined algorithm) using the strengths of the different instruments to be flown on the observatory in combination with other satellite data (e.g., Geostationary Operational Environmental Satellite (GOES)) will increase the extent and accuracy of rainfall measurements (i.e., rainfall areal coverage and distribution of intensities), and help define better the onset and evolution of convective storms and relate them to surface hydrology. The results reported here demonstrate that remotely sensed data can be used to estimate rainfall over a large scale in semi-arid regions.

Acknowledgments

The data reported here was acquired with support from the NASA TRMM Science Research Opportunities (NRA-90-OSSA-15) and the United States Geological Survey, EROS Data Center. Shawn Miller received a travel grant from IFAD to attend the workshop.

References

Brooks, K.N., Ffolliott, P.F., Gregersen, H.M. and Thames, J.L. 1991. *Hydrology and the management of watersheds.* Iowa State University Pess, Ames, USA.

Dickinson, R.E. and Emery, W. 1991. Interaction of terrestrial and atmospheric hydrological cycles in the context of the North American summer monsoon. Proposal No. 0890(40(1022B, University of Arizona, Tucson, USA.

Gifford, G.F. 1996. Rangeland watersheds-indicators of healthy ecosystems. *Grazingland hydrology issues: Perspectives for the 21st century.* Society for Range Management, Denver, Colorado, USA.

Emery, W. and Miller, S. 1993. *Satellite estimation of rainfall.* Internal Report, July 30, 1993. Colorado Center for Astrodynamic Research, University of Colorado, Boulder, USA.

Ferriday, J. (Unpublished) *Rainfall algorithm for use with TRMM data,* Ph.D. dissertation, Colorado Center for Astrodynamic Research, University of Colorado, Boulder, USA.

Moran, M.S., Clarke, T.R., Kustas, W.P., Weltz, M. and Amer, S.A. 1994 . Evaluating of hydrologic parameters in a semi-arid rangeland using remotely sensed spectral data. *Water Resources Research,* Vol. 30, No. 5, 1287-1297.

Moran, M.S., Weltz, M.A., Vidal, A., Goodrich, D.C. and Amer, S.A. 1993. *Evaluating energy balance of semiarid rangeland from combined optical-microwave remote sensing.* IEEE Symposium, CO-MEAS, March 22-25 1993.

Wentz, F.J.1992. Production of SSM/I Datasets, *RSS Technical Report 090192,* September 1.

Processing multitemporal satellite imagery for natural resource mapping, monitoring and management

17

D.J. Rogers, S.I. Hay and M.J. Packer

Synopsis

The paper discusses the problems and prospects of using multitemporal satellite imagery from the National Odeanic and Atmosheric Adminisrtation (NOAA) and Meteosat series of meteorological satellite to monitor soils and vegetation. Emphasis is placed on how to handle the vast amounts of data and how to interpret them. The developments necessary for making better use of the satellite imagery are outlined.

Key Point

1. *Multitemporal satellite images provide more or less instantaneous views of the earth-surface phenomena and, when appropriately composited, reveal the seasonal evolution of vegetation features. Processing these images for maximum use involves two distinct steps.*

   The first step seeks to reduce the sheer volume of data to manageable proportions, to provide clear, unambiguous and a preferably biologically meaningful set of variables. The second step involves the application of these derived variables to describe the land-surface phenomena we wish to study. Our research group uses temporal Fourier processing for the first step and various forms of discriminant analysis for the second step.

1. INTRODUCTION

For many years, high-resolution Landsat and SPOT images have found wide application in development project areas, often providing the only maps available for remote sites. Their high cost and relatively small coverage per scene, however, preclude their use over wider areas, as does the sheer volume of data involved. Low-resolution meteorological satellite images have been used in the last ten years as inputs to famine and drought early warning systems but, until relatively recently, were not readily available to the wider research community. Drought and famine forecasting were based on work showing how meteorological satellite data are related to plant photosynthetic activity, biomass and plant phenology (e.g., the 'greening up' of vegetation after seasonal rains). For example, when correlations were discovered between the same satellite image values and tsetse mortality rates, tsetse abundance, trypanosomosis incidence and prevalence at sites throughout Africa (Rogers and Randolph, 1991; Rogers, 1991; Rogers and Williams, 1993), the potential for satellite imagery to describe and monitor key features of tsetse, trypanosomosis and land-use patterns in Africa (and, by implication, the distribution of many other natural resources, pests and diseases) was clearly established. The Trypanosomosis and Land-use in Africa (TALA) Project was funded by the Overseas Development Administration (ODA) (UK) to explore this potential further, and to begin to work towards a set of guidelines by which habitat, vector and disease situations could be rapidly assessed, control programmes could be designed with more complete environmental information to hand and the impacts of suppression and eradication programmes could be monitored through time.

During the lifetime of the TALA Project, we have used several sources of satellite data, each more detailed or more accurate than the previous ones, or involving more channels of data, with each channel containing information about electromagnetic energy either reflected from, or emitted by, the earth's surface or by clouds and aerosols in the atmospheric column. We were particularly interested to discover good satellite correlates of land surface meteorological variables, such as land-surface temperature, rainfall or humidity, each of which has in the past been used to describe the distribution of either vegetation types, insects or insect-borne diseases. We also wished to explore alternatives to the ubiquitous measure of vegetation photosynthetic activity, the Normalized Difference Vegetation Index (NDVI) which, despite criticism, has survived many attempts to replace it with alternatives claiming greater accuracy. The NDVI is derived from channels 1 and 2 (visible and near-infrared channels, respectively) of the Advanced Very High Resolution Radiometer (AVHRR) on board the polar-orbiting NOAA series of meteorological satellites, and is now an integral part of drought and famine early warning systems. Other channels in the AVHRR receiver have been correlated with land-surface air temperature, whilst the geostationary Meteosat satellite produces images processed to give a monthly measure of the duration of cold cloudcover (i.e., Cold Cloud Duration, or CCD), which are related to rainfall (Snijders, 1991).

The most complete and carefully calibrated AVHRR dataset is available from the PATHFINDER programme of the North American Space Agency (NASA) (James and Kalluri, 1994) and we have recently completed the analysis of three years' worth of daily data which has allowed us to calculate a variety of vegetation and thermal indices that could not be calculated from composited 10-day or monthly data. We were thus able to examine the predictive power of a variety of raw satellite channels and the vegetation, vapour pressure and thermal indices that may be derived from them.

For further work, the multitemporal satellite data were first subjected to temporal Fourier analysis that describes each data stream in terms of its mean value and the amplitude and phases (i.e., timing) of the annual, bi-annual and tri-annual cycles that may be used to describe it. Details of this processing are given in Rogers, Hay and Packer (1996) and examples of the application of Fourier-processed imagery in studying ecological patterns and processes are given in Rogers and Williams (1994). Fourier processing achieves the important aim of data reduction without much loss of information, with the additional bonus that the Fourier descriptions have an obvious biological interpretation (unlike alternative data reduction techniques, such as principal components analysis).

The use of temporal Fourier-processed multitemporal AVHRR and Meteosat data in predictions of biological phenomena involves both binary (e.g., presence/absence) and multiple-valued (either ordinal or attribute) predicted variable data types. In both cases, various forms of linear and non-linear discriminant analysis have given accuracies when applied to the training set data, often exceeding 90%. The techniques applied to tsetse flies in Africa are described in full in Rogers, Hay and Packer (1996). However, several qualifications need to be stressed. First, linear discriminant analysis, which assumes a common covariance matrix of the predictor variables across all classes of predicted variable (and therefore linear discriminant axes or planes), is less satsifactory than non-linear discriminant analysis, which allows each predicted variable class to retain its own (often unique) covariance matrix of predictor variables (Green, 1978; Tatsuoka, 1971). Different covariance matrices for each of several distinct vegetation types could perhaps be expected a priori, but there are also often strong differences in particular elements of the covariance matrices of the predictor variable datasets for animal species' presence and absence; an indication that each species is not living in a simple 'subset' of general environmental space, but in an unique subset in which it is presumably in some way best adapted. Secondly, the use of observed prior probablities tends to improve overall predictive accuracies (Tatsuoka, 1971). In the absence of any specification of prior probabilities, discriminant analysis makes the reasonable assumption that any observation has an equal probability of falling into any one of the set of predicted categories. Incorporation of the expectation of occurrence of each category into the predictive process (i.e., the prior probabilities) generally improves the overall predictive performance of discriminant analysis, and may be estimated from the training set data when these are drawn at random from the distribution being descibed.

Finally, the calculation (or retention) of posterior probabilities, rather than the output of the unique attribute assignments characteristic of maximum likelihood methods, allows for reasonable uncertainty in the output classification. Thus posterior probabilities can be interpreted to imply that a particular pixel belongs to a particular class with a high probability, but may belong to more or less any class in the predicted variable dataset, albeit with lower probabilities (the sum of all posterior probabilities is normalized to 1.0). Whilst the process of normalization needs to be undertaken with caution (especially when what is being classified differs qualitatively from the training set data), it can (when used sensibly) provide some indication of real uncertainty in classification, as in the determination of genuine mixed pixels - or 'mixels' - that are so characteristic of the larger pixels of coarse spatial resolution meteorological satellite data. It remains to be seen whether the claims of the 'fuzzy logicians', that the posterior probabilities represent the actual proportions of the different pureend member types within each mixed pixel (e.g., Foody, 1992), are actually correct in any but the most simple cases (e.g., a pure forest to a pure grass transition, involving no other vegetation type). We suspect that in real-world applications, such as the highly-heterogeneous vegetation types seen in Africa, the overlap and lack of homogeneity of the covariance matrices of the spectral characteristics of the vegetation components of mixels preclude reliable fuzzy classification at the level of a single mixel.

In applying the above methods to describe the distribution of a natural resource, we therefore have a set of potential predictor variables derived from satellites, and a set of land-surface phenomena we wish to describe. Our application of discriminant analysis involves the forward step-wise selection of predictor variables, each variable being selected on the grounds that it increases the separation between predicted variable classes more than any other predictor variable in that 'round' of selection. Separation is measured by the Mahalanobis distance, which is a covariance-adjusted measure of separation (i.e., it allows for the covariance between predictor variables that is commonly encountered in satellite data). In the case of more than two classes of predicted variable, the Mahalanobis distances are summed, to give a Mahalanobis index of separation provided at each step of the variable selection process.

With the qualifications outlined above, Fourier analysis coupled with discriminant analysis, information is therefore provided that may be directly related to land-surface phenomena. Fourier analysis also partitions the variance of the satellite signal orthogonally, so that the contribution of annual, bi-annual and tri-annual components to the overall annual variation may be easily examined. This allows the production of seasonality maps, providing important insights into the spatial arrangement of habitat types in Africa. Finally, Fourier analysis readily lends itself to studies of environmental change over time. Each of the obvious changes in habitat type (e.g., gradual deforestation as land is brought into the cultivation cycle; degradation of vegetated habitats to bare soil; reforestation of annual grassland areas with perennial woodlands) is associated with obvious and predictable changes in Fourier components. It follows from this that judicious use of maps showing the difference in key Fourier components (e.g., amplitudes, phases), over the time-span of the data archive, should be able to reveal longer-term changes in habitat use.

The application of satellite imagery in predicting climate, vegetation and the distribution of organisms are briefly described here, together with comments on the potential for future developments.

2. SATELLITE MONITORING OF CLIMATE AND WEATHER

Details of the steps involved in producing the data layers used in the analyses reported here are given in Hay (1996) and in Hay et al., (1996). A great deal of image processing, involving meteorological station records from up to around 200 sites throughout Africa, has shown that satellite-derived surrogates of meteorological variables can explain an average of around 69% of the variance of monthly temperature records throughout Africa, around 63% of the variance of monthly saturation deficit (= vapour pressure deficit) readings, and around 65% of the variance of monthly rainfall figures (Hay, 1996).

2.1 Temperature

Hay (1996) found that out of three raw satellite data channels (AVHRR Ch3, Ch4 and Ch5) and three derived measures of land-surface thermal brightness temperatures, the Price method (1984) consistently provided the most reliable correlate of land-surface temperature. One example is shown in Figure 17.1. These correlations were improved further by the incorporation of station elevation as a second predictor variable.

Figure 17.1

The best correlation (1988 - 1990) between satellite-derived monthly maximum estimates of land-surface thermal brightness temperatures (using the Price method, 1984) and monthly air temperatures at ground level (from NOAA - NCDC records). These records are for December 1990 and involve 124 stations throughout Africa (r^2 = 0.74, p<0.0001).

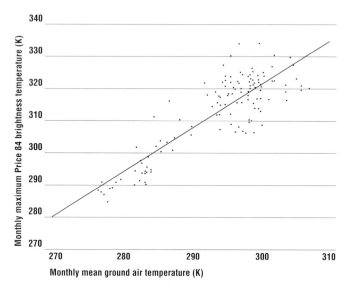

Source: Hay (1996)

2.2 Atmospheric moisture

Many important biological phenomena are related to atmospheric moisture, although there is no 'obvious' satellite data channel recording humdity. Instead, use is made of a relationship between radiance in AVHRR channels 4 and 5 and the total precipitable water content of the atmospheric column (Dalu, 1986). This in turn is converted to an estimate of dew-point temperature at the land-surface (Smith, 1966), and thence (using also the Price method 1984 estimate of temperature) to an estimate of Vapour Pressure (= saturation) Deficit (VPD) (Prince and Goward, 1995).

Hay (1996) found a strong relationship between satellite-derived estimates of VPD and meteorological station records of saturation deficit from the same network of sites in Africa. An example is shown in Figure 17. 2.

Figure 17.2

The best correlation (1988 - 1990) between satellite-derived monthly maximum estimates of land-surface VPD and monthly saturation deficit at ground level (from NOAA - NCDC records). These records are for November 1989 and involve 140 stations throughout Africa ($r^2 = 0.81$, $p<0.0001$).

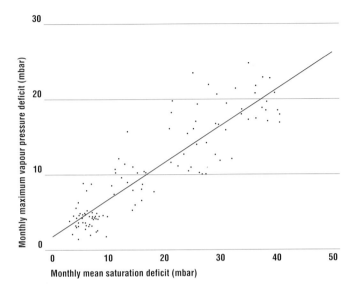

Source: Hay (1996)

2.3 Rainfall

Snijders (1991) has investigated the relationship between estimates of Cold Cloud Duration (CCD) derived from the Meteosat weather satellite and rainfall in a broad zone north of the Equator and south of the Sahara. Hay (1996) has extended this analysis throughout the continent; an example is shown in Figure 17. 3.

Taken together, these results demonstrate the potential for satellite imagery to monitor the traditional meteorological variables through time. The correlations that Hay (1996) found between the satellite predictors and ground-station records appeared to vary in a semi-seasonal fashion, suggesting that if the causes of such variation can be discovered, they can be removed from the estimates, thus improving them still further.

Figure 17.3

The best correlation (1988 - 1990) between Meteosat satellite-derived monthly CCD and monthly rainfall at ground level (from NOAA - NCDC records). These records are for January 1990 and involve 104 stations throughout Africa ($r2 = 0.84$, $p<0.0001$).

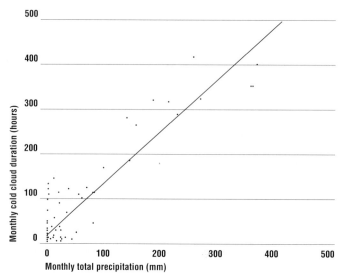

Source: Hay (1996)

3. SATELLITE MONITORING OF VEGETATION

3.1 Vegetation at the continental scale

Unsupervised classification of a series of whole Africa, images incorporating a variety of vegetation indices (e.g., Ratio Vegetation Index, or RVI, i.e., Channel 2/Channel 1 reflectances; Soil Adjusted Vegetation Index (SAVI), Huete, 1988; GEMI, Pinty and Verstraete 1992), has shown that the 'traditional' NDVI outperforms all others in producing vegetation bands most similar in appearance to the standard vegetation map of Africa (White, 1983), and is apparently least contaminated by 'noise'. One thing hampering further progress at the continental scale is the absence of reliable and widespread ground-truth data against which to test our predictions. White's map purports to present the natural vegetation zonation of Africa, unaffected by human impact, but this is increasingly an important factor in structuring landscapes and, therefore, the satellite signal they emit. Careful aerial surveys of selected areas of the continent would allow us to refine our predictions, as the following example shows.

3.2 Vegetation at the country scale: the example of Nigeria

An excellent set of ground-truth data from Nigeria (RIM, 1992; Wint, this volume) allowed us to test a variety of approaches to describing surface vegetation types. Initially, we used linear discriminant analytical methods to describe the range of percentage cover by a single vegetation type (e.g., woodland). The initial results were most encouraging, showing that there is a gradual change in the average values of key satellite predictor variables across the range of surface coverage by individual vegetation types. One example is shown in Table 17.1, where it can be seen that there is a monotonic increase or decrease in the most useful satellite predictor variables (a characteristic shared by all ten selected variables).

Maps produced using these predictor variables were, however, disappointing. Whilst grid squares with dominant vegetation types (i.e., where a particular vegetation type occupied > 70-80% of each grid square) were accurately predicted, those with lower percentage coverages were not. The mean values shown in Table 17.1 were associated with so much variation that classification accuracy diminished. The obvious reason for this is that grid squares not dominated by a particular vegetation type could be dominated by any one of the other eight or nine types present in the training set, each with its own unique satellite signal.

Table 17.1

Mean values of the 'top 5' satellite predictor variables for grid squares in the RIM (1992) aerial survey data from Nigeria, with different percentages of all woodland cover

% cover	NDVI max	Thermal amp 1	Thermal phase 1	Thermal min	Thermal mean
0 - 8%	0.34	6.14	2.07	27.85	34.25
9 - 26%	0.39	7.05	1.87	26.12	32.97
27 - 50%	0.43	7.93	1.72	24.74	32.00
51 - 74%	0.45	8.46	1.64	23.79	31.41
75 - 100%	0.47	8.54	1.57	22.9	30.68
Mean	0.41	7.61	1.77	25.10	32.2

*Thermal'refers to AVHRR Channel 4 maximum surface brightness radiance

Source: TALA Project

To overcome this problem we decided to concentrate only upon dominant vegetation types within each grid square, and the results are shown in Colour Plate 4 and Tables 17.2 - 17.4. These analyses were carried out using PATHFINDER data, but before Fourier analysis, while variable means and standard deviations (their maxima and minima) were used as predictors. The Gutman index is one of a number of measures of land-surface temperature.

Table 17.2 records the key satellite predictor variables when the threshold for defining dominant vegetation type is set at 50, 60 or 70%, together with two measures of predictive accuracy, the kappa and tau statistics (see Anderson et al.,

1976, for a discussion of land-cover classification accuracy). Elevation consistently appears as the most important variable, followed by a variety of the Channel 1, thermal and vegetation indices.

Table 17.2

The top predictor variables for Nigeria land-cover at the 50, 60 and 70% thresholds, and accuracy measures for the predictions.

Rank	Variable (70%)	Variable (50 %)	Variable (60 %)
1	Elevation	Elevation	Elevation
2	Ch1 SD	Ch1 SD	Ch2 max
3	Ch3 max	Ch1 min	Gutman max
4	Ch1 min	RVI max	GEMI mean
5	RVI mean	NDVI max	GEMI min
6	NDVI mean	SAVI max	Ch1 min
7	Ch2 SD	Price mean	Price min
8	Ch1 mean	GEMI max	RVI min
9	RVI min	Price min	Ch3 min
10	GEMI max	Ch2 mean	Price mean
Kappa	0.468	0.541	0.640
Tau	0.467	0.525	0.635

Source: TALA Project

Table 17.3 records the predictions in the form of a confusion matrix and Table 17.4 records the accuracy of predicting each vegetation type in terms of producer accuracy (i.e., the accuracy of identifying those grid squares known to be of a certain vegetation type) and consumer accuracy (i.e., the percentage correct of those grid squares identified as a particular vegetation type). The results are encouraging and mis-classifications may be easily understood. For example,

Table 17.3

Classification matrix of land-cover classes for the 60% threshold coverage showing the number of Nigerian sample grid-squares in each category.

Observed	1	2	3	4	5	6	7	8	Total
Predicted									
1. Bare ground	**0**	0	5	1	1	0	0	1	8
2. Grassland	0	**19**	3	2	1	0	0	0	25
3. Scrubland	0	0	**41**	2	4	5	0	1	53
4. Open woodland	0	7	21	**89**	34	6	0	5	162
5. Dense woodland	0	1	9	29	**168**	40	0	3	250
6. Forest	0	0	1	0	1	**86**	0	0	88
7. Mangrove	0	0	0	0	0	0	**12**	0	12
8. All cultivation	0	3	26	42	47	10	0	**120**	248
Total	**0**	**30**	**106**	**165**	**256**	**147**	**12**	**130**	**846**

Source: TALA Project

cultivation is often confused with various forms of woodland, a vegetation type in which (and under which) much cultivation takes place.

The success of this approach has allowed us to make predictions of land-cover types throughout West Africa.

Table 17.4

Classification accuracy of the land-cover classes in Table 17.6.

Class	Producer accuracy (%)	Consumer accuracy (%)
1. Bare ground	0.0	N.A.*
2. Grassland	76.0	63.3
3. Scrubland	77.4	38.7
4. Open woodland	54.9	53.9
5. Dense woodland	67.2	65.6
6. Forest	97.7	58.5
7. Mangrove	100.0	100.0
8. All cultivation	48.4	92.3

* N.A.= not applicable

Source: TALA Project

3.3 The distribution of animals - the tsetse fly in Africa

The distribution of organisms may be analysed in much the same way as the distribution of vegetation type. Results for four key species throughout Africa are recorded in Table 17.5; distributions of two species are shown in Colour Plate 5.

Table 17.5

The key predictor variables for the distribution of four species of tsetse throughout Africa

Rank	G. morsitans	G. palpalpis	G. tachinoides	G. pallidipes
1	DEM	DEM	DEM	DEM
2	Ndmax	NDm/CH4m	NDm/CH4m	Ndrange
3	NDm/CH4m	Ndmax	CCDmean	CH4a1
4	CCDmean	CCDmax	Ndmean	NDp1-CCDp1
5	Ndmean	Nda2	CH4min	Nda1/CH4a1
6	NDp1-CH4p1	Nda1/CH4a1	CCDmin	Nda1
7	CH4min	CH4min	Nda1/CH4a1	Nda2
8	CCDa2	NDp1-CH4p1	CCDa2	CCDa3
9	Nda3	CCDa1	CCDa1	Ndmean
10	Nda1	CCDa3	Ndrange	NDm/CCDm
Result/n	10	10	10	10
%correct	88	94	96	89
%false +	12	5	4	9
%false -	1	0	0	2
Sensitivity	0.97	0.98	0.96	0.87
Specificity	0.86	0.935	0.96	0.89

Source: TALA Project

One important conclusion from these studies is that the average conditions in areas of fly presence differ only slightly from those in areas of fly absence. The implication is that insect distributions may rapidly respond to even slight changes in local weather conditions and there is some evidence that this has already happened (e.g., the increasing incidence of high-land malaria, and the increasing altitudinal limits of tsetse flies).

3.4 Habitat monitoring: long-term changes in vegetation signals from satellites

The archive of multitemporal satellite data now extends back to 1982 and gives us the possibility of monitoring changes in land-surface vegetation cover through time. In theory, Fourier analysis is ideally placed to monitor obvious changes associated with the change from forest to woodland to grass or scrub, or the reverse of this process. This may be achieved by comparing key Fourier variables at two moments in time, i.e., the start and the end of the satellite data series. Differences between these two images are a record of changes taking place in the interim. One example, in Nigeria is shown in Colour plate 6, which records the difference in the Fourier mean and the amplitude of the annual cycle of NDVI changes. In the figure, increases in each variable over time are shown in green, and decreases in red.

At the continental level, there is a strong spatial patterning that suggests that the technique is picking up some signal rather than simply noise (which would give the images a more speckled appearance). The NDVI images show an increase in mean values in the moister parts of the continent between the two dates (a general reflection of recovery from the drought of the early 1980s?), and a general increase in the amplitude of the annual cycle of vegetation growth, though with some areas showing a marked decrease (e.g., parts of Côte d'Ivoire, the Central African Republic and northern Uganda/southern Sudan).

The Nigerian maps (Colour plate 6) show some regional detail of these changes. The mean NDVI increased over the period in question in most of the southerly regions, but appeared to decrease slightly in the regions along, and to the north of, the northern border. This decrease occurs over a period generally acknowledged to have become wetter, and is perhaps an example of Goward and Prince's observation (1995) that, whilst long-term rainfall patterns can be related to long-term vegetation patterns, shorter-term variations in each of these variables are less easily related to each other because of presently unappreciated time-delays in the response of vegetation to rainfall. It has been suggested (Willy Wint, personal communication) that the vegetation in the north of Nigeria's border is dependent upon groundwater reserves. Such reserves are likely to show a delayed response to drought and to the increased rainfall following drought, and this may help to explain the patterns seen in the different images.

Within Nigeria's borders, in the north of the country, the annual amplitude increased in the west, but decreased in the east (with a slightly earlier peak in both areas), whilst in the south there is a mixture of changes, especially pronounced in the Southwest. This southwestern region has experienced considerable change (in many cases decreases) in agricultural activity in the last 15 - 20 years, a phenomenon attributed to the impact of oil wealth.

Whilst this preliminary approach has shown the potential of this technique, there are clearly still many questions that need to be addressed at the research level. It is hoped that these satellite images have revealed important changes, the explanation of which will lead to a clearer understanding of the dynamics of natural vegetation through time, and a clearer appreciation therefore of the impact of humans on natural landscapes.

4. CONCLUSION

Remotely-sensed satellite imagery provides us with a new and exciting technology to monitor meteorological variables, land-surface types and the distribution and abundance of a variety of animals over space and time. There is clearly an urgent need to refine our present capabilities, in order to put into place monitoring schemes that will be ready to detect the increasing influence of humans on natural habitats, climate and weather. If we are to avoid disaster in the future, we must first understand the natural processes of our world, their dynamics and sensitivities to long- and short-term changes, and we must act to ameliorate (or reverse) the impact we have upon them.

Acknowledgements

Many people contributed to the work described in this report and everyone in the TALA Project is grateful to them. We should particularly like to thank Brian Hursey, Jan Slingenbergh, Tony Piccolo and Fred Snijders of FAO; Guy Hendrickx and Dr. A. Napala of Project GCP/TOG/013/BEL in Togo; Reg Allsopp, Professor Maggie Gill and Dr. Jonathan Wadsworth at the Natural Resources Institute (NRI); Drs A. Belward, D. Ehrlich, E.F. Lambin and J.P. Malingreau at the Joint Research Centre (Ispra, Italy); Drs C.O. Justice and C.J. Tucker at NASA; and the many people associated with the PATHFINDER programme who have made our project such an enjoyable one.

References

Dalu, G. 1986. Satellite remote sensing of atmospheric water vapor. *International Journal of Remote Sensing,* 7:1089-1097.

Foody, G.M. 1992. Classification accuracy assessment: some alternatives to the Kappa coefficient for nominal and ordinal level classifications. In: *Remote Sensing: from Research to Operation.* Proceedings of the 18th Annual Conference of the Remote Sensing Society. (eds. Cracknell, A.P. and R.A. Vaughan, A.P.) pp 529-538.

Goward, S.N. and Prince, S.D. 1995. Transient effects of climate on vegetation dynamics - satellite observations. *Journal of Biogeography* 22, 549-564.

Green, P.E. 1978. *Analyzing Multivariate Data.* The Dryden Press: Hinsdale, Illinois, USA.

Gutman, G.G. 1993. Multi-annual time series of AVHRR-derived land surface temperature. *Advances in Space Research* 14, 27-30.

Hay, S.I. 1996. An investigation of the utility of remotely sensed meteorological satellite data for predicting the distribution and abundance of the tsetse fly (Diptera: Glossinidae). *D. Phil thesis,* Oxford University (submitted).

Hay, S.I., Tucker, C.J., Rogers, D.J. and Packer, M.J. 1996. Remotely sensed surrogates of meteorological data for the study of the distribution and abundance of arthropod vectors of disease. *Annals of Tropical Medicine and Parasitology* 90, 1-19.

Huete, A.R. 1988. A soil adjusted vegetation index (SAVI). *Remote Sensing of Environment* 25, 295-309.

James, M.E. and Kalluri, S.N.V. 1994. The PATHFINDER AVHRR land data set - an improved coarse resolution data set for terrestrial monitoring. *International Journal of Remote Sensing* 15, 3347-3363.

Pinty, B. and Verstraete, M.M. 1992. GEMI, a non-linear index to monitor global vegetation from satellites. *Vegetatio* 101, 15-20.

Prata, A.J. 1993. Land surface temperatures derived from the advanced very high resolution radiometer and the along-track scanning radiometer 1. Theory. *Journal of Geophysical Research* 98, 16, 689-16, 702.

Price, J.C. 1983. Estimating surface temperatures from satellite thermal infrared data - a simple formulation for the atmospheric effect. *Remote Sensing of Environment* 13, 353-361.

Price, J.C. 1984. Land surface temperature measurement for the split window channels of the NOAA 7 advanced very high resolution radiometer. *Journal of Geophysical Research* 8: 7231-7237.

Prince, S.D. and Goward, S.N. 1995. Global primary production - a remote-sensing approach. *Journal of Biogeography* 22, 815-835.

Resource Inventory and Management (RIM). 1992. *Nigerian livestock resources.* Four Volumes. Report prepared by RIM Ltd. for the Federal Department of Livestock and Pest Control Services, Abuja, Nigeria.

Rogers, D.J. 1991. Satellite imagery, tsetse and trypanosomiasis in Africa. *Preventive Veterinary Medicine* 11, 201-220.

Rogers, D.J. 1993. Consultant Report to FAO. Unpublished.

Rogers, D.J., Hay, S.I. and Packer, M.J. 1996. Predicting the distribution of tsetse flies in West Africa using temporal Fourier processed meteorological satellite data. *Annals of Tropical Medicine and Parasitology* 90, 225-241.

Rogers, D.J. and Randolph, S.E. 1991. Mortality rates and population density of tsetse flies correlated with satellite imagery. *Nature* 351, 739-741.

Rogers, D.J. and Williams, B.G. 1994. Tsetse distribution in Africa, seeing the wood and the trees. In: (eds. Edwards, P.J., May R.M. and Webb, N.R.) *Large Scale Ecology and Conservation.* Blackwell Scientific Publications: Oxford, UK. pp. 249-273.

Smith, W.L. 1966. Note on the relationship between total precipitable water and the surface dew point. *Journal of Applied Meteorology* 5, 726-727.

Snijders, F.L. 1991. Rainfall monitoring based on Meteosat data - a comparison of techniques applied to the Western Sahel. *International Journal of Remote Sensing* 12, 1331-1347.

Tatsuoka, M.M. 1971. *Multivariate Analysis: techniques for educational and psychological research.* John Wiley & Sons: New York, USA.

White, F. 1983. The vegetation of Africa - a descriptive memoir to accompany the UNESCO/AETFAT/UNSO vegetation map of Africa. UNESCO, Paris.

Large-scale Saharan-Sahelian vegetation variations from 1980 to 1996 derived from ground precipitation and NOAA satellite data

18

C.J. Tucker and S.E. Nicholson

Synopsis

This paper examines a set of observations derived during 1980-1996 from the National Oceanic and Atmospheric Administration (NOAA) series satellite imagery and ground-based data in Saharan-Sahelian Africa. The Normalized Difference Vegetation Index (NVDI) was established and the 175 mm/yr isoline estimated for each year. Inferences are drawn from these data about the likelihood of systematic trends in precipitation.

Key points

1. *Ground precipitation records and satellite-derived vegetation index data from the NOAA-series of meteorological satellites show a high correlation from 1980-1996. This correlation enables a satellite-based estimate of the 175 mm/yr precipitation isoline to be determined for each year from 1980 to 1996.*

2. *The inter-annual variation in this boundary is substantial, varying between years of higher annual rainfall, such as 1980 and 1994, and years of very deficient annual rainfall such as 1984. We continue to study this interesting phenomena in Saharan-Sahelian Africa and are unable to draw any conclusions regarding systematic trends toward drier conditions for the 1980-1996 time period.*

3. *Satellite data, coupled with available ground rainfall measurements, have been used to study desert expansion and contraction in arid and semi-arid Africa on the southern side of the Sahara. In Sahelian Africa, substantial recovery from the 1984 drought was found. Since 1984, there has been a marked improvement in rainfall and hence vegetation production in the Sahel zone, with substantial inter-annual variation. These results cast doubts on the more extreme assumptions of Sahelian Zone desertification, in which the recovery from the combined effect*

of drought and overgrazing has been suggested by some workers to be a slow or impossible process.

1. INTRODUCTION

Desertification has been defined as the process by which more productive arid and semi-arid lands become less productive or more "desert-like". This can result from many causes, but generally is attributed to over-use by man and/or by climatic tendencies toward drier climates.

In the 1980s, international interest was focused on the southern side of the Sahara Desert, the Sahel Zone, which is the semi-arid grassland or steppe area immediately to the south of the Sahara. One of the prevalent assumptions at that time was the continuous expansion of the Sahara Desert to the south. We will now review some of the recent work on this topic extended to 1996. Previous descriptions of our work on this topic have appeared in Tucker et al., (1991) and Tucker et al., (1994).

The Sahara of Africa, the largest desert of our planet, is between 7 000 000 and 10 000 000 km² in size. The northern boundary has been arbitrarily set to follow the southern side of the Atlas Mountains to Biskra (Algeria), where it dips south-ward through Tunisia to the Gulf of Gabes and from there continues along the Mediterranean to the Suez Canal (McGinnies et al., 1968; Cloudsley-Thompson, 1984; Swift, 1975). The southern boundary stretches east to west at 16° to 17°N for 6 000 km, from the Atlantic Ocean (off Mauritania) to the Red Sea (off Sudan) and is a vegetation-zone boundary. At this boundary, there is a barely perceptible gradient of plants, animals and physiographic characteristics into steppe vegetation of the Sahel zone (Le Houérou, 1980; Monod, 1986), resulting from a mean annual precipitation gradient of 1 mm yr^{-1} km^{-1} from north to south.

Uncertainty in, and variation of, the location of the boundary between the Sahara and the Sahel zone have prevented precise estimates of the extent of the Sahara (N.B., we include in our figures for the Sahara the Nubian Desert of the Sudan, the Eastern and Western deserts of Egypt, the Libyan Desert, and all other sub-deserts of North Africa, contiguous to the Sahara.

Although deserts have a number of common features of climate, weather and a low density of vegetation, most workers have defined "desert" according to their discipline (Goodall and Perry, 1979; McGinnies, 1979; Shmida, 1985; Evenari, 1985). We use "desert" to be synonymous with "arid". "Semi-arid" represents the gradation of desert into "steppe" and denotes areas of less aridity, higher and more evenly-distributed rainfall, and higher levels of primary production. Steppe is also imprecise and its use varies widely (Evenari, 1985).

Largely anecdotal information has accumulated from early this century to the present, suggesting that the Sahara has expanded toward the south (Cana, 1915; Bovill, 1921; Stebbing, 1935; Rodd, 1938; Stebbing, 1938; Aubreville et. al., 1973; Eckholm and Brown, 1977; Smolowe, 1987; Norman, 1987; Ellis, 1987; Lamprey, 1975). The alleged expansion was attributed in part to climate variation (i.e., droughts) (Smith, 1986) and to land mismanagement such as overgrazing, increased cultivation and firewood cutting (Eckholm and Brown, 1977; Ellis, 1987).

This process of land degradation is called "desertification" by some (Kassas, 1970) and "desertization" by others (Le Houérou, 1968). The occurrence of a period of continuous wet years (1950 to 1968) followed by a period of continuous dry years (1969 to 1996) has also contributed to the controversy in the location of the southern Sahara boundary (Figure 18.1) (Nicholson, 1989; Lamb et al., 1986; Toupet, 1972).

Figure 18.1

Percentages of rainfall departures for the Sahel zone of Africa from 1900 to 1992. Note the run of wet years (c. 1950-1965) followed by a run of dry year (c. 1970 to the present).

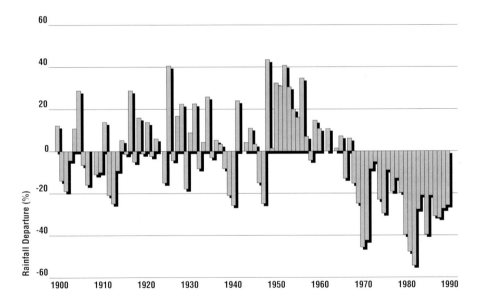

Lamprey (1975) compared the location of the southern boundary of desert vegetation in western Sudan in 1958 with its location in 1975. He estimated that the boundary had shifted southward by 90 to 100 km during the 17-year period, a desert expansion of 5.5 km yr[-1], and this value has been repeated often in the popular press (Smolowe, 1987; Norman, 1987; Ellis, 1987). However, a 1984 field study by Hellden (1984) in the same area found no evidence to support such an expansion.

In order to measure directly the changes in vegetation at the boundary, we used a satellite-derived vegetation index to map inter-annual changes in vegetative cover (and, by inference, rainfall) along the Saharan-Sahelian boundary from the Atlantic Ocean to the Red Sea for the period 1980 to 1996. We hypothesized that annual variations in rainfall would bring corresponding changes in the density of vegetative cover (Figure 18.2).

Figure 18.2

Relationships between the mean NDVI and mean annual precipitation for 1980-1994 for reporting stations in sub-Saharan Africa. The non-linear correlation coefficient between these variables is 0.93.

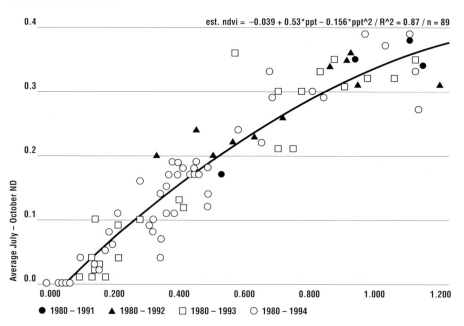

est. ndvi = −0.039 + 0.53*ppt − 0.156*ppt^2 / R^2 = 0.87 / n = 89

● 1980 – 1991   ▲ 1980 – 1992   □ 1980 – 1993   ○ 1980 – 1994

Source: Nicholson (1989), with additional data to 1992

Vegetation indices are commonly used spectral measures derived from remotely sensed data in the red and near-infrared spectral regions. The red spectral response is inversely related to the chlorophyll density, and the near-infrared spectral response is directly related to scattering in individual leaves and between leaves in the canopy.

Combinations of these two adjacent spectral regions provide compensation for differences in irradiance and an estimate of the intercepted fraction of the photo-synthetically active radiation or photosynthetic capacity (Tucker, 1979; Curran, 1983; Tucker and Sellers, 1986; Sellers, 1985; Monteith, 1977; Hatfield et al., 1984; Daughtry, et al., 1983; Asrar et al., 1986). These data have also been shown to be highly related to total primary production when summed or averaged over the growing season (Tucker et al., 1981; Asrar, et al., 1985; Tucker et al., 1985; Gosse et al., 1986; Prince, 1991). We used a satellite-derived vegetation index calculated from meteorological satellite data and expressed this index in terms of estimated annual precipitation (Figure 18.2).

2. THE AREA OF STUDY

The area we studied lies between 16° W and 39° E longitude and 10° and 25°N latitude. This area includes a sizable part of the Sahara Desert, as well as the Sahel. Precipitation varies from <100 mm/yr in the Sahara Desert to 400 mm/yr at the southern boundary of the Sahel zone; a precipitation gradient of 1mm yr^{-1} km^{-1} occurs from 18° N to 10° N (Le Houérou, 1980; White, 1983).

The Sahara Desert, the Sahel zone and their transition zone have been defined as: 0 to 100 mm yr^{-1}, Sahara Desert; 100 to 200 mm yr^{-1}, Saharan-Sahelian transition zone; and 200 to 400 mm yr^{-1}, Sahel proper. Rainfall in this area is uni-modal and occurs from July to October; the rest of the year it is dry (Le Houérou, 1980; Monod, 1986; White, 1983; Breman and De Wit, 1983).

We will use the 200 mm/yr precipitation isoline as the boundary between the Sahara Desert and the Sahel zone, realizing that this is actually the boundary between the Sahel proper and the Saharan-Sahelian transition zone. This is unavoidable as the utility of our satellite vegetation index approach is limited below the 150-200 mm/yr precipitation isoline, because of limited green vegetation.

3. DATA USED

Satellite data from the NOAA polar-orbiting meteorological satellites were used from 1980 to 1996. Data from the Advanced Very High Resolution Radiometer (AVHRR) (Channel 1 (0.55-0.68 µm), Channel 2 (0.73-1.1 µm) and Channel 5 (11.5-12.5 µm)); were used to calculate the NDVI. Data from NOAA-6 (1980), NOAA-7 (1981-1984), NOAA-9 (1985-1988), NOAA-11 (1989-1993), NOAA-9 (1994, but from the descending node with 09 00 hours over-pass time) and NOAA-14 (1995-1996) were used from July 1 to October 31 of 1980 to 1996. Daily AVHRR 4-km data were acquired for Africa; the NDVI was formed from Channel 1 and Channel 2 as (2-1)/(2+1); a cloud mask using

Channel 5 was applied labelling everything colder than 12°C as cloud; and the data was mapped to an equal-area projection with a 7.6-km grid-cell size.

The daily mapped data were formed into 10-day images and averaged for each year. Formation of composite images minimizes atmospheric effects, scan angle effects, cloud contamination and solar zenith angle effects (Holben, 1986; Ranson and Daughtry, 1987). Calibration corrections after Kaufman and Holben (1993) were applied. A total of 8 500 orbits of AVHRR data were used from a total of five different NOAA-series satellites.

4. RESULTS

NDVI data were computed for the Sahel zone, as well as a 1 000 000 km^2 area of the central Sahara, and plotted against the year (Figure 18.3). Rainfall, and hence primary production, decreased progressively from 1980 to 1984 in the Sahel zone (Figures 18.1 and 18.3). Nicholson has reported that 1980 had a rain-

Figure 18.3

Average vegetation index values for the approximate 200 to 400 mm/yr long-term mean precipitation zone and the Sahara Desert from 1980 to 1996. 1984 was an exceptionally dry year (see also Figure 18.1).

There is a direct relation between primary production and the vegetation index (Tucker et al., 1981; Asrar et al., 1985; Tucker et al., 1985; Gosse et al., 1986; Prince, 1991), precipitation and primary production (i.e., Houérou and Hoste, 1977; Rutherford, 1980; Seely, 1978), and hence precipitation and the vegetation index (Figure 18.2).

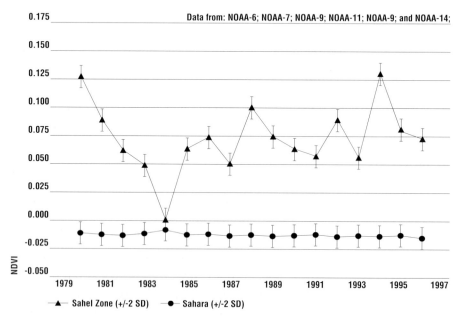

Source: NOAA-6; NOAA-7; NOAA-9; NOAA-11; NOAA-9; and NOAA-14.

fall departure of about -13% from the long-term mean precipitation for the Sahel zone, and 1984 was one of the driest years this century (Nicholson, 1989; Lamb et al., 1986). Higher mean NDVI values for the Sahel zone were found for 1985 to 1996 than for 1984; these values indicate that conditions improved in 1985 to 1996 as opposed to 1984. Significant variation of the NDVI was observed in the Sahel zone over the 17 years of observation; 1980 was the highest year of the NDVI and 1984 the lowest.

This observation is in agreement with the meteorological data of Nicholson (1989) and Lamb et al., (1986). Annual precipitation for all 17 years of our study was below the long-term mean (N.B., the precipitation for 1994 was close to the long-term mean).

Our data document a progressively southward movement of the Saharan-Sahelian boundary (i.e., the 200 mm/yr precipitation isoline) of 240 km (60 km/yr) from 1980 to 1984. This rate was computed by averaging the boundary location at each half degree of longitude from 15.5°W to 38.5°E (Table 18.1).

The average southward movement of the Saharan-Sahelian boundary (i.e., the estimated 200 mm/yr annual precipitation isoline) was 55 km from 1980 to 1981; 77 km from 1981 to 1982; 11 km from 1982 to 1983; and 99 km from 1983 to 1984. From 1984 to 1985, there was south-to-north movement (i.e., retreat of the desert) of 110 km, followed by a further northward movement of 33 km from 1985 to 1986.

In 1987, the mean position moved southward 55 km. In 1988, it moved northward 100 km; in 1989 and 1990 it again moved southward 44 and 33 km, respectively. The mean position of the southern boundary in 1991 was indistinguishable from the boundary in 1990. The mean position of the estimated 200 mm/yr precipitation boundary in 1992 moved northward 55 km from 1991, followed by an 110 km southward movement (expansion of the desert) from 1992 to 1993. From 1993 to 1994, there was a retreat of the desert (or movement northward) of our estimated 200 mm/yr precipitation isoline of 170 km, followed by an expansion or southward movement of our estimated 200 mm/yr precipitation boundary of 90 km from 1994 to 1995. We estimate that the error associated with our boundary determination is ± 4 pixels or 30 km.

While it is perhaps inappropriate to think of deserts expanding and contracting annually, clearly the coupled-use of satellite and ground data permit measurements such as these to be made. Climates, especially arid and semi-arid climates, are determined from mean climatic conditions. Our satellite data document, in a spatially-continuous manner, the tremendous inter-annual variation in precipitation and hence vegetation development on the south side of

Table 18.1

The area of the Sahara Desert and Saharan-Sahelian transition zone from 1980-1996, using the estimated 200 mm/yr precipitation isoline as the southern boundary

Year	Saharan area (km²)	Change relative to 1994 (km²)	Annual precipitation departure(%)	mm/yr	mean latitude (0.9)	and range of the 200- isoline (degrees)
1980	8,633,000	27,000	-13%	16.3	(0.9)	14.3 to 17.9
1981	8,942,000	335,000	-19%	15.8	(1.1)	14.1 to 17.6
1982	9,260,000	653,000	-40%	15.1	(0.9)	12.9 to 16.7
1983	9,422,000	815,000	-48%	15.0	(0.9)	13.3 to 16.7
1984	9,982,000	1,375,000	-55%	14.1	(1.0)	12.1 to 17.0
1985	9,258,000	652,000	-28%	15.1	(0.9)	13.3 to 17.3
1986	9,093,000	493,000	-21%	15.4	(0.8)	14.0 to 17.1
1987	9,411,000	804,000	-40%	14.9	(0.9)	13.3 to 16.8
1988	8,882,000	275,000	-21%	15.8	(0.8)	14.2 to 17.3
1989	9,134,000	528,000	-30%	15.4	(1.3)	12.8 to 17.6
1990	9,269,000	662,000	-32%	15.1	(1.1)	12.8 to 17.4
1991	9,072,000	472,000	-27%	15.6	(0.8)	13.5 to 17.0
1992	8,987,000	387,000	-25%	15.8	(0.9)	13.9 to 17.3
1993	9,593,000	1,005,000	-50%	14.8	(1.1)	12.9 to 16.9
1994	8,601,000	0 -	10%	16.4	(0.8)	14.5 to 17.8
1995	9,059,000	462,000	no data	15.7	(1.1)	13.8 to 17.6
1996	9,156,000	550,000	no data	(not determined as of 11/1/96)		

In the central Sahara, the Adrar des Iforas, Air and Tibesti mountain areas were included as were the desert areas for the Eastern Desert of Egypt and the Nubian Desert of The Sudan. Changes are relative to 1980. Nicholson's (1989) Sahelian mean annual precipitation departures from the long-term mean are given from 1980-1987. The northern boundary of the Sahara was the line running from Wadi Draa (29°N, 10.5°W) on the Atlantic coast along the Saharan Fault to Figuig (32°N, 2°W), in Morocco, from there to Biskra (35°N 6°E), in Algeria, and from there southward through Tunisia to the Gulf of Gabès (34°N, 10°E). Areas of cultivation on the Mediterranean coast were excluded, as was the Nile Delta and River Valley. We estimate the mean latitude position error to be ± 30 km. The error associated with the total Saharan area is estimated to be ± 200,000 km² and is the product of the north-south error (±30 km or ±0.3° of latitude) and the length of the southern boundary (6 000 km). The standard deviation appears in parenthesis.

the Sahara, which has been so well-documented by many workers in arid and semi-arid land research.

The estimated mean position of the 200 mm/yr boundary in 1996 was thus 70 km to the south of its position in 1994. Desert expansion varied in the 17 years of our analysis from 27 000 km² (1980) to 1 375 000 km² (1984), all relative to 1994. The 1994 expansion represents a 16% increase of the Sahara from its size in 1984. We estimated the area of the Sahara and the Sahara-Sahelian transition zone was 8 600 000 km² in 1994 (Table 18.1). The north-south position of the 200 mm/yr isoline varied greatly across the south side of the Sahara (Figure 18.4).

Figure 18.4

Summary of the estimated mean, the most northern, and most southern positions of the 200-mm/yr-boundary location from 1980 to 1995 at every 0.5° of longitude from 15.5° W to 38.5o E. See also Table 18.1.

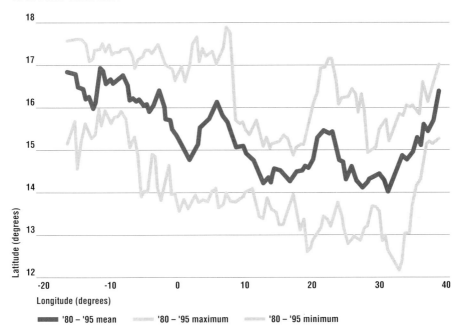

Variation was high from Mali through central Niger and from eastern Chad through western Sudan. Variation was low in southern central and southeastern Mauritania and from central Niger through western Chad. Rainfall, and hence vegetation distributions, vary in space as well as in time in this area.

The observed low variability in inter-annual movement of the estimated 200 mm/yr isoline in Mauritania, and from central Niger through western Chad, may have implications for detecting desertification. Detection of changes should be more effective in areas of lower inter-annual variability. Inter-annual variations mean that it would require a decades-long study to determine whether long-term expansion or contraction of the Sahara is occurring.

While our satellite data provide the measurement baseline against which to compare future data, it will be necessary to continue similar types of high-temporal frequency low-spatial resolution (i.e., 500-m, 1-km, 4-km) for the next decades. It is only by a continued systematic series of measurements that global processes, such as arid and semi-arid precipitation-primary production dynamics, can be understood. It should be clearly stated that for studying global processes, highly-detailed data collected over 2-3 years are much less useful than the adequate but simple data obtained over decades.

References

Asrar, G., Kanemasu, E. T., Jackson, R. D. and Pinter, P. J. 1985. *Remote Sens. Environ.* 17, 211.

Asrar, G., Kanemasu, E. T., Miller, G. P. and Weiser, R. L. 1986. *IEEE Trans. Geosci. Remote Sens.* GE24, 76.

Aubreville, A. *et. al.,* 1973. *Bois et Forets des Tropiques* 148, 3.

Bovill, E.W. 1921. *J. Afr. Soc.* 20, 175 and 259.

Breman, H. and De Wit, C. T. 1983. *Science* 221, 1341.

Cana, F.R. 1915. *Geograph.* J. 46, 333.

Cloudsley-Thompson, J.L. 1984. *Sahara Desert.* Pergamon Press, New York.

Curran, P.J. 1983. *Phil. Trans. R. Soc.* A-309, 257.

Daughtry, C.S.T., Gallo, K. P. and Bauer, M. E. 1983. *Agron. J.,* 75, 527.

Eckholm, E. and Brown, L.R. 1977. *Worldwatch Pap. 13,* 1 Worldwatch Institute, Washington, D.C.

Ellis, W.S. 1987. *National Geographic* 172, 140.

Evenari, M. 1985. In: Evenari, M., Noy-Meir, I. and Goodall, D.W. (eds) *Ecosystems of the World: Hot Deserts and Arid Shrublands* Elsevier, New York pp. 1-22.

Goodall, D.W. and Perry, R.A. 1979. *Arid-Land Ecosystems: Structure, Functioning and Management,* 1 Cambridge University Press, Cambridge.

Gosse, G. et al., 1986. *Agronomie* 6, 47.

Hatfield, J.L., Asrar, G. and Kanemasu, E.T. 1984. *Remote Sens. Environ.* 14, 65.

Hellden, U. 1984. *Drought Impact Monitoring.* Lund University Naturgeografiska Inst., Lund Sweden.

Holben, B.N. 1986. *Int. J. Remote Sens.* 7, 1417.

Kassas, M. 1970. *Arid Lands in Transition.* American Association for the Advancement Science, Washington, D.C. pp. 123-142.

Kaufman, Y.J. and Holben, B. N. 1993. *Int. J. Remote Sens.,* 14, 21.

Lamb, P.J., Peppler, R.A. and Hastenrath, S. 1986. *Nature* 322, 238.

Lamprey, H.P. 1975. Report on the desert encroachment reconnaissance in Northern Sudan, UNESCO/UNEP (Nairobi, 1975), pp. 1-16 *Desertification Control Bulletin,* 17, 1 (1988).

Le Houérou, H.N. 1968. *Ann. Alger. Geogr.* 6, 2 (1968).

Le Houérou, H.N. 1980. *J. Range Manage.* 33, 41 (1980).

Le Houérou H.N. and Hoste, C .H. 1977. *J. Range Manag.* 30, 181 (1977).

McGinnies, W.G., Goldman, B.J. and Paylore, P. 1968. *Deserts of the World* University of Arizona Press, Tucson.

McGinnies, W.G. 1979. In: Goodall, D.W. and. Perry, R.A (eds) *Arid-Land Ecosystems: Structure, Functioning and Management,* 1. Cambridge University Press, Cambridge pp. 299-314.

Monod, T. (1986). In: Evenari, M., Noy-Meir, I. and Goodall, D. W. (eds) *Ecosystems of the World: Hot Deserts and Arid Shrublands* Elsevier, New York. pp. 203-243.

Monteith, J.L. 1977. *Phil. Trans. R. Soc.* B-281, 277.

Nicholson, S.E. 1989. *Weather* 44, 47.

Norman, C. 1987. *Science* 235, 963.

Prince, S.D. 1991. *Int. J. Remote Sens.* 12, 1301.

Ranson, K.J. and Daughtry, C.S.T. 1987. *IEEE Trans. Geosci. Remote Sens.* GE-25, 502.

Rodd, F. 1938. *Geograph. J.* 91, 354.

Rutherford, M.C. 1980. *S. Afr. J. Sci.* 76, 53.

Seely, M.K. 1978. *S. Afr. J. Sci.* 74, 295.

Sellers, P.J. 1985. *Int. J. Remote Sens.* 6, 1335.

Shmida, A. 1985. In: Evenari, M. Noy-Meir, I. and Goodall, D.W. (eds) *Ecosystems of the World: Hot Deserts and Arid Shrublands* Elsevier, New York pp. 23-77.

Smith, S.E. 1986. *J. Soil Water Cons.* 41, 297.

Smolowe, J. 1987. *Time* 127 (33), 36.

Stebbing, E.P. 1935. *Geograph. J.* 85, 506.

Stebbing, E.P. 1938. *Geograph. J.* 91, 356.

Swift, J. 1975. *The Sahara.* Time-Life Books, New York.

Toupet, C. 1972. *C. R. Somm. Soc. Biogeogr.* 48, 39.

Tucker, C.J. 1979. *Remote Sens. Environ.* 8, 127.

Tucker, C.J. and Sellers, P.J. 1986. *Int. J. Remote Sens.* 7, 1395.

Tucker, C.J., Holben, B.N. and Goff, T.E. 1984. *Remote Sensing Environ.* 15, 255.

Tucker, C.J., Holben, B.N., Elgin, J.H. and McMurtrey, J.E. 1981. *Remote Sensing Environ.* 11, 171.

Tucker, C.J., Dregne, H.E and Newcomb, W.W 1991. *Science* 253, 299.

Tucker, C.J., Newcomb, W.W. and Dregne, H.E. 1994. *Int. J. Remote Sensing* 15(17):3547-3566.

Tucker, C.J., Vanpraet, C.L., Sharman, M.J. and Van Ittersum, G. 1985. *Remote Sensing Environ.* 14, 233.

White, F. 1983. *The Vegetation of Africa* UNESCO, Paris.

High resolution imagery for rangeland inventory and monitoring: a case study in Morocco

M. Aït Belaïd

Synopsis

This paper reviews in some detail the outcome of the Geostat-Maroc Project which aimed at the development of an integrated remote sensing and Geographic Information Systems (GIS) methodology to allow quick and accurate assessment of rangeland areas at a national level.

Key Points

1. *Rangelands occupy nearly 80% of Moroccan territory and provide about 30% of the feed requirements of the national livestock population. Rangelands are located in fragile ecosystems and subject to strong degradation after decades of environmental stresses (e.g., arid climate, poor soils, strong erosion, overgrazing, demographic expansion).*

2. *These ecosystems need rigorous management and frequent monitoring. In this context, the Geostat-Maroc Project was conducted to develop a methodology based on remote sensing and GIS techniques, which will provide regular rangeland acreage estimation in a quick and cost-effective manner.*

3. *Complete and repetitive coverage of rangelands with high resolution imagery is not feasible due to the high cost and volume of data. Therefore, an approach that combines statistical modelling and remote-sensing data was adopted for the Geostat-Maroc Project to assess rangeland acreage at the national level with reasonable accuracy (i.e., coefficient of variation is estimated to 8.5%).*

4. *In order to make a rangeland inventory using high resolution imagery, we developed a methodology in three main steps: (i) a technical study at the national level using GIS for rangeland zoning; (ii) a detailed thematic feasibility study on three SPOT test sites for vegetation mapping; and (iii) a statistical study to*

set up a suitable sampling plan (with SPOT scenes as the statistical units) and an extrapolation model. The methodology developed within the framework of the Geostat-Maroc Project can be applied in many other countries of the Mediterranean basin, the Middle East and many regions of Africa, Asia, America and Australia.

1. THE GEOSTAT-MAROC PROJECT

Natural vegetation analysis, in relation to agropastoral practices in arid areas, is of prime importance for desertification monitoring and control. It is interesting to study this phenomenon at a regional scale, in terms of inventory and monitoring, by using a satellite system with a large field of view, such as the National Oceanic and Atmospheric Administration's Advanced Very High Resolution Radiometer (NOAA-AVHRR). However, such a system has a low spatial resolution and it is difficult to characterize sparce vegetation with a spatio-temporal variability.

The use of a high-resolution system such as Landsat Thematic Mapper and SPOT Multispectral allows a better identification of rangelands, despite the difficulty of distinguishing from the signal between the contribution of vegetation and soil. Furthermore, a complete and repetitive coverage of rangelands is not feasible, due to the high cost of data acquisition and analysis.

The Geostat-Maroc Project adopted an approach such as the one used in Europe for agricultural statistic-gathering, combining high resolution satellite data (SPOT scenes) over a small number of sites and statistical modelling, to assess rangeland acreage with reasonable accuracy and affordable cost.

The study was conducted in Morocco, where the rangelands occupy nearly 80% of the territory and cover about 30% of the nutritional needs of national livestock. Natural vegetation and rangelands are located in fragile ecosystems and subject to drought and desertification.

The feasibility project, called Geostat-Maroc, was conducted jointly by Centre National d etudes Spaciales (CNES) and the Centre de recherches terraotres et spaciazle (CRTS), with many other Moroccan and French partners, including: Institut Agronomique et Veterinaire, Hassan II University, Departement of Environment (DE), ENSAT, INSEE and Scot Conseil.

2. GEOSTAT-MAROC METHODOLOGY AND RESULTS

The main components of the Geostat-Maroc Project are global rangeland zoning, detailed vegetation mapping and the statistical inventory of rangelands (Aït Belaïd and Lefèvre, 1995).

2.1 Rangeland zoning, using the Geographic Information System (GIS)

The first step of the project was rangeland zoning, which allows the territory to be subdivided into homogeneous zones according to specified criteria (e.g., soil types, land cover, climate).

The zoning procedure was conducted using the existing cartographic documents and GIS technology, which allows map digitizing, data analysis and archiving. The zoning map was produced with seven homogeneous strata by overlaying three different types of information: the bioclimatic map, the agropastoral map and the soil map. Other information was integrated in the database, such as: population; hydrography; administrative boundaries; and SPOT grid (CNES et ENSAT, 1992; Lacombe et al., 1995).

The synthetic product was used to generate a fragility map, with four degrees of fragility, according to the sensitivity of rangelands to degradation and overgrazing, for example.

2.2 Vegetation mapping, using high-resolution imagery

The second step consisted of a thematic study on three SPOT sites representative of the main 'steppic' regions in Morocco (Oujda, Khenifra and Ouarzazate provinces). The detailed thematic study has resulted in natural vegetation characterization and mapping (e.g., Stipa tenacissima, Artemisia herba-alba) by using multispectral SPOT data. The choice of the period of acquisition and the interpretation technique of these images are dependent on the knowledge of the sites, the phenology of species and atmospheric conditions.

The automatic analysis, based on supervised classification and ground truth, was conducted on the two first sites, using two SPOT scenes for each one in autumn 1991 and spring 1992. For these two cases, only one image of spring is sufficient for rangeland identification and mapping, because the vegetation coverage is very high (Aït Belaïd and Yessef, 1994; Aït Belaïd et al., 1994). At the Oujda site, seven classes were identified, of which five were vegetation species (Colour Plate 7), with a classification accuracy of 84%. At Khenifra, five classes were established, of which three were vegetation species, with a comparable accuracy of 83%. These accuracies can increase to 90% and 96%, respectively, if we consider only the two major species (*Stipa tenacissima* and *Artemisia herba-alba*).

The study of the Ouarzazate site is more complex, because of low vegetation coverage and high-seasonal variability. The study, in this case, was based on photo-interpretation, in order to identify the surface stages from the analysis of one image of summer. Ground observations allowed the possibility to establish a relationship between the predominant vegetation species and the corresponding surface stages. Thus, ten surface stages were identified, of which three were vegetation species, with an accuracy of 86% (Bennouna et al., 1995).

All the studies conducted in the three sites, using different methodologies (e.g., classification, photo-interpretation) have demonstrated - at the scale of 1/50 000 and an accuracy of 85% to 95% – the feasibility of rangeland mapping, which constitutes the input of the statistical model.

2.3 Statistical inventory of rangelands

The last step in the project focused on a statistical study, in order to set up a suitable sampling plan (with SPOT scenes as the statistical units) and build up an extrapolation model. The objective was to assess rangeland proportion or rangeland total area at the country level.

The statistical model (i.e., the number of SPOT scenes, sampling rate, number of segments, size of segments, extrapolation model) was developed according to the documents produced in the two previous steps, particularly the zoning map and vegetation map. In order to facilitate the statistical study, the two thematic maps were simplified to the following nomenclature :
• steppic rangelands;
• agricultural lands; and
• bare soil.

The methodology developed was based on the following double- sampling technique (Brion and Fournier, 1995):

(i)   random sampling of SPOT scenes, taking into account the zoning map and SPOT grid as constraints; instead of sampling images in the whole country, we decided a priori to sample a certain number in each stratum, in order to increase the accuracy of rangeland estimation; and

(ii)   systematic sampling of square segments, within the selected scenes at the first sampling; these segments can be localized in the field by using the Global Positioning System (GPS).

The statistical modelling allowed the definition of a sampling plan composed of 30 SPOT scenes distributed within the different strata, and each scene contained 30 segments of 4 hectares (ha) (200m x 200m) each. The extrapolation model made it possible to evaluate rangeland area successively at the level of segment, scene and stratum, right up to the national level. In Morocco, the proportion of rangelands in the studied area was estimated at 40% ± 7% (95% probability), using 115 "digital quick look" as SPOT data.

3. CONCLUSION AND PERSPECTIVES

In conclusion, the developed methodology integrating different types of data (existing documents, field observations, satellite data) and different types of processing (GIS, image analysis system, statistical model) provides the following solutions:

(i)   the detailed vegetation map, zone by zone, with a comparable scale of 1/50 000, accuracy ranging from 85 to 95%;

(ii)   the global zoning map at the country level using the existing documents or digital "quick look", with a scale of 1/2 000.000;

(iii)   the fragility map (overgrazing hazard), with a scale of 1/2 000.000;

(iv)   the statistical inventory of rangelands at the national level, with an accuracy greater than 90%; and

(v)   the development of the rangeland database, including the results of the different components of the project.

The results of the Geostat-Matroc Project, briefly presented, are more encouraging and of high-quality in terms of vegetation mapping with accuracy from 85 to 95% and the statistical inventory (with accuracy better than 90%). It is interesting now, after the success of the feasibility study, to deal with the operational implementation of the project.

The project was initially developed in Morocco where rangeland problems are very important. Naturally, it can be extended to the regional and continental level (e.g., zone of Observatoire du Sahara-Sahel, the Mediterranean basin, Middle East, and many other regions of Africa, Asia, America and Australia). The Geostat-Maroc Project dealt not only with rangeland inventory and monitoring but was also directly related to desertification monitoring problems and their consequences on natural resources and the environment, which are of prime importance to many regional and international organizations such as Observatoire du Sahara-Sahel (OSS), the Food and Agriculture Organization of the United Nations (FAO), the United Nations Environment Programme (UNEP) and the United Nations Educational, Scientific and Cultural Organization (UNESCO).

References

Aït Belaïd, M., Lefèvre, M.J., Husson, A., Yessef, M., Berkat, O. et El Gharbaoui, A. 1994. Faisabilité de la cartographie par télédétection des parcours steppiques à Alfa et Armoise. *GéoOservateur,* N° 4, Avril, Rabat, Maroc, pp. 37-46.

Aït Belaïd, M. et Lefèvre, M.-J. 1995. *Utilisation de données satellitales pour l'inventaire statistique et le suivi des parcours (Projet Geostat-Maroc).* MARISY'95, Ifrane, Maroc, 16-18 Octobre, pp. 321-325.

Aït Belaïd, M. et Yessef, M. 1994. *Analyse du Milieu Naturel à Faible Pluviométrie et Suivi des Parcours, Étude Thématique (phase A).* Projet Geostat-Maroc, rapport de synthèse, N° 1/94, CRTS, Rabat, Maroc.

Bennouna, T., Keammerer, M., Manière, R., Zouhri, A., et Lefèvre, M.J. 1995. *Méthodologie de Caractérisation des Parcours Sub-Désertiques, Région de Ouarzazate, Maroc.* Congrès International AFRICAGIS'95, Abidjan, 6-10 Mars, pp. 320-335.

Brion, Ph. et Fournier, Ph. 1995. *Étude Geostat-Maroc, partie statistique.* INSEE/SCEES, Mars, 27 p.

CNES et ENSAT 1992. Inventaire et suivi des terres de parcours, Étude thématique : stratification du territoire (Maroc). Projet Geostat-Maroc.

Lacombe, J.P., Aït Belaïd, M. et Lefèvre, M.J. 1995. *Un SIG pour le suivi des parcours en Mmlieux arides et semi-arides (Maroc).* AFRICAGIS'95, Abidjan, Côte d'Ivoire, 6-10 Mars, pp. 307-319.

Evaluating the vegetation of the Dirab using remote sensing and GIS: a case study in Saudi Arabia

20

A. Al-Shareef, M.A. Al-Noori and M.S. Samdani

Synopsis

This is an essay on the role and merit of an integrated remote sensing/Geographic Informnation System (GIS) approach to vegetation inventory and monitoring. It focuses on the Dirab area of Saudi Arabia. The objective of this study is to investigate the trends in land-use for agriculture purposes and, at the same time, to develop assessment strategies for use in monitoring natural vegetation.

Key Points

1. *The natural vegetation in desertic countries like Saudi Arabia is a precious resource. In a large country like Saudi Arabia, space imagery could be very useful in monitoring the vegetation. However, the usually poor vegetation cover makes this process difficult. On the other hand, space imagery can be very useful for agricultural areas with denser vegetation or other areas with dense natural vegetation.*

2. *Remote sensing data is an important source of information for monitoring temporal changes and updating the map planes. Using proper image processing, these data can be transformed into thematic information about features such as potential land-use, soils and vegetation cover. An image-processing module provides the facilities for pre-processing, image display enhancement, classification and geometric correction. GIS packages provide support for spatial data analyses for natural resources and socio-economic aspects of land use.*

3. *Multiple satellite images are now commonly used for detection of changes in natural and agricultural resources including crops, surface water bodies and disturbances by man for infrastructure development. GIS is an efficient way for*

delineating land use for various purposes, by using data generated by remote sensing and conventional methods. The results of such an exercise could be integrated with the socio-economic information to develop strategies for efficient utilization of available natural resources. Identification of physical, biological and socio-economic factors associated with desertification is an essential prerequisite for the development of a comprehensive database for a review of the past and for all future planning of land-use strategies.

1. INTRODUCTION

Images of our planet's surface from satellites are providing scientists with new tools to investigate the earth and its environment. Satellites such as Landsat offer several unique advantages to the planner, because the images which they provide cover a large area, are repetitive and are uniform in pictorial aspect and sun-angle. These images delineate many major features on the earth's surface, such as natural vegetation and crops, surface water, soils and geology. The synoptic view and high resolution provided by satellite remote sensing offer a viable technological solution for monitoring irrigated land and other areas under cultivation.

Two recently developed techniques, digital image processing and GIS, represent very valuable tools for combining map and statistical information. These techniques allow the integration of spatial and non-spatial data on vegetation with other information, such as soil type and water quality, so that the status of crops and soils can be monitored and lands can be classified according to their agricultural potential.

The Dirab area was selected to evaluate the use of remotely sensed data for monitoring agricultural areas, identifying changes in land-use patterns and assessing land degradation caused by irrigation systems. It is primarily a farming area developed as a result of Saudi Arabia's efforts to promote agriculture. This study focused on the changes occurring over the past decade (1987-96).

2. STUDY AREA

The area under study is 50 km west of the city of Riyadh and lies between 46°29'47" and 46°43'31" E longitude and 24°26'36" and 24°27'40" N latitude. It covers an area of 474.7 km² (47 426.312 hectares). Dirab has a dry continental climate with hot summers and cold to moderate winters. The average temperature is 35°C (97°F).

3. GEOLOGY AND LAND USE

The geology of the area is predominantly sandstone with subordinate limestone from the Mesozoic Age. The sedimentary formation which underlies Dirab is part of an extremely thick sequence of rocks that dip easterly off the Arabian Shield. The water-bearing sandstone and limestone beds store a substantial volume of water and constitute an important alluvial aquifer.

The general topography of this area is steeply undulating terrain dissected by valleys or wadis. There are two wadis in the area: Wadi Lida and Wadi Al-Awsat which are exploited mainly for their high agricultural potential. Wheat, alfalfa and other crops are grown primarily with the use of central pivot irrigation systems. However, the poor to fair quality of the water is not conducive to the growth of crops; and in some cases this has forced many farmers with large holdings to limit their agricultural activity.

4. MATERIALS AND METHODS

This study essentially consisted of collecting information from computer compatible tapes (CCTs) and field surveys; these data were processed and subjected to computer modelling to identify temporal changes in vegetation during 1987-96.

Data on the Dirab area (474.7 km^2) were downloaded from the CCTs and processed to make a false-colour composite file with a combination of bands 4, 3, and 2. The CCTs of the Landsat Thematic Mapper (TM) CCTs used for the digital analysis were made on four different dates (Table 20.1).

Table 20.1

Landsat TM images of the Dirab area, 1987-96

Dates	S No.	Path and Row
15/3/1987	1	166-43
17/4/1990	2	166-43
08/3/1993	3	166-43
20/2/1996	4	166-43

Remotely sensed data can be processed to correct geometric or radiometric distortions caused by the data being obtained from different platforms. Various digital image processing techniques were used to remove these distortions and obtain more accurate results within the image and to co-register the data sets.

Image enhancement techniques were used to improve the visual appearance of an image. Digital image processing techniques were found to be the most useful and satisfactory method for image enhancement. Enhancement techniques were applied separately to each band of multispectral images and were usually performed prior to visual interpretation. The individual enhancement bands were combined to produce a false-colour composite. Clustering techniques were used to interpret and classify each pixel of the image into one of a number of categories. The output was a map depicting categories/clusters based on two separate techniques: supervised and unsupervised. The unsupervised technique was used for the classification of the study area. This technique does not involve the use of any prior information about the area; rather, it employs a random selection of pixels and plots their digital number (DN) values. The computer programme then looks for natural "clusters" of points in the feature space. A map is produced and field work is subsequently undertaken to calibrate and label each category.

GIS was used to integrate a variety of other map data, rectified into a common format. Data sets were analyzed and then displayed for the study area. Thematic layers of information were manually interpreted and stored in the GIS using ARC/INFO software. These data include the following at a scale of 1:50 000:

(i)   a road network map;
(ii)   a soil map;
(iii)   a vegetation map; and
(iv)   a wadi map.

These maps were digitized manually and stored within the GIS. A land suitability map was subsequently produced based on the following procedure. Firstly, the base map (produced by the Aerial Survey Department, Ar-Riyadh in 1983) was obtained. Information on roads, soil, wadis and agriculture was systematically digitized to form an ARC/INFO database (i.e., coverage). Specific commands were used to select the coverages, display and analyze them and check for minor digitizing errors. As accessibility to infrastructure is a key criterion for the development of new agricultural areas, roads were buffered with a distance of 1.25 km on both sides. Finally, all coverages were overlaid to derive the potential land suitability map for agriculture. During the analysis, ARC/INFO software proved to be a powerful tool for combining and manipulating numerical and spatial data and for displaying these phenomena graphically as maps of the study area.

5. RESULTS AND DISCUSSION

A detailed trends/pattern map for the Dirab region displaying areas under agricultural crops was generated from Landsat TM data using ERDAS-image processing software. As expected, the remotely sensed data provided significant information about the changes and trends in agricultural land use that have taken place within the last decade.

After completion of several field investigations and analysis of the satellite images, it was found that there have been abrupt changes in the pattern of land cover. For example, while the area under agriculture increased very rapidly during 1990-93, it suffered a severe decline in the period 1993-96 (as evident from the 1996 satellite image). These changes are presented in Table 20.2, which shows the acreage under cultivation calculated using the satellite images of the entire study area.

Table 20.2

Area under cultivation in the Dirab area, 1987-1996.

Date of image	Cumulative area (ha)
15/3/1987	1181.07
17/4/1990	1212.57
08/3/1993	2054.79
20/2/1996	912.06

The sharp decrease in the land area under cultivation from 1993 to 1996 is due to several factors. Sand encroachment onto farmland was one factor that could be observed from the images. The other cause was the expansion of building activities, mostly due to the construction of new habitations (e.g., homes, resort areas and motels).

6. CONCLUSION

Remotely sensed imagery provides the resource manager with opportunities to view large contiguous areas simultaneously and frequently, due to its synoptic coverage (i.e., ability to view large areas) and its high temporal resolution (i.e., periodicity). The spectral qualities of these satellites provide unique perspectives on the land cover of the earth's surface. Information derived from such analysis can be used to provide policy-makers with timely guidance on the nature, rate and direction of changes taking place.

With respect to agricultural land, these data permit fairly easy identification of short and long-term changes occurring (e.g., in the extent and types of vegetation), possible agricultural limitations (e.g., low soil moisture) and the association with other land-cover classes. Thus, at the national or regional level, insights can be gained as to the critical parameters to be monitored, and indicators of natural resource degradation can accordingly be developed. Finally, long-term policies can be proposed for the development of areas such as Dirab. At the local level, the information gleaned can be used to provide farmers with valuable recommendations concerning the use and development of their holdings.

References

Alhadeff, S.J. 1988. *Development of a statewide geographical information system to support environmental management decision (Abstract)*. GIS Symposium on Integrating Technology and Geo-Science Applications. pp. 26-30, September 1988. Sheraton Denver Tech. Center Denver, USA pp.36-37

Anonymous, 1979. *A guide to agricultural investment in Saudi Arabia*. A report from the Ministry of Agriculture and Water, Kingdom of Saudi Arabia.

Curran, P.J. 1988. Image Processing. In: *Principles of remote sensing*, English Language Book Society/ Longman, Hong Kong. pp. 176-266.

Chakarborti, A.K. 1993. Strategies for watershed management planning, using remote sensing techniques. *Journal of Indian Society of Remote Sensing* 21 (2): 87- 97.

Colwell. R.W. 1993. Remote Sensing application in agriculture. In: *Manual of remote sensing*, American Society of Photogrammetry. 210 Little False Street, Falls Church, Virginia. pp. 2210-2218.

Gritzer, J.H. 1986. *Evaluation firewood and grazing resources in Kgateng District Botswana using remote sensing and geographic information system technology*. Proceedings, at the Twentieth International Symposium on Remote Sensing of Environment, Nairobi, Kenya, 4-10 December 1986. Vol. 11: 677-786.

Homer, C.G. 1996. *Vegetation cover-type mapping of Nevada*. Proceedings, ERDAS 1996 User's Group Meeting, 10-13 March, Atlanta, Georgia, USA.

Johansen, C.J. and Sanders, J.L. 1982. Remote sensing application for agricultural resources. In: *Remote sensing for resource management*. Soil Conservation Society of America, pp. 379-420.

Schlemmer, M.R., Blachmer, T.M. and Schepers, J.S., 1996. *Remote sensing and GIS tools for site-specific management*. Proceedings ERDAS 1996 User's Group Meeting, March 10-13, Atlanta, Georgia, USA.

Swain, P.H. and Davis, S.M. 1978. Biological and physical considerations in applying computer-aided analysis techniques to remote sensor data. In: *Remote sensing, the quantitative approach*, McGraw-Hill, USA. pp 228-286.

Tappan, G. 1986. *Remote sensing and mapping of the vegetation and landuse of Senegal*. Proceedings, Twentieth International Symposium on Remote Sensing of Environment, Nairobi, Kenya, 4-10 December 1986. Vol. 11: 483-487.

Monitoring the pastoral resources in the Sahelian zone: a case study in Senegal

A.M. Niang

Synopsis

For the last ten years, the Ecological Monitoring Centre/Centre de suivi écologique (CSE) has been conducting regular monitoring of the Senegalese environment. The pastoral monitoring used by CSE is presented in two stages: (i) a statement of all techniques and programmes that enable the presentation of yearly status, in order to update the pastoral maps and to better choose the transhumance management; and (ii) a case study on a pastoral unit judiciously chosen around a borehole, which will serve as pretext to illustrate an example of a community-based pastoral management plan.

Key Points

1. The monitoring surveys are based on the use of imagery from the National Oceanic and Atmospheric Administration (NOAA)/Advanced Very High Resolution Radiometer (AVHRR) satellite to extract the Normalized Difference of Vegetation Index (NDVI). These data are calibrated to determine the growth of the biomass production available for the rangelands at the end of the rainy season.

2. The survey reconnaissance flights are coupled with aerial photography and videography to count livestock for the evaluation of food needs. These flights enable CSE to confirm or validate the satellite data regularly collected.

3. The ground control sites are distributed over all ecoclimatic zones of the country to measure the herbaceous vegetation and tree production. These sites also provide data on the floristic diversity of the rangelands and their dynamism and the use of information issued from different early warning programmes available at CSE, i.e., the monitoring of agricultural production, fire breaks and rainfall with remote sensing.

1. INTRODUCTION

As in other Sahelian countries, the pastoral resources of Senegal are highly depen-dent on both inter and intra-annual climatic variations. Variability of climate, and particularly rainfall, translates into a high vulnerability of pastoralists and their herds, which are dependent upon scarce water and biomass resources (Behnke, et al., 1993). To improve livestock production and alleviate vulnera-bility, government policies have been implemented to augment water supplies during the 8-9 month dry season in Senegal. Among the numerous water-management interventions made in the pastoral zones, the creation of boreholes has perhaps had the most profound impact, by sedentarizing populations and concentrating herds around these water points during the dry season. As a result of sedentarization, increasing concerns about forage availability and land-degra-dation have been raised. Thus, although boreholes and other water-related inter-ventions have been helpful in lowering climatic-related vulnerability, these are not enough to satisfy fully the biomass needs of pastoralists and their livestock. In order to complement existing development programmes, the CSE has imple-mented a pastoral monitoring programme over the past ten years to:

(i)   create a database available for potential clients and partner institutions that will help lead to sustainable management of the pastoral resources;

(ii)   define the most appropriate methods for monitoring and managing pastoral resources; and

(iii)   apply these methods in pastoral units, in order to facilitate decision-making for monitoring and managing pastoral resources.

The CSE uses such techniques as remote sensing, aerial census and field surveys to support monitoring and management of pastoral ecosystems. Ground validation is routinely carried out as a means to check and calibrate remotely-sensed data and to supplement the CSE's growing database on herd sizes, trends, and pastoral conditions. This has enabled the CSE to provide specific services and information related to pastoral resources such as:

(i)   the monitoring and assessment of rangelands;

(ii)   the counts of livestock for zoo-technical monitoring; and

(iii)   land-cover or land-use maps of pastoral units.

The following sections present a description of the field and remote sensing methods used to estimate and map rangeland production and livestock numbers, the detailed results of recent surveys in several pastoral zones and a specific case study of the pastoral unit of Thiel, which is located in the northern part of Senegal.

2. MONITORING AND ASSESSING RANGELAND VEGETATION PRODUCTION

2.1 Methodology

Each year the CSE produces a vegetation production map based on data provided by polar-orbiting NOAA satellites. This map represents the final product of CSE's annual biomass campaign, and is based upon a combination of different levels of data collection and processing, including:

(i)   the satellite level in which the NDVI is calculated using the red and near-infrared channels of NOAA/AVHRR;

(ii)   the ground level in which above-ground harvest measurements are made on the herbaceous and tree strata at ground sites distributed throughout the study area; and

(iii)   the calibration of image data in which harvest measurements from ground sites are used to develop a linear regression, relating temporal sums of NDVI to biomass production.

2.2 Vegetation production for 1995

The results of the 1995 vegetation map are shown in Colour Plate 8. The map, which shows zones of low production in grey tones and high values in dark green, provides an estimation of the amount of dry matter produced per hectare each year (see map legend). Since the rains were abundant during the wet season of 1995, vegetation production in the natural rangelands was generally satisfactory. CSE field surveys in the Ferlo (the pastoral zone that contains over half of the nation's livestock), suggested that, not only was the quantity sufficient but also that the quality of rangeland vegetation was adequate during much of the dry season. In such cases where resources are adequate, management generally calls for avoidance of fire and overgrazing. In the south, as is normally the case, vegetation production was elevated relative to the north; however, the fodder in the southern zones lignifies very quickly after the rains and remains under constant threat of fires. Furthermore, the quality of the fodder is generally inferior to that found in the north of the country. Under such conditions, policy recommendations generally include selective harvest and conservation of fodder in pastoral management schemes.

3. ANIMAL COUNTS AND ZOO-TECHNICAL MONITORING

3.1 Animal counts

3.1.1 Data collection

In the absence of a precise demarcation of the ten pastoral units, CSE analyzed data from overflights of the zone located within a radius of 20 kilometres (kms) around the boreholes for each unit. The flight lines were 3 km apart, which allowed tightly spaced sampling. The results were considered reliable following the application of a student's t-test. The plane used was a CESSNA 206, with high wings and a maximum flight time of five hours. The flights were done at a low altitude (i.e., 122 metres (m)) and at a constant speed of 180 km/h. In addition, the aircraft was equipped with a Global Positioning System (GPS) that allowed precise navigation along flight lines. Observations were done in the transects, corresponding to 150 m wide for each of the two observers. Next, observers were provided with tape recorders and cameras to record and film areas where the number of animals exceeded ten. The sampling units were spaced at 30 seconds. They corresponded to the same length as the one covered by the plane during 30 seconds and at a width of 300 m, representing the total obtained from the two observers. The following animals were recorded: cattle, small ruminants[1], donkeys and horses. Camels were very scarce and thus were not recorded separately.

3.1.2 Animal counts: data processing

Films were developed as slides and then studied under a microscope for a detailed count of livestock present. This allowed calculation of correction factors for each species and for each observer. This relationship between the number of animals counted on the photograph and the visual estimation for the same livestock type is necessary to compare the results of different observers and to arrive at global estimations of stocking rates. The information is then entered into CSE's computers to test statistical reliability as indicated above. Specific estimations, gathered for each point, were allocated an averaged value and a geographical reference (UTM projection) using the computer software. This program allows the computer to select all the points within each unit and calculate the livestock density per km^2 for each species. Often the number of horses and donkeys is very low and thus not statistically valid for purposes of reporting. However, these animals are taken into account in the estimation of the number of Tropical Livestock Units (TLUs) in the ten pastoral units surveyed.

1/ This term concerns the sheep and goats that are difficult to differentiate at high altitude.

3.1.3 Results of the analysis

Table 21.1 shows that the majority of cattle were concentrated in the three pastoral units of Mbar Toubab (48 949), Kamb (36 831) and Amali (30 067), which include 47% of the total bovine population (as opposed to 53% for the seven others). The concentration of cattle around the pastoral units, located near the Ferlo Valley, can be explained by the movement to the valley of animals from Mbeuleukhe village at the time of counting. Moreover, the area around the Lake de Guiers shows the highest cattle density (39 head/km²) within Mbar Toubab. In fact, the availability of surface water in this area favoured the development of an herbaceous layer that remains green in the dry season, justifying the presence of a high number of herders leading their animals to this high-quality forage. High numbers of cattle have been located in the pastoral unit of Thiargny where the available fodder was very high (i.e., 1 280 kg of dry matter/km²). On the other hand, the survey team found that for the pastoral unit of Tessekre there was only 10 734 head/km², due to the lack of good pastoral land (it had a very low fodder production - 837 kg of dry matter /km² and the early dry fodder). Cattle numbers were also very low at Thiel (12 969 head), despite an adequate fodder production (1 064 kg of dry matter/km²).

Table 21.1

Total livestock units (TLUs) in the ten pastoral units surveyed

Pastoral unit	Number of Cattle	Number of Small Ruminants	Total (TLUs)
Thiel	12,969	49,408	16,469
Thiargny	26,692	72,136	29,371
Velingara	22,273	89,647	27,719
Tessekre	10,734	38,753	12,987
Amali	30,067	57,309	30,128
Kamb	36,831	94,647	39,487
Mbar Toubab	48,949	62,643	43,803
Yare Lao	22,179	79,649	26,653
Atch Bali	21,663	47,995	22,512
Revane	13,308	48,724	15,552

Source: CSE

In some areas, it was noted that pastoralists had moved their herds out of the traditional pastoral zones of the Ferlo toward areas of higher biomass such as Velingara. Three explanations are generally given for this movement:

(i)   the malfunctioning of boreholes;

(ii)   the reduction of fodder due to bush fires; and

(iii) the scarcity of boreholes, except in the southeast where the majority of registered livestock are located.

The CSE surveys also noted that the proportion of small ruminants to cattle seems to have increased, confirming the tendency of the cattle breeders to favour smaller animals which, beside their higher fertility rates, seem to adapt better to drought (CSE, 1994). Thus, the survey found 94 647 head of small ruminants at Kamb (i.e., three times the number of cattle), followed by Velingara, Thiargny and Mbar Toubab, with 89 647, 72 136 and 62 643 head, respectively. The smallest number was registered at Tessekre (38 753 head) and at Thiel (49 408 head). The expression of the results in TLUs (Table 21.1) shows a high concentration of animals in the pastoral unit of Mbar Toubab (43 803 TLUs for a density of 34.87 TLUs/km^2) and in Kamb (39 487 TLUs, as opposed to Tessekre and Revane where there were only 12 987 TLUs and 15 552 TLUs, respectively).

3.2 Comparison of production and stocking rates at the pastoral-unit level

Primary pasture production data in six pastoral units permit assessment of the rangelands in areas of high stocking rates. Table 21.2 shows that among pastoral units surveyed only Mbar Toubab was overstocked (stocking rate/carrying capacity > 100) relative to biomass availability. However, inter-annual comparison suggests that the pastoral unit of Mbar Toubab was less overstocked than the previous year, and subsequent field surveys suggest that the pastoral units of Thiargny and Thiel may have been overstocked at the end of the rainy season.

Table 21.2

Pasture production of the ten pastoral units surveyed

Pastoral unit	Total biomass	Usable biomass	Herd size (TLU)	Carrying capacity	Stocking rate / Carrying capacity (%)
Thiel	2,129	710	16,469	54,609	30
Thiargny	2,130	710	29,371	54,609	54
Velingara	2,041	580	27,719	41,867	66
Tessekre	1,651	550	12,987	41,867	31
Amali	1,975	658	30,128	48,308	62
Kamb	1,927	642	39,487	48,308	82
Mbar Toubab	1,619	540	43,803	41,867	105
Yare Lao	1,241	414	26,653	31,400	85
Atch Bali	1,152	384	22,512	28,545	79
Revane	1,678	559	15,552	41,866	37

Source: CSE

3.3 Demographic (zoo-technical) monitoring

3.3.1 Methodology

Ground surveys were concentrated in north-east Senegal, where approximately 18% of the country's total livestock is found. Livestock were randomly chosen to enable determination of the evolution of the herd and zoo-technical parameters and the impact of the population changes on the surrounding livestock. It should also be noted that in the following sections, the absolute differences in animal counts between years were due to the number of samples gathered, and thus relative differences (expressed as percentages or rates in Tables 21.3-7) should be used in comparing inter-annual changes in herd size and composition.

Table 21.3

Composition of cattle

Year	Category	Size	Percentage
1993-94	Calves	345	20
1,717	Young bullocks, Young bulls, heifers	349	21
	Bulls and bullocks	107	6
	Cows (4-10 years old)	722	42
	Cows (+ 10 years old)	194	11
1994-95	Calves	87	21
417	Young bullocks, Young bulls, heifers	66	17
	Bulls and bullocks	23	6
	Cows (4-10 years old)	202	48
	Cows (+ 10 years old)	39	9

Source: CSE

The livestock were visited regularly and all events were noted on a livestock sheet. After the initial annual census, periodic observations were made on the herds, in order to note events that had occurred. At the end of each observation series, a synthesis is done for each pastoral unit. This synthesis allows calculation of the evolution and the productivity of herd parameters. The sheets obtained from the sampled cattle allow calculation of only certain zoo-technical parameters. These include the fecundity rate, death rate and the zoo-economical parameters.

3.3.2 Results and analysis

The examination of herd composition over the last two years shows that the number of young animals is far less than that of older animals. In general, this situation does not favour the expansion of herd sizes.

Calves are considered as such from 0-1 year old. Young bulls, steers and heifers are considered as such from 1-3 years old. At over 4 years old, animals are considered as adults and the pyramid is established on this basis. Examination of Table 21.3 shows clearly that cows are kept much longer than other animals. To simplify the interpretation, females are represented by negative values. Among females, it was found that animals over ten years old represent 11% of the total population. In the study area, the age of first calving of the female reproducers is four years. Two categories of reproducing females can thus be distinguished: cows of 4-10 years old and cows of more than 10 years old.

Table 21.4

Composition of herds according to sex and age

Males			Females		
Year 1993-94	size	%	Year 1993-94	size	%
Calves	142	8	Calves	203	12
Young bulls/steers	106	6	Heifers	243	14
Bulls/bullocks	107	6	Cows (4-10 years old)	722	42
			Cows (over 10 years old)	194	12
Year 1993-94	size	%	Year 1993-94	size	%
Calves	49	12	Calves	38	9
Young bulls/steers	31	7	Heifers	35	8
Bulls/bullocks	23	6	Cows (4-10 years old)	202	48
			Cows (over 10 years old)	39	9

Source: CSE

Table 21.5 shows that the fecundity rate was positive during 1995. This can be explained by the abundant and rich grazing lands comprised of grasses (Gramineae) and leguminous species (e.g., Zornia sp.), which provide high-quality forage and are sought after by the livestock.

Table 21.5

Fecundity rate of cows

Years	No. of births	Cows, beg. of year	Cows, end of year	Mean values	Fecundity rate
1993-94	492	916	845	880	56
1994-95	143	241	228	235	61

Source: CSE

Table 21.6 illustrates that the conservation of females over ten years old appeared to have a negative effect on the livestock productivity, since females aged over ten years old are in a status of physiological stress which is often incompatible with reproduction. Furthermore, old animals lose much of their weight during the dry season. This affects their reproductive quality and greater time is required after the arrival of the next rainy season to regain the weight attained at the end of the previous wet season.

Table 21.6

Fecundity rate of cows according to the categories of females

Years	No. of births	Cows, 4-10 years old	Cows, over 10 years old	Rate 1	Rate 2
1993-94	492	694	880	71	56
1994-95	143	200	235	72	61

Source: CSE

Table 21.7 reflects that the average for two years at the 10% rate (i.e., 10 bulls for 100 females) is well above the fixed norms estimated at four bulls for 100 females. This suggests that cattle breeders did not castrate non-reproducing males.

Table 21.7

Distribution of bulls and reproducing females

Years	No. of bulls	No. of reproducers	Percentage
1993-94	80	916	9
1994-95	26	235	11

Source: CSE

3.3.3 Mortality factors

Generally speaking, the death rates vary according to the different categories of animals. The mortality rate is much higher with the young and especially males. Deaths also vary according to season. Mortality is more likely during the hot dry season. The primary causes of death are physiological stress, disease and accidents. As opposed to the dry season of 1993-1994, the death rate during 1994-95 appeared to be low (Table 21.8).

Table 21.8

Total mortality of cattle

Years	Initial number	Mortality	Percentage
1993-94	1,717	132	8
1994-95	417	43	10

Source: CSE

Table 21.9 shows that the 0-1 year old death rate is low compared to norms estimated at 20-40%. The year 1994-95 had been marked by a high rate compared to the previous year.

Table 21.9

Mortality of young animals aged 0-1 year old.

Years	Initial number	Mortality	Percentage
1993-94	492	32	6
1994-95	230	32	14

Source: CSE

The study of the frequencies shows that the death was higher among cows during 1993-94, but that during 1994-95, deaths were higher among young animals (Table 21.10).

Table 21.10

Mortality according to sex and age (frequency based on the total number of deaths).

Years	Category of males	No.	Mort.	%	Fr.	Females	No.	Mort.	%	Fr.
1993-94	Calves	187	19	10	14	Calves	305	13	4	10
(132 deaths)	Young bulls/steers	248	18	7	14	Heifers	446	16	4	12
	Bulls/bullocks	107	11	10	8	Cows	916	55	6	42
1994-95	Calves	122	20	16	46	Calves	109	12	11	28
(43 deaths)	Young bulls/steers	31	3	10	7	Heifers	35	2	6	5
	Bulls/bullocks	23	2	9	5	Cows	235	4	2	9

Source: CSE

No. = number   Mort. = mortality   % = percentage   fr. = frequency

3.3.4 Market (zoo-economical) factors

The exploitation of cattle relates to the number of animals removed from herds. It includes the voluntary exploitation resulting from decisions made by pastoralists themselves and the urgent exploitation necessary to deal with wounded or sick animals.

The working rate of the cattle refers to the amount of selling, slaughter and gifts of animals. Available data enable the definition of the working rate reported as the size at the beginning of the year. The high working rate during 1994-95 may be explained by the rate of cereal production needed to overcome this period. In fact, agropastoralists were obliged to sell some of the animals in order to buy these provisions (Table 21.11).

Table 21.11

Working rate of cattle

Years	Initial size	No. of animals sold	Gifts	Working rate	Selling rate
1993-94	1 717	172	28	12	10
1994-95	417	56	38	23	13

Source: CSE

During 1993-94, sales mainly involved males and young animals over one year old. The high sales of males and young animals indicate that pastoralists give more importance to maintaining heifers. During 1994-95, in addition to sales of the young males, pastoralists also tended to sell old female animals (Table 21.12).

Table 21.12

Animal sales by category

Years	Category of animals	No. of animals sold	% animals sold
1993-94	Young (males)	90	52
	Young (females)	25	15
	Adult (males)	42	24
	Adult (females)	15	9
1994-95	Young (males)	33	59
	Young (females)	5	9
	Adult (males)	3	5
	Adult (females)	15	27

Source: CSE

4. CASE STUDY: CARTOGRAPHY OF THE PASTORAL UNIT OF THIEL

4.1 Base map

4.1.1 Methodology

The field data coordinates of mapped attributes were collected using a GPS. Thus, the villages, wells and ponds of each pastoral unit have been visited in order to register their coordinates. The GPS used gave an accuracy of ± 100 meters. The procedures used to elaborate the base map included the following:

(i)   transformation of geographical coordinates into UTM coordinates;
(ii)   data entry of the base information from the National Geographic Institute/Institut Géographique National map (1:200 000);
(iii)   creation of the database (locations, ponds, boreholes and drills); and
(iv)   creation of a buffer, based on a radius of influence around boreholes (around 20 km).

4.2 Soil map

4.2.1 Methodology

From the file created by the buffer, a buffer zone around the borehole is extracted and the soil types that were gathered in the survey of each pastoral unit of Thiel were elaborated.

4.2.2 Results and analysis

The analysis of these soil maps shows the different types of soil found in each pastoral unit of Thiel (Table 21.13). This information permits soil types to be related to vegetation and helps to explain the agro-sylvi-pastoral practices of each pastoral unit. Generally, it is worth noting that ponds are located on the following three types of soils: hydromorphous; tropical ferruginous; and lithosols on cuirass. However, it should be borne in mind that fossil river valleys serve as drinking points during the wet season.

Table 21.13

Soil characteristics of pastoral units of Thiel.

Soil type	Areas (ha)	%
Hydromorphous soil on clay material	638	7.6
Hydromorphous soil on sandy material	8 730	10.4
Tropical ferruginous soil, not or weakly-leached, with linear ponds	27 533	32.7
Tropical ferruginous soil, not or weakly-leached, without linear ponds	13 474	16
Tropical ferruginous soil, weakly-leached and well-drained	1 888	2.2
Tropical ferruginous soil, weakly-leached and poorly-drained	31 991	38

Source: CSE

4.3 Synthesis maps

4.3.1 Methodology

Synthesis maps were obtained from the overlay of layers such as the soil and base maps.

4.3.2 Results and analysis

The study of the maps of pastoral units enables identification of the exact location of ponds according to the types of mapped soils. The absence of ponds in the sandy units is a common feature and this helps to explain the lack of natural water bodies in the pastoral unit of Tessekre, which is typically characterized by eolian soil formation.

4.4 Land-cover maps

4.4.1 Methodology and image processing

The land-cover maps currently realized from SPOT and Landsat images provide information on vegetation formations and infrastructure. The processing of these images, including rectification and resampling, was done using CHIPS software, which is produced and supported by the Institute of Geography, University of Copenhagen. Non-supervised classification was carried out, and histograms of the various image channels were examined to determine suitable land-cover classes. The analysis of image statistics using ERDAS software indicated 30 spectral classes based on signature extraction. Ground verification allowed characterization of each class, according to its correspondence with land-cover observed in the field.

4.4.2 Ground truthing

Ground truthing was carried out which allowed:

(i)   verification of the mapped units at various points georeferenced by GPS; and

(ii)   characterization of the mapped units as related to the vegetation formation, which was assessed using the principal species and their abundance-dominance methods (Bonham, 1989).

4.4.3 Results and analysis

Table 21.14 provides information on the landcover found in the pastoral units, which is based on:

(i)   natural vegetation (including its level of degradation);
(ii)   agricultural area;
(iii) bare soil;
(iv)   settlements;
(v)   water points; and
(vi)   the tracks.

These elements help to elaborate the natural and infrastructural resources available for each pastoral unit.

Table 21.14

Land cover in the pastoral units of Thiel

Pastoral Units	Coverage (%)	Areas (ha)	Proportion %
Bare soils	0	2,668	3.19
Agricultural areas	0	18,829	22.51
Shrub savanna very dense on depression	+75	17,738	21.21
Dense shrub savanna	50 to 75	9,125	10.91
Bare tree savanna	10 to 25	2,725	3.26
Bare tree savanna	10	8,377	10.02
Bare shrub savanna	+75	3,803	4.54
Very dense tree savanna on depression	50 to 75	9,733	11.63
Bare tree savanna	10 to 25	8,178	9.77
Bare tree savanna	10	2,467	2.94
TOTAL			100

Source: CSE

5. CONCLUSIONS

Information on the status of the pastoral resources helps decision-makers and planners to determine appropriate resource use and future development interventions. This paper presents the results of recent pastoral surveys done by the CSE and underlines the usefulness of remote sensing and ground surveys for accurate, real-time monitoring of herd sizes and distributions, biomass availability and mapping of land cover and infrastructure.

By comparing herd densities with biomass production estimates obtained from field and AVHRR data, the results of CSE's recent pastoral monitoring campaigns suggest that overstocking of cattle was relatively rare in the ten pastoral units studied. Interestingly, this result is consistent with national-scale estimates for 1991 prepared by the CSE (Consere, 1996), which show that overstocking nationwide was relatively uncommon and found in only a few small areas in the main agricultural zone (the "peanut basin") and in the Senegal River Valley. Thus, results obtained at two different scales (national and local) indicated that overstocking is relatively infrequent in the main pastoral zone, the Ferlo. However, this does not mean that overstocking is always a rare phenomenon. Malfunctioning boreholes throughout the Sahelian region, for example, often produce concentration of herds around the few remaining water points during the middle and end of the dry season, which in turn may lead to severe overstocking and compaction and degradation of soils (Behnke, et al., 1993).

In addition to the analysis of carrying capacity, demographic, zoo-technical, and market (zoo-economic) data are presented, which help to explain short-term fluctuations in livestock composition. These, and other results, indicate that monitoring of vegetation production should be complemented by market and demographic surveys, in order to understand fully short-term herd dynamics.

References

Behnke, R.H., Scoones, I., and Kerven, C. 1993. *Range ecology at disequilibrium: new models of natural variability and pastoral adaptation in African savannas.* Overseas Development Institute, London.

Bonham, C. 1989. *Measurements for Terrestrial Vegetation.* John Wiley & Sons, New York.

Centre de Suivi Ecologique (CSE). 1994. PAPEL Systematic Reconnaisance Flight Report. Dakar, Senegal.

Conseil Superieur Des Ressources Naturelles et de l'Environnement (Consere). 1996. *Phénomène et effets de la sécheresse et de la desertification au Sénégal.* Etude N°96/001, Sécheresse et Désertification (CONS-001), Rapport N° 01. Dakar, Senegal.

Rapid resource assessment and environmental monitoring using low level aerial surveys

22

W. Wint

Synopsis

This paper considers the role of the integrated (low-level) aerial and ground survey for rangeland resource assessment, in the context of recent advances in remote sensing. It attempts to identify the 'niche' for which this role is best suited. Examples are taken from more than 50 surveys carried out throughout sub-Saharan Africa between 1984 and 1994, in order to demonstrate the scope, adaptability and suitability of the methods available, especially for the censuses of livestock and human habitation. The future usefulness of the low-level aerial survey, in the context of 'high tech' resource assessment techniques, is considered.

Key Points

1. *A range of techniques is available for rangeland resource assessment and environmental monitoring: from satellite imagery, aerial photography and aerial observation to ground truth studies; and from total coverage to random, stratified or systematic sample surveys. Each technique has its own advantages and drawbacks in terms of the resolution, cost, personnel and logistic support required, and (most importantly) the parameters that can be assessed reliably and cost effectively.*

2. *A number of potential and actual applications of the data collected by this methodology are described, including: estimating and mapping human and livestock populations and land cover; establishing the role of livestock in relation to their agro-economic environment; defining livestock and agricultural systems; assessing land degradation; and 'ground truthing' remotely sensed vegetation data. Land use can also be assessed by this technique, either visually (e.g., during a livestock survey, at no additional cost) or photogrammetrically.*

3. *Because such survey techniques are based on sample counts, large areas can be covered rapidly, and substantial databases can readily be accumulated. This information can easily be amalgamated with other remotely sensed or cartographic data.*
4. *There remains a role for low-level aerial survey techniques, despite recent advances in remote sensing technology.*

1. INTRODUCTION

Sustainable use of rangelands requires access to reliable baseline information. These data are provided by rangeland resource assessment and monitoring of a variety of types of information, including: the distribution, productivity and composition of natural vegetation and agricultural land; rainfall and temperature regimes; edaphic and hydrological data, rangeland utilization by wild and domesticated animals; land tenure and ownership; and socio-economic information and marketing.

Rangelands are not, however, static entities, but usually are subject to major seasonal variations, as well as longer-term cycles of drought and recovery. Given the inexorable rise in the human populations that exploit the rangelands, there is often a general medium to long-term trend towards overgrazing and degradation. It is, therefore, not enough to furnish baseline data alone and a temporal perspective is essential if planning for sustainable rangeland exploitation is to be feasible.

A properly planned rangeland resource assessment and environmental monitoring programme must include both an initial study to establish prevalent resource levels and, if possible, establish broad historical trends; and a longer-term monitoring exercise to maintain the currency of the information and identify ongoing trends. The techniques used for each of these two phases may differ, provided the various methods produce compatible and comparable information.

Techniques available range from the use of satellite imagery, aerial photography, videography and aerial observation to ground-based studies; from total coverage to random, stratified or systematic sample surveys. Each technique has its own advantages and drawbacks in terms of the resolution, cost, personnel and logistic support required, and (most importantly) the parameters that can be assessed reliably and cost-effectively.

This paper considers the role of low-level aerial survey techniques, as initiated in the early 1980s and developed to date, and attempts to identify the 'niche' for which they are best suited.

2. AERIAL SURVEYS

2.1 High-level survey

High-level surveys are usually flown at heights of some 5 000 to 10 000 feet (ft) above ground level (agl) and are primarily suited for cartography (i.e., the production of maps), using high-resolution photography (both digital and conventional), or airborne radar and radiometry sensors. Such techniques are frequently used for vegetation mapping, geological and hydrological assessment, or by dint of stereo photography, for the production of topographic maps. This technique has, until relatively recently, been the basis of most national map series.

Because of the comparatively high unit cost - in the region of tens to hundreds of dollars per square kilometre - high-level aerial surveys are increasingly used for military purposes or for surveys of areas measured in hectares (ha) rather than square kilometres (km²), and are less widely commissioned for large areas. Despite the clarity consequent upon their potentially high resolution (i.e., in the order of one metre), high-level aerial survey techniques cannot readily be adapted for the assessment of animal populations.

2.2 Low-level survey

Low-level aerial surveys are normally flown between 400 and 2 000 ft agl, and are most often designed to collect numerical information about target animal populations and distributions over large, often remote areas, in a short period. The air crew usually consists of a coordinator/navigator, pilot, and two observers or photographers. The survey technique is usually based on a systematic reconnaissance flight (SRF) sampling pattern that provides uniform coverage of an entire region and enables a geographically coordinated gridded database to be established. As a result, unit costs are substantially lower than for high-level coverage (e.g., around USD 2-5 per square kilometre), and are less susceptible to interference from atmospheric dust or clouds.

Key features of this technique are its repeatability, and that it does not rely on any previous knowledge of the area concerned. Repeat surveys at different times of the year allow seasonal changes in distribution and abundance to be determined.

2.2.1 Sampling strategies

SRF surveys are able to obtain a wide range of information, through visual observation, or by photographic or videographic means. The essence of the technique rests on systematic flights over a whole survey zone, but using sampling rather than total coverage of the area concerned. A systematic sample from a patchy population ensures that all parts are represented in the correct proportions, whereas a random sample may fall in areas of high or low density more often than the proportion of such areas in the population would suggest.

Furthermore, a systematic sample provides more or less constant accuracy throughout the sampling frame, unless there are regular and periodic spatial patterns in the population's distribution. This is extremely unlikely to be the case for any natural system.

As far as stratification is concerned, (i.e., the sampling of different sectors of a survey site at different intensities), there are arguments both for and against this strategy. The points in favour of stratification are essentially that areas with low populations can be sampled at low intensity, whilst those with high numbers can be covered more intensively, and thus with greater precision.

This, however, presupposes some advance knowledge of the distribution of a population within the survey site. It is also complicated by the very real possibility that different target populations have different distribution patterns. The choice of a particular stratified strategy might, for example, increase the precision of cattle population estimates but would have the reverse effect as far as camels were concerned. Similarly, stratification in favour of cultivated land could adversely effect the reliability of estimates of woodland or forest. Thus, if the provision of overall distribution maps and population estimates for a range of parameters is required, then all the advantages rest with unstratified sampling.

In view of these arguments, the default technique generally adopted follows standard procedures of SRFs, described by Norton-Griffiths (1978) and Clark (1986), in which a series of parallel flight lines are flown over the given region at an equal distance apart. Each flight line is divided into sectors of equal length to form a sampling grid, often based on the Universal Transverse Mercator (UTM) projection.

The aircraft is usually flown along the centre line of each grid and observations are made from, or photographs taken of, a fixed sample band (Figure 22.1). The size of each cell depends on the desired sample intensity for a given survey. The grid-cell sizes commonly vary from 1 x 1 km, to 20 x 20 km, which result in sample percentages of between 2% and 50%, according to flying height and strip width.

The major consequence of choosing a systematic sampling pattern is that the calculation of the error term is somewhat complex, as it has to be calculated from what is, statistically speaking, a single estimate of the target population for the whole survey area. The population estimates and associated standard errors (SEs) of aerial survey data may be calculated using either the Jolly Ratio Method

Figure 22.1

Aerial Survey Grids

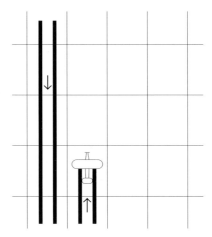

(which uses the flight line as the sample unit), or the Marriott 4-Cell Method, for which the grid cell or 'sub-unit' is the sample unit. The relative advantages of each are discussed at length in Marriott and Wint (1985), and depend on the spatial integrity of the survey area, as well as the distribution pattern of the population within it.

Both methods will tend to give similar SEs if the target animals are evenly spread throughout a survey area, or if they are rare and found in isolated large groups. The Jolly SE estimates will tend to be lower, if the targets are quite abundant and aggregated in large herds regularly spaced throughout the area. The Marriott SE estimates will tend to be the lower if there is any spatial trend in numbers from one end of a flight line to the other, or if there are substantial areas of high density, surrounded by less well-stocked regions.

It should be emphasized that both methods are statistically conservative, and give rise to SEs well above the inherent errors of the sampling strategies used. There is thus a case for using whichever method provides the lower calculated SE. It is also stressed that, although the calculated standard errors may differ, depending on the method adopted and the underlying statistical assumptions, the size of the estimated population is not affected.

The aircraft flies in parallel lines over the study area, and observers record from fixed sample bands to each side. The flight lines are divided into equal sectors, to create a grid-cell lattice, by which each record is located.

The formulae for the total population, the variance and the Jolly standard error are:

Population Total: $\qquad$ $Y = Z \cdot R$

Population Variance: $\qquad$ $Var\,(Y) = \dfrac{N(N - n).(s^2_y - 2.R.s_{yz} + R.s^2_z)}{n}$

where: $\qquad$ Y $\;$ = total population estimate.

$\qquad$ N $\;$ = potential number of sample units in the survey region.

$\qquad$ n $\;$ = actual number of sample units surveyed.

$\qquad$ Z $\;$ = area of the survey region.

$\qquad$ z $\;$ = area of any one sample unit.

$\qquad$ y $\;$ = number of animals counted in that unit.

$\qquad$ R $\;$ = ratio of the animals counted to the area searched ($\Sigma y/\Sigma z$).

and:

$\qquad$ s^2_y = variance of animals counted between sample units.

$\qquad$ s^2_z = variance of sampled area between sample units.

$\qquad$ s_{yz} = covariance between counts and areas of each unit.

Note that, for the Jolly estimate, flight lines can be defined in either the horizontal or vertical orientation, and given the conservatism of the method, it is acceptable to use the direction which gives the lowest SE.

The relevant formula for the Marriott standard error is:

$$Var\,(Y) = \Sigma \frac{(4y(i,j)-y(i-1,j)-y(i+1,j)-y(i,j-1)-y(i,j+1))^2}{20n^*}$$

where:

$\qquad$ Y $\;$ = total population estimate.

$\qquad$ i,j = coordinates of a grid point.

$\qquad$ y $\;$ = number of items recorded for a given grid.

$\qquad$ n $\;$ = number of grid points with four surrounding neighbours.

The standard error is the square root of the variance of the estimate, based on the difference between sample value (y) at point (i,j) and the average of its four neighbours, provided they all fall within the overall survey sample.

2.2.2 Photography and videography

Low-level aerial photography (LLAP) can be carried out using either video or small-format (35 mm) still cameras. As videography is the subject of a separate workshop paper, only small-format still cameras will be considered here.

LLAP surveys have been used largely for estimating crops or natural vegetation cover, with vertically mounted cameras, usually equipped with wide-angle lenses to maximize the sample size. Telephoto lenses can also be fitted to permit the ancillary identification of individual crops. The cameras have data backs to imprint time and frame identifiers on each photograph, and with intervalometers which control the exposure frequency. Typically, such surveys would be flown at 2 000 ft agl, giving frame dimensions of 900 m x 600 m on the ground, so that a continuous strip coverage can be produced from exposures as intervals of 20-30 seconds (or approximately 1.5 hours per bulk film).

A survey of substantial size can require several thousand photographs from which the requisite data must be extracted, which precludes the use of digital photography unless very substantial data storage and processing power is available. Thus, photo-interpretation is most effectively done manually, and is carried out by point sampling of the projected colour images at a scale of 1:1 000. Each slide is projected onto a matt-white screen with a 6 x 4 array of 24 cross-hair sample points, being the number closest to 20 (the minimum number of replicates required) that fit in a regular, and thus unbiased, lattice within the shape of the photograph.

Because the ground coverage of each frame is dependent upon the flying height, which can vary by 100 feet or more, this technique is not suited to absolute measures of vegetation cover, but rather to estimating percentage cover. Interpreters thus classify each sample point into one of several mutually exclusive and easily distinguishable land-cover categories, such as: tree canopy; shrub cover; farmland; and other (e.g., bare ground, water, or grassland). The occurrence of a number of additional features anywhere within a frame, such as severe erosion, major towns, roads and large rivers, may also recorded.

2.2.3 Visual observation

Attempts have been made in recent years to use satellite imagery and conventional aerial photography to estimate animal populations. However, the availability of satellite imagery and the resolution of both imagery and photography are generally such that they are not appropriate for the assessment of livestock or wildlife populations. High-resolution aircraft-mounted video has also been tried in a number of areas, with limited success, as the equipment needed to stabilize the video platform is expensive, prone to malfunction and produces tapes which require a substantial amount of time to analyze. As a result, animal populations are best assessed using visual observation.

2.2.4 Methodology

Only the animals within a fixed strip of ground on either side of the aircraft, delineated by viewing frames, are recorded. Each observer is also required, wherever possible, to take photographs of all herds (in excess of ten) falling within the ground sampling strip. These photographs can be used in two ways: either by using them as the primary source of counts; or as a means to calculate observer counting error that can then be applied to all observer counts. The first of these is less reliable in areas with significant vegetation cover, as animals may be obscured from the lens, and a calibration exercise must be carried out to provide correction factors for different cover levels and types.

Observers, by contrast, have a more flexible field of view as they can look forward and backward along the strip, and are therefore able to see (and count) the animals sheltering under trees and bushes. Comparison of subsequent accurate photocounts with the estimates recorded by observers during the survey allow an individual counting bias to be determined for each parameter recorded. These biases are used to correct those estimates for which clear photographs are unavailable. Calculated observer biases are usually less than 5%, and commonly between 1% and 2%.

Although the technique was developed for the estimation of animal populations, it can be effectively used to count human habitations, or indeed any target that is visible from the air (Tables 22.1). Rural habitation may be divided into village and pastoral dwellings. In many cases, distinctive sub-types may also be distinguished; for example, Fulani rugas and Twareg tents in West Africa, Beja tents in The Sudan and Tiv huts in Nigeria. Major urban centres and large towns are not easily estimated visually, and are better assessed photographically.

Table 22.1

Information typically collected from the air

WITHIN THE SAMPLE BAND		
Numbers	Animals	Cattle, sheep and goats, horses and donkeys, camels, wild animals
	Habitation and Settlements	Villages, rooftops of selected architectural types, Compounds, tents of selected architectural types
	Other	Corrals, tar roads, all weather roads, tracks Rivers and open water, wells
WITHIN EACH GRID		
		Presence of open water, % cultivation, % grassland, % burned ground, gully and sheet erosion score (0-5) % open canopy woodland, % savanna woodland, grass cover, indicator plant species (e.g., Calotropis spp) Flying altitude, direction and time

These paramaters are not an exhaustive list, but are indicative of those data commonly collected during SRF surveys.

Whilst visual observation is primarily used for estimating animals and human habitation, it may also be used to collect estimates of land cover, though within each survey grid rather than within the observation strips. Typical cover types assessed are: land within the cultivation cycle (active cropping plus fallow); bare ground; grassland; scrub; open woodland; dense woodland; and forest.

As these are assessed visually by the front-seat observer, the estimates are obviously not as precise as those provided by photogrammetric methods. They are, however, sufficiently accurate to provide useful information and, equally importantly, involve little if any incremental cost.

2.2.5 Data accuracy

Data accuracy is shown by repeated estimates of permanent habitation levels that should change little from year to year. For example, in the Bahr el Ghazal region of Chad, the 1991 and 1993 estimates for permanent numbers were 79 700 and 82 800 km^2 respectively; and for Niger State of Nigeria, permanent habitation estimates for 1989 and 1990 were 17.5 and 17.8 per square km^2, respectively.

The accuracy of the visual vegetation estimates may be assessed either by comparing repeated measures of the same parameter, or by comparing the visual estimates with those derived from a different methodology. For example, in the Bahr el Ghazal region of Chad, woody vegetation was assessed in 1991 at 14.3%, and in 1993 at 13.6%. In Gongola State, Nigeria, percentage grassland was estimated in 1983 and 1984 at 14 and 17%, respectively; and in Niger State of Nigeria, cultivation was estimated in 1989 and 1990 at 20 and 21%, respectively. These comparisons provide reasonable grounds for believing that these vegetation and land-use parameters are sufficiently precise to be meaningful.

During the course of 1990, active cultivation in northern Nigeria was assessed visually, and through the interpretation of aerial photographs together with concurrent Landsat MSS satellite imagery. A comparison of the results from both techniques is illustrated in Figure 22.2. As can be seen, the mean percentages assessed are almost identical, and the regression line between the two shows a highly significant and linear correlation. This suggests that, once again, visual estimates of land use are accurate and reliable.

The photographic survey of 1990 also assessed the percentage of tree canopy cover within each photograph. This measure differs from the percentage of open or dense woodland assessed visually, but comparison of the two sets of data can be made to ensure that there is a linear relationship between the land-use categories and the canopy cover. The same comparison can also be used to calculate the average percentage canopy cover that each visual vegetation category represents.

Figure 22.2

Comparison of visual and photographic cultivation estimates

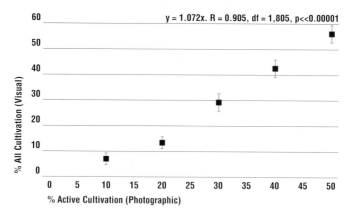

Mean %:- Visual = 32.5, SE = 1.14. Photographic = 32.05, SE = 0.47. T= - 0.72, ns

Figure 22.3 demonstrates a clear linear relationship between photographic and visually assessed parameters, and the slopes of the two fitted regression lines suggest an average canopy cover of approximately 40% for open woodland, and 60% for dense woodland. Given that the visual estimates also assessed closed canopy forest and the non-wooded vegetation categories, this implies that open woodland represents 5 to 50% canopy cover, and dense woodland 50 to 95% canopy cover.

Figure 22.3

Comparison of visual and photographic woodland categories

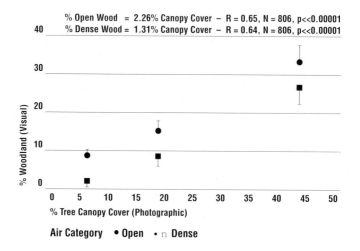

2.3 Integrated surveys

Low-level aerial surveys alone, both photographic and visual, have significant limitations. Photographic techniques can provide percentage of vegetation cover, but little crop or forest production data. Visual counts of animals are limited to larger species, and do not distinguish between sheep and goats. They are also, for example, unable to assess the numbers of animals under cover in villages.

These limitations can be overcome through integrating aerial survey techniques with ground survey methods designed to collect information which cannot be obtained from aerial reconnaissance, such as the proportion of sheep and goats in small ruminant herds, or to provide data which can be combined with aerial counts to give estimates of parameters which would otherwise be impractical. An example is the number of poultry kept in rural villages. Air counts give the number of habitations in a sample grid; ground counts provide the number of birds per habitation. Combining the two figures gives village poultry population estimates and distributions. This integrated air/ground approach provides an objective basis for resource assessment and a better understanding of local production systems. Table 22.2 illustrates parameters that may be collected by the ground element of an integrated livestock survey.

Integrated surveys can also be used to differentiate between the large ruminants associated with human settlement, and those more pastorally managed animals that are found away from villages. This distinction is made by ensuring that the aerial survey observers either record animals seen within village boundaries separately from those elsewhere, or exclude such livestock from the aerial counts altogether. If the latter course is adopted, then the estimates of total livestock numbers are calculated by adding the numbers derived from aerial counts to those derived from the ground survey and aerial habitation records. If it is assumed that the aerial counts represent pastorally managed animals, then the two sets of figures can be used to give an indication of the populations of animals managed by transhumant/nomadic pastoralists (the "pastoral" element) and those managed by mixed farmers or settled agropastoralists ("village" animals).

Ground survey can also be integrated with aerial survey techniques to produce estimates of vegetation standing crop. A fuelwood survey of northern Nigeria, covering some 322 000 km², relied on the integrated use of low-level aerial photography, ground validation and satellite imagery. Over 5 000 photographs were taken and assessed for the proportion of tree canopy cover, from which the canopy area was calculated for each of six land-use categories identified from satellite imagery.

In addition, some 6 700 trees, of 140 species in nearly 150 sample sites, were measured for canopy and trunk dimension. Using available conversion tables,

Table 22.2

Illustrative ground survey parameters: integrated livestock survey

Numbers per habitation		Presence or absence of:	
Camels		Pack oxen	
Cattle:	Zebu	Horse mills	
	Muturu	Water drawing	
	Others	Browse cutting	
Goats		Night grazing	
Sheep		Theft	
Horses		Dairying species:	Camels
Donkeys			Cattle
Pigs			Sheep
Chickens			Goats
Turkeys		Fattening stock:	Cattle
Pigeons			Sheep
Guinea-fowl			Goats
Ducks		Ploughing with:	Camels
Guinea			Oxen
Dogs			Bulls
Cats			Carting
Rabbits		Keeping of female:	Camels
Giant rats			Cattle
Tortoises			Goats
Fish-wells			Donkeys
Snail Farms		Dairy products:	Fresh milk
Fish ponds			Butter
Bee hives		Purchase of:	Supplementary feeds
			Mineral blocks

Source: Unpublished

these ground data were then converted to wood volumes per unit area of canopy which, when combined with the estimated area of canopy, allowed the estimation of wood volumes per square kilometre for each land-use category.

Estimated wood volumes in grassland and shrubland were 4 to 6 m³/ha; in cultivation and shrub/grassland were approximately 7 to 9 m³/ha; rising to some 22 and 50 m³/ha in woodland and dense woodland, respectively. These figures compared well with other field estimates for small areas in the study area, but concealed a wide variability in relation to ecological conditions.

The results demonstrate the value of the integrated use of satellite imagery, sample photography and selective ground truthing in providing rapid, reliable and cost-effective assessments of vegetation cover, wood volume and land use for large areas. The method clearly has relevance and applications in many other regions.

2.4 Data utilization

Resource assessment is primarily used to establish baseline data or to provide the information required for development planning and targeting. The information can be utilized in a range of additional ways. Because data derived from aerial or integrated surveys are standardized and geo-referenced, they can readily be amassed into archives and examined for internal correlations and relationships, as well as analyzed in relation to other types of geographical information. The following sections provide five examples.

2.4.1 Livestock and their environment

An analysis of over 50 livestock surveys in sub-Saharan Africa between 1984 and 1993, covering over 2 million km^2 (much of it twice or more), examined the seasonal distribution levels of livestock in the regions surveyed (Figure 22.4). The driest areas (with less than 250 mm precipitation per year) had the lowest live-stock biomass - an average of 1.28 Tropical Livestock Units (TLUs) (320 kg) per square kilometre. However, a doubling of rainfall to 500 mm was associated with a fourteen-fold increase in livestock levels to 18.29 TLU (approximately 4 600 kg) per square kilometre. Peak values were reached at around 825 mm rainfall per annum, after which biomass density declined with increasing rainfall. These biomass values are comparable with those reported by Coe et al., (1976), Bell (1982 and 1985) and Fritz and Duncan (1993), but their observations were confined to the arid and semi-arid zones, with less than 1 000 mm per annum.

Figure 22.4

Sub-Saharan survey area

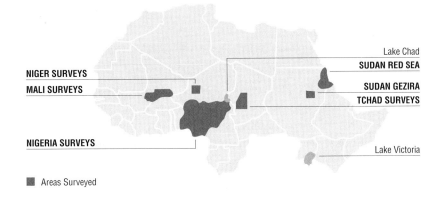

Areas Surveyed

Only minor differences were revealed in the seasonal distribution of biomass in relation to rainfall (Figure 22.5). At the macro-level, this implies that a high proportion of animals were resident, or at least remain within the same rainfall zone throughout the year, and that long distance seasonal movements were relatively uncommon (unless, of course, livestock movements in one direction are offset by equal and opposite movements in the other, which seems somewhat unlikely).

Figure 22.5

Seasonal change in livestock biomass distribution

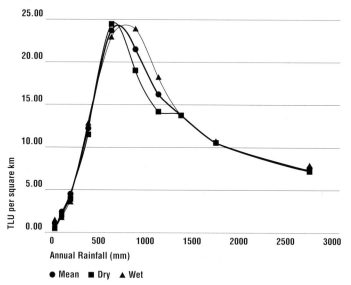

On closer inspection, seasonal differences were largely confined to the 750-1250 mm rainfall band, corresponding to the interface between semi-arid and sub-humid zones, where wet season biomass densities were 25-30 % higher in the wet season than in the dry season. In contrast, arid and humid zones showed only very modest changes in seasonal biomass densities. These observations reflect a seasonal flux of livestock into the southern semi-arid and northern sub-humid zones during the wet season, which is perhaps somewhat surprising, but may indicate the return of transhumant herds from dry season pastures.

Table 22.3 compares livestock biomass densities for each of the major agroclimatic zones obtained from contemporary field surveys, with Jahnke's more subjective assessments, derived from the FAO's Yearbook of Production (1979); Higgins et al., (1978); and OAU/STRC/IBAR (1976). Major differences are apparent, with Jahnke's figures some 30% lower, overall, and substantial under-representation of livestock biomass in both semi-arid and sub-humid zones.

Table 22.3

Livestock biomass density by agro-climatic zone*

| Agroclimatic Zone | Total (ERGO 1995) | | | Jahnke (1982) |
	Dry	Wet	Mean	1979
Arid	4.2	4.6	4.4	3.5
Semi-Arid	21.7	23.5	22.6	14.4
Sub-Humid	14.0	15.6	14.8	6.3
Humid	8.9	9.2	9.0	9.1
Total	7.6	8.3	7.9	5.59

*Densities are in TLU per square kilometre
Source: data compiled from field survey; FAO (1979); Higgins et al. (1978); and OAU/STRC/IBAR (1976)

The variable composition of livestock biomass in each of the four agroclimatic zones is shown in Figure 22.6, as the relative proportions of camels, cattle and small ruminants. Camels are largely confined to the arid zone, although some extend into the semi-arid zone. Cattle account for around two-thirds of livestock biomass in the arid, semi-arid and sub-humid zones, although the proportion declines with increasing humidity, as the contribution of small ruminants increases. Their relative proportions are reversed in the humid zone, where small ruminants account for some 80% of livestock biomass.

Figure 22.6

Livestock composition by agroclimatic zone

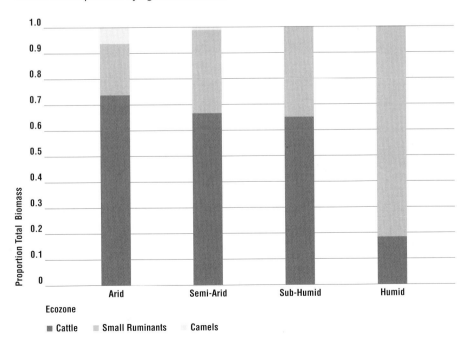

A large number of statistically significant correlations between livestock (cattle, camels, small ruminants) and environmental parameters (rainfall, grass cover, grassland, open woodland, dense woodland, forest, cultivation and rural settlement) can be generated. Only some of the more significant and interesting relationships are considered, relating to livestock biomass as a whole, rather than individual species.

The three most significant bivariate correlates of livestock biomass distribution were: percentage cultivation, or land-use intensity (accounting for 54% of variance); density of rural settlement (51% of variance); and mean annual rainfall (37% of variance).

The strongest association found was between the livestock biomass and percentage of land under cultivation (Figure 22.7). Not only is there a more or less even incremental rise in biomass density across the complete spectrum of cultivation levels, but the degree of variation, as shown by the vertical bars (indicating two standard errors), is surprisingly low.

Figure 22.7

Livestock biomass: % cultivation

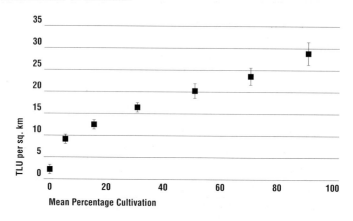

Log10 (y)=0.3014 + 0.5561 Log10(x).R^2=0.535; N=3663; p << 0.0001

Statistical levels of significance are astronomical for this level of association, with probabilities of chance occurrence much less than 1 in 1 000 000. There is, therefore, little room for doubt that livestock tend to congregate where land is cultivated.

Not surprisingly, there is also a strong positive correlation between livestock biomass levels and the density of rural settlement, as recorded by aerial survey, in terms of the number of rooftops per square kilometre (Figure 22.8), although the

Figure 22.8

Livestock biomass: habitation density

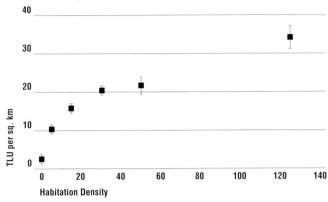

Log10 (y)=0.3582 + 0.5897 Log10(x).R^2=0.507; N=3663; p << 0.0001

linkage is marginally weaker than for cultivation. The relationship is slightly less robust than for cultivation, with greater variation in more densely settled areas.

The most significant result of these analyses is thus to show that livestock numbers are much more closely associated with the consequences of human activity – either percentage cultivation or habitation density – than they are with the extent or distribution of natural grazing. This pattern also holds true for the subset of livestock that are more pastorally managed – those that have tradition-ally been thought to concentrate in areas where natural grazing is widespread.

Furthermore, the similarity between the trends established for all livestock and the pastorally managed element suggest that there is little reason to view the latter as a special case, affected by factors specific to the pastoralist management system. This conflicts with many traditional views which hold that pastoralists minimize the risk to their animals by following the best of the natural grazing. Rather, it suggests that cultivation, or the vegetation associated with it, has, over much of the Sahel at least, become the most predictable source of livestock fodder, obviating the need to travel long distances in search of less certain natural resources.

If this is indeed the case, and if, as seems inevitable, human activity continues to expand in the future, then the trend away from dependence upon extensive rangelands is likely to continue. It therefore seems essential that future develop-ment planning addresses the interface between livestock and cropping as a higher priority than has been the case to date (Bourn and Wint, 1994).

2.4.2 Livestock, human activity and land degradation

Ecologists, economists and others have long debated the linkage between the size of human populations and the degradation of their environment. However, population densities per se, or population growth, have not been correlated with soil erosion, water impurity, deforestation and other major ecological changes (Tiffen et al., 1994; Mortimore, 1989; Clarke and Rhind, 1992).

The data set examined in the preceding section includes measures of percentage erosion only for Nigeria during 1990, and demonstrates a striking association between erosion and three predictor variables. Stepwise, multiple regression (Equation 1) reveals that the extent of bare ground in a survey grid is the primary predictor of erosion levels. The next strongest predictor is the percentage of active cultivation (excluding fallow), followed by livestock biomass per square kilometre.

Equation 1:
$$Lg10 \, (\% \, Erosion) = -1.03 + 0.265 Lg10 \, (\% \, Bare \, Ground) + 0.198$$
$$Lg10 \, (\% \, Active \, Cultivation) + 0.216 \, Lg10 \, (Livestock \, Biomass \, per$$
$$km^2) \quad R^2 = 0.206; \, DF = 3, \, 1916; \, p \ll 0.0001$$

The statistical significance of the relationship is overwhelming: R^2 is 0.54 with in excess of 1 900 data points, as compared to a threshold value of 0.02 at the 1% level of significance. The level of erosion is thus most severe in areas with little natural vegetation, presumably those more arid and agriculturally marginal regions, and its incidence within these regions is highest where there are both extensive cultivation and high livestock numbers.

2.4.3 Land-use change

The assessment of land-use change requires that compatible sets of information are available from two periods sufficiently far apart that the differences between them are greater than the errors inherent in their estimation. Various classifications of Nigerian vegetation have been published since the 1950s, but most are rather broad and unsuited to the present task. An exception is the set of maps published by the Federal Department of Forestry, which provides a detailed assessment of vegetation and land-use patterns for the whole country during 1976/77, based on Side Looking Airborne Radiometry (SLAR). A dataset which is compatible in spatial terms, comparable in the parameters assessed and also covers the whole country, is the one available from the Nigerian National Livestock Resources Survey of 1990 (Resource Inventory and Management Ltd, 1992). It was conducted on behalf of the Federal Department of Livestock and

Pest Control Services, for which land-use cover was estimated during the course of a low-level aerial survey.

The aerial survey data are based on visual estimates of five major land-use categories within each of 2 280 survey grids covering the whole country. A comparison with photographic assessments and between repeated visual surveys confirms their reliability.

In order to match aerial survey estimates with the SLAR data, two steps were needed: (i) recording the amount of each SLAR vegetation category within each survey grid; and (ii) then matching the SLAR categories with the aerial survey data. The first stage was effected by overlaying the aerial survey grids onto each of the 69 SLAR vegetation maps, subdividing each into 100 cells, then recording the predominant vegetation category within each cell and calculating the percentage of each cell covered by each vegetation category. Matching the SLAR and aerial survey data was achieved by a combination of regression and distribution analyses. The degree of land-use change was calculated by subtraction of the two sets of matched figures.

The results show a rise in cultivation levels of approximately 2.1% compound per annum, (p.a.) and a fall in the extent of natural vegetation types: grassland by 2.3% p.a.; scrub by 1.1% p.a.; woodland and mangrove forest by 0.6% p.a.; and closed canopy forest by 2.1% p.a. Settlement also increased substantially, at an estimated compounded annual rate of 6.9%. Projections, using these estimated rates of change, suggest that, by the year 2020, just over half of Nigeria will be cultivated, less than a third will be covered by woodland and settlement will amount to about 5% of the country's land area.

2.4.4 Agricultural system definition, display and identification

Geo-referenced data of the sort produced by integrated air and ground survey is well suited to internal examination of relationships of the sort described in the previous section. It is also amenable to interrogation using conditional statements to locate, for example, all data points with animal densities falling between prescribed thresholds in densely populated areas. These sorts of queries can be used both to define and map agricultural systems, and indeed to validate the defining criteria. The possibility thus arises of defining the production systems so often used by agricultural development planners, so that they have a basis in actual data and have a real geographical identity, rather than being founded on hypothesis and assumption.

Figure 22.9 depicts such a process, whereby small ruminant density is first plotted against human habitation density and rainfall, in order to give a three-dimensional surface which is a visualization of the interrelationships between the three parameters derived from survey data from a substantial part of the Sahel. This can be used to identify criteria that describe coherent small ruminant systems, in this case illustrated as two discrete peaks or regions of the surface plot.

Figure 22.9

Agricultural system definition

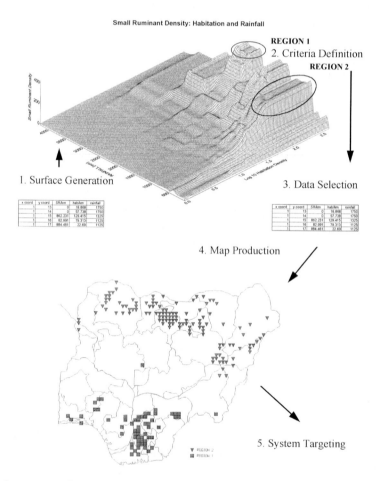

The locations of corresponding values for the defining criteria (rainfall and habitation density) can then be identified within a particular geographical area (in this case Nigeria) and these can then be mapped to assess their geographical coherence and realism.

A second example of agricultural system definition might be the development of tsetse-control strategies in selected African countries. This process needs to take account of such issues as where to prioritize areas for control, and which type of control (targets, community participation, or aerial spraying) is most appropriate. In this example, human and cultivation data are derived from the aerial survey data set, whilst up-to-date tsetse survey data for Togo has been used to model the distribution of the tsetse (G. palpalis) using environmental data from remote sensing satellites (Rogers et al., 1994). The satellite data can be used to derive predictions of the probability of occurrence of this species of tsetse throughout Nigeria; these predictions are shown as the coloured overlay on the three-dimensional surface in Figure 22.10, in relation to cultivation, rainfall and cattle density in Nigeria.

Figure 22.10

Tse-tse-risk surface

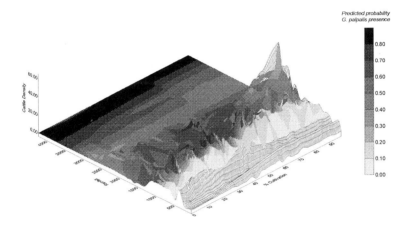

On this surface it is interesting to note the relative restriction of cattle to areas with less than approximately 2 000 mm rainfall annually, and their concentration, within these regions, in areas of higher rather than lower levels of cultivation. A number of other features are noteworthy. The band with more than an 80% probability of tsetse occurrence contains negligible cattle numbers; and the peaks of cattle density occur largely in those parts of the surface where tsetse are predicted to be relatively unlikely to occur.

Reading from this surface, the major regions where tsetse control appears to be required are those with high cattle densities and with a high probability (i.e., more than 70%) of tsetse presence. The three-dimensional surface shows that these areas are limited to regions with between 1 250 and 1 400 mm rainfall and with between 10 and 35% cultivation or areas with 1 500 to 1 600 mm rainfall and with 35 to 45% cultivation.

Such areas are shown as 'Region 1' (Map 22.1) Nigeria. If the tsetse probability threshold is lowered to 60% then most of the 1 250-1 600 mm rainfall band, with less than 65% cultivation, is included in the area to be targeted for tsetse control. These areas are shown as 'Region 2' on the map.

By incorporating data from other parts of Africa which may support different agricultural management practices, the relevance of the predictions produced could be applied to a substantially wider geographical area.

Map 22.1

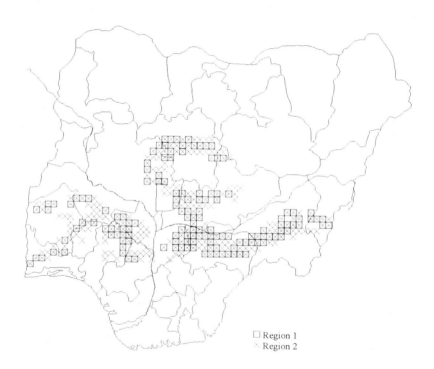

☐ Region 1
× Region 2

2.4.5 Satellite image information

In any assessment of temporal trends, it is desirable to have information from more than two data points. Data from intermediate points in time may confirm apparent trends, or identify them as curvilinear or cyclic, rather than merely linear. Research currently in progress at the Department of Zoology, Oxford University (Rogers et al., 1996), suggests close links between the 1990 aerial survey assessments of vegetation cover and the vegetation indices derived from

1987-1989 Advanced Very High Resolution Radiometer (AVHRR) imagery obtained by the National Oceanic and Atmospheric Administration (NOAA) series of meteorological satellites.

The results summarized here quantify the observed links between Fourier-processed AVHRR data for 1987-1989, and the 1990 aerial survey data extrapolated to 1988 on the basis of known rates of change in percentage vegetation cover. Details of the Fourier processing, and its use in the interpretation of seasonal changes in vegetation cover, are presented in another workshop paper and will not be elaborated upon here.

Table 22.4 and Figure 22.11 demonstrate a highly significant match between the two sets of information. This shows the Fourier analysis can be used with some confidence to extract the extent of the various land-use types in general terms. However, some of the categories are less accurately predicted, particularly cultivation, which Fourier analysis substantially underestimates. This is most probably because farmland, especially in the south of the country, returns a similar NDVI-signature to natural background vegetation, and is thus difficult to differentiate from it.

Table 22.4

Comparison of Fourier and aerial survey vegetation percentage, 1988

Vegetation %	Air	Fourier
Grass	6.09	7.29
Scrub	13.47	13.63
Active Cultivation	24.17	16.17
All Cultivation	31.37	17.91
Parkland	16.02	10.68
Open Wood	20.41	17.02
Dense Wood	25.79	23.05
All Wood	43.06	35.42
Forest + Wood	49.79	47.99
Closed Canopy Forest	8.34	12.10
All Forest	6.59	9.16
Air Grass*	7.88	9.17
Air Cultivation*	32.18	18.32
Air Scrub*	14.07	13.83

*Includes bare ground

It is envisaged that this stage of the analysis will be refined further, most notably by treating the various vegetation types within the different ecological zones separately. This may well enhance the precision of the calibrations, and allow for more accurate estimations of land-use cover.

Figure 22.11

Comparison of Fourier and aerial survey estimation of percentage land use, 1988

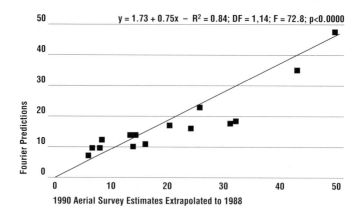

$y = 1.73 + 0.75x - R^2 = 0.84; DF = 1,14; F = 72.8; p<0.0000$

Fourier Predictions

1990 Aerial Survey Estimates Extrapolated to 1988

3. DISCUSSION AND CONCLUSIONS

The preceding discussion has demonstrated that low-level aerial survey is a practical technique for estimating a wide range of livestock, land cover and habitation parameters. Although some of the worked examples presented here are not primarily related to rangeland areas, the techniques are directly transferable to rangeland monitoring, either through photography or through visual observation.

In isolation, however, the methodology has limitations, in that it is unable to produce estimates of, for example, animal numbers in villages, nor can it provide production or productivity data. The technique is, like many other monitoring methods, most effective if it is combined with others, particularly satellite imagery and ground survey, whereupon it becomes a powerful weapon in the arsenal of resource assessment, because of its adaptability, repeatability and ease with which the data derived from it are integrated with other sources of geographical information. If we add to these advantages its comparatively low cost, its reliance upon relatively few specialist skills or equipment, and its rapidity, then low-level aerial survey is an attractive option.

The question is whether the relatively simple technology that aerial survey represents will be superseded by more advanced technology, especially by the use of remotely sensed satellite imagery and digital photography. Both these highly sophisticated applications undoubtedly have the potential to provide accurate assessments of vegetation; assuming that remotely sensed data are sufficiently well-calibrated, and that enough processing power and data storage is available to interpret the information. However, to date, neither is commonplace and substantial research efforts will be required to make them so. Furthermore, if these techniques are to be available to developing countries, extensive technology transfer and training would be required.

Whilst all things are, of course, possible, it seems unlikely that either satellite imagery or digital photography will be able to replace aerial and integrated air and ground survey in estimating animal populations, because the resolution required to detect even the larger species makes their use over large areas unrealistic. The fixed lens/sensor viewing angle means that many animals are obscured by vegetation.

It appears, therefore, that there will be a place for aerial survey in agricultural resource assessment for some time to come. If so, it seems only sensible to continue to use it to obtain land-cover data, given that the incremental cost of doing so is negligible, and that the results obtained are not only adequate for most, if not all, monitoring purposes, but also represent a potential source of much needed calibration for satellite remote-sensing technologies.

If this is to be the case, then low-level aerial survey has an important role to play, in conjunction with other resource assessment methods, not only to ascertain the population levels and (perhaps more importantly) the distribution patterns of animals in relation to resources, such as rangeland grazing, cultivation, or human habitation, but also to validate other remote-sensing methods. A recent IFAD environmental assessment study in Jordan has identified just such an example (ERGO, 1995), whereby the majority of the data required would be collected through satellite imagery, together with the requisite ground truthing, whilst the aerial survey component would provide livestock-related information needed to assess rangeland utilization.

References

Bell, R.H.V. 1982. The effect of soil nutrient availability on community structure in African ecosystems In: Huntley, B.J. and Walker, B.H. (eds) *The Ecology of Tropical Savannahs.* Springer, Berlin. pp 193-216.

Bell, R.H.V. 1985. Carrying capacity and off take quotas. In: Bell, R.H.V. and McShane Caluzi, E. (eds) *Conservation and Wildlife Management* Washington, US Peace Corps.

Bourn, D. and Wint, W. 1994. *Livestock, land use and agricultural intensification in sub-Saharan Africa* Pastoral Development Network Discussion Paper. Overseas Development Institute, London.

Clarke, J.I. and Rhind, D.W. 1992. *Population data and global environmental change.* ISSC Series: 5, ISSC/UNESCO, Paris.

Clarke, R. 1986. *The handbook of ecological monitoring.* Oxford Scientific Publications, Clarendon Press, Oxford.

Coe, M.J., Cumming, D.H. and Phillipson, J. 1976. Biomass and production of large African herbivores in relation to rainfall and primary production *Oecologia* 22:341-354.

Environmental Research Group Oxford (ERGO) 1995. *Environmental assessment for the identification of a pastoral resource assessment component for the national programme for range rehabilitation and development* Report prepared for the Ministry of Agriculture, Hashemite Kingdom of Jordan, and the International Fund for Agricultural Development, Rome, Italy.

Food and Agriculture Organization of the United Nations (FAO) 1979. Yearbook of Production. FAO, Rome.

Fritz, H. and Duncan, P. 1993. Large herbivores in rangelands *Nature* 364, 292-3.

Higgins, et al., 1978. *Report on the agro-ecological zones project. Volume 1: methodology and results for Africa.* World Soil Resources Report 48. FAO, Rome.

Marriott, F.C. and Wint, G.R.W. 1985. *Sampling and statistics in low level aerial survey.* Report prepared by Resource Inventory and Management Ltd, for the International Livestock Centre for Africa (ILCA/CIPEA), Addis Ababa, Ethiopia.

Mortimore, M. 1989. *Adapting to drought: farmers, famines and desertification in West Africa.* Cambridge University Press.

Norton-Griffiths, M. 1978. *Counting animals: A series of handbooks on techniques in African wildlife ecology.* Handbook no. 1. African Wildlife Leadership Foundation, Nairobi, Kenya.

OAU/STRC/IBAR 1976. *African Cattle Distribution Map. Nderito and Adeniji.* Organization of African Unity, Scientific Technical and Research Committee, Inter-African Bureau for Animal Resources, Nairobi.

Resource Inventory and Management Ltd. 1992. *Nigerian Livestock Resources (4 volumes).* Report to the Federal Department of Livestock and Pest Control Services (FDLPCS), Abuja, Nigeria.

Rogers, D.J., Hay, S.I. and Packer, M.J. 1996. Predicting the distribution of tsetse flies in West Africa using temporal Fourier processed meteorological satellite data. *Annals of Tropical Medicine and Parasitology,* 3: 225-241.

Rogers, D.J., Hendrick, G. and Slingenbergh, J.H.W. 1994. Tsetse flies and their control. *Revue Scientifique et Technique de l'Office International Epizooties,* 13: 1075-1124.

Tiffen, M., Mortimore, M. and Gichuki, F. 1994. *More people, less erosion: environmental recovery in Kenya.* Wiley and Sons, Chichester, UK.

The integrated use of remote sensing for ESON rangeland and desertification assessment in Saudi Arabia

23

E. Weiss

Synopsis

The Environmental Support of Nomads (ESON) project is funded and directed by the Meteorology and Environmental Protection Administration of the Kingdom of Saudi Arabia. The primary project objective is to ensure that the use of these lands by animal herds does not result in increased desertification.

A new analytic methodology for the detection of desertification of arid rangelands was developed specifically for this project. These systems include two satellite sensors and an airborne video suite designed specifically for the ESON project.

Key Points

1. *Due to the naturally desertic condition of Saudi Arabia's rangelands, the changes which the project was trying to assess are more subtle than would be the case for other, less desertic areas. A new methodology was developed to try to cope with this situation.*

2. *The conceptual framework for the analysis is the use of the Coefficient of Variation (CV) and maximum value composite of the monthly Normalized Difference Vegetation Index (NVDI) as a measure of the vegetative biomass; a higher NVDI CV for a given pixel means a greater change in vegetative biomass in the ground area represented by that pixel. Linear regression was used to determine the trend in CV values for each pixel over the 12-year period for which data were available; pixels with a negative slope are considered to represent ground areas with decreasing amounts of vegetation, i.e., they are becoming more desertified.*

3. *Results are validated by tests of statistical significance and by comparison of the theoretical results to vegetation change and land-cover data from remote sensing systems, and from reconnaissance flights over selected areas. These desertification*

*trend results are then combined with land cover, land use and range capability
information to provide an assessment of desertification status and hazards.*

1. INTRODUCTION AND PROJECT BACKGROUND

Much of the land area of the Kingdom of Saudi Arabia is used for livestock
grazing by nomads for at least part of the year. There is a particular concern that
the rangelands must not be allowed to degrade through overgrazing or other
activities of man. Human-induced problems are regularly cited as among the
primary causes of desertification and these effects may be more varied and
pronounced in lands which are themselves arid or semi-arid.

For example, Nahal (1995) lists overgrazing, agricultural development, the
creation or movement of human settlements and mineral/petroleum extraction as
among the primary causes of desertification. He notes that the arid and semi-arid
rangelands of Syria and Iraq contain three times the amount of livestock that can
be supported by the carrying capacity of the range. He further notes that "this
heavy pressure on the natural rangelands is one of the main reasons for the deterioration of the plant cover and the rapid progress of desertification", adding that
"the changes that have taken place in recent years in nomadic pastoral systems and
which have been reflected in traditions and rights have reduced the possibility of
controlling natural rangelands and contributed to their deterioration".

One of the primary objectives of the ESON study, funded and directed by
MEPA (Saudi Arabia), has been to ensure that the Saudi Arabian rangelands will
support continued utilization by the indigenous nomad groups. The ESON
project, largely limited to analysis of four specific areas, referred to as study areas
1, 2, 3 and 4, has focused on identifying environmental risks (such as those identified by Nahal) early enough in the deterioration process, in order to mitigate and
reverse any existing damage while preventing further degradation of the rangelands. The location of these areas within Saudi Arabia is shown in Figure 23.1.

This ambitious set of goals first required the definition and identification of
those sub-areas within the ESON study areas that are experiencing (or are at risk
of) desertification. Desertification is usually defined as the loss of biological
productivity of arid and semi-arid lands (Kassas, 1995). In the case of the rangelands of the Saudi Arabia, desertification may be interpreted as the reduction of
natural vegetation. (Of course, this definition does not apply to those areas in
which the natural vegetation is deliberately removed for such reasons as the
development of irrigated agriculture or the construction of human dwellings or
commercial enterprises). Thus, the ESON Anti-Desertification Study was
required to develop analytic methodologies for detecting and identifying those
areas that are experiencing a decline in levels of natural vegetation.

Figure 23.1

Location of ESON study areas within Saudi Arabia

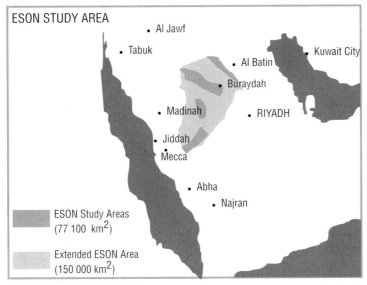

ESON STUDY AREA

- Al Jawf
- Tabuk
- Al Batin
- Kuwait City
- Buraydah
- Madinah
- RIYADH
- Jiddah
- Mecca
- Abha
- Najran

ESON Study Areas
(77 100 km^2)

Extended ESON Area
(150 000 km^2)

Detection of declining vegetation levels in Saudi Arabia poses formidable technical problems. The primary reason for this is the naturally desertic condition of much of the country's rangeland; i.e., the natural vegetation levels are already very low. This makes the detection of subtle, long-term changes even more difficult. The size of the areas of interest and the need to look at changing conditions over longer time intervals, necessitate the use of remote sensing satellite systems with data available for at least the past decade. This need for longer temporal data series imposes a forced reliance on a data set of low-resolution satellite imagery for assessing vegetation cover.

Data from the National Oceanic and Atmospheric Administration's (NOAA) Advanced Very High Resolution Radiometer (AVHRR) are available from 1980 onward, but at low spatial resolution (7.6 km per pixel). It is necessary to use data from this system rather than data from the more recently developed and higher spatial resolution systems (e.g., Landsat or SPOT), because a consistent record over a long time interval is needed to detect changes of interest. Additionally, the measure traditionally utilized in remote sensing of vegetation levels and growth cycles, the NVDI, is only available at this lower resolution for large areas over longer time intervals. This compounds the difficulties in performing this assessment, because the use of low-resolution imagery complicates the detection of small or sparse features such as desert vegetation (Marsh and Hirosawa, 1994).

Finally, many of the changes associated with desertification within Saudi Arabia have most probably been going on for much longer than the period for which remote sensing data is available. When some of the rangelands began to be degraded due to overgrazing, the vegetation levels were higher; thus, the initial degradation was probably more severe, with greater percentage reductions in vegetation. These early changes would most likely have been more easily detected. As the process continues, the reduced levels of vegetation make each subsequent reduction more difficult to detect. Consequently, detection of these processes becomes more difficult as time passes. In the case of the ESON study areas, the rangelands have been in continuous use for long periods, with increasing nomad and animal populations accelerating the continued exploitation of these lands.

The Office of Arid Lands Studies (OALS) obtained two AVHRR datasets for this analysis. AVHRR Global Area Coverage (GAC), with an effective (projected) spatial resolution of 7.6 km was acquired in the form of dekadal (i.e. 10 days), the maximum value NDVI composites. Thus, for each pixel in each image, the maximum NDVI value for the ten-day period is provided. These data covered the period from 1982 to 1991 and 1993 to 1994. In addition, OALS was able to purchase from NOAA more recent Local Area Coverage (LAC) data for the period from March 1994 to June 1995. These data have a spatial resolution of 1.1 km.

Objectives and methods of analysis were derived to accommodate the availability of data. In addition, data developed through companion efforts involving analysis of Landsat Thematic Mapper (TM) imagery, airborne video Systematic Reconnaissance Flights (SRF) and the generation of land-cover and land-systems maps were also utilized in the ESON Anti-Desertification Study. Final objectives of the study therefore, included: (i) analysis of the long-term (1982-1994) AVHRR GAC dataset to detect changing vegetation levels over a 12-year period; (ii) analysis of the AVHRR LAC dataset available from March 1994 to June 1995 to assess more recent cover conditions, and the relationship between NDVI and range utilization for periods of coincident SRF airborne video data; (iii) integration of land-cover information derived from Landsat TM with the long time-series GAC data to map desertification status; and (iv) integration of range capability information with the long time-series GAC data to map desertification hazards.

2. ASSESSING VEGETATION AND DESERTIFICATION WITH AVHRR DATA

Beginning in 1978, NOAA has operated a series of polar-orbiting satellites primarily designed to monitor weather conditions. These satellites acquire data for any spot on earth twice daily. The AVHRR, one of the sensors on-board the satellites, has also been used extensively to monitor surface vegetation cover. Prior research has demonstrated that the red (0.58-0.68 m) and near-infrared (NIR) (0.72-1.1 m) spectral channels of the AVHRR can be used to detect and monitor vegetation. Chlorophyll in actively growing vegetation is a strong absorber of red radiation and the cell-wall structure of healthy leaves strongly reflects NIR radiation. Therefore, greater photosynthetic activity will result in lower reflectance in the red band and higher reflectance in the NIR. It is for this reason that the red and NIR regions of the electromagnetic spectrum are the primary bands utilized in remote sensing of vegetation.

By combining these two spectral regions in a ratio or difference, the NDVI, the sensitivity to photosynthetic activity is enhanced. While a variety of vegetation indices has been utilized over the past two decades, the NDVI is the most commonly applied index as:

$$NDVI = (NIR-RED)/(NIR+RED)$$

By normalizing the difference between the channel values, NDVI can be scaled between -1 to +1. Water typically has an NDVI value less than 0, bare soil values are between 0 and 0.1 and vegetation values are over 0.1. Of course, the NDVI value for a particular pixel will be based on the composition of that pixel, and may thus have a value which reflects the mix of ground-cover types that occur in the ground area represented by that pixel.

Typically, the data are calibrated and corrections are made to the AVHRR Red and NIR channel data prior to calculation of the NDVI (Che and Price, 1992). The NDVI values are then composited to minimize the effects of cloud cover, atmospheric aerosols and non-optimal illumination and viewing geometries (Holben, 1986). NASA pre-processes the channel data to correct for these effects prior to computing NDVI from the (corrected) channel data. The resultant NDVI can be interpreted as a measure of vegetation vigour and/or density.

AVHRR NDVI data have been successfully utilized to monitor regional to global-scale vegetation patterns, (Tucker, 1979; Tucker, 1986; Marsh, et al., 1992). AVHRR NDVI data have also been successfully employed to assess vegetation conditions in arid and semi-arid lands (Prince, 1991; Hobbs, 1995) and the relationship between NDVI and vegetation response to rainfall (Nicholson, et al., 1990). More problematic results are reported in the assessment of desertification and land degradation (Tucker, et al., 1991; Bastin, et al., 1995). The success and failures represented by this prior research provided the background that helped suggest the concept for an analytical method to detect and identify areas undergoing desertification. This methodology was developed specifically for this study, but should be applicable to assess desertification in any setting.

2.1 AVHRR GAC data analysis

The data source for the project was a CD-ROM of GAC NDVI data in the Hammer-Aitoff projection produced by the Africa Real Time Environmental Monitoring Information System (ARTEMIS) group of the Food and Agriculture Organization of the United Nations. This dataset was designed for studies of the African continent, but the entire Arabian peninsula is included on the images. The images are available for every 10 days (dekadal) from January 1982 until June 1991. These images have been corrected for sensor drift. FAO also provided uncorrected data for 1993 through 1995. Data is not available for the period July 1991 to December 1992 because the quality of the images was adversely affected by aerosols from the Mount Pinatubo eruption in the Philippines. In addition, the 1995 data were not included in the study because the quality of the new NOAA-14 GAC data are suspect.

Since the data are provided as NDVI values, a limited amount of pre-processing on the GAC data was necessary. A subset of only Saudi Arabia was first extracted from each image. In order to further remove cloud and aerosol contamination, the dekadal NDVI values were composited up to monthly images with a maximum-value composite (MVC). The monthly MVC was created by selecting, for each pixel, the maximum NDVI value for the month (with a maximum of the three dekadal values for that month). Sensor-drift corrections for the 1993-1994 data were derived by looking at time-series statistics for areas in Saudi Arabia known to have a very low deviation in NDVI over time. Corrections were then applied to the appropriate images.

One useful way to identify vegetation in NDVI images is to look at "temporal signatures", or time-series plots of the NDVI levels of the pixels in the image. As vegetation grows, NDVI increases, and as the vegetation dies back, NDVI decreases. Thus, the cyclic increase and decrease of NDVI over time in a given area is characteristic of vegetation growth cycles, and is therefore taken as an indication of the presence of vegetation. Since much of the vegetation in arid environments is seasonal, a distinctive curve can often be seen showing high values during the growing season and lower values the rest of the year. This cyclic fluctuation of NDVI values is reflected in the temporal NDVI histories showing the minimum and maximum NDVI values for each month over the entire Arabian peninsula and surrounding area. These values were taken over the period 1982-1990; for each year, the monthly NDVI values were generated for each month as described above, and then the average of all of the nine NDVI minimum and maximum values for each month (1982-1990) were computed. Thus, for each pixel, the NDVI values for January represent the minimum and maximum of the maximum January values for the years 1982-1990, on a pixel by pixel basis. The ESON study areas are also outlined in Figure 23.1. Inspection of the data reveals that NDVI values throughout the image change from month-to-month, possibly reflecting the vegetation growth cycles in different areas of the image. The differences from area to area are due to differing amounts of vegetation and rainfall, soil types, terrain elevations and land-use patterns (including changes related to irrigated agriculture and grazing).

To determine a baseline for vegetated areas, those pixels whose monthly NDVI values vary over the year consistently with yearly vegetation growth cycles must be identified. It is not enough to merely find those pixels whose NDVI values change over the months, because some fluctuation in the NDVI values may be due to non-vegetative effects, and must therefore be ignored. To help to isolate the pixels of interest, the range of NDVI values can be examined.

The differences between the maximum and minimum NDVI values vary among ESON study areas. This reflects both the different vegetation potential of the four areas and the presence of irrigated agriculture, particularly in Area 2. There are relatively high minimum-NDVI values and very high maximum-NVDI values in Area 2, due to the irrigated agriculture, which is not dependent on rainfall, and so has relatively high NDVI levels throughout the year.

For most areas of Saudi Arabia, maximum rainfall levels occur in December, January and February. Allowing a lag period for this rainfall to result in vegetation growth or "green-up", the growing season was taken to be January-February-March. The dry season throughout most of the peninsula extends from May to September; the vegetation will be at its driest at the end of this period.

The maximum difference in NDVI values can therefore be calculated as the difference in NDVI values between these two periods.

Other data analyzed for this study also indicate that some areas in the southern portion of the Arabian peninsula have higher rainfall levels throughout the period March-August than December-February. Consequently, these regions will have higher NDVI levels in September than in the January-March period.

Unfortunately, with the predominance of soil rather than vegetation in arid regions, a simple analysis is precluded. Therefore, some method for separating the soil signature from vegetation had to be derived. In an earlier analysis, the dry season (September) NDVI was subtracted from the main growing season (January-February-March maximum) NDVI. This worked quite well for identifying those areas that had significantly different NDVI levels between the two seasons. However, not all vegetation fell neatly into those seasons; in particular, the rangeland areas of primary interest here could not be identified by this method.

3. DETECTION AND ANALYSIS OF DESERTIFICATION

Initial research efforts on the ESON project, briefly discussed above, were aimed at developing analytic methods utilizing NDVI for identifying vegetated areas, and distinguishing these from areas of bright soil (soil with strong signatures in the red and/or infrared parts of the electromagnetic spectrum). These methods employed different statistics, generated from the NDVI, to determine which areas exhibit NDVI temporal signatures consistent with vegetation growth cycles. The statistics used included the average NDVI value or the maximum NDVI value over a defined period of vegetation green-up, the standard deviation of these values and the difference between the minimum and maximum NDVI values over the time period.

All of these earlier methods and statistics were designed to identify vegetated areas; they were not aimed at identifying areas that are undergoing a decline in vegetation levels. Development of a methodology to assess degradation of vegetation cover (i.e., desertification), derived specifically for this project, is discussed below.

3.1 Development of a GAC NDVI indicator of desertification

In order to detect the process of desertification, or a reduction in biological production in the study areas, it is necessary to detect declining levels of vegetation. This has been done for the ESON study by identifying areas with statistically significant declines in the variation of the vegetation-growth cycles.

Initial investigations of MVCs created from the AVHRR GAC data identified areas with temporal signatures indicative of vegetation growth. These cycles were reflected in the NDVI MVCs as cyclic increases and decreases in NDVI levels. The greater the variation between the maximum and minimum NDVI values, the greater the level or robustness of vegetation that can be inferred. However, it is possible that unusual rain (i.e., rain at an unexpected time or in an unusual amount), sensor problems or drift, or data artifacts, could cause a single erroneous high or low-NDVI value that could yield a misleading difference between these values.

A more stable measure of the vegetation growth cycle is the Coefficient of Variation (CV) of the NDVI values. The CV is used to compare the amount of variation in different sets of sample data. These samples are often sets of time-series data, in which case the CV represents a measure of pixel-level NDVI variation over time. This, in turn, is interpreted as a measure of changing vegetation dynamics over time, and has been used to assess vegetation changes and ecosystem boundaries (Tucker, et al., 1991b).

Individual NDVI values for single pixels at different times can be combined to produce a CV image. This image is generated by computing the standard deviation (F) of the set of individual NDVI values and dividing this by the average, or mean (:) of these values for each pixel in the image. Thus, the value for each pixel in the CV image is given by: CV = F/:. Note that the CV will be by definition a dimensionless quantity, and that by dividing by the mean, all CV values will be at the same scale of magnitude. This facilitates comparisons of data collected over different periods.

Because the CV is used as the measure of vegetation-growth cycles, changes in this parameter can be used to identify changes in the growth cycles in an area. Thus, declining values of the CV of NDVI values in an area reflect a loss of biological production. Comparison of these figures helps to reveal the clear temporal sensitivity of the CV of NDVI.

The next step was to establish a means of detecting and quantifying changes in CV. One method for identifying a continued decline in the CV values over time is based on linear regression. This method determines the equation of the straight line that best fits the set of annual CV values for each pixel. In other words, the CV regression line for each pixel reflects the overall long-term trend in the data. If the CV values exhibit a statistically significant decrease over time, it is possible to conclude that the vegetation growth cycles are declining, i.e., the area imaged in that pixel is undergoing desertification. If, on the other hand, the slope of this regression line shows a statistically significant increase, then it can be concluded that vegetation growth cycles are increasing in that area. This could result from either an increase in rainfall or, in the case of the rangelands within Saudi Arabia, a protected area that has been closed to grazing for some time, or the development of irrigated agriculture (with its more dense and vigorous vegetation).

However, methods must also be employed to ensure that the detected changes in CV values for a given area over some time period are statistically valid and not just a consequence of erratic, statistically "noisy" NDVI data. This would help to confirm that changes indicated by the slope of the regression lines for the different pixels are statistically significant. This confirmation can be in the form of the statistical confidence level at which one can conclude that the slope represents a real trend, and is not just an artifact of the data.

This is done by performing a t-test of the value of the slope. This tests whether the data used to compute the regression line will permit a conclusion of statistical significance at the desired confidence level. Insight into the effects of applying confidence levels to the data may be seen by creating histograms of the slope values for an image covering the four study areas showing increasing confidence levels (e.g., 0%, 60%, 75%, 90% and 95%). The histogram, or frequency distribution of CV regression slope values for all of the pixels, with no minimum confidence level (0%) is roughly "bell-shaped", with a mean value and a preponderance of slope values of less than 0.0, (i.e., there seem to be more areas undergoing some level of degradation than regeneration, or growth in vegetation).

The curve for a minimum confidence level of 75% represents far fewer pixels at all slope values; this reflects the deletion of those pixels for which the calculated slope cannot be considered statistically significant at the 75% confidence level. These low confidence slope values may thus be an artifact of the data (CV values), rather than a reflection of real processes affecting the land. The largest decrease in frequency counts occurs near the slope level of 0.0. This is to be expected, since in those areas in which the vegetation levels remain more or less the same (slope of CV regression line=0.0), irregular deviations (statistical "noise") would be expected to include both positive and negative values that cumulatively, would be expected to largely cancel each other out. Thus, many of the lowest confidence level data will have slopes with values near 0.0; these were precisely the preponderance of pixels eliminated by imposing a minimum confidence level. The figure also reveals that, at a minimum confidence level of 90 or 95%, the number of statistically significant pixels is reduced even further.

By examining the cumulative percentage of pixels still considered valid after the different confidence levels are applied, we can quantify the percentage of statistically significant pixels. At 95% confidence level, we can consider approximately 25% of the data significant; at 90% confidence level approximately one-third (35%) of the pixels; and at 60% minimum confidence level, over 85% of the pixels are retained. This information demonstrates the cumulative effects of using AVHRR GAC data over a time period, reflecting only part of the fairly subtle land-cover changes that may be occurring in the study areas. It further shows that, as the confidence levels at which one wants to assert conclusions increases, the size of the areas (number of pixels) about which those conclusions can be made decreases.

For a more complete discussion of the concepts of linear regression, t-tests and confidence levels, the reader is referred to standard texts on econometrics, such as those by Kennedy (1992) or Ramanathan (1992).

The analytic concepts discussed above were tested by comparing the predicted, theoretical results to actual data for areas on the ground, for which actual vegetation changes were known, from Landsat TM images or from the systematic reconnaissance flights. These areas of vegetation change included a military exclosure on the northern boundary of ESON Study Area 1 and a region of irrigated agriculture in Study Area 2.

The irrigated agriculture areas in the north-central portion of Study Area 2 exhibit positive CV regression line slopes for the 12-year GAC data record; this is the period in which much of this agricultural region was developed. Thus, as an area becomes more heavily utilized for irrigated agriculture, the overall levels of vegetation increase, leading to increases in CV and, therefore, positive regression-line slopes. Outside the irrigated agriculture areas, the results are more mixed, with some areas improving, others degrading, and others remaining about the same. This is what was expected, since only the irrigated areas should show widespread, positive changes in vegetation levels.

The results from these two test sites confirm the theory and methodology used for the subsequent analysis of desertification for the ESON project.

4. DEVELOPMENT OF DESERTIFICATION STATUS MAPS

The preceding section discussed the development of a method for identifying areas undergoing desertification. To provide a more useful analysis product, it was necessary to reinterpret these data in terms of the status/ground cover and anticipated hazards to these areas. These analysis steps are described in this section and in Section 5, respectively.

Creation of desertification status maps for the four ESON study areas was a two-step process. The CV slope information derived from the 7.6 km resolution AVHRR GAC dataset directly assesses the changing condition of vegetation cover over the period 1982 through 1994. Although this information is directly applicable to understanding desertification in the study areas, the coarse spatial resolution ($\sim$58 km^2 per pixel) of the original data diminishes the ability to interpret the results. Therefore, the second step in the creation of the desertification status maps involved integrating the GAC slope data with higher spatial-resolution land cover maps derived from the Landsat TM data, as part of a separate ESON analysis. The resultant CV slope maps for ESON Study Area 3 exhibit a blockiness as a result of the large GAC pixel size.

Quantitative analysis of the CV slope maps for the four study areas follows. Study Area 1: 93% of the land area exhibit near-zero slope, indicating relatively stable conditions overall, 5% has relatively minor negative slopes and 1% has positive slopes. Study Area 2: 41% of the land area has near-zero slope, 3% has negative slopes and 55% has positive slopes, which for the most part correspond to areas of irrigated agriculture. Study Area 3: 84% of the land area exhibit near-zero slopes, 9% has negative slopes and 6% has positive slopes. Study Area 4: 48% of the land area has near-zero slopes, 51% has negative slopes, with over 20% in the most negative slope classes and only 1% of the area exhibits positive slopes. These data are summarized in Table 23.1.

Table 23.1

Percentages of the ESON study areas with different values for the slope of inter-annual CV

ESON Area	CV Slope near 0.0 (Near Constant CV)	Positive CV Slope (Increasing CV)	Negative CV Slope (Decreasing CV)
1	93	1	5
2	41	55	3
3	84	6	9
4	48	1	51

These results clearly indicate that Study Area 4 has experienced, or is experiencing, the most severe land degradation while areas 1, 2 and 3 have relatively small (< 10%) areas of apparent degradation. Study Area 2 is unique in its large amount of area with positive slopes (> 50%), which reflects the development of irrigated agriculture in the region.

The final Desertification Status Maps were then created by integrating the CV slope information layers with general land-cover information. The seven land-cover classes originally mapped utilizing the Landsat TM data were grouped into three more general but distinctive classes. This generalization of the land-cover classes was considered prudent given the limited spatial detail available from the GAC CV data. The three classes defined for this purpose are "Outcrop/Rocky Plain", "Sandy Surfaces" and "Vegetation". These classes were separated on the basis of soil retention of rainfall, which is extremely important to range production in the study areas. The distinctive Vegetation class consists of all agriculture areas, as well as natural vegetation. This class is unique in its ecological and economic value and vulnerability to exploitation. The "Outcrop/Rocky Plain" class combines the original Rock Outcrop and Rocky Uplands and Plains land-cover classes. These classes have very low water infiltration rates and can not retain rainfall as well as the other classes (except in small isolated areas of wind-blown sand). The "Sandy Surfaces" class combines all of the predominately sandy soil classes. [Follow-up studies may wish to examine whether the Rocky Uplands and Plains class might be more appropriately grouped with the Sandy Surfaces class or as a fourth and separate class. Further refinement of the data may also lead to a more consistent identification of ephemeral stream courses with riparian vegetation].

Final desertification status maps for the four ESON study areas were created by identifying areas of no change (near-zero CV slope), areas with declining vegetation cover (negative CV slope) and areas with improving vegetation cover (positive CV slope), for each of the three general land-cover classes - Outcrop/Rocky

Plain, Sandy Surfaces and Vegetation. The colour key for these maps was designed so that each of the three land-cover classes has three unique colours representing "no change", "decline" and "improvement". In addition, the colour key was constructed so that all areas of no change are represented in white, gray or black; improving areas are in shades of green; and all declining areas are in shades of yellow/orange/magenta. In this way the desertification status maps convey degradation or improvement, based upon land cover originally mapped at 30 m spatial resolution.

Analysis of these maps gives a clear indication of the nature of both the declining and improving surfaces within the four ESON study areas and establishes their geographic setting and location. Table 23.2, below, provides the quantitative results for the desertification status maps by total area in square kilometres and percentages of total area for the four study areas. These data indicate that Study Area 1 is the most stable (94% unchanged); only 5% of the area is becoming more desertic and the areas is on Sandy Surfaces. Study Area 2 is unique in that close to 50% of the area is mapped as improving. This improvement is due to the development of irrigated agriculture and is found on vegetated (7%), sandy (25%) and rocky (23%) surfaces. Approximately 84% of Study Area 3 appears unchanged; while 10% of the area, evenly split between Outcrop/Rocky Plain and Sandy Surfaces, is degrading, approximately 6% of the area is improving. Study Area 4 exhibits the most extreme desertification, with over 50% of the surfaces mapped as declining; most of these are the most useful Sandy Surfaces (40%), with Outcrop/Rocky Plain contributing the remaining 11%.

Table 23.2

Quantitative summary of the desertification status maps.

Status Class		ESON Area 1 Area (km^2) : %	ESON Area 2 Area (km^2) : %	ESON Area 3 Area (km^2) : %	ESON Area 4 Area (km^2) : %
Outcrop	Declining	46 : 0	454 : 1	597 : 5	2119 : 11
	No Change	2503 : 27	6582 : 20	3579 : 29	1377 : 7
	Improving	77 : 1	7689 : 23	497 : 4	3 : 0
Sand	Declining	450 : 5	476 : 1	584 : 5	7308 : 40
	No Change	6206 : 67	6830 : 21	6668 : 55	7512 : 41
	Improving	35 : 0	8221 : 25	243 : 2	152 : 1
Vegetation	Declining	0 : 0	143 : 0	< 1 : 0	0 : 0
	No Change	< 1 : 0	142 : 0	2 : 0	0 : 0
	Improving	< 1 : 0	2224 : 7	< 1 : 0	0 : 0

5. DEVELOPMENT OF DESERTIFICATION HAZARDS MAPS

Development of the desertification hazard maps for the four ESON study areas also utilized the 1982-1994 GAC CV slope datasets. To assess desertification hazard, or perhaps more appropriately the risk of desertification to the land surfaces, the range capability maps that were derived from the land cover data and integrated with digital soils information were further integrated with the CV slope datasets. The rationale behind creation of the hazards map is that the GAC CV slope data accurately portrays areas of degradation or desertification over the period 1982-1994, while the range capability maps rate the surfaces on the basis of the capability of the range to support vegetation growth and thus grazing. The range capability maps utilize five rating classes - "Very Low", "Low", "Medium", "High", and "Very High". Values from 1 (Very Low) to 5 (Very High) were then assigned to these classes and arithmetically multiplied by the CV slope values for each pixel for each study area. The resulting maps provide levels of risk on the basis of range potential. For example, areas of high range-potential with large negative CV slopes will have a greater risk value than areas of low range-potential with the same slope value. In a sense, these "risk" values may be considered as future "payoffs"; they reflect both the undergoing desertification or improvement processes and the potential "cost" or "gain" if these processes are allowed to continue. In this context, the higher the "payoff", the better the outcome vis-a vis desertification.

The range of risk values was then level-sliced into nine classes. One class was established for near-zero risk values representing no apparent risk; four positive slope classes represented decreasing risk; and four negative slope classes represented increasing risk. To help further define the current risk on the hazards maps, the composite positions of sheep/goat and camel herds identified from the SRF missions were superimposed on the risk map. These data are from four missions flown during the winter, spring, fall and summer of 1995, and were selected to represent herds identified over four seasons of one year. In this way, areas mapped as having high risk of desertification that also had herds present during the past year can be considered as most endangered, while areas mapped as low risk with herds present may be of less concern. Obviously, the dynamic nature of herd movement forces any conclusions concerning herd positions in relation to risk to be strictly for this past year.

The final desertification hazards maps for the four ESON study areas were developed. Analysis of these maps indicates that the total areas at risk range from approximately 10% for Study Area 2, to 82% for Study Area 4. Study Area 1 has 56% of the surface mapped at risk and Study Area 3 has 39% mapped at risk. Apart from Study Area 2, herd positions are most often associated with areas at risk.

6. CONCLUSIONS AND RECOMMENDATIONS

Desertification of arid and semi-arid lands is an increasing problem both within Saudi Arabia and throughout the world. The ecological and socio-economic impacts of desertification are problems that must be addressed with as much information as possible. Analysis efforts on behalf of MEPA and the ESON project were designed specifically to provide information where little existed before.

Satellite-remote sensing data are the only source of relatively long-term (10-15 years) views of the earth's surface and are therefore used extensively for mapping land-cover change. In particular, data are available from the NOAA AVHRR sensor dating back to the early 1980s. These datasets provide useful information on vegetation cover through the use of maximum value composites of the NDVI. However, identifying areas that are becoming more desertic, within an arid environment where vegetation cover is minimal, is a difficult problem. This difficulty is compounded by the use of low spatial-resolution data sets. No established techniques existed to solve this problem, utilizing available multitemporal NDVI datasets.

Previous ESON-sponsored research had shown that the Coefficient of Variation (CV) of NDVI could be utilized to assess the presence of sparse vegetation in arid environments. The CV for 1982 through to 1994 was used to base an assessment of vegetation cover change or desertification on the slope of the CV over this time period. This methodology was tested and found successful over two areas within Study Areas 1 and 2, where it was known that vegetation cover had increased. This methodology was then applied to develop both the desertification status and hazards maps.

The desertification status and hazards maps provide a clear indication of both the degree of desertification within the ESON study areas and the areas of rangeland most at risk. Study Area 4 is the region having experienced the greatest land-cover degradation (> 50%), and is the area most at risk. Results also indicate that Study Area 1 has undergone the least desertification (< 5%) but this area also faces significant risk based upon range capability and herd densities.

Only isolated areas of Study Area 2 appear to have degraded since 1982, while much of the area is mapped as improving (> 50%) as a result of the significant development of irrigated agriculture in the region. However, if these agricultural fields are allowed to go fallow, they would certainly be mapped as becoming more desertic in any future analysis. A relatively small (10%) portion of Study Area 3 appears to have declined, but much of that area is also at risk.

References

Bastin, G.N., Pickup, G., and Pearce, G. 1995. Utility of AVHRR data for land degradation assessment: a case study. *International Journal of Remote Sensing,* 16(4):651-672.

Che, N. and Price, J.C. 1992. Survey of radiometric calibration results and methods for visible and near infra-red channels of NOAA-7, -9, and -11 AVHRRs. *Remote Sensing of Environment,* 41:19-27.

Hobbs, T.J. 1995. The use of NOAA-AVHRR NDVI data to assess herbage production in the arid rangelands of Central Australia. *International Journal of Remote Sensing,* 16(7):1289-1302.

Holben, B.N. 1986. Characteristics of maximum-value composite images from temporal AVHRR data. *International Journal of Remote Sensing* 7(11):1417-1434.

Kassas, M. 1995. Desertification: a general review. *Journal of Arid Environments,* 30:115-128.

Kennedy, P. 1992. *A Guide to Econometrics* 3rd Edition. The MIT Press, Cambridge, USA..

Marsh, S.E., Walsh, J.L., Lee, C.T., Beck, L. and Hutchinson, C.F. 1992. Comparison of multi-temporal NOAA-AVHRR and SPOT-XS data for mapping land cover dynamics in the West African Sahel. *International Journal of Remote Sensing,* 13(16):2997-3016.

Marsh, S.E. and Hirosawa, Y. 1994. Remote sensing of desert environments. *Journal of the Society of Instrument and Control Engineers* (Japan), 33(10):875-879.

Nahal, I. 1995. Desertification and its effects in the Arabian Peninsula. *Desertification Control Bulletin* No. 27, pp. 53-57.

Nicholson, S.E., Davenport, M.L. and Malo, A.R. 1990. A comparison of the vegetation response to rainfall in the Sahel and East Africa, using normalized difference vegetation index from NOAA AVHRR. *Climate Change,* 17:209-241.

Prince, S.D. 1991. Satellite remote sensing of primary production: comparison of results for Sahelian grasslands 1981-1988. *International Journal of Remote Sensing,* 12:1301-1311.

Ramanathan, R. 1992. *Introductory econometrics with applications.* 3rd Edition. The Dryden Press, Harcourt Brace and Jovanovich, Fort Worth, Texas.

Tucker, C.J. 1979. Red and photographic infrared linear combinations for monitoring vegetation. *Remote Sensing of Environment,* 8:127-150.

Tucker, C.J. 1986. Maximum normalized difference vegetation index images for sub-Saharan Africa for 1983-1985. *International Journal of Remote Sensing* 7(11):1383-1384.

Tucker, C.J., Dregne, H.E. and Newcomb, W.W. 1991a. Expansion and contraction of the Sahara Desert from 1980-1990. *Science* 19 July 1991: 299-301.

Tucker, C.J., Newcomb, W.W., Los, S.O. and Prince, S.D. 1991b. Mean and inter-year variation of growing season normalized difference vegetation index for the Sahel 1981-1989. *International Journal of Remote Sensing* 12(6):1133-1135.

part IV

*Experience in sustainable
rangeland development*

Sustainability of the resource base is the key to continued use of grazed drylands. For centuries, traditional systems of land-use were able to be sustained but population growth, technological innovation, changing values and government intervention have now led to a breakdown of the tradition.

Emphasis in this section is placed on traditional pastoralists, especially the Bedouin, whose way of life is in transition to a more market-oriented, technologically-advanced system.

The eight chapters in this section draw on examples from Jordan, Saudi Arabia and elsewhere, to show how culture and tradition act as a cohesive force among traditional Bedouin and to demonstrate how people have adapted to changing environments and government policies.

The effect of the desert locust, Schistocerca gregaria (Forskal), on the productivity of rangeland in the Red Sea coast of The Sudan and its population management through environment-friendly control tactics

24

M.O. Bashir, I.A. El Rahim Sorkati
and A. Hassanali

Synopsis

This paper reports on experiments designed for a further understanding of the ecology and control of the desert locust. Filed studies of rangeland vegetation at several sites were aimed at quantifying the impact of desert locusts. The impact was two-fold: the direct effect on biomass production; and the indirect effect on palatability of attacked plants and dietary preference by small ruminants.

Key Points

1. *The desert locust, since Biblical times, has remained a major pest of concern to all the world. Its ravages are severe on poor farmers and rangeland in marginal areas. The species earns its status due to explosive reproduction coupled with astonishing mobility and lack of respect for national boundaries.*

2. *Investigations by ICIPE in the study area revealed that the desert locust nymphs consume 40 to 50% of their body weight, depending on their stage and the host plant species, palatability and preference. During the middle of each stage, consumption is high and it is very low before and after each moult.*

1. INTRODUCTION

The desert locust (*Schistocerca gregaria*) is one of the most feared pests on earth. The species still plays havoc in its invasion domain that covers 29 million km^2. The species is more serious in marginal lands where productivity is low and even more serious in marginal rangeland. These areas constitute desert land areas with low rainfall (100 to 200 mm/annum), which is suitable for desert locust population growth and outbreaks.

Assessment of pest damage to pasture is well-documented. Good information is available in rich pasture areas for many species (Bullen, 1966; Bullen, 1970). Assessment of damage due to locusts is limited, even on crops (let alone on pasture). It is virtually non-existent in pastures in marginal areas. Control of the species still depends on the dissipation of pesticides in sensitive marginal areas. Recently, the trend is to steer away from such practices and an integrated approach is advocated (Joffe, 1995). This requires precise information on assessment of damage, economic thresholds and research and field application of alternate, environment-friendly means of control. In this respect, the ICIPE has conducted intensive research into the semiochemicals of the desert locust and started its trials as novel means of managing of populations of this species.

The following study deals with the evaluation of damage and change in the composition of pasture and non-pasture vegetation in biotopes attacked by the desert locust. The study was conducted in the Red Sea coast of The Sudan during the period from 1990 to 1995.

2. METHODOLOGY

2.1 The study area

The investigations on desert locust damage to pasture were conducted in two major Khors, Hosheri (19º 24" N, 37º 19" E) and Handob (19º 13" N, 37º 17" E) that lie 23 and 50 km, respectively, west of Port Sudan. Inhabitants of the two areas are small ruminants and camel raisers.

In 1990, attack by the desert locust was extensive in the two Khors. Breeding in both areas resulted from invading swarms from western Sudan. Hopper bands were observed marching from the foot of mountain ranges towards the coastal plain in defined lines. The bands did not cover the whole area in their marching.

2.2 Vegetation measurements

In 1990, annual and perennial plants in marked transects in the attacked and unattacked zones were surveyed before the bands moved in, and after they moved and caused the damage. Surveys in the same transects continued every year until 1995. They were conducted four weeks after the rains with the establishment of vegetation. The observations included: plant frequency; plant density; tree cover; and the number of fruits per marked sample trees in the attacked and unattacked transects.

Plant frequency refers to the occurrence or non-occurrence of the plant species. This is obtained by measurements along the surveyed transects by the loop and pace-sampling techniques. In the loop technique, observation points were taken at 1 m intervals using a 0.75 inch diameter loop along a 100 meter of stretched tape. Hits were recorded for plants, bare soil, debris or rocks when they fell within the circumference of the loop. In the pace-sampling technique, records were taken every pace which is stretched equivalent to 1 m.

Plant density was assessed within a 1 m² quadrat, thrown randomly within the marked transect, and the number of each plant species was recorded. The absolute and relative density of the various species was then calculated.

Tree cover was assessed by counting the individuals of each species within a 10 x 10 m quadrat and the number of species per hectare(ha) was then computed.

The number of fruits and flowers per tree in the attacked and unattacked transects was counted every year on specific marked trees. Trees of comparable size, by diameter and height, were investigated in both zones. In case of the *Capparis*, the number refers to the average number of flowers and fruits per major branch, four branches sampled per tree. Data were obtained only from Hosheri as few trees occur in Handob.

3. RESULTS

3.1 Attack by the desert locust

In 1990, attack by the desert locust was heavy in the Handob and Hosheri areas. The marching nymphs were several km long and more than 300 m wide, with a density varying from 100 to 1 500 individuals per square meter. They moved in waves, but were eventually controlled by the use of airplanes and manual spraying. The pesticide "propoxur" was in heavy use. Roosting nymphs were estimated to amount to 2 500 individuals per 1 m² and completely covered trees of all sizes. An average of 10 000 roosting individuals per tree was estimated at the beginning of the infestation. *Acacia tortilis* and *Convolvulus hystrix* were heavily defoliated. *Capparis decidua* were debarked. The annual and perennial plants were heavily attacked. The most affected species were *Heliotropium, Crotalaria, Tribulus, Corchorus* and grasses, except *Panicum*. Other forbs were not affected as they do not seem to be preferred by locusts.

3.2 Vegetation measurements

Vegetation measurements were made in 1990, before and after the attack by locusts, in the marked and replicated transects in Handob and Hosheri. Every year until 1995 the measurements were again taken four weeks after the rains in the same transects.

The relative frequency of bare soil, rocks, debris and plant cover in the attacked and unattacked transects are presented in Table 24.1 (Handob and Hosheri sites). The data indicates the different nature of the two localities. In Handob, the soil is sandy loam with few rocks and the vegetation cover is rich compared to Hosheri, where the soil is sandy with appreciable rocks and gravel and the vegetation cover is relatively low. In both localities, the attack by the desert locust drastically reduced the vegetation cover by more than 50%. Recovery was apparent only after the fourth year in both areas.

Table 24.1

Frequency of bare soil, rocks, debris and plant cover in attacked and unattacked transects at two sites (1990-1995)

	Hosheri		Handob	
Attacked	Mean	STD	Mean	STD
Bare soil	62.59	6.26	54.07	7.27
Rocks	1.63	1.37	1.63	1.37
Debris	4.80	4.01	4.60	4.01
Plants	31.18	8.16	39.70	9.58
Unattacked				
Bare soil	47.28	4.53	44.76	6.70
Rocks	9.85	1.85	1.13	0.97
Debris	2.15	0.60	3.80	1.38
Plants	40.72	3.76	50.31	6.90

STD = Standard deviation

Table 24.2 shows the tree and shrub cover in the two areas. It also reveals the different nature of the areas. In Hosheri, more trees are found with the dominant species being *Calotropis procera* followed by *Acacia tortilis*. In Handob, *Calotropis* dominates, followed by *Arthrocnemum glaucum*.

Table 24.2

Mean number of trees and shrubs per hectare, Handob and Hosheri, in 1990

	Handob	Hosheri
SPECIES		
Acacia tortilis	2	15
Convolvulus hystrix	1	5
Arthrocnemum glaucum	15	2
Prosopis glandulos	2	5
Capparis decidua	7	5.5
Leptadenia pyrotechnica	0	3
Commiphora sp.	0	1
Cadaba longifolia	1	4
Calotropis procera	20	26
Suada monoica	11	-
Total	59	66.5

Analysis of the relative frequency of forbs and grass showed that in Handob, the most dominant four plant species by order are *Heliotropium, Zygophyllum, Dactyloctenium, Arthrocnemum* and *Panicum*. In Hosheri, the most dominant ones are *Heliotropium, Crotalaria, Zygophyllum* and *Dactyloctenium*. During the locust attack, dominance by these species was changed. Immediately after the attack, in Handob, *Arthrocnemum* was dominant, followed by *Zygophyllum, Panicum and* then Cassia. In Hosheri, *Zygophyllum* was dominant, followed by *Heliotropium, Calotropis* (seedings) and then *Panicum*. The normal dominance seen before the attack was not restored in both areas until 1994.

The analysis of the relative frequency of grass and forbs in the form of annuals, perennials and palatable and unpalatable species, with respect to small ruminants (goats and sheep) and camels revealed that changes in the ratio of relative frequency of forbs to grass was not consistent during and after the attack in both areas. The frequency of palatable species, with respect to small ruminants, was significantly reduced after the attack and in the following two years in both areas. Analysis of flower and fruit production of attacked and unattacked trees in Hosheri showed that although *Capparis* was heavily attacked, flower and fruit production was low for only two years. By the third year, productivity of initially attacked trees was comparable to unattacked ones. Fruit production in *Convolvulus* was significantly low for three years. *Acacia tortilis* was the most affected species. The drop in fruit production was highly significant for three years.

4. DISCUSSION

The desert locust (*Schistocerca gregaria*) is a notorious pest of field crops and pasture. Its control is a high-priority task in many countries in Africa and Asia. However, information on crop loss is slight despite detailed information on the infested surface being available. The detailed assessments of damage on pasture by grasshoppers and some locust species is available in developed countries but meagre in developing ones. Unpublished work (Suliman, pers. comm.) showed that the species *Aiolopus simulatrix* removes substantial biomass of sorghum, sesame and other species of natural forbs. It was based on computation of the daily consumption in relation to body weight.

Similarly, (Mustafa pers. comm.) showed that biomass removal by the tree locust *Anacredium melanorhodon melanorhodon nymphs* on *Acacia* spp. was based on body weight and the size and number of individuals in the band. Information is meagre on the damage by the desert locust on pasture vegetation in developed countries. Investigations by ICIPE in the study area revealed that desert locust nymphs consume 40 to 50% of their body weight, depending on their stage and the host plant species, palatability and preference. During the middle of each stage, consumption is high and it is very low before and after each moult. The aggregate weight-duration of the different instars was computed to be 0.6521 g and 0.598 g for the solitary and gregarious phase, respectively. Tests with 35 different plant species from the area revealed that, on average, for all tested species a biomass equivalent to 43.3% of the gregarious nymph body weight is consumed daily (i.e., 0.259 g). Taking the average duration from first instar to fledging to be 43 days in winter, then one individual consumes 11.137 g of plant biomass to complete development. During the investigation, the average number of roosting nymphs per *Acacia* was estimated to be 10 000 individuals. Although nymphs do not remain all day on *Acacia* and *Convolvulous* trees, they could potentially remove approximately 2 590 g of biomass per day. In addition, roosting nymphs tend to destroy and waste an appreciable amount of plant leaves while feeding and roosting on *Acacia* and *Convolvulous*.

Therefore, it is not realistic to judge biomass loss only by attributing it to direct consumption. Precise biomass studies on host plants important in the life system of the desert locust and the estimation of loss to solitary and gregarious desert locust nymphs and adults, are in preparation by ICIPE in the Red Sea area.

From these simple calculations, damage by the desert locust to pasture in the two biotopes in the Red Sea area is substantial. The investigated area is very poor in pasture resources. Nevertheless, local people are mainly small ruminants and camel raisers. Their limited holdings are cultivated with millet and vegetables and then only during years of heavy rains and/or benevolent flooding from in the Khors. The exact number of animals in the two Khors is not known. In the Port Sudan district that includes the two areas, the total number of animals is 187 000 head. This figure includes 11 700 camel, 78 000 sheep and 97 000 goats.

The results indicated that, at the initial attack, locusts caused substantial damage that mainly affected the small ruminants. One of the dominant and palatable forbs, *Crotalaria microphylla,* is competed for by both the locusts and the small ruminants. The relative frequency of palatable grass and forbs was almost halved during the attack and continued to be low for three years after it. In addition, the two browse species of trees utilized by small ruminants (*Acacia tortilis* and *Convolvulus hystrix*) which form only 5% and 30% of the palatable tree cover in Handob and Hosheri, respectively, were completely defoliated in the initial attack. The recovery of these species required three years. This indicated that the desert locust is a serious competitor of small ruminants on the meagre desert vegetation resources of the areas. More seriously, the aftermath of the attack by this pest lasts for three years after which the normal biodiversity ratio of the vegetation returns to normal. Camels do not seem to be affected as this animal has a broad list of food plants, most of which are not approached by locusts.

Control of the desert locust in the area depends on the use of pesticides. The use of these lethal chemicals in fragile desert habitats is very serious. Many concerns have been raised about the use of pesticides in the control of locusts and grasshoppers (Matterson, et al., 1991; Everts, 1990; Joffe, 1995; and TAMS consultants, 1989). OTA (1990) and USAID (1991) consider placement of the desert locust control within the context of Integrated Pest Management (IPM), a desirable goal.

However, a number of research gaps have to be addressed to achieve this goal. These include detailed information on desert locust population dynamics; the probability of locust attack in a given area; crop loss and economic thresholds; and the impact of production loss and alternate control agents (Joffe, 1995). One of the alternate methods of the desert locust include the use of pheromones in disrupting behaviour, leading to solitarization of nymph bands and adult swarms.

Investigations on insect semiochemicals long revealed their successful use in control and monitoring tactics. This was dominated by the use of sex pheromones and food lures. The potential of alarm pheromones and other behaviour-moderating pheromones in disrupting essential life system patterns and in control, are being realized. Laboratory investigations on locust semiochemicals at the ICIPE, sponsored by IFAD, have yielded substantial information on locust chemical ecology and behaviour (Mahamat, et al., 1993; Inayatullah, et al., 1994; and Torto, et al., 1994). Verification of this information is being undertaken under field conditions at the ICIPE field station in Port Sudan.

Promising results were obtained in the use of some products as behaviour-disrupting tools to achieve degregarization and predisposing nymphs to biotic, natural and other control factors were obtained (Bashir, 1996). Results of the ongoing ICIPE research on phase markers, and sex and oviposition pheromones will also improve practical locust survey methods in the locust-affected countries. These findings will also help in the development of components for the model dealing with gregarization.

More investigation is needed on the evaluation of damage by the desert locust and other species on pasture in areas where resources are meagre. There is a need for the development of alternate control methods, testing and improving the field application of promising ones. These alternate methods are needed in the design of an integrated management strategy to conserve the already fragile habitats in marginal rangelands.

References

Bashir, M.O. 1996. Preliminary investigations on the effect of a component of the desert locust adult gregarization pheromone on gregarious nymphs. Symposium on the role of research in the integrated biological control of the desert locust. Univ. of Juba, The Association of Arab Research Councils and the Sudanese National Research Center, Khartoum, 3-5, October 1995. In Press.

Bullen, F.T. 1966. Locusts and grasshoppers as pests of crops and pasture- a preliminary economic approach. *Journal of Applied Ecology,* 3: 147-168.

Bullen, F.T. 1970. *A review of the assessment of crop losses caused by locusts and grasshoppers.* Proceedings of the International Study Conference on Current and Future Problems of Acridology, London, pp. 163-169.

Everts, J.W., Ed. 1990. *Environmental effects of chemicals in locust and grasshopper control. A pilot study.* ECLO/SEN/003. NEM Project Report. FAO Rome.

Food and Agriculture Organization of the United Nations (FAO). 1985. Report of a consultation on desert locust plague prevention in the central region, Rome, 28-30 May 1985. FAO, Rome.

Inayatullah, C., El Bashir, S. and Hassanali, A. 1994. Sexual behaviour and communication in the desert locust, *Schistcerca gregaria* (Forskal) (Orthoptera : Acrididae): Sex pheromone in solitaria. *Environ. Entomol.,* 23: 1544-1551.

Joffe, S. 1995. *Desert locust Management: A Time For Change,* World Bank Discussion Paper no. 248, World Bank. Washington, D.C.

Keith, J. and Mullie, J. 1990. The effect of Fenitrohion and Chlorpyrifos on birds in savannah of Northern Senegal In: Everts, J. (ed) *Environmental effects of chemicals in locust and grasshopper control. A pilot study.* ECLO/SEN/003. NEM Project Report. FAO Rome.

Mahamat, H., Hassanali, A., Odongo, H., Torto, B. and El-Bashir, S. 1993. Studies on the maturation-accelerating pheromone of the desert locust *Shistocerca gregaria* (Orthoptera: Acrididae). J. Chem. Ecol. 4: 159-164.

Matterson, P.C. 1991. *Field studies of the environmental impact of locust/grasshopper control programmes in Africa.* IITA-BCP/CAB IIBC Workshop on biological control of locusts and grasshoppers, Cootonou, Republic of Benin, April 29-May.

Office of Technology Assessment (OTA). 1990. *A Plague of Locust , Special Report.* U.S. Congress, Office of Technology Assessment, OTA-F-450. Washington, DC, Government Printing Office.

TAMS Consultants. 1989. *Locust and grasshopper control in Africa/Asia. A programmatic environmental assessment.* Report for USAID. TAMS Consultants, Inc., New York, NY and Arlington, VA.

Torto, B., Obeng-Ofori, D., Njagi, P.G.N., Hassanali, A. and Amiani, H. 1994 . Aggregation pheromone system of adult gregarious desert locust, *Schistcerca gregaria (Forskal). J. Chem. Ecol,.* 20: 1749-1762.

United States Agency for International Development (USAID). 1991. *Review of environmental concerns in A.I.D. programs for locust and grasshopper control.* USAID, Washington, DC.

The socio-economics of pastoralism: a commentary on changing techniques and strategies for livestock management

Y. Ahmad

25

Synopsis

This essay is wide-ranging and deals with nomadic pastoral in the past and present. The author argues the case for programme and policy interventions that are multi-disciplinary, process-driven and focused on a minimum threshold of critical objectives.

Key Points

1. *A clearer understanding of the socio-economics of nomadic pastoralism is needed if the application of recent technological advances in rangeland monitoring is to yield maximum potential benefits to nomads and their home countries. To understand and consider viable nomadic pastoralism in the context of a healthy support environment, several distinct features need to be understood, which requires going beyond the more traditional control of livestock numbers in terms of a hypothetical concept of rangeland carrying capacity.*

2. *Stock numbers can continue to be governed by the pastoralists' traditional strategy of enhanced mobility and accessible communications that optimize advantages and opportunities offered by changing climatic and episodic conditions. Grazing systems could remain essentially event-driven. Attention should however be paid to understanding the special needs of pastoral nomads, particularly in terms of cultural values and the need to involve them in the processes of change and development with a potential to affect them.*

3. *One conclusion which has emerged generally from development activities that impact on the environments is that economy-wide policies, such as policy and programme interventions for the sustainable use of rangelands or for desertification control, help enhance social stability. This, in turn, will yield environmental*

benefits. Instability, combined with land-use pressures, undermines the sustainable use of natural resources.

4. *While the mechanics of information-gathering and enhancing mobility have changed with time, the basic strategies for livestock management and production have remained the same. In recent years, however, a number of complex concerns have emerged that render effective livestock production more difficult and burdensome for pastoral nomads. These concerns include: a rapid increase in human population in pastoral communities; a more sedentary way of life; an increasing need for technology to deal with pressing problems of management; and rapidly-changing political, economic and social conditions. As a result, policy and programme interventions are required that are multidisciplinary, process-driven, and focused on a minimum threshold of critical objectives.*

5. *Man and nature are always in search of a liveable balance, but mishaps are more likely to happen because of the "discontinuous" nature of the relationship between the pressures generated by human activities and the tolerance levels of ecosystems. It is unlikely that damage inflicted on dry rangelands by overgrazing will be irreversible, because even a minor change in rainfall or other climatic conditions will often bring about a rapid response in terms of vegetation and alter expectations. It is, nevertheless, worthwhile when faced with risk and uncertainty with such critical consequences, to follow the precautionary principle and take action on a broad front to ensure that unexpected surprises do not occur.*

1. INTRODUCTION

The application of innovative and presently evolving technologies in rangeland monitoring is a critical concern and, quite rightly, a major pre-occupation of this workshop. Enormous advances have been made in recent years in climate and other environmental forecasting. But for these advances to be of maximum benefit to pastoral nomads, the use of the resulting data must be based on a clear understanding of the socio-economic underpinnings of pastoralism. Policy-makers are often not aware of the economic and social management "tools" and cultural levers available to mobilize community energy and coordinated action in terms of economy-wide development programmes. There is a steep learning curve in understanding the role of socio-cultural contexts, but it is a road worth travelling if we are to achieve meaningful progress.

A distinguishing feature of nomadic pastoralism is that the evolution and impact of economic and social change does not necessarily follow a steady state. Nomads often reflect a continuing effort at adjustment between the physical and natural forces on the one hand, and the gradual evolution of deep-seated perceptions, customs and cultural forces on the other hand. It is necessary in this situation to accept periods of little or no change followed by shifts that could be relatively rapid, towards a new equilibrium (Blench, this volume; Ngaido, et al., this volume).

Clearly, the problems of rangeland management and of pastoral development are much more complex than the reduction of land degradation through the control of livestock numbers, based on some ill-defined and unenforceable concept of carrying capacity of the rangelands. There is much to be said in favour of the traditional strategy of stock movements for the maximization of livestock production and returns, based on the spatial and temporal distribution of forage. Such an "opportunistic" movement of livestock can come about in response to rainfall variability or other episodic events, such as rangeland fires or the outbreak of diseases. In reality, the grazing systems in a region are essentially event-driven. Adjustment policies for the pastoral nomads must, therefore, not only take account of the shift between equilibrium and non-equilibrium dynamics within the region, but they must also be open to evolve with time.

Another distinguishing feature is that pastoral nomads, like other groups of the relatively poor, have special needs that must be specifically recognized and respected (Al-Eisa, this volume). These include: access to ownership of natural resources and other forms of capital; an increase in the productivity of capital through improved infrastructure; and accessibility to health, sanitation and social services, a lack of which, for example, is severely felt and which acts as a major impediment to economic and social change as it is the absence of a safety net for the pastoralists and their families. The remedy requires the provision of social investment funds. The cost of the necessary measures is likely to be high in the region, because of a lack of effective environmental monitoring, poor resource management in the past, inefficient extension services, and inappropriate macro-economic policies. There is much to be said in favour of preparing in advance an in-depth analysis of the scale and structure of a full range of identified needs before proceeding with policy and programme interventions (Geerken, et al., this volume).

The basic rationale for social investment in nomads comes from the realization that the means and the ends of long-term development, and of economic and social change, requires emphasis in equal measure on the quality of human resource development and the quality of the resources made available for the purpose. Such an approach must consequently focus attention on the distinct steps needed for nomads to diversify and flourish in an enabling environment. The single concept that should cut across all strategic development agendas in this field is the importance of building local-level capacity in natural resource management. It requires both training and organizational arrangements. The latter is a sensitive issue and there is no attempt here to offer advice from outside.

But it is also an essential condition for effective and efficient resource allocation. What instruments and policy frameworks are to be considered and eventually used for the purpose are for individual countries to decide.

The ecological fate of desertified, arid and semi-arid lands has tended to fluctuate with climatic variability on the one hand, and the level of interaction by local communities on the other hand. The sustainable use of rangelands and desertification control are critical issues because the means of subsistence for over 20% of the world's population is at risk. Moreover, most of the threatened people are also those who are the most vulnerable of the country's population, namely, the poor and the marginalized. It is estimated that more than 133 million people may be forced to migrate because of land degradation within a short period, but it is impossible to determine how many may have been forced to abandon their lands already (though the figure is expected to be in the millions).

The interaction effected by local communities, however, is not only an economic problem but also a socio-cultural one for which broad-based solutions must be sought. Fortunately this critical aspect of the problem has been recognized, to its credit, by the UN Convention to Combat Desertification (CCD). It is not surprising that more than 100 countries signed the Convention in June 1994 in Paris. According to the terms of the definition agreed by world leaders at the 1992 Earth Summit in Rio de Janeiro and spelled out by the Convention, desertification is "land degradation in arid, semi-arid and sub-humid areas resulting from resource problems, including climate variations and human activities", such as, overgrazing, overcropping, poor irrigation, deforestation and the cultivation of marginal lands. In keeping with this definition, the objectives of the Convention are: (i) to seek an improvement in the management of the ecosystems; and (ii) to ensure that international aid flows are more responsive to the needs of the threatened regions.

Because nomads live or languish according to how well they can assess risk and uncertainty, they are more sensitive – and more sensitized – to natural changes than most other population groups. This is why rangeland monitoring and its evolving techniques are potentially of such critical importance to nomads. Measures for the sustainable development of rangelands, and certainly anti-desertification programmes, must take a close look at both directly related variables (e.g., changes in vegetation cover, depths of topsoil, species composition) and indirectly related variables (e.g., intensity and distribution of precipitation, prices of agricultural commodities, human migration) as the basis for remedial action. But authorities must also proceed on the basis of a cost/benefit analysis of how to respond to the perceived threats. A number of decision-making problems arise as we try to balance the costs of early action against delayed or no action. The Climate Change Convention deals with this problem of uncertainty by adopting the precautionary principle. Article 3(3) states: "When there are threats of serious or irreversible damage, lack of full scientific certainty should not be used as a reason for postponing such measures".

It is worth reminding ourselves, however, that there are a number of major issues of public policy that have so far not been resolved either in the developing or the developed world. Furthermore, in recent years, large and complex global changes in the perception of social needs have taken place. They involve the ageing of populations. They also involve the gradual dwindling of the capacity of national governments not only to provide for general and individual welfare, but also, and more specifically, to create economic opportunities and jobs and to generate social protection. These changes are still going on and new ones are likely to be in the offing. Eventually, a consensus may arise on the most appropriate role of the state, private enterprise, media and civil society. Within such a framework of roles and responsibilities, it will become more realistic to explore and develop future policy options on such far-reaching and critical problems of global import as desertification. Further development in the techniques of rangeland monitoring must undoubtedly continue. Climatic variability has so far played a dominant role, but in the light of the global climate change problems and the unprecedented pressures generated by world population increase, the existing patterns may well change. It is worthwhile, in any event, to address far-reaching issues, such as those we are considering today, in a contingent manner.

2. IMPORTANCE OF CULTURAL VALUES

The role of traditional cultural values in the definition of economic and social change has not received the consideration by policy managers it deserves. There is a deeply rooted conviction in traditional societies that models for productivity and stability, equivalent to sustainable development, must not only generate economic growth, but must also ensure its equitable and just distribution. In the drive towards economic betterment, the imperatives of "modernity" should not override the traditions of society. It is accepted that such an approach would have certain costs. Sustainable growth requires us to minimize these costs to the extent possible and desirable, for example, without sacrificing basic cultural values. Past experience shows that "modernization" strategies, by themselves, could often, at worst, be misconceived; at best, not be based on sustainable targets and objectives. They may come from not fully understanding the multifaceted nature of the problems that face us, or from a lack of focus on the priorities. In any event, much more attention needs to be paid to the manner in which traditional cultural values are treated (or manipulated) in the decision-making process at present.

The balance of available evidence in the region seems to indicate that, if economic change and development of the pastoral nomads is in harmony with their traditional cultural values, there is more likelihood of a rewarding move upwards, (in the continuum of their continuing struggle with nature), towards stability, productivity and growth. These trends need to be studied, their weaknesses and strengths identified, and support for the more dynamic elements strengthened.

Needless to say, a major educational effort is implicit in the introduction and development of such an approach and a broader time-horizon is indicated. But these efforts are more likely to lead to a productive and process-oriented strategy in the long run than the current approaches applied.

A focus of many of the elements of the strategy must be on cost-effective opportunities for improving the status and income of nomads. The favoured strategy must take into account two types of costs involved: the costs of the rehabilitation and regeneration of the pasturelands as such; and the costs of activities focused on the socio-cultural context of the target groups (e.g., in the case of the nomads, to allow them to develop in harmony with their religious beliefs and organizations, manners and customs, and systems of valuation, whether expressed or implicit). The second type of costs could be viewed as an attempt to focus social spending on neglected groups. They could also be regarded as costs of transition, but not transition at any cost, i.e., at the expense of primary education, basic health care, and the nutritional needs of children. If it is to answer certain key questions at the outset and broker a solution on crucial cultural issues, the strategy must be based firmly on the identification, evaluation and effective funding of the second type of costs involved, largely ignored with the plea of budgetary constraints so far, and not merely by paying lip service to them. It is interesting to note how the assessment of essential societal needs, and their reflection in budgetary allocations, have evolved over time. Twenty years ago, expenditures on education, health and social care were considered controversial, much as expenditures on policy and programme interventions for environmental and natural resource concerns are considered today. It is a moot issue, although likely, that a similar evolution of societal needs will eventually cover ecological concerns.

Many of the current programmes of economic and social change for the pastoral nomads appear to be based more on the symptoms, than the causes, of their underdevelopment and marginalization. A new assessment, new budgetary allocations and a new regulatory framework are necessary to ensure the proper participation and protection of the pastoral nomads. The models of production and consumption and the values that support them, notably the primacy of the economic over cultural and social ones, are in effect a source of the key problems of underemployment and social exclusion, and not a solution.

Traditional cultural values are viewed as largely irrelevant in the analysis and planning for economic development, and hence often are neglected. But when economic development and growth must take into account environmental and natural resource constraints and opportunities, (as it must if it is to be long-term and sustainable), other dimensions come centrally into play. One of these dimensions is the amalgam of perceptions, beliefs and customs of the people concerned (Blench, this volume; Ngaido, et al., this volume). Another is the close involvement and contribution of the people. These essential elements are to be sought in the traditional cultural values of the local communities. For this reason, there is finally an increasing recognition that policy and programme interventions for the sustainable management of dry rangelands and desertification control must relate clearly, and in a primary way, to traditional cultural values, especially when these values are as strongly held as is the case with the pastoral nomads.

3. INVOLVEMENT OF PASTORAL NOMADS IN DEVELOPMENT ACTIVITIES

Apart from cultural values, it is possible to identify in the light of recent development experience (largely through World Bank projects), a broad spectrum of policy interventions that could guide the economic change and development of pastoral nomads. In summary, there appears to be two particularly efficient conditions for success. The first is encouragement for more active involvement by those affected by development activities in the decision-making process. The second is the establishment of an institutional framework to deal with the major agricultural and natural resource problems of targeted groups. These two conditions constitute what has been called the "social scaffolding for sustainability".

The case for the involvement of those affected by development activities in the decision-making process revolves around a nexus of three basic considerations: (i) an improvement in the purposes of the activity to be undertaken; (ii) an enhancement of national help to the poor and the disadvantaged groups involved; and (iii) an enlistment of their willing cooperation and support in the realization of objectives of development intervention. The latter is a critical parameter that depends on strengthening a feeling of identification with the project. When identification is not there or when it is weak, the chances of success for the development intervention are minimal. Identification of this nature will only come when the policy and programme interventions are conceived, as a result of felt needs, by the people affected by them.

There is increasing recognition among experts, both at the national and international level, that it is important to gauge the preferences and priorities of the local communities and to provide an enabling environment for them to realize their objectives. This is based on the gradual realization that much can be gained through an understanding of the way in which local communities, pastoral nomads included, view public services such as health and education, administrative institutions, and infrastructure. In recent times, attempts have also been made to develop techniques to assess the perceptions of local groups, both as to the nature of specific development activities to be implemented and the effectiveness of the proposed operational instruments to be used. These techniques are based, among others, on social and beneficiary assessments. But much work still needs to be done on these types of assessments through improvements in their conception, design and application to practical problems.

What does involvement of this nature mean in practice? There are many ways to proceed and there is no consensus on the nature and content of the process of "involvement". But perhaps it is useful to follow a "best practices" approach, both in terms of the design of integrated conservation and development activities, and training in methods. It is a matter of record that very few projects of rangeland management and pastoral development worldwide have stemmed from the conscious involvement of local communities. This is the net consequence of neglecting to take into account social and cultural considerations, a neglect strengthened by the lack of institutional capacity and technical expertise.

It is worthwhile, in this connection, to consider the concept of "social capital" and to keep under review, from an early or conceptual stage of policy formulation, its different components, notably: the stock of techniques, inter-relationships; organizational arrangements; beliefs and perceptions; and, above all, the confidence and commitment of the affected groups, like the nomads, to come to terms with their fragile natural resource base. The fact of the matter is that throughout history traditional pastoral cultures have managed, through their own empirically developed techniques of farming and herding, to wrest a living from unfriendly and unforgiving soils, while maintaining the productivity and resilience of their rangelands. This is no mean achievement, especially considering that it was done without the aid of the sophisticated, recently developed, technical and scientific tools for rangeland monitoring.

It will be worthwhile for countries implementing the CCD, and the agencies supporting them, to take a close look at these traditional techniques from the point of view of their potential for transferability. Fortunately, there is a greater willingness nowadays to respect traditional cultural values and to learn from traditional techniques and practices.

In practical terms, institutional capacity-building is concerned not so much with the way in which an institution is set up or with its organizational structure.

It is more concerned with its standing and its support within a community, which is expressed in terms of funding, its responsibilities and mandate stated in unambiguous language, and the technical knowledge and skills available to it. Above all, capacity stipulates the ability and willingness to operate effectively over multi-disciplinary issues and across jurisdictions. In order to play its proper role, institutional capacity-building, especially in terms of the sustainable management of dry rangelands, must focus on the development of a public awareness strategy, (particularly of disaster awareness), and the initiation of contingency planning systems, supported by information and monitoring networks.

4. CHANGING STATUS OF PASTORAL NOMADS

A change in balance between settled agriculture and nomadic pastoralism appears to have been ongoing in the region since the early years of the present century. The process of change has not been due to any perception of ecological damage caused by the pastoral nomads to rangelands through excessive use leading to land degradation, but due to the political reality of governments preferring settled farmers who could be taxed and conscripted to nomads outside the political community who might presumably pose a danger to order.

There has also been a second factor at work. In the interface between agriculture and pastoralism, an increasing sophistication and diversity in the consumption patterns and preferences of the population led inevitably to a decreasing demand for the main products of the rangelands or rather to a shrinking profits from them, as compared to those from agricultural crops. The market for camels began to shrink with the advent of modern transportation (e.g., the coming of railways, network of roads, automated vehicles), which struck a substantive blow at the traditional use of camels for transport. The demand for sheep and goats continued, and may have increased as the population grew, but capital was profitably invested in the growing of crops. As a result, the numbers of livestock in proportion to human population have decreased dramatically all over the region, even though 99% of the pastoral households today own sheep for cash value to meet their family needs.

The nomads have lived a largely self-contained existence with strict observance of traditional rites and obligations. Nevertheless, during the 1920s and 1930s, according to a noted historian of the region, Albert Hourani, "nomadic pastoralism virtually disappeared as an important factor in Arab society". This does not mean that nomads are no longer to be found or that they have been fully integrated into the mainstream of economic life. The development and management of livestock production continues to be followed through reliance on "opportunistic" stock movements. The techniques utilized for the purpose have evolved with time. A generation ago, the more talented young men of the extended family were sent out to scout for rainfall areas and vegetative cover; today, young men are working in oilfields or construction sites, sometimes across the border in other countries. There is also a reliance on trucks for transporting livestock and on telephones for tracking climatic and other conditions. In this process, the pastoral nomads are actually settling down to a more profitable existence with a family house in their ancestral village and access to schooling for their children.

Thus, while techniques have changed, the long-standing strategies for livestock management have not. These strategies are based on the need to respond as rapidly as possible to changing climatic and vegetative conditions, through enhanced mobility and such means of information gathering as may be available. Grazing systems cannot be replaced easily by prescriptions to reduce land degradation through the control of excessive livestock numbers. Such prescriptions are usually ignored. Carrying capacity and critical loads are useful concepts in broad scientific analysis.

In 1994, the concept of critical load was effectively used as the basis for a protocol to a treaty limiting the release of nitrous oxides from large combustion plants, automobiles and other sources in Europe. These are equilibrium concepts, but equilibrium is not the normal state of the ranges in drylands. The key to the success and survival of the pastoral nomad lies in the keenness of his observation of variations in vegetation and precipitation in time and over different parts of the rangelands and on his successful (or unsuccessful) exploitation of observations. Information exchange and transportation have always been, and still remain the major instruments for rangeland management. For this reason also, there is little doubt that in due course the pastoral communities will become more involved and participate directly in the adaptation and use of the new technologies for rangeland monitoring.

Meanwhile, policy and programme interventions are needed to help pastoral nomads overcome a number of emerging concerns that have made effective and efficient (in the economic sense) livestock management more difficult for them. These concerns include: the rapid increase in human populations in pastoral communities; a more sedentary life on the pasturelands; the increasing need for technology to deal with emerging problems; and changing political, economic and social conditions. These concerns are not static. They are changing in nature and impact as their incidence becomes more burdensome and they interact with one another. Time is not on the side of the nomads and early action is indicated, if we are to avoid an accelerated deterioration in economic and environmental conditions. Bad management decisions stemming largely from the lack of local participation and poor foreign advisory services (through unqualified experts, for example), often contribute to a worsening of these concerns.

5. ENVIRONMENTAL IMPACT OF HUMAN ACTIVITIES

It is commonly accepted that our understanding of the environmental impact of human activities, whether interventions in nature or environmental support for development policies and programmes, remains limited. Some of the impacts could be irreversible, others synergistic. It is necessary, in this situation, to proceed with caution. One conclusion, however, that has emerged repeatedly from development initiatives that impact on the environment is that economy-wide policies (such as policy and programme interventions for the sustainable management of dry rangelands and the control of desertification), help to enhance social stability at the local and national levels. They thus yield substantial environmental benefits because instability undermines the sustainable use of natural resources. In contrast, social stability, based on the maintenance and promotion of cultural values, leads to a longer-term perspective by all users, (particularly the most vulnerable) of the resource base.

One of the main objectives of policy and programme interventions is to improve the income flow of the pastoral nomads over time. But such is the interlocking nature of the activities involved that, in so doing, they will also produce other advantages and disadvantages, in reality costs and benefits, requiring a trade-off. Complications may arise, both in the short and long term. In the short term, the impact of adjustments on poverty, and especially on employment and underemployment, may generate pressures on open-access resources. In the long term, public policies, such as those we are considering, would certainly induce changes and also increase pressures on the environment.

It is essential to take these interlinkages into account, at an early stage, and plan to reduce the resulting pressures through a number of specific remedial measures, such as: the introduction of a system of livestock marketing that takes account of unpredictable shifts of forage and the financing and infrastructure necessary for such a system; better technology for monitoring; and a new approach to the maintenance of mobility as a critical instrument for livestock management. The latter effort is likely to be the most difficult, and at the same time the most pressing within the region at the present, because it involves the vexing problem of a reform of pastoral land tenure.

But apart from costs, unexpected and very large benefits may also arise with momentous impact on global and regional well-being. It is worthwhile to estimate these benefits and factor them in along with the costs.

6. CONSERVATION OF FLORA AND FAUNA IN DRY RANGELANDS

A global benefit of great importance that the policy and programme interventions are likely to produce relates to the conservation and sustainable use of biodiversity in the arid and semi-arid rangelands. Arid lands are roughly defined, in this context, as those lands receiving 0.25 centimetres (cm), and semi-arid lands as those receiving between 25 and 50 cm of rainfall annually.

Although there is a consensus that conservation and sustainable use of flora and fauna in dry rangelands is a priority concern, their continuing destruction through unrestricted hunting and overgrazing is a marked phenomenon of these regions.

The loss of species is a classic example of irreversibility. While conservation and sustainable use of biodiversity may not yield quantifiable results in the short term, they produce substantive social and ecological benefits, including the protection and enhancement of a vital, life-sustaining part of the environment. The loss of the world's unique genetic heritage is compounded by the fact that we have no certain knowledge of what we are losing, at what rate, and at what cost to the present and future generations. Some species are seen to be repositories of key genetic material, others are seen as of marginal genetic significance. But our knowledge in this field is quite limited.

The present approach to conservation through the creation of biosphere reserves and protected areas is both inadequate and unsatisfactory for its purposes. While it is accepted that the cost of protecting all the species, genes and ecosystems could be prohibitive, the present strategy of saving only a select few on an ad hoc basis is discriminatory and unscientific. The present approach is also unsatisfactory because the selection of sites for the establishment of protected areas and biosphere reserves is not based on the latest available tools of technical and scientific assessment and monitoring, and there is no attempt to seek long-term and practical accommodation between the needs of herders and of wildlife. The establishment of protected areas and biosphere reserves are currently viewed in the great majority of their locations by local communities as outside imports, cultural impositions, from which they seldom benefit. This is a perception which imposes an unnecessarily heavy burden on conservation efforts.

For environmental management and conservation in particular to succeed, there is a need for the willing co-operation of all the parties involved namely: government agencies; local "users" of the natural resources, including flora and fauna; and local communities. The challenge is to get all parties to agree on common paths in which capacities are tapped, responsibilities are shared and everyone is expected to receive some benefits (and bear some costs) for the conservation and sustainable use of biodiversity.

In reality, the distributional incidence of costs and benefits of biodiversity conservation and sustainable use is seldom shared in a fair and responsible manner. Indeed, one of the major problems facing the implementation of the Framework Convention for Biodiversity Conservation, approved at the Earth Summit in Rio de Janeiro in 1992, has been the lack of an agreed mechanism to correct the present imbalance in the distributional incidence of costs and benefits at different spatial (and temporal) levels.

It is possible to identify three broad spatial levels for the consideration of costs and benefits:
• local;
• regional/national; and
• global.

There arises a difference in interests and incentives from the asymmetry in both economic costs and economic benefits at the three levels.

At the local level, although there are considerable variations from site to site, the overall benefits tend to be somewhat narrow and defined. These benefits are, generally speaking, related to direct consumption use, notably of food, herbs, medicinal plants, supplementary income from tourism or recreational activities in protected areas. At the same time, the economic costs, both indirect costs involving damages arising, in the most common example, from the protected wildlife in the area, and the opportunity costs, i.e., benefits foregone (both for direct consumption use by herders and for conversion of areas placed in protection for extending agricultural use or carrying out mining and other profit-making activities), as a result of lost access to the resources of the protected area, are at once concrete, easily perceived and burdensome.

It is essential to find a resolution of the problem of asymmetry of interests at different levels and particularly at the local level, which requires in essence an acceptable accommodation between the needs of wildlife and those of pastoralists (in their role as herders).

The basic problem that must be resolved is a two-dimensional one. It is necessary to make the need for conservation measures understandable and acceptable to the pastoralists. But that is only one aspect of what needs to be done. According to the findings of a team of eminent biologists studying experimental prairies in the US, published in the journal *Nature* (February, 1997), the increase in the number of species increased the productivity and stability of the ecosystem. The study concluded that the more species an area had, the more biomass or plant material it produced and the better it retained nitrogen, the most crucial of nutrients and the basis for long-term growth. The conclusion supports the suggestion made by Charles Darwin in *The Origin of Species*, that more diverse ecosystems were also likely to be the more productive ones. The second aspect of what needs to be done, thus, is to complement the perception of the link between the number of species and the productivity of ecosystems. This requires us to devise strategies and the technical means for the most effective use of rangelands and their resources, such as, sharing the resources on an optimal curve between the grazers (cattle and sheep) and the browsers (camels and goats), keeping in mind the needs of both domestic animals and wildlife.

In order to be successful in these efforts, institutional support will be needed for the nature conservation programmes through the development of an integrated protected areas system, boundary demarcations, ecodevelopment in and around protected areas, and further research.

Empirical evidence suggests that the proper management of natural resources must be seen both from the point of view of "protection" and "production". While the natural resources are being protected, they must also be made more productive. The test of sustainability lies in the proper mix of protection and production. In the final analysis, the effort for accommodation must be made by the pastoralists and they will only achieve it, i.e., share the grazing in an equitable manner with all the claimants including wildlife, if they see a clear advantage in it for themselves. This can only come from a commonly perceived increase in the productivity of the rangelands.

7. CONCLUSION

It will be seen that in dealing with the complex and rapidly changing socio-economic problems facing the pastoral nomads, policy and programme interventions should be multidisciplinary in character, and they should be process-driven. They should also attempt to cover a minimum threshold of critical objectives focused on improving the productivity and resilience of the rangelands. Within a broad programme of this nature, the interventions should support the design of planning and implementation procedures in order:

(i) to slow and, if possible, reverse the worsening of the quality of soil, water and other natural resources;

(ii) to protect, conserve and restore the genetic density of the targeted regions;

(iii) to develop institutions of research, reforestation and technology generation;

(iv) to strengthen environmental legislation and institutions involved in the task;

(v) to mobilize adequate resources to correct damages, such as erosion and soil degradation caused by the indiscriminate conversion of land for agricultural use;

(vi) to ensure environmentally sound investments in the rehabilitation and development of irrigation and drainage schemes;

(vii) to help in the establishment of soil and water management demonstration centres in agro-ecological zones, where potential problems have been found; and

(viii) to identify innovative ways of providing pastoral nomads with access to credit to improve the management of their natural resource base, particularly through micro-credit schemes on pastures and rangelands.

In establishing the inter se priority of the interventions to be undertaken and their effectiveness, it would have been helpful for us to have had available a generalized understanding of the carrying capacity of the dry rangelands. Unfortunately, as already noted, there is no consensus on the use and reliability of the models for estimating carrying capacity, especially in regions of high climatic variability. The policy issue that arises is whether the damage that has already been inflicted on the rangelands is irreversible (i.e beyond some projected level of carrying capacity) and there is, therefore, no justification for further investments, or whether they are seen as suffering a temporary setback from which they could recover to produce adequate returns on investment.

Documented evidence suggests that a change in rainfall or other climatic conditions often bring about a rapid response in the dry rangelands. Vegetation cover is often found to switch over considerable distances with even a modicum of precipitation. It appears unlikely, therefore, that irreversible damage to dry rangelands is a probability within time frames of relevance to us.

As the Desertification Convention makes it clear, action to deal with land degradation in desertified, arid and semi-arid lands is required in two parts. It is necessary to follow climatic conditions closely and to have pastoral nomads involved in the use of recently developed technologies for rangeland monitoring. Secondly, policy and programme interventions are needed to cope with emerging problems of economic and social adjustment.

From the long-term and ecological point of view, however, the bottom line must be that when faced with risk and uncertainty of such critical consequences, it is worthwhile to follow the precautionary principle and take immediate action on a broad front to ensure that unexpected and unpleasant surprises do not occur. Such mishaps are the more likely to happen because of the "discontinuous" nature of the relationship between the pressures generated by human activities and the threshold levels of tolerance of ecosystems. The actual collapse of ecosystems could be extremely burdensome in both human and financial terms; anticipatory and preventive policies are far more reliable and far less costly than curative ones.

References

Al-Eisa, A. 1997. Changes and factors affecting Bedouin movement for grazing (this volume).

Blench, R.M. 1997. Rangeland degradation and socio-economic changes among the Bedu of Jordan: results of the 1995 IFAD survey (this volume).

Ngaido, T. Nordblom, T. Osman, A.E. and Gintzburger, G. 1997. A policy shift toward sustainable resource development (this volume).

Finan, T.J. and Al-Haratani E.R. 1997. Modern Bedouins: the transformation of traditional nomad society in the Al-Taysiyah region of Saudi Arabia (this volume).

Geerken, R., Ilawa, M., Jaja, M., Kauffmann, H., Roeder, H., Sankary, A.M., and Segl, K. 1997. Monitoring dryland degradation to define and implement suitable measures towards sustainable rangeland management (this volume).

Modern Bedouins: the transformation of traditional nomad society in the Al-Taysiyah region of Saudi Arabia

26

T.J. Finan and E.R. Al-Haratani

Synopsis

This is a paper tracing the history of the nomadic Bedouin pastoralists and the impact of modernization. It is based on a large empirical study in central Saudi Arabia, including several months of participant observation among the Harb tribesmen. The paper examines the impact of modernization upon changes in rangeland management strategies and, in turn, upon the livelihood of local Bedouin groups. It further enquires into the environmental consequences and suggests several options that seek to reconcile the persistence of the Bedouin as a social category in Saudi Arabia with environmental sustainability.

Key Points

1. Since the unification of the Kingdom of Saudi Arabia, traditional strategies of rangeland management have been significantly altered. Tribal boundaries and local control over water sources have disappeared, creating a situation of open ranges accessible to all groups and eliminating local management strategies.

2. At the same time, economic growth in Saudi Arabia has introduced capital-intensive forms of herding and more intense market integration of Bedouin groups into a wider economic systems. Moreover, the government subsidies on feed grains have expanded economic opportunities and reduced the traditional risks of nomadic pastoralism. The Bedouin have experienced a major transformation from an essentially nomadic existence to one that resembles a market-oriented ranching strategy.

3. The environmental consequences are significant, with land degradation being a common feature.

1. INTRODUCTION

The position of the tribal nomads in society remains an issue of great complexity in the modern Kingdom of Saudi Arabia. From a historical and politico-cultural perspective, the Bedouin provide a symbol of enduring resilience and a sense of fierce independence that inspires public pride and private admiration among all Saudis. From a socio-economic perspective, however, the Bedouin have been marginalized by the process of rapid development that has benefited the rest of the Kingdom, and particularly the educated urban population. The popular Bedouin image of brave self-reliance is belied by the reality of illiteracy and poverty and, in terms of its livelihood system, an increased dependence on public assistance. In the context of this ambivalence there arises a question of how traditional Bedouin society will adapt to the inevitable forces of modernization and integrate itself into a wider national context. The Bedouin question places an important focus on the role of public policy in promoting sustainable livelihood systems in a fragile desert environment, while facilitating Bedouin participation in the socio-economic mainstream.

There are two non-controvertible facts about the pastoral tribes of Saudi Arabia. The first is that tribal pastoralists still comprise a significant portion of the total national population, in terms of both numbers and influence. The national average share of tribal nomads in the total population is estimated at 25% (Cole, 1981), and they are a vocal, if dispersed, constituency in the political arena. The second fact is that the Bedouin pastoralists have been undergoing a major transformation over the last few decades, beginning with the Public Lands Decree of 1953 that prohibited the maintenance of traditional rangeland reserves (hema) and abolished exclusive tribal rights over their tribal lands (dirahs) (Cole, 1981). This transformation was accelerated by the process of rapid economic growth that began in the 1970s with the emergence of oil wealth. In effect, rangeland is now a common property resource, available in principle to all those who wish to use it, and (as a consequence of economic growth) the technology of range use has intensified dramatically.

This paper has a dual purpose. It first documents the impact of policy change and modernization on the economic well-being of a select group of nomadic pastoralists in the Al-Taysiyah region of north east Saudi Arabia. The rulers of the Kingdom have had a long and complicated historical relationship with their Bedouin populations and have targeted several forms of assistance and opportunities to different tribal groups. At different times, public policy has attempted to: locate Bedouins in settlements with enhanced access to education and health care (e.g., the Harrad and King Faisal projects); to promote agricultural activities among the nomads; and to improve the viability of herding practices. Partially in response to such public efforts, the Bedouin have substantially changed their traditional herding and rangeland management strategies. In this paper, we examine these changes and their economic consequences. At the same time, we acknowledge that these nomadic pastoralists live in and utilize the resources of a fragile arid environment, and changes in range management bear potentially serious implications for the sustainability of that natural resource base. It is commonly asserted throughout the Kingdom that current herding and rangeland practices have resulted in the overgrazing of available vegetation and the general deterioration of the rangeland. Here we seek the Bedouin appraisal of this argument of environmental degradation.

In summary, this paper presents a case study from a single nomad group in a traditional rangeland region, in an attempt to: determine current economic status of the Bedouin; identify changes in their livelihood strategies related to the impacts of modernization; and assess the sustainability of these changes within the reality imposed by a harsh and uncertain environment. Finally, we will investigate possible areas of government assistance that would preserve the economic sustainability and cultural integrity of the Bedouin within an increasingly complex and urban society.

2. METHODOLOGY OF THE STUDY

This paper is the result of an anthropological study carried out within the target area of the Environmental Support of the Nomads (ESON) Project (Figure 26.1) shows the location of Al-Taysiyah within the ESON area). In January 1995, a research team consisting of technicians from the Meteorology and Environmental Protection Administration (MEPA) and the University of Arizona conducted a rapid appraisal of the entire ESON region, in order to prepare a preliminary assessment of Bedouin livelihood systems (Finan, 1995) and to identify an appropriate region for a more detailed case study. During this field visit, 27 nomadic camps from six different tribes (Ben Rashid, Dawassir, Harb, Mutair, Otaybah and Shammar) were interviewed. On the basis of this appraisal, it was decided to concentrate research on the Al-Taysiyah region, since it was considered a traditional rangeland for nomads and representative of the modernization processes occurring among nomadic groups throughout the Kingdom. Specifically, the rangeland surrounding the Bedouin village of Al-Zabirah was selected.

During the summer of 1995, Mr. Eisa Al-Haratani, a PhD candidate from the University of Arizona, conducted a five-month field visit to Al-Taysiyah, the traditional dirahs of the Wuhub, Ben Auf, and the Bani Ah clans of the Harb tribe. During this period of the field work, 84 Bedouin families were contacted and interviewed. A formal survey instrument was applied to all camps, and more detailed key informant interviews were carried out with several of the Bedouins. The field researcher resided with the Bedouin and employed the traditional anthropological technique of participant observation. After initial contacts were established and suspiscions were allayed, the researcher was warmly accepted by the local population. During part of this time, Dr. Mohammed Habib of the Department of Geography, King Abdul-Aziz University, joined Mr. Al-Haratani in the field and contributed significantly to the success of the study.

Figure 26.1

Map of the ESON study area.

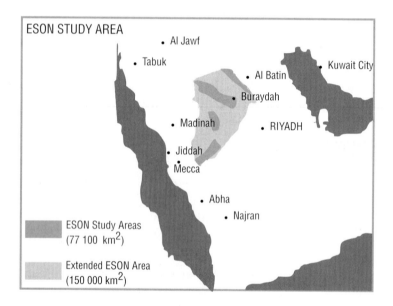

While this region is often visited by the Otaybah, Mutair, and Dawassir tribes during the winter and spring, the research team only encountered Harb camps in the hot summer season. Of the 84 families interviewed, five were categorized as "nomadic", in the sense that they practiced regular migrations in search of winter pastures to the north; three were sedentary Bedouin families who reside in Al-Zabiran, but travel to their herds daily; and the rest were classified as "semi-nomadic", in the sense that they remain in the general area of the dirahs, moving only short distances to procure new pastures or clean campsites.

3. BEDOUIN ECOLOGY: A CONCEPTUAL FRAMEWORK

To systematically understand the changes that have affected Saudi Arabian nomads over the last few decades, it is useful to think of the nomad camp (i.e., household or family) as a decision-making unit that functions within an environment (both physical and institutional) that is fixed over the short run. Bedouin households make decisions and devise livelihood strategies that are based on their perception of this environment as an exogenous variable. Thus, for example, a nomad cannot – over the short run – change the rangeland. It either rains or it does not rain. In the same way, a nomad cannot change institutional factors, such as market prices and locations, Bedouin traditions, clan affiliation, and public regulations and laws. For example, under the traditional system, individual nomad camps did not make unilateral decisions regarding time and routes of migration; rather, such decisions were taken in unison with the other camps of a specific kin group. Thus, individual decision-making was constrained by a wider group consensus because of the large amount of cooperation required by the system itself. In other words, these physical and institutional (including cultural) environments define the choice of possible strategies from which an individual can decide in the quest to improve family well-being. These relationships are depicted in Figure 26.2.

Figure 26.2

The ecology of Bedouin pastoralism

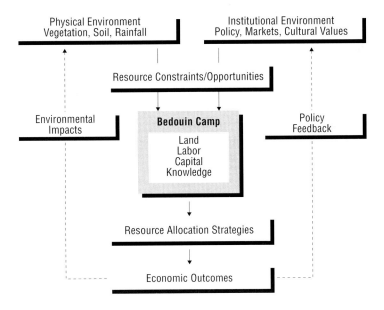

As Figure 26.2 suggests, the Bedouin household does have flexibility of choice within the existing environmental bounds, by manipulating the allocation of household resources such as land, labour, capital, and knowledge. For example, a nomad camp decides the size and composition of its herd, the particular grazing strategy to be pursued in a given year (or season), the division of family labour between different pastoralist activities and other employment alternatives, and the use of different herding technologies (i.e., the acquisition of capital items, such as trucks and tankers). The range of allocative strategies open to an individual nomad family is a function of access to the necessary resources. Thus, families that have fewer resources in relation to their neighbours will also have fewer strategies available to them within a given environmental context. Inversely, the richer families have a wider array of possible strategies.

Bedouin resource decisions generate impacts on household well-being – at least over the short run. In practice, a nomad sells off lambs or increases the herd, buys a truck, seeks a loan from a fellow tribesman, sends a child to school, or moves to a new rangeland, and these decisions can be assessed in terms of their economic contribution to the livelihood of the household. But, as Figure 26.2 further suggests, these decisions may also affect the physical environment (through resource degradation) or the institutional environment (through influence).

Rainfall data have only recently been systematically collected by government weather stations, thus estimates of rainfall for Al-Taysiyah must be derived by extrapolation from nearby stations in Al-Dasim and Hail. These data are presented in Table 26.2, and they indicate a pattern typical of arid and semi-arid regions where available rainfall is highly concentrated into a brief season. More than half of annual rainfall occurs during the spring months of March to May, while there is virtually no rainfall during the summer season. Rains arrive from the north (Hail, for example, experiences significant precipitation in the fall season), which traditionally influenced the northern nomadic routes. Tribes located to the south move north to meet the rains (and emergent pastures), then follow them down to their dirahs for the summer and the rainless season.

Table 26.1

Vegetation in Al-Taysiyah identified by local Bedouin.

Local Name	Scientific Name	Plant Type	Land Form / Soil Type	Season	Animal Preference	Status
Adhir	Artemisia monosperma	shrub	deep sand	year round	small ruminants	disperse
Alanda	Ephedra alata	shrub	calcareous gravel	year round	all	disperse
Arfaj	Rhanterium epapposum	shrub	shallow sands	spring	all	disperse
Arta	Calligonum comosum	shrub	deep sands	year round	all	disperse
Awsaj	Lycium shawii	shrub	rocky plains	year round	camel	disperse
Hadaj	Cucumis postulatus	shrub	sandy soils	year round	all	disperse
Hamat	Arnebia hispidissima	shrub	shallow and deep sands	year round	all	disperse
Ja'dah	Teucrium polium	shrub	rocky plains	winter	all	dispers
Mussay	Cyperus conglomeratus	shrub	deep sand	year round	all	disperse
Nuqd	Arvillea garcini	shrub	silt floors of wadis	year round	all	disperse
Nusi	Stipagrostis plumosa	grass	shallow, stable sand	year round	small ruminants	disperse
Qaysum	Achillea fragrantissima	shrub	rocky plains	year round	all	disperse
Qirdi	Ochradenus baccatus	shrub	rocky plains	spring	small ruminants	disperse
Ramram	Heliotropium bacciferum	shrub	shallow sands	year round	small ruminants	common
Remth	Haloxylan salicornium	shrub	shallow to deep sands	year round	camel	common
Ribl	Plantago albicans	grass	shallow or deep sands	spring	small ruminants	disperse
Rukhama	Convolvulus oxyphyllus	shrub	sandy wadi floors	spring	all	disperse
Sabat	Stipagrostis drarii	grass	deep sand	year round	small ruminants	common
Sadan	Neurada procumbens	grass	shallow to deep sands	winter/spring	small ruminants	common
Samnah	Carthamus oxyacantha	shrub	disturbed soils	spring	small ruminants	rare
Shafallah	Capparis spinosa	shrub	silty soils over limestone	summer	all	rare
Shih	Artemisia judaica	shrub	sand or wadi floor	year round	small ruminants	rare
Sidr	Ziziphus mummularia	shrub	silty basins	year round	camel	common
Silla	Zilla spinosa	shrub	wadis and silt basins	winter/spring	small ruminants	common
Talh	Acacia raddiana	tree	wadi floors	year round	camel	disperse
Thumam	Panicum turgidum	grass	well-drained sands	year round	all	disperse

Source: ESON

Table 26.2

Rainfall and temperature data from the project region.

Climatic Characteristic	Al-Qasim	Hail	Riyadh
Annual Rainfall (mm)	168.5	138.5	96.1
% in winter	31.7	25.8	32.1
% in spring	53.4	45.1	64.6
% in summer	0.1	0.2	1.2
% in fall	14.3	28.6	3.2
Annual Temperature (CO)	24.6	21.9	26.0
winter average	13.4	11.2	15.3
spring average	24.2	21.5	26.3
summer average	34.0	31.4	35.5
fall average	25.8	23.6	26.9

Source: MEPA (1981-1995)

4. TRADITIONAL PASTORALIST ADAPTATIONS IN THE AL-TAYSIYAH

The Harb tribe arrived in tha Al-Taysiyah region relatively recently. While the origins of the tribe lie in modern-day Yemen, the Harb were well-known as transporters during the time of the caravan trade that connected Mecca and the rest of the peninsula with India and countries to the north. As a consequence, the Harb spread out into the western desert around Mecca and Madinah, which became the central location of their tribal lands. During the struggles for unification, the Harb were allies of the Al-Rashidi, the rivals of the Al-Saud family; however, after the ascendency of the royal family and the creation of a modern monarchy, the Harb were given Al-Taysiyah in a gesture of reconciliation. Today, the region is divided into three sub-clans of the Harb tribe – the Wuhub, Ben Auf, and Bani Ah. Each clan lays claim to its own rangeland and wells, and tend not to venture into each others' domains.

The Bedouin nomad livelihood system has been described by Al-Gain (1974) and Al-Gain et al., (1994), among others, as a rational use-adaptation to a fragile ecosystem. The low precipitation and sparse vegetation of the Arabian Peninsula, in general, and the central deserts, in particular, impose severe constraints on the economic exploitation of this environment. The traditional nomadic adaptation was built upon the ability to move quickly, upon a highly sophisticated indigenous knowledge base, and upon an efficient (albeit informal) information system. These preconditions for success required a livestock herd capable of surviving within a desert ecology of sparsely distributed vegetation and water sources. Tribal boundaries restricted free movement across the desert and forced different ethnic groups either into negotiated political alliances or into warfare.

At the same time, tribal groups were able to manage their rangelands, and there is some evidence that pasture restrictions and protected reserve areas were observed.

In terms of our conceptual approach presented above, the environment carried a more immediate influence over traditional nomadic strategies than did institutional factors (other than the system of tribal proprietary rights). The Bedouin nomads followed routes generally determined by "normal" rainfall patterns within their own dirahs rather than into the dirahs of the neighbouring tribes with whom agreements had been struck. In the case of the Naflid, for example, the Otaybah and more southern tribes (such as the Dawassir and the Al-Murrah) moved to the northern Ad-Dahna and As-Somman regions to take advantage of the winter ranges, than moved back to the southern ranges fed by summer moisture. The Harb and Shammar moved toward Jawf in the northwest during the winter rains, then back to the Hail region during the summer. The timing of movement, the specific location, and the duration in a given spot were all determined ad hoc by the unique characteristics of that year.

The traditional Bedouin nomad camp could cover large distances (1 500 km or more), and exploit a wide swath of rangelands. Signs of rainfall (e.g., distant lightning), or word-of-mouth information, would initiate the nomadic movement toward a specific region. Specific decisions about the direction and timing of a move were made at the sub-clan level in the majus of the local sheikh. Often a scout (assas) was sent out to explore potential rangelands and to prepare an appropriate route. The camps usually traveled within sight of each other, and the progress was gradual, averaging about 30 - 50 km a day. The camps moved from water source to water source, usually in a wadi or sheib bottom, grazing the surrounding pastures. Commonly, it would take up to two months to reach the general destination, and, once there, the nomads would remain in the vicinity as long as the available forages permitted. If reports of lusher rangelands arrived, the camps would move on.

This pastoral livelihood system depended critically upon the effective and accurate flow of information and upon a detailed knowledge of the environment, its soil and vegetation. Despite the absence of modern mass communication, the specific locality of rainfall was rapidly disseminated as nomads mover throughout the desert. In fact, scholars of Bedouin society have interpreted the traditional and formal hospitality of the Bedouin in terms of its effectiveness as a communication system. Nomads welcome visitors so enthusiastically and insist on sharing coffee and tea, in part to obtain information about the localities that the visitors have passed through. Similarly, the complex networks of alliances between tribes and sub-tribes also functioned to get critical information circulated rapidly. At the same time, there was a high premium placed on Bedouin indigenous knowledge of rainfall and temperature patterns, desert vegetation, local geohydrology, the distribution of water wells and water-holes, camel physiology, and, of course, the political ethnic map of his region. The desert ecology is highly dynamic. For example, certain species of range vegetation are associated with specific land types; and certain species are consumed when green, others when dry; and certain shrubs become available only when a specific combination of moisture and temperature obtains.

The Harb, for example, like to set their camps on the edge of differing ecologies, such as, at the point where sand dunes give way to rocky plain, thus providing access to distinct vegetation communities. The decision to raise Najdi or Naimi breeds of sheep is also related to their knowledge of the specific adaptability of each breed. A similar knowledge is required for the obtention of water. Certain nomads have a special talent for recognizing land formations that might hold water, where wells could be dug and where traditional water-gathering structures could be constructed. Throughout the Al-Taysiyah region, small stone-lined wells and short containing walls attest to the traditional water strategies of the Bedouin herders.

Given the complex interrelationship between pasture and water, the camel was the animal of preference because of its ability to utilize rough desert vegetation, to move quickly, and to resist several days without water. The camel was also the major form of transportation, and it essentially carried all household belongings (including the tent) from place to place. At the same time, camel meat (particularly the young camel) and milk were the primary economic outputs, being both consumed and (occasionally) marketed. Small ruminant herds, for their part, were less mobile and more demanding in terms of forage and water. The traditional camp maintained sheep and goats, primarily for family consumption (milk, meat, ghee, and butter), but also to exchange with villagers for wheat flour and other basic necessities.

A further characteristic of the traditional Bedouin nomad livelihood was its high level of self-sufficiency. Up until unification, most Bedouin were not sedentary. Tribes maintained a central 'home' usually located in an oasis town or near a major tribal well, but the nomads spent most of the year on the move. The different camps interacted with sedentary peoples in marketplaces, where animal products were exchanged for grain and other basic necessities. For the most part, however, the tribes were self-sufficient, being able to produce or procure their own food and necessities without reliance on government intervention. After unification, public employment, oil-related employment, and royal subsidies came to play an important role in the camp economy. As the nomads became increasingly integrated into a wider national economy, they also became increasingly dependent on government assistance to maintain their welfare.

In summary, the traditional Bedouin family, while culturally associated with its dirahs, spent much of the year in "foreign lands", following the rains, seeking adequate rangeland near the next water source, and subsisting on the consumption and marketing of animal products. At the tribal level, the natural resource base was managed through the maintenance of tribal boundaries and wells and through the creation of alliances that permitted access to non-tribal pastures (and wells) at certain times of the year. At an individual camp level, resource management strategies were determined by: the mobility and biology of their animals; access to information; profound knowledge of the vegetation and the hydrogeology of the desert; and intra-clan cooperation.

From a political-ecological perspective, the constraints of this livelihood system assured the sustainability of the environment in two ways. Firstly, since animals can only move a certain distance before returning to drink water, more distant rangelands would not be grazed or only utilized sparingly in a given year, due to the absence of a watering source. Rangeland ecologists argue that this environmental restriction on range utilization provided an important source of seed for range restoration year after year. Secondly, the biophysical, climatic, and social constraints also clearly limited the population within the region. Both the numbers of people and the numbers of animals were low. Although reliable data are not readily available, Heady (1972) offers an estimate of a population perhaps slightly higher than one million, based on a 1966 aerial survey of 227 000 nomad tents throughout the Kingdom. Each camp was also constrained in terms of the number of animals that it could water, feed, and manage, and herd sizes were often less than a hundred camels (with much smaller numbers of sheep and goats).

This traditional Bedouin livelihood system changed dramatically, firstly with the opening of tribal boundaries and then with the emergence of an oil economy in the Kingdom. In the first case, open access to tribal lands eliminated tribal-level management of the natural resource base. In principle, any Bedouin group could use the range resources of another tribe without the necessary forging of alliances or the fear of reprisal. Thus, when rains were reported in a given region, all nomads could converge on the range. Moreover, the traditional range reserves were also prohibited (although the Harb did not have any in Al-Taysiyah).

The opening of tribal lands did not, however, break the other physical constraints associated with nomad pastoral strategies, such as the scarcity of water distance, and animal physiology. Further change accompanied the increasing flow of oil income after 1960, as the Bedouin population became engaged in a process of modernization and integration into larger society. With increased access to government wells and, particularly, to motorized transport, the individual constraints on mobility were eliminated, providing any camp the opportunity to utilize virtually any available pasture. Integration into larger society – especially through wider participation in the educational system – also brought more nomad camps into a non-pastoral economy and greater access to diverse employment possibilities.

In effect, as the model in Figure 26.2 presents, modernization profoundly altered the policy environment within which Bedouin families could devise their resource allocation strategies. New channels of resource access were made available through both direct and indirect policy decisions. On the one hand, the rulers of the Kingdom introduced a specific "Bedouin policy", which attempted to encourage settlement and to increase access to health and education services. While the effort to transform nomads into sedentary agriculturalists was not widely successful, the value of education and health care was quickly assimilated by the Bedouin populations. At the same time, indirect policies, such as the recruitment of Bedouins into the National Guard (an important income source), investments in water wells and roads, and, since 1979, the subsidized sale of feed barley, have redefined the physical and economic constraints to pastoralism. The case of the Harb the in Al-Taysiyah demonstrates that these external changes have transformed the nature of nomadism in the region.

5. CURRENT PASTORALIST LIVELIHOOD SYSTEMS IN THE Al-TAYSIYAH

The rapid appraisal of field-work carried out in early 1995, during an above-average rainy season, identified the converging presence of nomadic tribes from regions south and south-west of Al-Taysiyah, including Otaybah and Dawassir. The research team also encountered numerous urban merchants from Riyadh, who had transported their herds to the region to take advantage of the emergent new pastures. By the summer of that year, these tribes (and merchants) had left the Al-Taysiyah, and the remaining nomad camps were Harb (with a single exception). All the 84 respondents in the survey were from the three Harb sub-clans.

At a most basic level, the survey sought to describe the general characteristics of the pastoral livelihood system and the transformations that the Bedouin have experienced over the last three decades. Several critical impacts of modernization were readily apparent. Firstly, the nature of Bedouin mobility has changed. Whereas traditional camps moved long distances in search of range and water, present Harb camps in the Al-Taysiyah only shift within the boundaries of the region itself, in fact within the dirahs of their respective sub-clans. On the other hand, short distance mobility has been exceedingly increased. The first pick-up truck appeared in Al-Taysiyah in 1964, and now every Bedouin camp has at least one such vehicle. With access to transport, many families travel dozens of kilometres daily to obtain water, to take children to village schools, to attend markets, and, ironically, to herd their livestock. With this change in mobility, most nomads now practice a form of livestock management more similar to ranching than to nomadism as it is conventionally defined.

A second impact of modernization has been the change in herd composition and a more market-oriented pastoral strategy. The importance of camels has been reduced in most camps to a romantic vestige of a previous era. The Al-Taysiyah nomads, as is the case elsewhere, have shifted the herd composition toward small ruminants, principally sheep, which are raised for the urban markets. In the traditional system, animals were occasionally exchanged for foodstuffs and the overall need for cash money was limited. Now, however, nomad pastoral decision-making is very much dictated by markets and sheep and barley prices. Consequently, the Al-Taysiyah Bedouin have become much more dependent on cash transactions. The current pastoral system requires large amounts of capital for investment in fixed assets, as well as working capital, to purchase feed and fuel, pay herders, acquire breeding stock, and pay veterinary expenses.

A third general characteristic of "modernized" Bedouin in the Al-Taysiyah region is cultural, or anthropological, in nature. In contrast to traditional pastoralist systems, the contemporary nomad has opportunities outside of herding. With access to education, many younger Bedouin have sought their livelihoods in more urban environments, where they might practice herding as a complementary or recreational activity rather than an economic one. As a consequence, the demographic structure of the nomad camps has shifted toward an older generation, with a growing absence of young people. In this same cultural sense, it appears that nomads have also become more individualized in their economic behaviour. Decisions to move camp or to seek new pastures do not require the same degree of inter-family consensus as the traditional system did, most likely because the same degree of interdependence does not exist.

In the following section, these impacts of modernization will be discussed in greater detail with specific reference to the Al-Taysiyah nomad population. In an effort to understand the level of diversity among the nomad camps, we have classified the sample into two sub-groups who are defined by the size of their respective herds. The first group is comprised of those camps that reported 450 sheep/goats or less, while the second group has herd sizes of over 450 animals. The assumption that drives this classification is that families with larger herds are wealthier and will have incorporated the re-orientation more thoroughly, whereas the small herds will belong to the older, poorer and more traditional nomads.

5.1 Demographic characteristics of the Al-Taysiyah Bedouin

An important indicator of the impacts of modernization on the Al-Taysiyah nomads is the elevated age of the family heads. As Table 26.3 illustrates, the average age of the head of camp was 58 years for the entire sample, while the heads of camps with small herds tended to be somewhat older. The oldest head was 90 years of age and the youngest was 19 years old. The median number of people residing in a camp was eight people, with a slightly smaller number for the families with smaller herds. The minimum camp size encountered in the sample was a single person and the largest family had seventeen people. The Harb customarily live in a long single tent divided functionally. The public compartment is the majlis, with one component for storage and food prepara-tion, and another private component for the women and family members. These characteristic tents were once hand-sewn by Harb women using camel hair. The tents are now purchased from Europe. Larger camps will have several tents, and some camps have tents for guests or for storage. The average camp in the sample had 1.3 tents, while the wealthier camps had a slightly larger number. It is impor-tant to note that individual families, even when closely related, tend to respect their distance from each other, so that herds do not get entangled. A herd size of 450 small ruminants was the median value for the sample.

Table 26.3

Demographic characteristics of Al-Taysiyah nomads by size of livestock herd

Demographic Characteristics	Nomad Camp by Size of Herd		Total Sample
	450 Sheep or Less	More Than 450 Sheep	
Sample Size	46	36	84
Age of Camp Head **	61	55	58
Number of Tents	1.2	1.5	1.3
Size of Family	7.2	8.3	7.7
Distance from Al-Zabirah (kms)	32	34	33
Children in School (% of camps)**			
boys only:	28.6	40.0	33.8
girls and boys:	21.4	28.6	24.7

Source: Al-Taysiyah Field Study

a/ two camps did not report their herd sizes and thus were excluded from the category.

** difference significance at the .10 level of confidence

The Al-Taysiyah camps in the sample were distributed near the Wadi Al-Hasaki, about 30 km on average from Al-Zabirah. This village is especially important because it is an administrative centre, and its well provides water to the nomad tanker trucks. It has schools (for boys and girls) and a small market and service centre where basic staples can be purchased and vehicles repaired. The interviewed nomads travel frequently to the village, even from the furthest camp over 80 km away. There is no difference between the wealthier and the poorer camps, in terms of distance between their camps and the village.

Another critical measure of change among the Bedouin is education. Most of the nomad families place a high value on education for their children (although most of the older generation is illiterate). Nearly 60% of the families reported that their children (boys or girls) were currently in school or had attended school. Among the wealthier camps, 40% had boys in school and another 28% provided both boys and girls with education. The proportion of the poorer camps with educated children was smaller for both boys and girls. In-depth interviews with nomad families also suggested that detailed indigenous knowledge of the environment and its flora and fauna is not systematically passed on from generation to generation as it was under the traditional system. Fathers clearly prefer formal education and indicated that the motive for sending their children to school was to enhance their opportunities outside of pastoralism. Those camps that did not provide an education for their children pointed to the need for family labour to care for the livestock. In fact, approximately 60% of those families without a hired expatriate herder do not send their children to school. In general, however, education and the income-earning potential it creates are perceived by the Al-Taysiyah nomads as an attractive alternative to pastoralism.

5.2 Economic characteristics of Al-Taysiyah Bedouin

The Bedouin in the Al-Taysiyah region are mostly part semi-sedentary pastoralists. With the changes wrought by modernization, the pastoralist household now resembles a capital-intensive economic firm with strong integration into regional input and output markets. As Table 26.4 summarizes, the average nomad camp in the Al-Taysiyah has 433 sheep and goats. Following our classification into poorer and wealthier camps, the latter group of Bedouin maintains an average of 650 animals, while the poorer families have about 250 head. It was not possible to discriminate the exact proportions of sheep and goats in these small ruminant herds, although we have estimated from observation that about 10% of total herd consists of goats. In general, sheep are sold for their meat and represent the majority of the herd and economic value. Goats are kept for their milk, from which ghee (samen), butter (zibdah) and dried milk biscuits (iqt) are prepared.

Ghee and butter are sold in urban markets, particularly by the poorer camps, and consumed domestically. Around 40% of the sample still herds camels, and the average herd size for those who own camels is 36 animals. It is interesting to note that while more wealthier camps run camel herds, the number of animals per herd is not different from the poorer camps. This fact supports the argument that camels are raised more for their sentimental value, as a consumption benefit rather than for their economic advantages as a marketed good.

In terms of capital assets, every nomad camp has at least one pick-up truck and most have more than one. The wealthier camps featured in Table 26.4 have an average of 1.7 pick-ups, while the poorer camps have 1.3 vehicles. These multi-purpose pick-ups are used for transporting animals and feed, herding, and for meeting general transportation needs (e.g., taking children to school, visiting neighbours). Virtually all nomad camps also have a water tanker which is a critical component of the current livelihood system. About 60% of the wealthier families and 15% of the poorer camps have large transport trucks. These are used to haul animals to pasture and the transport feed. At many times a nomad family will also rent its truck to others for a fee. While making allowances for the date of purchase and the common pattern of acquiring used vehicles, the sample reported a capital investment in vehicles of nearly Saudi Ryals (SAR) 195 000 to SAR 214 000 for the wealthier group and SAR 174 000 for the poorer group. This level of capital investment makes the modern pastoral livelihood system very different from the traditional adaptation. Around one half of the sample has contracted expatriate herders to provide necessary shepherding labour. Most of these hired herders come from India (for sheep) or The Sudan (for camels) on multi-year contracts, and they are paid around SAR 500 per month[1]. They tend to live in tents away from the nomad camp and near the herds. It is evident from the data that the use of contracted expatriate labour for pastoral activities is related to the "ranching" orientation of the current system. The wealthier camps are twice as likely to hire expatriate herders compared to the poorer camps, and urban merchants who have large investments in herds depend almost exclusively on this source of labour.

In economic terms, the investment requirements of the current Bedouin enterprise are large in terms of cash and capital. Under the assumption of an average cost of 300 SAR for each stock animal, the entry cost of an 450 head herd, including vehicles and necessary working capital, is one half million nyals.

1/ The employees also pay a SAR fee for recruiting and transporting the worker, who usually arrives with a two-year contractual obligation.

The Al-Taysiyah Harb tend not to utilize the formal banking system to acquire capital, thus they rely upon traditional forms of access to capital. More than two-thirds of the sample reported that they borrowed money from friends or fellow tribesmen. As Table 26.4 indicates, the poorer camps are relatively more dependent on borrowing to meet their capital needs. Slightly more than one-quarter of the sample also had access to some form of non-herding income, either a salary or a pension payment. Nomads have traditional ties to the National Guard, and many families receive a stipend through this avenue or some other form of public employment. Moreover, ride-price is still practiced in the Al-Taysiyah region. Whereas in the past, it was traditionally paid in animals (camels and sheep), ride-price is now a cash transaction. In some camps, the value of ride-price can exceed SAR 100 000. Thus, while the success of the traditional system demanded detailed knowledge of the physical and political environment, the success of the "modernized" Bedouin system relies more on business acumen and access to capital.

Table 26.4

Economic characteristics of Al-Taysiyah nomads by size of livestock herd

Economic and Wealth Characteristics	Nomad Camp by Size of Herd		Total Sample
	450 Sheep or Less	More Than 450 Sheep	
Number of Sheep/Goats	257	659	433
Camels: % of Camps	40	50	44
Number of Animals	36	36	36
Number of Pick-up Trucks	1.4	1.7	1.6
Water Trucks (% of Camps)	95.7	100	97.3
Large Trucks (% of Camps)	15.2	58.5	34.1
Total Estimated Vehicle Investment ('000 SAR)	174	214	194
Expatriate Herders (% of Camps)	34.8	72.2	51.2
Borrowed Money (% of Camps)	78.3	52.8	67.1
Salary or Pension (% of Camps)	26.1	30.6	28.0

Source: Al-Taysiyah Bedouin Survey

This study also estimated the flow of income from the Bedouin livelihood systems. Tables 26.5 and 26.6 are built upon a set of assumptions regarding the wealthier and the poorer nomad camps that were derived from empirical observations in the field. The analysis examines the economic outcomes of the representative enterprises that these assumptions describe. Both representative camps are assumed to have small camel herds (30 animals). For the small ruminant herds, goats constitute 10% of the animals, while the *Nadji* breed of sheep makes up the rest. Females are assumed to have 1.3 births per year, and some young females are retained to reconstitute the breeding stock. Average prices for sheep

Table 26.5

Income flows from a representative 250-herd camp in Al-Taysiyah

Animal Type	Sheep	Goats	Camels
Number of Animals	230	20	30
Female Reproducers	120	15	20
Births/Year	160	20	18
Animals/Marketed	120	10	12
Price per Animal	SAR 350	SAR 200	SAR 2,000
Marketed Value	SAR 42,500	SAR 2,000	SAR 24,000

Animal Type	Sheep+Goats	Camels
Gross Animal Income	SAR 44,500	SAR 24,000
Marketed Ghee	SAR 8,000	n.a.
Cost of Barley [a]	SAR 33,000	SAR 33,000
Veterinary Costs/year	SAR 600	n.a.
Annual Fuel Costs	SAR 5,700	n.a.
Net Animal Income	SAR 13,200	(SAR 9,000)

Source: Al-Taysiyah Bedouin Survey

a/ *For small ruminants: 5 bags/day for 300 days at a cost of SAR 22/bag;*
   for camels: 5 bags/day for 300 days at a cost of SAR 22/bag.

Table 26.6

Income flows from a representative 650-herd camp in Al-Taysiyah

Animal Type	Sheep	Goats	Camels
Number of Animals	600	50	30
Female Reproducers	400	40	20
Births/Year	500	50	18
Animals/Marketed	400	40	12
Price per Animal	SAR 350	SAR 200	SAR 2,000
Marketed Value	SAR 140,000	SAR 8,000	SAR 24,000

Animal Type	Sheep+Goats	Camels
Gross Animal Income	SAR 148,000	SAR 24,000
Cost of Barley [a]	SAR 85,500	SAR 33,000
Cost of Herder [b]	SAR 6,000	n.a.
Veterinary Costs/year	SAR 1,500	n.a.
Annual Fuel Costs	SAR 7,000	n.a.
Net Animal Income	SAR 47,700	(SAR 9,000)

Source: Al-Taysiyah Bedouin Survey

a/ *For small ruminants: 13 bags/day for 300 days at a cost of SAR 22/bag;*
   for camels: 5 bags/day for 300 days at a cost of SAR 22/bag.

b/ *Herder costs are calculated at SAR 500 per month plus,*
   an annualized start-up cost of SAR 1,000 per year.

were estimated at SAR 350, for goats SAR 200, and for young camels SAR 2 000. It is further assumed that this poorer camp sells SAR 8 000 of ghee during the winter and spring seasons when goat milk is more plentiful. The imputed value of meat, skins, milk and milk products consumed by the family do not enter into these calculations, although their importance to the overall welfare of the household is recognized.

On the cost side for the poorer group, it is estimated that 50 small ruminants consume one bag of feed barley daily for 300 days a year. For camels, one bag feeds six animals daily. As Habib (1995) reports, the barley price in Hail is SAR 17 for a bag of 50 kg, but the price in Al-Zabirah is SAR 22 per bag. This latter price has been used in the analysis. No expatriate herders were included in these representative budgets (only 30% of these camps hire herders), but veterinary expenses were estimated at about SAR 600 per year. Fuel costs were estimated on reported fuel expenditures per vehicle type and quantity. Water costs tend to be free (from Al-Zabirah well) or negligible, and were not included in the analysis.

For this small-scale enterprise, the economic returns to capital and labour average about SAR 13 200, considered to be a poor income in the current Saudi Arabian economy. The camel component of this system produces an economic loss, and it would be necessary to reduce camel barely consumption to about 200 days in order to reach a "break-even" point. These budgets clearly demonstrate the extent to which the current Bedouin livelihood is tied to markets and the modern economy. At the same time, however, these results do not incorporate the factor of risk, particularly due to animal disease. Over 90% of the sample lost sheep to disease last year, and most complained about as-sommel, a particularly dangerous disease that has appeared since the Gulf War. Some camps report losses as high as 300 sheep over the past year.

The wealthier camps with 650 animals earn substantially larger profits. The return to capital and management of around SAR 47 700 is economically attractive, not only to Bedouin nomads but also to merchants with available investment capital. For this group, it was assumed that the ghee and butter products are not marketed. Again, this type of enterprise is fully dependent on functioning input and output markets and is vulnerable to high degrees of risk. It is, for most purposes, a modern-day ranch.

The level of profitability of these two representative nomad systems is determined to a large extent by the cost of feed barley, which accounts for 85% of all variable costs. Barley is sold throughout the Al-Taysiyah region, in both the villages and at frequently travelled points along local roads. Since 1973, the Government has strongly subsidized the barley price, which has been sold in the region at levels as high as SAR 60 per bag. At any price over SAR 30, these live-

Table 26.7

Bedouin seasons in the Al-Taysiyah regions

Local Names for Seasons	Roman Calendar	Arabic References	Number of Days	Characteristics			
				Rainfall	Vegetation	Animal	Barley Comsumption
Qaidh	June-September 15	Muharam to Rabiya II	104 15	no rain	dry grasses (summer)	fewer (hamiss)	medium animals
Kharif	September-October 10	Rabiya II to Jamad I	25	no rain	leaf drop on perennials	fewer animals	medium
Wasm ("expecting")	October-December 20	Jamad I to Jamad II	50	rains begin	germination (nafel)	females covered	medium
Murbaniah/ Shatwi	December-January 10	Rajag to Shaban 10	40	cold and rain (winter)	leaf drop (artah, araj)	females drop lambs	high
Shabth	January10-Febuary	Shaban	21	cold and rain	slow growth	lambs	high
Aquarib ("scorpion")	Febuary	Ramadan	28	rain, cold	talah, naged	lambs	low for stock animals
Azar/ Rabiya ("green")	March -April 10	Shawal	40	rain and spring temperature best pastures	ramam arfaj	fattened for market	high for fattened animals
Saif ("warming")	April 10-June	Qaidah/Hadj	57	rain diminishes	nasi, hamath, azar	Sale of animals	low

Source: Unpublished

stock systems fail to be profitable. Thus, Bedouin dependence on public policy to maintain the profitability of their production systems is critically important. Without the barley subsidy, the modern Bedouin system, as it is currently configured, would cease to exist.

5.3 Range and herd management practices of the Al-Taysiyah Bedouin

Under the current conditions of nomadism in Al-Taysiyah, the Bedouin have adjusted their grazing and herd management practices to the economic incentive structure. With increased local mobility, the camps can move their herds easily to any available pasture then truck in water. A nomad family makes the decision to settle in a given area based on the availability of vegetation and the composition of the rangeland. There is a direct trade-off between the use of barley and profitability, and for every week (fewer than the 300 days in the analysis) that animals can be pastured rather than fed, there is an increase in profit of about 4%. Thus, there are strong economic incentives to maximize their utilization of a given rangeland. In a given camp, most Bedouin practice a rotational grazing pattern that is determined by the number of camps in the area and the spatial distribution of different plant species. Herds are moved in one direction one day, then in an opposite direction on the following day, and so on in a circular fashion, until the herd returns to the original spot. When the pasture grasses have been exhausted, the family scouts nearby areas to determine if the camp should be relocated. The animals either return to camp daily or stay with a herder in the range. The nomad owner goes to the animals daily, often taking water and feed. Animals being readied for market are kept in confinement in pens and fed more barley for rapid weight gain.

Table 26.7 presents a local calendar of the nomad year and indicates the dynamic nature of herding practices. Timing and location are critically essential to a pastoralist system. Rains begin in the late fall in Al-Taysiyah, during a season that the nomads call wasm (or "expecting"). Annual grasses begin to appear with the arrival of the rains, but the temperature retards growth. So while grasses have germinated and the shrubs have begun to bud, only limited amounts of biomass are available. During the spring season, azar (or "green"), the desert enjoys the most luxuriant phase of its annual cycle. Both annuals and perennials flourish and nomads from other tribes begin to arrive with their trucks, herds, and camps. During this time, the animals require less barley and less water as Table 26.7 suggests. Lambs have dropped and now enter into a fattening stage (with barley) in preparation for the Hadj market, at the time of the year when the demand for live animals is at its highest. With the onset of qaidh (the summer months), the animals graze the dried annual grasses (harniss) and browse shrubs and trees. Within this pattern, barley is fed to maintain the stock during the periods of poor pasture, then feeding is intensified during the period of reproduction, lambing, and milking. Levels of feeding are then reduced as the rangeland produces more biomass. During periods of drought, the barley feeding is extended throughout the year, and herd sizes are reduced.

Of great concern to the nomads is the increasing level of mortality among the small ruminant herds. While only 20% of the camel herders lost an animal over the last year, almost 85% of the camps with sheep lost animals to disease. As previously stated, the Bedouin complain of the disease, as-sommel, which they associate with the consequences of the Gulf War and the fires in the Kuwaiti oil fields. The median number of animals lost to this disease was 53 for the entire sample, while the wealthier families lost 65 animals and the poorer camps lost 39 sheep. The economic consequences of this epidemic are severe for all the camps, and the nomads feel that there is no treatment available.

In summary, the current practices of the Al-Taysiyah nomads can be interpreted in terms of a more intensified use of the rangeland resource. It is clear that within a given dirah, the area which a given sub-clan considers to be its territory, more animals are being grazed and none of the range is set aside either intentionally or unintentionally for conservation purposes. Some of the Al-Taysiyah nomads travel to other regions during part of the year, but these pastures also attract other nomads. At the same time, the logic of grazing is driven by a market orientation that attempts to maximize the number of animals, supplement pasture grass with feed barley (and alfalfa and wheat straw), and prepare animals for the Hadj market season. This strategy has proven itself viable, if risky, and the economic outcomes are positive in the current physical and policy environment. It is evident, however, that the resource allocative strategies depicted in Figure 26.2 are driven by short-run incentives rather than by a long-run conservation ethic.

6. THE ECOLOGICAL IMPACTS OF MODERNIZATION

There is wide concern that the efforts to promote the economic health of the Bedouin may come at the expense of the environmental health of the desert. In this study, the research team attempted to identify Bedouin perspectives on changes in their surroundings. For most of the Al-Taysiyah Harb, the quality desert has deteriorated during their lifetime. In places where wildlife abounded, such as the revered Houbara bustard and the gazelle, few can be found now. The Bedouin relate anecdotally that rabbits, and even gazelle, could once hide in the annual grasses. Rains were much more frequent, more consistent, and more bountiful. Now, some plant species, such as arfaj, have become much less common than before. To some extent, this reduction in range biomass is related to the increased use of the resource. Several Bedouin stated that when the rains arrive, too many outsiders converge on the range, and the grasses do not have the chance to develop. Others pointed to the increasing presence of urban-dwelling merchants who maintain large herds as economic investments. While the Bedouin themselves assert that they protect their patrimony, the outsiders from the cities and other lands kill trees and destroy wood shrubs for fuelwood to sell in the cities. Thus, while the scientific evidence has not yet documented the degradation of pasture lands, the qualitative information from this survey does suggest that the current systems, regardless of the size of the herd, are using the system very intensively and, perhaps, exceeding the carry capacity of this fragile range.

7. CONCLUSIONS: THE FUTURE OF NOMADISM

The Al-Taysiyah Bedouin, like other nomad groups in the Kingdom of Saudi Arabia, face a difficult future. On the one hand, public policy and the impacts of modernization have protected their livelihood from extinction, and they are able to survive at reasonable levels of economic well-being. They have responded to current economic incentives and have been able to overcome many of the constraints associated with the traditional livestock livelihood system. In many ways, modernization has transformed the Bedouin into a tent-dwelling rancher, with a capital-intensive enterprise that hires outside labour and depends critically on market conditions, as much as on range conditions. This transformation, however, has also changed the nature of nomad decision-making. Herd management strategies and grazing practices reflect the demands of short-term economic maximization, rather than long-term conservation. Herd sizes are large, water is free, range access is open, and cash is needed to pay the expenses. This combination favours the short-term option on natural resource management that is observed among the Al-Taysiyah Bedouin.

At the same time, there is increasing competition for the Bedouin in a modern world. Urban residents with available capital are moving into livestock herding for profit. These capitalists seek the economic benefits without the rigours of the lifestyle. Other interests are competing for the desert, such as city recreationists, agriculturalists and now those with conservation interests such as the Wildlife Conservation Agency, which is in the process of claiming rangeland for the recuperation of wildlife species. Such pressures. combined with the exodus of young Bedouin to urban areas, will continue to place the Bedouin existence in jeopardy.

For policy-makers, choices are equally challenging. In a society that values the Bedouin lifestyle for its cultural contribution to national identity, new solutions are needed to assure the sustainability of this livelihood. It is inevitable that such sustainability will require a redefinition of the Bedouin place in their desert and in their society.

References

Al-Gain, A. 1974. The In-Situ Development of the Bedouin nomads: A Bayesian decision analysis. Ph.D. Dissert. University of Arizona. Tucson.

Al-Gain, A., A. Al-Lisa and M. Fogel. 1994. Maintaining a traditional heritage through the environmental support of nomads. Unpublished paper presented to King Saud University. Riyadh.

Cole, D.P. 1981. Bedouin and social change in Saudi Arabia. *Journal of Asian and African Studies XVI*, 1-2, pp. 128-49.

Finan, T.J. 1995. *Impacts of modernization on Saudi Arabian bedouin groups: an anthropological study.* Report presented to the Hefzi Est. for Trading and the ESON Project. Jeddah, Saudi Arabia.

Habib, M.A. 1995. *A survey of the economic resources and the socio-economic conditions of the nomadic population in Al-Taysiyah area, Hail Governate.* Report presented to the Environmental Protection General Directorate, Meteorology and Environmental Protection Agency (MEPA), Jeddah, Saudi Arabia.

Heady, H.F. 1972. Ecological Consequences of Bedouin Settlement in Saudi Arabia. In: Farvar, M.T. and Milton, J.P. (eds.) *The careless technology: ecology in international development.* Garden City. NY: The Natural History Press.

Meteorology and Environmental Protection Agency (MEPA) 1996. Environmental Support of the Nomads (ESON): *Information Circular* 1:3. Jeddah, Saudi Arabia.

Changes and factors affecting Bedouin movement for grazing

27

A. Al-Eisa

Synopsis

This paper is an overview of recent changes in the lifestyle, economy and prospects for Saudi Arabia's traditional pastoralists, the Bedouin. Changes are reflected in grazing strategies, labour arrangements, consumption patterns and dependence on motorized transport. The use and importance of barley to the Bedouin culture is reviewed.

Key Points

1. *Although most of the rangelands in Saudi Arabia are located in remote areas and are known for their harsh environment and scarce resources, the rangelands play an important part in the national economy.*

2. *Many of the traditional Bedouin have now settled, but a large number pursue a nomadic or semi-nomadic lifestyle. This latter group is the largest user of rangelands and the people are best adapted to live there.*

3. *Changes in lifestyle, mobility and dependence on motorized transport have affected the way people use the rangelands. In the past, every tribe had its own territory for grazing. In dry times, that particular tribe could move to the territory of another tribe provided that certain conditions were met. Some of these traditional "rules" have been abandoned as pastoralists have come to depend on cheap barley as an alternative to long-distance movements in times of drought.*

4. *Barley supplements have become an important factor in Bedouin society, because grazing on Saudi Arabian rangelands, with the exception of some mountainous areas, is limited to the short rainy seasons.*

1. INTRODUCTION

The badia (rangelands) are very important to the national economy of Saudi Arabia and to the Bedouin herders, who depend on them for raising their animals. However, the productivity of most natural range areas in the country, with the exception of ranges associated with mountains, is low and is limited to the rainy seasons.

Despite the harsh environment and scarce resources available, Bedouins in the past maintained a flourishing culture based on nomadic pastoralism. At the same time, they conserved the natural vegetation and condition of the range by keeping stocking/grazing at sustainable levels. Among the factors which contributed to this situation were that their herds were mainly camels with only a small number of sheep, and rangeland access and use was controlled under the hema reservation system.

Traditionally, utilization of the vegetation of the drier areas took place under the tribal hema system which restricted the timing, frequency and intensity of grazing, and was instrumental in the maintenance of the rangeland (Jaubert and Bocco, 1994; Draz, 1985). Social change has led to a breakdown of tribal structures, and the abandonment of controls on the use of the rangelands (Blench, this volume).

Government policies aimed at increasing meat production have supported the provision of subsidized feedstuffs (barley grain), and, with modern transport facilities, feed and water are now transported to semi-permanent populations of people and livestock in the more remote areas (Leybourne, 1994; Abdulla and Al-Hajooj, 1995). This has led to severe degradation of the vegetation through overgrazing and the use of shrubs for fuel. As in the wetter areas, the reduction in the vegetation has caused more runoff of the sparse surface water and an escalation of soil erosion, by both water and wind, as large areas are laid bare.

Under this communal hema system of rangeland conservation, every tribe had its own designated territory for grazing. When dry periods occurred, a tribe was allowed to move to areas assigned to other tribes under specified conditions (a description is beyond the scope of this paper). Although the hema system was abolished, providing unlimited access to all grazing areas, many Bedouins still prefer using securely limited areas such as those that used to be their traditional reservations.

After the unification of Saudi Arabia and the subsequent changes in social, cultural and economic conditions, Bedouin life changed substantially. These pastoralists began raising more sheep to profit from the increasing demand for meat. In addition, the use of trucks to transport animals and water tankers opened up formerly inaccessible areas of the badia. These circumstances exacerbated the degradation of grazing lands already devastated by severe periods of drought, which occurred in the 1950s and 1960s. Bedouin herds deteriorated, thus lowering the nomads' living standards. The Government of Saudi Arabia attempted to compensate for the shortage of natural forage by providing barley at subsidized prices; the goal was to assist the Bedouins to rebuild their herds.

This paper reviews the use and importance of barley to the Bedouin culture, and identifies several recent factors affecting the movements of these pastoralists.

2. USE OF BARLEY

As noted above, the reliance on barley as a fodder crop has increased and has assumed major importance in sustaining Bedouin livestock production. The provision of subsidized fodder has contributed to a large increase in the livestock population of Saudi Arabia. Without the subsidy, it would be uneconomical for many Bedouins to raise animals. Even with the subsidy, however, the Bedouin often make use of the open ranges to reduce their feed expenditures, especially poorer nomads for whom the price of barley is still relatively high. This in turn has put heavy pressure on the already deteriorated natural rangelands.

Several techniques are used by the pastoralists to reduce their expenses for purchasing barley. First, they use the badia when the forage condition is good. Second, they mostly feed barley to animals designated for sale and to the young or pregnant sheep. The rest of the animals are fed under a system known as ghob, in which barley is fed only on alternate days. Usually, the barley is fed at a ratio of one kilogramme (kg) per head daily.

Many Bedouin are only able to afford barley because they have additional sources of income, i.e., they may obtain financial assistance from their capable sons and/or be eligible for Social Security benefits (i.e., for Bedouins over 60 years of age). In addition, they may sell their animals to obtain the needed cash, as well as to reduce the herd size commensurate with the amount of barley they can afford.

3. FACTORS AFFECTING BEDOUIN MOVEMENTS

Fully nomadic pastoralists do not grow forage crops, but instead rely upon their native pastures, purchased feed and on seasonal movement of their flocks to areas with higher rainfall. There are several major factors which influence the movements of Bedouins in Saudi Arabia. These include: the preference for traditional pastures; the availability of barley; financial conditions (including herd size); and the enrollment of children in schools.

3.1 Use of traditional pastures

Despite the unimpeded access to open rangelands, many Bedouins elect to remain in their tribal grazing areas when rainfall is adequate. This fact was demonstrated by surveys conducted in 1996. This field-work showed that the Bedouins in Jandaliah and Taisiah were primarily from local tribes. This was because rain had fallen on most of the grazing areas in Saudi Arabia. By contrast, in spring of the previous year (1995), Bedouins from many different tribes flocked to these two areas because the rainfall there was more abundant than in the rest of the country.

3.2 The availability of barley

Although the Government has strongly supported programmes to provide subsidized barley through legal distributors, there has nonetheless been a shortage of barley in the past few years. The local arrangements for the distribution of barley were such that only local Bedouins in each territory were supplied; no outsiders could obtain supplies legally. Consequently, many Bedouins grazed their animals in good pasture areas temporarily, after which they would return to their traditional grazing areas to be eligible for obtaining the subsidized barley.

3.3 Financial conditions and herd size

Herders who own 250 heads or more of sheep are able to sell some of their animals to purchase barley, small trucks and other items, without significantly affecting the size or productivity of their herd. Thus, they are much better off than herders with smaller flocks. These well-off Bedouins usually confine their herd's grazing movements to traditional areas for most of the year; they can afford to supplement natural pasture with purchased fodder. However, based on data collected from personal interviews, the majority of Bedouin herders own herds of fewer than 150 heads. This group often spends some time outside of their traditional pastures in order to be less dependent on barley, which (as noted above) is relatively expensive and often difficult to obtain.

3.4 Education of Children

Enrolling children in school necessarily limits the movement of Bedouin families, and is considered a hindrance to moving herds long distances from traditional areas. The choice of whether to send children to school is largely based on economics. Aging Bedouins, as well as those who have large herds of sheep, generally pay less attention to the education of their children because they need their help in raising the herd. Pastoralism is only economically viable for those who own large herds. Thus, the majority of Bedouins who have herds of less than

150 heads are eager to educate their children in the hopes of finding an alternative to nomadic desert life.

Another economic motive for Bedouins to send their children to school is Social Security benefits. These benefits are linked to the education of children: the amount of money received depends on the number of children in the family and documented proof of enrolling boys in school.

4. SUMMARY

Despite the scarcity of resources in the badia, the Bedouin continue living in their rural areas, raising animals partly on purchased barley. Without the economic subsidies which they receive (from government feed subsidies, the Social Security fund and the remittances provided by their children), it is unclear whether this traditional nomadic culture would be viable.

References

Abdulla, S.H. and Al-Hajooj, A. 1995. Dependency of barley as a feed source and the economic impacts of a cut in subsidy on nomadic operations. In: Omer, S. Razzaque, M.A. and Alsdirawi, F. (eds). *Range management in arid zones.* Keegan Paul, London pp. 285-300.

Al-Gain, A. 1985. Integrated resource survey in support of nomads in Saudi Arabia. *In:* Whitehead, E., Hutchinson, C., Timmerman, B. and Varady, R. (eds). *Arid lands today and tomorrow.* Proc. Int'l Res. And Develop. Conf., Tucson.

Draz, O. 1985. The *hema* system of range reserves in the Arabian peninsular: its possibilities in range improvement and conservation projects in the Near East. FAO, Rome.

El Shorbagy, M.A. 1997. Impact of development programmes on deterioration of rangeland resources in some African and Middle-eastern countries (this volume).

Jaubert, R. and Bocco, R. 1994. The reintroduction of traditional dryland resource managenment systems: a critical analysis of the "Hema" project in Syria. In: *Proceedings of the UNESCO/IUSSPIIGU Conference on Population and Environment in Arid Regions.* Amman, Jordan, 24-27 October 1994.

Leybourne, M. 1994. The dynamics of the agro-pastoral population in the northern Syrian steppe. In: *Proceedings of the UNESCO/IUSSPIIGU Conference on Population and Environment in Arid Regions.* Amman, Jordan, 24-27 October 1994.

Weiss, E. 1997. The integrated use of remote sensing for ESON rangeland and desertification assessment in Saudi Arabia. (this volume).

Economic analysis of nomadic livestock operations in northern Saudi Arabia

28

S.H. Abdalla, A. Hajooj and A. Simir

Synopsis

The economic consequences of changes to the pastoral system in Saudi Arabia are the subject of this study. It presents economic analyses, including investment, production rates, off-take, income and expenditures and the returns to nomadic pastoralists.

Key Points

1. *Traditional nomadism as a production system no longer exists in Saudi Arabia. Dependency on range forage as a basic feed resource has declined from 100 to less than 20%. Nomadic movements have been mechanized and operations commercialized.*

2. *A great shift from traditional camel-rearing to sheep-raising took place. Herd sizes increased manifold to suit the new economic conditions. Expansion in the sizes of production operations, in addition to other social changes, resulted in a growing demand for foreign labour.*

3. *The new system of mechanized nomadism requires high levels of capital investments and cash to run livestock enterprises. Production levels are generally low. The availability of cheap barley feed, machinery and labour expenses will be the most important factors determining production expenses. These factors tend to favour large-size operations for economy of scale. In determining the size of a viable unit that can support a nomadic family, the social traditions must be considered.*

1. INTRODUCTION

Traditional nomadism as a production system no longer exists in Saudi Arabia. Dependency on range forage as a basic feed resource has declined from 100 to less than 20%. Nomadic movements have been mechanized and operations commercialized. This paper presents the results of field-work among 11 groups of nomadic pastoralists, and analyzes the economics of their operations.

2. METHODOLOGY

A sample of 11 nomadic operations were selected, comprising five *Naimi* and four *Najdi* sheep operations and two camel operations. Flock sizes varied from 350 to 3 600 head for Naimi, and from 122 to 203 for *Najdi* operations. Camel herd sizes were 65 and 112 head. The Widyan and gravel plains of the Hamad were the main grazing areas of the Naimi operations while the deep sand dunes of the Nafud were the main grazing areas of the *Najdi* sheep and camels.

Primary data were obtained at the beginning of the survey on investments and management resources used in each individual operation. Data on production rates, expenses and returns were recorded on a monthly basis for each operation for a complete year. Management practices and production problems were also considered.

3. RESULTS

Tables 28.1 to 28.4 present details and summaries of investments, production rates, off-take, income, expenses and returns of nomadic livestock operations.

Depending on flock size, the estimated value of investments per operation ranged from SAR 288 534 to 1 893 050 for *Naimi*; 87 225 to 153 700 for *Najdi*; and from SAR 406 000 to 1 084 750 SAR for camel operations. Investments in animals varied from 43 to 90% of total invested capital in sheep operations, compared from 63 to 100% in camel operations. Investments in machinery (mainly vehicles) was also significant and ranged from 6 to 41%. Total investments per head ranged from SAR 525 to 896 for sheep, and from SAR 6 246 to 9 685 for camels.

Based on the number of lambs born alive per 100 mature ewes in the flock at the beginning of the year, lamb crop varied from 63 to 90 for *Naimi*, and from 102 to 152 for *Najdi*. Calf crop in camel operations varied from 16 to 28. Although the lamb crop in *Najdi* operations was boosted up by the high kidding rates of goats, which constituted 10 to 25% of the *Najdi* flocks, the production rates in *Najdi* operations were still higher than in the *Naimi*. Death losses were higher in ewes (8% average) relative to younger animals in all sheep operations. This high mortality rate in breeding ewes could be one of the emerging problems

Table 28.1

Investments in nomadic livestock operations

Item	*Naimi* operations Flock sizes					*Najdi* operations Flock sizes				Camel operations Herd sizes	
	350 head SAR	500 head SAR	660 head SAR	1200 head SAR	3600 head SAR	122 head SAR	128 head SAR	152 head SAR	203 head SAR	65 head SAR	112 head SAR
Sheep											
Ewes	126,000	150,000	225,000	450,000	1,250,000	16,000	40,000	32,000	60,000	–	–
Weaner Lambs	24,000	60,000	80,000	126,000	481,000	16,000	9,000	24,500	21,000	–	–
Bucks	8,000	4,000	10,000	20,000	24,000	500	1,400	1,600	1,500	–	–
Sub-Total	158,000	214,000	315,000	596,000	1,755,000	32,500	50,400	58,100	82,500	–	–
Goats											
Dams	–	–	–	–	–	3,750	4,000	–	–	–	–
Weaner Kids	–	–	–	–	–	3,900	1,620	–	–	–	–
Bucks	–	–	–	–	–	350	350	–	–	–	–
Sub-Total	–	–	–	–	–	8,000	5,970	–	–	–	–
Camels											
Dams	–	–	–	–	–	–	–	–	–	320,000	560,000
3 year old	–	–	–	–	–	–	–	–	–	24,000	21,000
2 year old	–	–	–	–	–	–	–	–	–	30,000	30,000
Yearlings & Calves	–	–	–	–	–	–	–	–	–	12,000	33,000
Bulls	–	–	–	–	–	–	–	–	–	20,000	10,000
Sub-Total	–	–	–	–	–	–	–	–	–	406,000	654,000
Horses and Donkeys											
Horses	–	–	–	–	–	–	–	–	–	–	–
Donkeys	600	600	1,200	1,200	1,800	–	–	–	–	–	–
Sub-Total	600	600	1,200	1,200	1,800	–	–	–	–	–	–
Machinery+Equipment											
Water Tankers	65,000	70,000	70,000	90,000	90,000	–	–	35,000	30,000	–	220,000
Trucks	21,000	30,000	–	30,000	–	–	–	–	–	–	135,000
Pick-up Trucks (4w.d.)	–	–	–	–	–	32,000	20,000	34,000	33,000	–	29,000
Pick-ups	18,000	12,000	21,000	15,000	23,000	–	–	–	–	–	–
Livestock equipment	934	630	580	1,040	3,250	725	1,570	1,050	200	–	750
Sub-Total	104,934	112,630	91,580	136,040	116,250	32,725	21,570	70,050	63,200	–	384,750
Dwellings											
Tents	25,000	10,000	10,000	26,000	20,000	14,000	9,350	8,000	8,000	–	16,000
Total Investments	288,534	337,230	417,780	759,240	1,893,050	87,225	87,290	136,150	153,700	406,000	1,054,750

Table 28.2

Investments per head of animal in semi-nomadic operations

Item	Naimi operations - Flock sizes									
	350 head		500 head		660 head		1200 head		3600 head	
	SAR/head	%	SAR/head	%	SAR/head	%	SAR/head	%	SAR/head	%
Livestock	453.1	55.0	429.2	63.3	479.1	75.7	496.7	78.6	488.0	92.8
Machinery+ Equipment	299.8	36.4	225.3	33.4	138.8	21.9	113.4	18.0	32.3	6.1
Dwellings	71.4	8.6	20.0	7.0	15.2	2.4	21.7	3.4	5.6	1.1
TOTAL	824.3	100.0	674.5	100.0	633.1	100.0	631.8	100.0	525.9	100.0

Item	Najdi operations - Flock sizes								Camel operations - Herd sizes			
	122 head		128 head		152 head		203 head		65 head		112 head	
	SAR/head	%	SAR/head	%	SAR/head	%	SAR/head	%	SAR/head	%	SAR/head	%
Livestock	332.0	46.4	440.4	64.6	382.2	42.7	403.7	53.5	6246.2	100.0	6107.1	63.0
Machinery+ Equipment	268.2	37.5	168.5	24.7	460.9	51.4	311.3	41.3	–	–	3435.3	35.5
Dwellings	114.8	16.1	73.0	10.7	52.6	5.9	39.4	5.2	–	–	142.9	1.5
TOTAL	715.0	100.0	681.9	100.0	895.7	100.0	754.6	100.0	6246.2	100.0	9685.0	100.0

Item	Naimi operations Flock sizes				Najdi operations Flock sizes				Camel operations Herd sizes	
	124 head		311 head		127 head		153 head		103 head	
	SAR/head	%	SAR/head	%	SAR/head	%	SAR/head	%	SAR/head	%
Livestock	483.9	55.9	501.6	38.8	366.9	39.2	454.4	46.9	5388.3	83.1
Machinery+ Equipment	349.8	40.4	768.5	59.5	481.9	51.5	514.4	53.1	1017.5	15.7
Dwellings	32.3	3.7	22.5	1.7	86.6	9.3	–	–	77.7	1.2
TOTAL	866.0	100.0	1,292.6	100.0	935.4	100.0	968.8	100.0	6483.5	100.0

Source: MAW

of heavy dependency on barley feeding. Lamb mortality and abortion rates were generally low (less than 5%), except in two of the operations where one operator lost 56% of his lamb crop as a result of an outbreak of foot-and-mouth-disease, while the other suffered a 12% abortion rate because of sheep-pox infection.

The number of animals removed from the herd for sale or home consumption was high. Percentage off-take varied from 8 to 29% for ewes, and from 15 to 71% for yearlings and lambs. Percentage off-take in camels varied from 11 to 41% for young animals, and from 0 to 20% for breeding females.

Receipts from animal sales, the value of animals consumed at home and the increase in herd inventory were the main components of gross income from nomadic operations.

Livestock sales were the main source of cash income for the nomadic families, but some operatiors received additional income by working as security guards or

Table 28.3

Herd structure, production rates and off-take in nomadic livestock operations

Item	Naimi operations Flock sizes					Najdi operations Flock sizes				Camel operations Herd sizes	
	350 head SAR	500 head SAR	660 head SAR	1200 head SAR	3600 head SAR	122 head SAR	128 head SAR	152 head SAR	203 head SAR	65 head SAR	112 head SAR
Breeding males: Females ratio *	1:28	1:88	1:45	1:45	1:83	1:28	1:32	1:40	1:43	1:40	1:18
Percentage of breeding ewes in the herd	80	69	68	75	69	45	75	53	64	62	63
Percentage of weaner lambs for replacement & herd growth	17	30	30	23	30	45	23	46	34	37	34
Percent of lamb (kid/calf) crop**	76	72	90	63	77	152	129	135	102	28	16
Twining rate	4	1	3	1	–	36	14	1	6	–	–
Percent of Death losses:											
Ewes (Dams)	6	9	10	6	2	4	6	16	7	3	3
Weaner lambs (calves)	3	0	0.7	2	0.1	0	1	6	11	0	0
Suckling lambs (calves)	4	56	4	2	2	0	3	5	7	0	0
Abortion	0.4	0.6	3	12	0.1	0	3	0	4	0	0
+ Percent off-take:											
Ewes (Dams)	25	29	16	26	8	9	11	0	16	0	20
Yearlings and lambs (Calves)	33	15	20	41	31	26	71	25	30	11	41

*   Only mature breeding females were included.

** Lamb crop is defined as the number of lambs (kids/calves) born alive
     as a percent of mature breeding ews (dams)

\+   Off-take is the number of animals removed from the herd and sold or consumed.

at other outside employment in the government service. Gross income varied from SAR 35 350 to 94 540 in the *Najdi* operations; SAR 58 950 to 712 449 in the *Naimi* operations; and from 5 400 to 127 000 in camel operations. The value of animals slaughtered and consumed at home constituted an important part of gross income in the small operations (up to 26%). The value of home consumption varied from SAR 6 800 to 40 000 in sheep operations.

Data on expenses included: (i) feed costs; (ii) livestock purchases and other expenses; (iii) machinery-operating expenses; (iv) hired labour; (v) other miscellaneous costs; and (vi) non-cash costs (depreciation on machinery and equipment, tents and decrease in inventory). Cash expenditures varied from SAR 14 151 to 43 792 in *Najdi* operations; SAR 49 425 to 175 060 in *Naimi* operations; and

Table 28.4

Summary of investments, gross income, expenses, net returns and rate of returns to capital

Item	Naimi operations Flock sizes					Najdi operations Flock sizes				Camel operations Herd sizes	
	350 head SAR	500 head SAR	660 head SAR	1200 head SAR	3600 head SAR	122 head SAR	128 head SAR	152 head SAR	203 head SAR	65 head SAR	113 head SAR
Gross Income											
Cash Sales	63,510	43,550	74,660	288,464	427,049	29,540	26,030	11,150	26,970	5,400	125,000
Perquisits	6,800	15,400	12,400	18,400	40,000	10,000	21,600	10,000	8,800	–	2,000
Increase in livestock inventory	8,300	–	67,100	–	245,400	55,000	–	14,200	12,700	–	–
Total	78,610	58,950	154,160	306,864	712,449	94,540	47,630	35,350	48,470	5,400	127,000
Expenses											
Cash costs: feeds	13,766	26,415	34,150	56,965	84,562	11,032	4,926	9,380	8,825	–	19,037
Livestock purchases	–	–	–	–	–	28,720	–	–	–	–	25,000
Other livestock expenses	540	400	650	650	1,060	–	325	–	–	–	75
Machinary expenses	13,419	12,441	15,750	22,566	34,738	3,980	6,500	8,744	4,766	–	8,208
Hired labour	21,600	27,600	32,400	39,250	54,100	–	2,400	3,500	3,150	–	15,840
Misc.	–	–	–	–	600	–	–	–	–	–	–
Total Cash Costs	49,325	66,856	82,950	119,431	175,060	43,792	14,151	21,624	16,741	–	68,160
Non Cash Costs											
Depreciation	13,676	15,315	11,235	24,120	32,911	4,540	3,533	4,400	4,100	–	22,808
Decrease in inventory	–	32,600	–	79,200	–	–	4,200	–	–	26,700	79,50
Total Expenses	63,001	114,771	94,185	222,751	207,971	48,332	21,884	28,224	20,841	26,400	170,468
Net Earnings	15,609	(55,821)	59,975	84,113	504,478	46,208	25,746	9,326	27,629	(21,000)	(43,468)
Net Income	8,809	(71,221)	47,575	65,713	464,478	36,208	4,146	(674)	18,824	(21,000)	(45,468)

* indicates negative value
Source: MAW

SAR 0 to 58 160 in camel operations. Feed, machinery and labour expenses were the most important production expenses and constituted from 95 to 90% of total production costs. These three items were about equally important in *Naimi* operations, but feed costs gained more importance relative to the other costs in large operations. In *Najdi* operations, labour was a minor expense.

Feed costs in *Naimi* operations varied from SAR 13 766 to 84 562, and constituted 22 to 41% of total production expenses. Cash machinery expenses varied

Table 28.5

Summary of production expenses and net income

Item	Naimi operations - Flock sizes									
	350 head		500 head		660 head		1200 head		3600 head	
	SAR	%	SAR	%	SAR	%	SAR	%	SAR	%
Production Expenses										
Feeds	39.33	22	52.83	32	51.74	36	47.47	40	23.49	41
Livestock expenses	1.54	1	0.80	1	0.98	1	0.54	–	0.29	–
Machinary expenses	70.27	39	53.51	32	39.37	28	36.74	31	18.24	32
Hired Labour	61.71	34	55.20	34	49.09	34	32.71	27	15.03	26
Dwellings	7.14	4	2.00	1	1.51	1	2.17	2	0.55	1
Total expenses	180.00	100	164.34	100	142.69	100	119.63	100	57.60	100
Net earnings	44.60		(111.64)		90.87		70.09		140.13	
Net Income	25.17		(142.44)		72.08		54.76		129.02	

Item	Najdi operations - Flock sizes								Camel operations - Herd sizes			
	122 head		128 head		152 head		203 head		65 head		112 head	
	SAR	%	SAR	%	SAR	%	SAR	%	SAR	%	SAR	%
Production Expenses												
Feeds	90.43	57	38.38	28	61.71	36	43.47	42	–	–	169.97	29
Livestock expenses	–	–	2.54	2	–	–	–	–	–	–	0.67	–
Machinary expenses	53.44	33	70.57	51	79.89	47	38.75	38	–	–	262.64	45
Hired Labour	–	–	18.75	14	23.03	13	15.52	15	–	–	141.43	24
Dwellings	16.39	10	7.81	5	6.58	4	4.93	5	–	–	14.28	2
Total expenses	160.26	100	138.15	100	171.21	100	102.67	100	–	–	588.99	100
Net earnings	268.65		201.14		61.36		136.10		(323.08)		(388.10)	
Net Income	210.51		32.39		(4.43)		92.75		(323.08)		(405.96)	

from SAR 13 419 to 34 738, and constituted (with depreciation 31) to 39% of total production expenses. Labour expenses varied from SAR 21 600 to 54 100, and constituted 26 to 34% of total production expenses.

In *Najdi* operations, feed costs varied from SAR 4 980 to 11 032, and constituted 28 to 57% of total production expenses. Machinery costs varied from 3 980 to 8 744 SAR, and constituted 33 to 51% of total production expenses. Labour costs varied from 0 to 3 500 SAR and constituted 0 to 15% of total production expenses (Table 28.5).

Table 28.6

Summary of return on capital and rate of return

Item	Naimi operations Flock sizes					Najdi operations Flock sizes				Camel operations Herd sizes	
	350 head SAR	500 head SAR	660 head SAR	1200 head SAR	3600 head SAR	122 head SAR	128 head SAR	152 head SAR	203 head SAR	65 head SAR	112 head SAR
Total investments	288,534	337,230	417,780	759,240	1.893,050	87,225	87,290	136,150	153,700	406,000	1.084,750
Gross income	78,610	58,950	154,160	306,864	712,444	94,540	47,630	35,350	48,470	5,400	127,000
Total expenses	63,001	114,771	94,384	222,751	207,971	48,332	21,884	28,224	20,841	26,400	170,458
Net returns	15,609	(55,821)*	59,975	84,113	504,478	46,208	25,746	9,629	27,629	(21,000)*	(43,468)*
Value of family labour	24,000	24,000	12,000	24,000	72,000	12,000	12,000	12,000	12,000	24,000	12,000
Return to capital	(8,391)*	(79,821)*	47,000	60,000	432,478	34,208	13,746	(2,674)*	(15,629)*	(35,000)*	(55,468)*
Rate of return to capital	(2.9%)*	(23.7%)*	11.20%	7.90%	22.80%	39.20%	15.70%	(2%)*	10.20%	(8.6%)*	(5.1%)*

* indicates negative value
Source: MAW

Total production expenses per head varied from SAR 58 to 180 in *Naimi* operations; SAR 103 to 171 in *Najdi*; and from SAR 0 to 589 in camel operations.

Net earnings were positive for all sheep operations, except one *Naimi* operation which lost 56% of its lamb crop as a result of foot-and-mouth-disease. Both camel operations resulted in net losses.

Net earnings from *Najdi* operations ranged from SAR 9 326 to 46 208 and net income of SAR -674 to 36 146. The difference between net earnings and net income reflects the importance of the value of home consumption in these small operations. Net earnings from *Naimi* operations ranged from SAR 15 609 to 504 478 and the net income from SAR 8 809 to 464 208. Net earnings per head varied from SAR 61 to 269 in *Najdi* operations, and from SAR 45 to 140 in *Naimi* operations (Table 28.6).

After subtracting the value of family labour and operator's management from net earnings, the rate of return to capital varied from -3 to 22% for *Naimi* operations; -2 to 39% for *Najdi*; and -5 to -9% for camel operations.

According to family budgets obtained from nomadic operators, a family in the Nafud area required from 6 000 to 10 000 SAR per year to meet cash living expenses, while those in the Hamad required twice this amount (SAR 12 000 to 20 000). Since net income per operation shows the amount which is available for family living expenses, only five of the eleven studied operations provided sufficient net incomes to meet family living expenses.

The four sheep operations that produced insufficient net income levels were small-size operations with less than 500 head. Due to the generosity and social traditions among Bedouin, the number of animals slaughtered and consumed at home were more than necessary for subsistence. The estimated average amount of meat consumed by a nomadic family was 568 kg; that is, a meat consumption per capita of 63 kg, compared to the national red meat consumption per capita of 28 kg. This high consumption rate of meat, dictated by social traditions, reduced cash-income levels in the small nomadic operations and available income per family living expenses.

4. CONCLUSIONS

In general, the new system of mechanized nomadism requires high levels of capital investment and cash to run livestock enterprises. Production was generally low in *Naimi* operations. The availability of cheap feed barley, machinery and labour will be the most important factor determining production expenses. These factors tend to favour large-size operations for economy of scale. In determining the size of a viable unit that can support a nomadic family, the social traditions must be considered.

References

Al-Shareef, A.G. 1997. Development of range resources and its role in combating desertification in Kingdom of Saudi Arabia (this volume).

Blench, R. 1997. Rangeland degradation and socio-economic changes among the Bedu of Jordan: results of the 1995 IFAD Survey (this volume).

Al-Eisa, A. 1997. Changes and factors affecting Bedouin movement for grazing (this volume).

El Shorbagy, M.A. 1997. Impact of development programmes on deterioration of rangeland resources in some African and Middle eastern countries (this volume).

Development of range resources and its role in combating desertification in Saudi Arabia

29

A.G. Al-Shareef

Synopsis

This paper discusses the results of an evaluation of the rangeland rehabilitation programmes undertaken by the Range and Forestry Department of the Ministry of Agriculture and Waters (MAW) of the Kingdom of Saudi Arabia. Water spreading and reseeding have been undertaken at numerous sites.

Key Points

1. *Rangelands occupy an area of 170 million hectares (ha), which represents 75% of the total area of the Kingdom of Saudi Arabia. During the last few decades, vegetation cover of Saudi Arabia has been deteriorating due to the malpractices of man and his tendency to over exploit the natural resources under wide climatic variations.*

2. *The Ministry of Agriculture and Water has felt the need for adequate preventive and curative measures to conserve natural resources and combat desertification. Through its Range and Forestry Department, it had to launch an ambitious programme to conserve, improve and manage rangeland resources. Since drought is always the major drawback in the arid areas of the country, the Range and Forestry Department has resorted to water spreading as a means of utilizing surface run-off to augment soil-moisture content. In this context, it has executed earthen dikes and dams in 104 sites in different regions of the country. As for range reseeding, the department has reseeded 73 sites with 54 forage species. As it is also concerned with the protection and conservation of natural vegetation, the Department has protected 35 range sites to allow the vegetation to improve by natural succession.*

1. INTRODUCTION

It has been estimated that the human population may exceed six billion by the turn of the century and continue to grow exponentially, reaching nine billion by the 2030s. Over this period of time, therefore, the number of people who will need to be fed will increase by 50%. The food requirements of this immense populace, many of whom will be at risk of starvation, will need to be met through the increased exploitation of natural resources. Due to the urgency of meeting these food needs, it is likely that intense agricultural development will occur regardless of the capability to ensure that future generations will be able to enjoy a similar quality of life, or of the ability of the environment to maintain vital ecological functions.

At the global level, acute environmental problems have already arisen, directly and indirectly, from the misuse and overexploitation of resources. Pollution of the atmosphere and terrestrial and marine ecosystems is unmistakably linked to man's activities. Two egregious examples are the depletion of the ozone layer and carbon dioxide-induced global warming. Because of their synergistic, often irreversible nature, these impacts pose an imminent danger to mankind, and are appropriately the subject of persistent international dialogue and bargaining.

At the local level, overuse of renewable natural resources through overgrazing, excessive logging, deforestation and farming of marginal land has caused unprecedented losses in vegetative cover, which in turn contribute to dessication, erosion, and – ultimately – desertification. The situation is further aggravated by the depletion of groundwater reservoirs and the pollution of soil and water by the fertilizers, pesticides and disinfectants used in intensive agricultural systems. Saudi Arabia has a harsh, arid climate and very limited water supplies. One of the country's most important natural resources is its rangelands with their fragile soils and indigenous vegetation. This paper reviews major studies and discusses practical applications related to the conservation and rehabilitation of natural range resources.

2. FACTORS AFFECTING THE DIVERSITY AND DISTRIBUTION OF NATURAL VEGETATION IN SAUDI ARABIA

The natural vegetative cover of a region is a product of many interacting factors. The most important natural factors are geographical, geological (soil type, depth and texture) and climatic (precipitation, temperature, evaporation rates, solar radiation and wind). The critical anthropogenic factors affecting vegetation in arid lands are the grazing of animals and land use activities such as agriculture, urbanization and tourism. The following sections highlight the main elements which have influenced the distribution of plant communities in Saudi Arabia.

2.1 Geography

Saudi Arabia comprises an area of approximately 2.25 million km^2, bordered by Jordan, Iraq, Yemen and Oman and surrounded by the waters of the Red Sea and the Arabian Gulf. This location places the country within the boundaries of two main biogeographical regions, the Saharo-Sindian and Sudano-Decanian. These regions cover the northern, central and eastern portions and the southern and southwestern portions of the country, respectively. Furthermore, the country borders several other vegetative regions, as follows:
- the Irano-Touranian region in the northeast;
- the Euro-Siberia region in the north;
- the Mediterranean region in the northwest;
- the moist tropical region in the south; and
- the Sino-Japanese region in the east.

This has resulted in the occurrence of many plant species, normally found in other vegetative regions of the world. In the Saharo-Sindian region, the Arabian desert species are dominant, mixing with Mediterranean and Irano-Touranian species. In the Sudano-Decanian region, African, Arabian and Indian species grow along side species belonging to other regions.

2.2 Geology and topography

The Arabian peninsula is characterized by two major geological formations: the Arabian Shield to the west and the Arabian Shelf to the east. Due to these differing rock formations, there is a great disparity in soil parental material between the western and eastern areas. This, in turn, affects the general land features of the country, which include:
- mountains and rocky areas to the west and southwest;
- plateaux extending from the northern to the central areas; and
- depressions and basins between the plateaux and the mountains.

This unique situation, in which expansive tracts of land are either elevated or depressed, has effectively obstructed the flow of surface and underground water from west to east. In consequence, a distinct division of natural habitats is found. These habitat types include the coastal strip; the eastern, central, northern and western plateaux; the western mountain range and the great sand deserts.

Within all of these geographical divisions, smaller habitats are formed within the larger ones due to the presence of wadis (valleys) and watercourses, and to factors such as altitude, latitude and soil depth, type, slope and salinity. These features cause significant differences in the composition and distribution of species and in the overall structure of the animal/plant community.

2.3 Climate

Despite the country's location in the western continental desert belt (which is particularly hot and dry throughout the year, but especially during the summer), the vastness of the area and varied topography actually produce wide variations in climate. Most areas receive rainfall during the winter and spring seasons. The southwestern region, however, receives an additional amount during the summer, which raises its annual precipitation range to 400-500 mm. At lower elevations and in the rain shadow of mountains, annual average precipitation decreases to 150-200 mm. Other areas receive less, with the extreme being the vast Nafud and Rub al Khali desert areas, which are usually confined to the bounds of 25-50 mm of rainfall annually.

There are vast variations in temperature among regions according to their latitude and altitude, while relative humidity varies mostly according to a region's proximity to the coast and mountains. All these factors influence evaporation rates and hence soil moisture, which in turn governs the distribution and types of plant communities. The southwestern Asir mountains support rich juniper forest communities, while the wadis and watercourses at lower elevations support acacia woods and shrub species. Other highly adapted plants occupy the remaining areas of sand deserts and arid lands.

2.4 Anthropogenic factors

The activities of man and his livestock are considered the most important biological cause of the deterioration of natural range vegetation in Saudi Arabia. Over the past 20 years, the number of livestock in the country increased significantly, and prior limitations on the use of range were largely removed. The use of trucks to transport animals over large distances and water tankers to provide mobile water supply has enabled the exploitation of remote range sites formerly inaccessible to nomads. Recently, large tracts of rangeland, especially those near wadi beds, watercourses and low floodplains, have been converted into agricultural land. This has substantially reduced the size of usable range, exerting more pressure on the plant cover in these highly productive areas. Together with the collection of firewood, heavy grazing has exposed extensive areas to complete destruction and desertification, with the resultant loss of most indigenous vegetation.

3. SAUDI ARABIA'S EFFORTS TO MANAGE AND PROTECT RANGELAND RESOURCES

Several legislative decrees have been issued in Saudi Arabia to ensure the conservation of natural resources and the protection of environmental stability. The major enactments which bear upon the rangelands include: the Fallow Land Use Act (Royal Decree No. M/26 dated 6/7/1398 H.); the Forestry and Range Act (Royal Decree No. M/22 dated 3/5/1398 H.); and the Water Source Conservation Act (Royal Decree No. M/34 dated 24/8/1400 H.).

The Ministry of Agriculture and Water (MAW) has primary responsibility for the management of range resources. To date, its efforts have concentrated on the gathering and analysis of basic data, the rehabilitation of depleted rangelands through reseeding, the adoption of specific protection measures and the improved use of rainwater.

3.1 Collection and analysis of basic vegetation data

A primary mission of the Ministry is to provide data on vegetation and animal resources (i.e., qualitative and quantitative parameters of the rangelands) relevant for scientifically sound development and management programmes. This has been accomplished by conducting a survey and inventory of these resources, using both national and international research organizations. The following phased steps were taken:

(i) 1966-71: The country was divided into eight hydrologic zones; an inventory of natural resources, including rangelands and forests, was completed in six of these zones.

(ii) 1971-83: A resource inventory was carried out in areas of the Arabian Shield, extending north and south of Tuhama and Ummal Radhma. Studies of Zone 1 were renewed and expanded to the Al Hamad basin and to the borders with Kuwait, Iraq and Jordan. A forest inventory of the southwest highlands was conducted with the aid of aerial photography.

(iii) 1983-96: Emphasis has been placed on studying range and forestry project sites and on evaluating the carrying capacity and productivity of range resources, the nutritional value of range vegetation and the feeding behaviour of animals.

These studies identified the actual condition of the range resources in terms of vegetative cover, dominant species (DM), productivity and carrying capacity, as shown in Tables 29.1 and 29.2.

Table 29.1

Rangeland condition and productivity

Condition	Percentage of total area	Total area in ha	Average ha productivity Kg/DM/yr	Total production ton/DM /yr
Excellent	8	14,238,000	180	2,562,480
Good	31	52,545,000	120	6,305,400
Moderate	33	55,087,500	88	4,847,700
Poor	29	47,639,500	25	1,667,022
Total	100	169,510,000	-	15,382,602

Source: MAW

Table 29.2

Number of livestock in Saudi Arabia, 1992

Type of animal	Traditional Range bred	Specialized Farm bred
Cattle	148,069	56,298
Sheep	6,022,721	1,023,441
Camel	416,865	–
Goat	3,349,995	–
Total	9,937,650	1,079,739

Source: MAW

3.2 Reseeding of depleted rangelands

Reseeding efforts to reverse the loss of valuable range vegetation were initiated in 1965. These efforts continued until 1975, albeit intermittently and in limited areas (i.e., the Siecid Reserve in Taif, the Awassy Range Improvement area in Arar and the Harrady Livestock Project). In 1980, MAW launched a renewed, extensive reseeding programme in several areas of the country; 73 locations were treated at 16 diverse range sites.

Due to the unavailability of local seed, seeds of 54 different species were imported during 1981-89. Most were perennial grasses, perennial herbs, shrubs and trees suited to the country's conditions. By 1990, local production of range seeds commenced. Three main reseeding methods were employed: hand broadcasting of herbaceous plant seeds followed by ploughing to a depth of 5-6 cm; the use of contour seeders with deep-disc ploughing (to depths of 40-70 cm); and the use of contour pitting seeders which make small pits 10-12 cm deep for planting shrubs or trees. These methods were used on open and fenced ranges, both with and without rainwater spreading systems.

The capacity for seed germination, growth and establishment differed greatly among the different species. In general, the degree of successful germination under natural conditions was 56% (attained by 30 out of 54 species). Failure to germinate was mostly due to the insufficiency, and occasionally the absence, of precipitation during one or several seasons. This became evident from comparing the higher germination success rate in the moist southwest to the lower rate in other, drier areas. However, some species showed a superior capacity to germinate in a much wider range of habitats than others. These included: *Cenchrus ciliaris; C. setigerus; Sporobolus airoides; S. cryptandrus; Panicum antidotale; P. turgidum; P. coloratum; Oryopsis hymenoides; Melilotus officinalis; Sorghostrum mutans; Pennisetum orientalis; Salsola vermiculata* and *Egragrostis lehmoniana.*

On the contrary, other species were substantially limited by extant environmental conditions. The following species flourish only with reasonable amounts of rain and mild temperatures: *Leucaena leucocephala; Acacia victoria; A. georginae; Agropyron elongatum; A. cristatum; Styposanthus humilis; Opuntia spp*, and *Ficus indica.*

The seeding method also influenced germination success through its effect on soil moisture, as shown in Table 29.3. The hand broadcasting method, which was preceded by ploughing, gave fewer individual plants per unit area than the contour seeder method. Germination success was limited because the ploughing loosened the soil, exposing it to wind erosion at sites which received no rain, and allowed the seeds to be blown away or eaten by insects and birds. In addition, the number of plants which became successfully established after germination was comparatively low with the hand broadcasting method (i.e., only 12 species representing 22% of the total number planted, and 40% of the number that germinated were successfully established).

Table 29.3

Forage yield, plant density, and soil moisture contents in reseeded range sites.

Description	Untreated	Treated by ripping	Contour lines
Forage Yield kg/DM/ha/yr	0	73.00	339.00
Plant Density	0	1.26	1.96
Soil Moisture	0.7	0.14	0.17

Source: MAW

For the purposes of this paper, the term 'established' means the persistence of the plant after germination until seed casting, even if exposed to light or moderate grazing during the first year of growth. Such resistant species of forage plants would be considered suitable for reseeding depleted rangelands in Saudi Arabia. These include: *Acacia victoriae; Artemisia herba alba; Atriplex halimus; A. leuco-clada; A. glauca; A. canascens; Conchrus ciliaris; C. setigerus; Cynodon dactylon; Opuntia spp; Ficus indicus; Panicum turgidum;* and *Salsola vermiculata.*

The number of established species was significantly greater in protected (or fenced) areas than at open sites. This exhibits the importance of protection from overgrazing and repeated grazing at early plant growth stages. It was noted that well-established species were ones with local relatives, implying that emphasis needs to be placed on indigenous species for rangeland reseeding programmes. Only when such indigenous species are absent should environmentally fit exotic species be considered for introduction.

3.3 Measures taken to protect rangelands

The historical means of controlling grazing of common rangelands in the Arabian peninsula was the use of the hema (reservation) system. Under this system, strict tribal principles were delineated concerning the extent of each tribe's reservation and the associated grazing rights and regulations. The hema system effectively protected the rangelands; however, they were abolished in 1953 for social and economic reasons. Ever since, it has been the prerogative of every Saudi citizen to use the rangelands without any restrictions.

Under such uncontrolled use, all areas of suitable vegetation were subject to intense grazing pressures, when in fact the livestock herds had already exceeded the optimum carrying capacity of the range. Moreover, during this period several dry cycles occurred, causing an unprecedented level of deterioration.

MAW has recently resorted to the protection of selected range sites for research, for conservation of certain vegetation types and to serve as fodder reserves for use during droughts. A total of 35 exclosures spread throughout 14 different locations and covering between 25 and 8 700 ha (250 and 87 000 donums) were established. Other areas which have been protected include forest lands, national parks, game reserves and sand-stabilization areas. Certain vegetation parameters were obtained periodically from inside and outside the protected areas. These included measurements of primary productivity and plant cover and density (Table 29.4), and evaluations of the desertification hazard (Table 29.5).

Table 29.4

Productivity, plant cover and density in some protected and open rangelands

Year	Dry matter production kg/ha/yr		Percentage plant cover		Density	
	Protected	Open	Protected	Open	Protected	Open
1984	26	68	1	3.9	0.07	0.46
1990	294	6.5	32	0.27	8.8	0.40

Source: MAW

Table 29.4 summarizes the results of readings obtained during 1984-1990, both inside and outside of 12 exclosures. The major findings which emerged are that, during this period:

- primary productivity of open range sites showed a greater than tenfold decrease, from 68 to 6.5 kg/DM/ha/yr, while the corresponding measurements of protected sites showed more than a tenfold increase from 26 to 294 kg/DM/ha/yr;
- the percentage of ground cover decreased from 3.9% to 2.7% in open sites but increased in the exclosures from 1.0% to 32%; and
- there was a decline in plant density in open rangelands from 0.46 plants/m^2 to 0.03 plants/m^2, compared to the increase recorded in protected sites from 0.07 plants/m^2 to 2.8 plants/m^2.

Table 29.5

Some measurements of desertification hazard in some protected and open rangelands

Element measured	Protected range	Open range
Plant cover litter (%)	74	6.5
Depth of erosion gullies (c,)	0	2.6
Depth of sand silt (c,)	0	2.5
Cover rocks and pebbles (%)	0	1.2
Bareground (%)	25.5	79.5

Source: MAW

Table 29.5 presents elements used to determine the potential for desertification as measured at protected and open range sites. The major findings are that:
- ground cover and litter percentages were vastly higher in protected sites;
- erosion gullies were only found on the open range sites;
- wind erosion was similarly found only on open range sites, where the height of sand accumulation was 2.5 cm; and
- the percentage of ground with bare rocks or pebbles decreased from 1.2% in open range to zero in the exclosures; and the percentage of bare ground in protected areas was less than one third of that in open sites.

3.4 Rainwater distribution and spreading measures

Prior to approximately 1985 (during the period 1400-1405 H.), MAW constructed 32 earthen dykes across wadis and streams of varied slope and depth. These were located in nine different areas and ranged in height from 2.5 to 4.0 metres (m). From 1405 H. to date, the Ministry constructed 105 contour earthen dykes in 18 locations with heights ranging from 70 to 120 cm.

A detailed evaluation of these measures is beyond the scope of this paper. In general, however, the dykes improved the water spreading process, thus increasing the soil moisture in the surrounding area. This greatly encouraged the growth of perennials and annuals, leading to an increase in plant density and cover compared to areas without water spreading measures. An improvement in range plant productivity was also observed. Because the foliage of the plants was retained for a longer period after the rainy season, the grazing period was extended and the nutritive value was raised above normal.

4. CONCLUSIONS

A variety of range improvement techniques, including reseeding, application of protective measures and the construction of rainwater spreading systems, were implemented by MAW either singly or in combination with other treatments. Based on the results obtained from comparing treated and untreated or unprotected areas, these measures make a significant contribution to enhancing the quantity and quality of natural range vegetation. The reseeding treatment contributed to a remarkable increase in forage production, which ranged from 73 to 339 kg/DM/ha/yr, compared to a range of 0 to 6.5 kg/DM/ha/yr. Reseeding success rates differed according to the type of seeding method used. The use of seeders proved more successful than hand broadcasting, while seeding along contour lines was shown to be superior to pit seeding when the site treated is a flat plain with a mild gradient.

The use of protective measures, such as the establishment of exclosures, generally augmented the percentage of plant cover and density and the frequency of key species. However, these improvements varied significantly from site to site, depending largely upon site characteristics, the nature and type of vegetation or dominant species present and the degree of deterioration at the time of implementing the protection measures. Range protection efforts clearly reduced wind erosion and runoff, indicating the potential effectiveness of these approaches in reducing the rate of desertification.

References

Al-Shareef, A.K. 1996. *Role of Ministry of Agriculture and Water in developing rangeplant vegetation of the Kingdom of Saudi Arabia.* The International Conference on Desertification in the Arab Gulf Countries. State of Kuwait, 23-26 March 1996. (In Arabic with English summary.)

Al-Shareef, A.K. 1989. *Role of Ministry of Agriculture and Water in rehabilitation of desert of the Kingdom of Saudi Arabia.* Symposium on Desert Studies in the Kingdom of Saudi Arabia. "Scope and Concerns". King Saud University, Riyadh. 21-23 November 1989. (In Arabic).

Al-Shareef, A.S. 1977. Geography of the Kingdom of Saudi Arabia (Part I). Dar El-Marrekh Publ. Riyadh. (*In Arabic*).

El-Shorbagy, M.A. and Al-Shareef, A.K. 1994. Rangeland Management in the Kingdom of Saudi Arabia. "Extent and Implementations". King Saud University, Riyadh. 2-4 October 1994. (*In Arabic*).

El-Shorbagy, M.A. 1986. *Phytogeographical Region and its solution to vegetation and rangelands of Arab countries.* Report of the first training course on plant genetic resources of arid zones. ACSAD/R/48/4/1986. (In Arabic).

El-Shorbagy, M.A. 1983. The Primary Survey of Rangeland Resources on Arabian Gulf States. Saudi Arabia. ACSAD/R/24 – 26/1982. (*In Arabic*).

Ministry of Agriculture and Water (MAW) 1975-1992. Various technical reports.

Rangeland degradation and socio-economic changes among the Bedu of Jordan: results of the 1995 IFAD Survey

30

R. Blench

Synopsis
The paper describes the pastoral system of the Bedu of Jordan as it existed in 1995, and summarizes the reasons for the changes that have occurred over recent years. The likely course of future development is outlined.

Key points
1. *The classic literature on the Bedu in Jordan and neighbouring countries has shown regular patterns of transhumance, following traditional routes and associated with particular tribal and sub-tribal groupings. This situation has been shown as if it still existed in quite recent reports. However, in reality, it has all but broken down in favour of a more opportunistic system using trucks and telecommunications to exploit remote pastures.*
2. *The main reasons for the changes in the Bedu behaviour can be summarized as follows:*
   - *Availability of trucks to move animals and water;*
   - *Telecommunications to assess the availability of pasture;*
   - *Closing of the national frontiers to the pastoralist movement;*
   - *Breakdown of traditional authority systems; and*
   - *A relatively liberal political climate.*

1. INTRODUCTION: THE HASHEMITE KINGDOM OF JORDAN

The Hashemite Kingdom of Jordan has a land area of some 90 000 km² and a human population of nearly 4 million. Situated between 29° and 33°N and between 35° and 40°E, it is bordered by Syria in the north, Iraq in the east, Saudi Arabia in the south and east, and Israel and the West Bank in the west. Map 30.1 shows a general political map of the Hashemite Kingdom of Jordan.

Jordan has long been heavily dependent on the service sector, both internally (tourism, transport, trade) and externally (via a highly educated expatriate population sending money back). This pattern underwent a dramatic change after the Gulf War, following the return of large numbers of expatriate workers and the consequent boom in housing and expansion of the urban population.

Of the entire land area of Jordan, only 5% is estimated to be arable. The agricultural sector contributes some 7% of the gross domestic product GDP and has a substantial export element. However, Jordan also has a policy of subsidies on basic foodstuffs, flour sugar and rice and until recently, on animal feed, notably barley and wheat bran. Public expenditure in the agricultural sector has generally been declining and levels in the rangeland areas are very low indeed. There have been a number of projects initiated for the rangelands but none are presently very active.

Map 30.1

Map of the Hashemite Kingdom of Jordan, showing the location of the IFAD Rangeland Rehabilitation Project

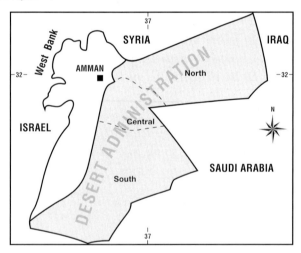

2. BACKGROUND TO THE RANGELANDS

2.1 Extent of the rangelands

The land area of Jordan's rangelands depends largely on the definition adopted. An inclusive definition joins together much of the desert proper, the steppe region and the highlands, regarding the spaces between cropped land as 'range'. In this case, some 97% of the land area of Jordan can be considered 'rangeland'. Alternatively, only the regions unsuitable for rainfed cropping, with rainfall below 200 mm annually, are defined as range which gives a figure nearer 80% of the total land area.

The decade since 1985 has seen an acceleration of all types of agriculture, gradually eating into the area of the rangeland. The practice of "pseudo-cropping", especially along the Syrian border, has effectively excluded both natural forage and livestock from significant areas of former rangeland and it is natural to regard these areas as extensions of the cropped area of the steppe. Similarly, in the Jordan valley, intensive cultivation has caused the disappearance of all but the smallest strips of natural forage, and livestock production now depends on feeds and vegetable residues. This process cannot be reversed and this former rangeland can be regarded as permanently eliminated.

The rangeland which is still available for producers, and for which it is possible to reverse the process of degradation, is the region known in Jordan as the badia. Nearly all of this region has rainfall under 200 mm, and the great majority is under 50 mm. Although crossed by some major roads for long-distance trade, the vast majority of the badia has virtually no infrastructure and no development at all. The land is technically government land and permission to put up permanent structures is rarely granted.

2.2 Physical and biological resources

The original description of the bioclimates of Jordan goes back to Long (1957). Shehadeh (1985) has compiled a more up-to-date description of the climate of Jordan.

2.2.1 Rainfall

The rainfall and associated parameters have been described in some detail in Shehadeh (1985) and IFAD (1993). Almost all of the badia falls within the 100-200 mm isohyets. There are few stations in much of the east and south east, otherwise it is likely that these regions would fall below 50 mm annually.

Analysis of the actual rainfall data from 1970-71 to 1993-4, within the rangelands, suggests that there has been no significant overall change in the trend of rainfall in the last quarter-century (Blench, 1995). However, the contrary is widely believed and is also used to explain the poor state of pasture in the rangelands.

2.2.2 Geomorphology

The broad categories into which the badia is divided are highland, steppe and desert. The highlands with high rainfall and high population densities are only marginally covered by the survey, as some livestock producers who exploit the badia live in this region. The steppe is represented by a narrow band, perhaps only 20 km wide, between the highlands and the desert proper.

The harra, black basalt plains that cover a great proportion of the northern badia, remain a difficult environment to exploit for subsistence. The sometimes large, evenly scattered stones, make the movement of humans and ruminants difficult, and a track has to be cleared for a vehicle to pass. Nonetheless, such clearways have been made and herds can be moved in to graze the annual grasses that penetrate the stone cover. Where the stones are large, herds are small and goats are preferred to sheep because of their sure footing.

2.2.3 Flora

The main floral regions of Jordan have been classified into some thirteen types (Eisawi, 1985). However, many of these occur only in the highland areas. The rangelands and their western edge can effectively be divided into seven categories. These are as follows;

(i)   Juniperous forest;
(ii)   Mediterranean non-forest;
(iii)   Steppe;
(iv)   Hammada. This subdivides into three distinct categories:
         Runoff hammada - *Wadis* and pools,
         Pebble hammada - the plain is covered with pebbles or stones, usually of black basalt, and
         Sand hammada - sandy plains with scattered plants;
(v)   Sand dunes. Confined to Wadi Araba and Wadi Rum. It consists almost entirely of shrubs and bushes which act to fix the sand dunes;
(vi)   Hydrophytic vegetation. This occurs principally around Azraq Oasis; and
(vii)   Mudflats. The mudflats or qa'a are virtually lifeless plains of cracked mud scattered throughout the badia. The largest one is due east of Al-Jafr in the southeast.

Vegetation zones are a major determinant of livestock distribution. In particular, the pattern in the rangelands has eliminated cattle, a major pastoral species in other parts of the world. The hammada deserts, where annuals dominate, favour sheep and the wadis and dune vegetation are where goats predominate.

2.2.4 Fauna

The Jordanian rangelands used to be quite rich in both small and large mammals and reptiles. These are described in Mountfort (1965), and to a lesser extent in Hatough, Eisawi and Disi (1986). Although small mammals such as rodents survive, and indeed flourish in the reserved areas, large mammals have undergone a significant decline due to hunting and habitat destruction.

2.3 Land use in the rangelands

2.3.1 Pastoralism

The single most significant economic use of the rangelands is pastoralism. The most important animal herded is sheep, although goats are more numerous further south. This represents a major change from camel production, which was predominant until the 1940s. Camels are still kept in certain areas, but their numbers are much reduced. This change has almost certainly affected the vegetation patterns, since the large thornbushes that camels graze cannot be eaten by sheep and goats. The controlled system of land use in the rangelands, the hema system, persisted until the early twentieth century in some form, but grazing is now virtually uncontrolled.

2.3.2 Agriculture

One of the most visible uses of the Jordanian rangelands is for agriculture. Given the extremely low rainfall, this area is not usually regarded as suitable for agriculture. Despite this, cropping is common all along the western edge of the rangelands. The most common pattern is rainfed winter barley and the ploughing of undisturbed rangeland is usually associated with this pattern. Yields are so poor that it is difficult to demonstrate that such production is economic and its function may be as much to bolster land claims as to provide cereals. IFAD (1993) refers to this practice as "pseudo-cropping".

Irrigated cultivation is usually based on drip-fed systems, using large rubber hoses with smaller feeder hoses and drawing water from artesian sources. This is most apparent in the region between the Mafraq to As-Safawi road and the Syrian border. The artesian wells, as most in the northern border region, depend on the watershed with its source in the Jebel Druze. The watershed continues as far as Saudi Arabia, where, however, the water is saline. Extremely high rates of extraction are increasing the salinity gradient in Jordan and it is likely that within a few years much of the water from these wells will be unsuitable for agriculture.

2.3.3 Hunting

Hunting with both dogs and falcons has long been part of the culture of the Bedu pastoral nomads. Large numbers of wild animals probably survived until vehicles became common. A combination of modern rifles and fast transport reduced mammal populations to remnants, mostly around the edges of reserves. Hunting has not been eliminated, as the numbers of salugi dogs attest.

2.4 Sources of degradation in the rangelands

This section enumerates all the sources of degradation of the rangelands, cited by livestock producers or noted during the survey. These are assigned very different degrees of importance by producers, whose views reflect their own concept of responsibility for resource management.

2.4.1 Grazing and overgrazing

The level of grazing is determined as much by the accessibility of the area as the actual plant cover. For example, the harra areas of the northern badia are covered in large stones that are extremely difficult for both animals and vehicles. As a result, patches of harra remain almost ungrazed because the costs of reaching them are too high. Similarly, in the southern wadis, some are so remote and windswept that pastoralists avoid them. The vegetation in these wadis is visibly in better condition than elsewhere.

2.4.2 Plastic waste

The use of synthetics for all types of industrial and commercial purposes has increased considerably in Jordan in the decade since the mid-1980s. No public ethos of recycling, or even litter prevention, exists in many parts of the country. Hence, many agricultural areas and adjacent rangelands are covered in plastic waste. Apart from plastic bags, the black plastic laid in strips to reduce evapo-transpiration in fields under drip irrigation is left to blow into the rangelands once the harvest is collected.

Apart from the aesthetic aspect, plastic waste is extremely dangerous for ruminants, especially goats, as they will eat it. The plastic becomes twisted around their intestines and effectively strangles them. Owners living adjacent to agricultural areas, cited swallowing plastic as the single most important cause of death in their flocks.

2.4.3 Declining rainfall

There is a widespread conviction throughout the entire region that the present state of the rangelands is due to declining rainfall. This is emphatically not the case. It is certainly true that there is an important seed reserve in the badia regions and a year of exceptional rainfall, such as 1994-5, caused the appearance of herbs and other perennials not seen for more than a decade.

Declining rainfall has an important function, as far as producers are concerned; it absolves them from responsibility. The idea frequently propounded was that if only the rainfall would return to "normal" levels then grazing would return to "former" levels. Since rain is at "normal" levels, this is best described as a convenient fantasy.

2.4.4 Cutting of woody vegetation

The disappearance of almost all large specimens of woody vegetation has meant that households in the badia are pressed to find wood for the principal fire. This fire, used for cooking the morning coffee, has an important symbolic value for the tent, as much of the actually cooking is done in the haram using gas cylinders. Cut wood is sold in the larger settlements on the roads, but in remoter areas it is difficult to buy or transport. As a result, branches are cut from shrubs, especially Artemisia herba-alba. However, the frequent cutting has led to a shortage of burnable wood and the response has been to use hoes to dig up the woody roots to burn. Swenne (1992) has documented the extensive uprooting of woody shrubs in the Shobak area, which is far more accessible by road than the more remote parts of the badia.

This strategy is little short of disastrous, since the plant is permanently destroyed. The soil-fixing properties are also lost, leading to greater erosion. Although some Bedu complain about this practice, and many can see, when pressed, that it is contributing to long-term degradation, there are no communal sanctions operating to prevent this practice. Such sanctions would in any event be difficult to enforce, since this degradation occurs most commonly where tents are scattered and there is no effective community.

2.4.5 Gathering of wild plants

The practice of gathering herbs for food and medicinal purposes is still widely practised throughout the Jordanian rangelands. Sometimes these are gathered in large sacks and sold. The scale of this is hard to determine and probably only causes very local declines in plant populations. Plants are usually gathered by tearing off the heads rather than by cutting them down at the roots, so the effect is similar to grazing.

2.4.6 Can the rangelands recover?

Initiatives for the conservation of the Jordanian rangelands are not new – indeed there is a long history of reports recognizing the problems and proposing solutions. Most notable among these reports are those by Park (1955), Tuttle (1971), Draz (1979), and Juneidi and Abu-Zanat (1993). In each case, the authors noted the erosion and degradation in the rangelands and proposed action to arrest the situation. Actions following these reports seem to have been minimal.

Indeed, since these reports, it is safe to say that the situation has become substantially worse. Almost certainly, there has been a major expansion in both the size and number of sheep flocks with a correspondingly greater pressure on range resources. The greater availability of water-tankers and trucks has meant that pastoralists are able to reach regions previously inaccessible, especially in the *harra* pebble desert. At the same time, the gradual tightening of restrictions on cross-border movement has meant that the pasture resources of the broader region are no longer available to Jordanian producers.

Whether the range can fully "recover" is unknown, due to an absence of baseline data. Moreover, the grazing regime of sheep and goats is very different from the grazing of antelope and camels which contributed to its evolution. However, evidence from protected areas and border zones is unequivocal that biodiversity can be greater and biomass much increased with proper management.

3. SOCIO-ECONOMIC BASELINE SURVEY OF THE JORDANIAN BEDU

3.1 Objectives and methods

A socio-economic baseline survey[1] of Jordan's badia rangelands was conducted in 1995, as part of the preparation for a project or the conservation of the rangelands. This survey aimed to devise the socio-economic matrix into which a feasible project could be slotted for providing baseline data against which the overall impact of the project could be measured.

The principal method was the administration of two questionnaires: a community and a household questionnaire. The community questionnaire was administered in an informal manner to senior figures in the community who were also livestock producers. In preference, they were asked to call as many other producers as was practical; thus an open-ended discussion could evolve.

The household questionnaire was designed to elicit basic numerical data on livestock numbers, inputs and expenditures and to allow estimates of the cash income from livestock. It also explored basic issues of sedentarism versus migration and livestock holdings. It did not look at overall household income, as this would have required a considerably more detailed investigation of kinship and residence patterns.

The information gathered was based on recollections of 1994, so in general it could not be checked except on the rare occasions where producers kept written records. There is every reason to believe that the majority of producers answered reasonably honestly. The questionnaires included a certain degree of self-checking, so internal checks often revealed inconsistencies. In some cases, the questionnaire was rejected on the spot and left incomplete, in other cases it was eliminated during data entry. Overall, some 10% of the questionnaires were thrown out.

3.2 Livestock producers in the badia

Livestock producers using the rangelands are divided into the Bedu, who may be described as occupationally specialized pastoralists, and the village producers who by and large combine livestock production with agriculture. Such a distinction is not clear cut, as many villages, (especially in the steppe regions) consist of Bedu who have settled within the last few generations. Similarly, although the Bedu generally have larger herds than the settled producers, this is not invariably the case.

3.2.1 Bedu

Livestock production in the rangeland areas of Jordan is largely in the hands of the Bedu. Although sharing many cultural features with the settled populations, (fellahin) their distinctive systems of production have set them apart since the earliest records of this region.

The Bedu are divided into numerous tribes, (ashira) of varying size, and these are subdivided into clans and lineages, (qabila). Until recently, these affiliations have constituted the single most important organizing principle in the Bedu social organization, defining livestock production strategies, patterns of migration, marriage and warfare, as well as access to pasture.

There is a substantial literature on the Bedu of this region, most notably Musil (1928), Marx (1978), Lancaster (1981), Chatty (1990), Lancaster and Lancaster (1990), and Abu Jaber et al., (1987). Except for the latter, these works tend to focus on specific tribal units. Moreover, despite publication dates they refer to the 1970s or earlier, prior to the profound changes that have overtaken Jordanian society since 1975.

Important changes that have gradually occurred over the course of this century include:
- Increasing settlement of the Bedu on the marginal lands;
- Switch from camel production to sheep production;

- Collapse of traditional migration patterns through widespread use of motorized transport; and
- High level of dependence on imported feeds.

All these factors have had the effect of transforming Bedu society, both economically and socially.

3.2.2 "From camel to truck"

This evocative phrase, taken from the monograph by Chatty (1986), describing the transformation of pastoral society in south Lebanon, is equally applicable to the Bedu of this entire region. With few exceptions, the rangelands-based Bedu seem to have specialized in camel production until the 1940s. The monograph on the Rwala by Musil (1928) describes a society based around camel production with horses kept as prestige animals. At that date, the term 'Bedu' appeared to be coincident with camel production, as Musil notes that sheep producers were called Al-Frejje.

The appearance of vehicles as early as the 1920s began to make a major economic impact in the 1940s. The camel had as its major function transport, especially of water. Once it was evident that this function could be fulfilled more effectively by the truck, camel production was threatened. As the need for money became more pronounced, the products of the camel, hair and milk were observably less marketable than the products of sheep.

The virtual demise of the camel as an economic element in the lives of livestock producers was sealed by a major drought between 1958 and 1962. Lancaster (1981) estimates that at least 70% of the camels died during this period. Combined with the disappearance of the raiding economy and the increased demand for ruminant meat in the growing urban areas, camel production never recovered. The Bedu are generally perceived as small ruminant producers today, specializing above all in sheep, a perception which is amply confirmed by the survey (Table 30.1).

Table 30.1

Percentages of households owning different livestock species

n=664	All n=664		North n=313		Central n=157		South n=194	
	No.	%	No.	%	No.	%	No.	%
Sheep	644	97.0	309	98.7	152	96.8	183	94.3
Goats	543	81.8	234	74.8	130	82.8	179	92.3
Camels	37	5.9	3	1.0	7	4.46	27	13.9
Donkeys	460	69.3	229	73.2	92	58.6	139	71.7
Chickens	297	44.7	126	40.3	73	46.5	98	50.5

3.2.3 Village producers

Down the central spine of the Jordanian steppe are villages which are primarily agricultural, but with variable holdings of domestic animals. They have long traditions of exploiting rangelands, that were traditionally attached to a particular community or group of communities. These rangelands were used seasonally when crop residues were not available and the animals were often herded collectively.

Although such villagers perceive themselves as having tribal affiliations, they do not link themselves with pastoral groups. Their social organization is very much the same as villagers in the intensive agricultural areas. Few of them move long distances with their animals, although this is necessary for those whose herds grow to very large numbers.

3.3 Livestock holdings

The majority of livestock producers in Jordan probably have just a few animals to meet ceremonial obligations, and those which can be tended effectively within the family and fed on household and agricultural wastes. The survey focused on owners with more than 30 head of either sheep or goats, on the grounds that such flocks were likely to make an impact on rangeland use and exploitation. This should be borne in mind when assessing the mean figures for livestock holdings.

3.3.1 Determinants of livestock holdings and distribution

As has been suggested above, the dominant domestic species is sheep. Ninety-seven percent of all the households surveyed owned sheep, as opposed to only 82% owning goats. Table 30.1 shows the percentages of households owning different species overall and in different regions.

Numbers of horses and cattle are too small to be treated in this way. The survey noted 15 households owning 20 horses and 8 households owning 14 cattle.

These figures show trends for some species only. For example, sheep are kept at virtually the same frequency in all parts of the rangelands (Table 30.2). Goats and camels, however, show a marked upward trend from north to south (Figure 30.1 and Tables 30.3 and 30.4). Donkeys represent an essential work-animal needed everywhere and ownership patterns show virtually no inter-regional variation.

These results suggest, as would be expected, that sheep predominate in the higher rainfall rangelands, whereas goats and camels are more important as rainfall decreases. The mean size of sheep flocks peak in the 75 and 100 mm isohyets, represented largely by the northern *badia*. Below this figure, the vegetation becomes too difficult to digest for sheep. The higher rainfall zones are too densely settled to permit such large flocks, except on a feedlot basis.

Table 30.2

Mean herd size by rainfall in zones for all households possessing sheep

1994 Zone (mm)	n	Mean Herd Size
All	644	296.7
< 50	53	197.7
< 75	24	711.0
< 100	178	419.4
< 200	302	241.0
< 300	68	168.0
< 400	13	254.6

Table 30.3

Mean herd size by rainfall zone for all households possessing camels

Zone	n	Mean Herd Size
All	37	7
< 50	21	9
< 75	1	16
< 100	6	10
< 200	7	4
< 300	2	3
< 400	0	0

Figure 30.1

Percentage of households owning goats by region

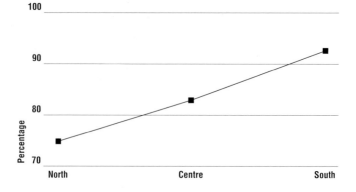

Table 30.4

Mean herd size by rainfall zone, 1994 for all households possessing goats

Zone	n	Mean Herd Size
All	543	38.6
< 50	55	73.6
< 75	21	71.3
< 100	146	40.2
< 200	258	30.8
< 300	51	27.9
< 400	12	17.3

3.3.2 Flock size

Sheep predominate numerically in the Jordanian rangelands and herds are very large indeed by the standards of pastoralists worldwide, especially in the northern badia. Table 30.5 shows the mean flock size for the entire sample of households contrasted with the flock size for households owning that species.

Table 30.5

Mean flock size recorded by the survey, 1995

Species	All	For Households with this species
Sheep	287.9	296.8
Goats	31.6	38.6
Camels	0.56	8.2
Horses	–	1.3
Donkeys	1.13	1.5

Source: IFAD Survey

Table 30.6 provides the overall mean, and then the mean herd sizes, in different regions for each species.

Table 30.6

Mean flock/herd size by region different livestock species

n=664	All owners		North		Central		South	
	n	Mean	n	%	n	%	n	%
Sheep	644	296.7	309	424.8	152	211.7	183	151.5
Goats	543	38.6	234	35.7	130	35.1	179	45.0
Camels	37	7.7	3	6.3	7	11.4	27	7.5
Donkeys	460	1.5	229	1.6	92	1.4	139	1.5
Chickens	297		126	18.7	73	18.4	98	12.5

Source: IFAD Survey

Sheep show a marked upward trend from south to north (Figure 30.2). Goats, however, show little variation in the north-central region but increase markedly in the south. Although there are markedly more camels in the south, the mean herd size does not change significantly, suggesting that constraints on camel herd size may be more to do with labour than feed. As with ownership percentages, there is no significant difference in the size of donkey herds between the different regions.

Figure 30.2

Mean sheep flock size by region

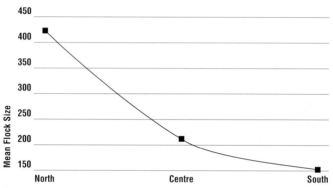

Source: IFAD Survey

3.3.3 Conversion to a common unit

The principal domestic species, both consuming natural forage and purchased feeds, are sheep, goats and camels. All other species, such as donkeys, represent a very small fraction of the total feed consumed. Donkeys are rarely fed purchased feeds but graze on the same shrub vegetation as camels.

To calculate the potential impact of grazing on the environment, it is useful to convert all species to a single unit. Unfortunately there are a diversity of ways of achieving this, which produce rather dissimilar results. The formula used in this report is the one proposed by the United States Agency for International Development (USAID) in their policy review of the low rainfall zone (USAID, 1992) as:

> Unit = 1 sheep or 1 goat
> 1 camel = 13 units
> Small Ruminant Units are thus sheep + goats + 13 x camels

This formula is similar to that used for Tropical Livestock Units (TLUs). Using this conversion, a mean herd size in small ruminant units (SRUs) can be calculated for the entire sample (Table 30.7). To obtain the figure for mean SRUs the herds were individually summed according to the formula above and the mean taken of those sums. This allows expenditures such as feeds and veterinary services to be averaged over SRUs.

Table 30.7

Conversion to SRUs n=664

Species	Mean Herd Size
Sheep	296.7
Goats	38.6
Camels	7.7
SRUs	325.3

Source:IFAD Survey

3.4 Household structures and labour availability

3.4.1 Size and structure of households

The size and structure of households in the rangeland areas is not an easy variable to analyze because of the complex relations with collateral branches of the family (Lancaster, 1981 contains more detailed descriptions relating to the Er-Rwala Bedu). The householders were asked about members of the family present and those away working. However, schoolchildren or aged relatives may stay in the concrete house in the west, while parts of the family migrate with the tent. There is a constant flux of family members between the badia and the permanent house, and an ever-changing labour resource. Results for this part of the survey should, therefore, be taken as indicative rather than absolute.

Table 30.8 shows the mean household size for the entire survey. The number away working is given in the second column and the mean for total members, present and away in the third column. Members working away or abroad do not contribute labour, but they are usually extremely punctilious about sending monetary contributions to the family and their presence is thus felt economically.

Table 30.8

Mean household size present and total

n=664

Region	n	Present	Away	Overall
All	664	10.5	1.0	11.5
Highland	10	6.5	1.4	7.9
Steppe	405	10.2	1.2	11.4
Badia	249	11.1	0.7	11.9

Source: IFAD Survey

The professions of absent household members suggest something about the alternative occupations available to livestock producers. Soldiering was the most common form of work, but otherwise government service and casual labour are the only other options (Table 30.9).

Table 30.9

Professions of migrant household members

n=283		
Region	Number	%
Soldier	203	71.7
Government Official	47	16.6
Unskilled Employment	29	10.3
Other	4	1.4

Becoming a merchant or trader, especially in livestock products, is a common option for Bedu, but such merchants normally cease producing animals.

3.5 Migration

3.5.1 Traditional classifications of migration

One of the most distinctive features of pastoral production is migration; highly visible in certain seasons, it is usually described in some detail in descriptive studies. One of the staples of such studies is the "migration map" with arrows criss-crossing the map showing seasonal movements of the herds.

In Jordan, the traditional classification of migration is threefold:
(i)   Migration from the mountains to the valleys westward;
(ii) East-West transhumance; and
(iii) Nomadism, i.e., all-year-round movement.

This has been described in various sources including Nesheiwat (1991). Mountain-valley transhumance, also called "vertical" transhumance, is outside the scope of this study and will not be further discussed.

It is hard to judge the reality of such a system in the past. However, it is evident that by 1995 it had broken down irretrievably. A combination of the use of vehicles to move flocks, the rise of detribalized producers with no respect for the traditional system of grazing rights, and the use of modern communications to establish areas of potential grazing, have all combined to produce a considerably more fragmented system of migration.

3.5.2 Tribal migration

An analogous staple of the literature on migration is tribal migration. This argues that particular tribes have specific migration routes which they follow most years. The usual product of this view is the migration map with arrows assigned to particular tribes.

As with annual migration patterns, it is hard to judge the reality of this in the past, but the present survey does not support such a view. Economic individualism has meant that individual members of particular tribes decide both whether to go on migration and, if so, where. Hence the scatter of individuals from a wide variety of tribes encountered, especially throughout the northeast, where the good rains in the winter of 1994-5 attracted numerous herders from all over Jordan.

In the villages, producers with large herds who do not identify themselves as Bedu, nonetheless make use of the rangelands in good rainfall years. The case history in Box 30.1 gives an example of such a producer.

Box 30.1	Mohammed S. is a resident of a village near Tafila. He owns some 300 sheep, as well as a substantial farm and a house. He does not regard himself as Bedu and will criticize Bedu intrusions into grazing lands attached to the village. However, he makes use of the badia grazing every year to reduce expenditure on purchased feeds. To find out where rain has fallen and grazing is consequently good, he makes extensive use of the telephone and of a network of contacts. After identifying a region of pasture, he uses his lorry and water-truck to graze his sheep there for as long as the forage lasts. Although he considers himself a member of a tribe, the Er-Hwetat, he will go to any area of the country and does not consider it necessary to ask permission or even to enquire into traditional grazing rights in the region where he plants his sheep.
Case history: a new urban nomad	

Source: IFAD Survey

3.5.3 Migration versus sedentary production

By contrast, one of the striking findings of the survey was the large number of livestock producers who have ceased to move. Of the entire sample, only 216 households (32.5%) migrate in any way. Many of those questioned had ceased migration in recent years due to the costs and problems associated and the availability of subsidized feed. Table 30.10 shows the numbers migrating, broken down by region. It might seem surprising that a lower percentage in the badia migrate but this includes pastoralists who are permanently resident in the desert and who simply move around a central encampment.

Table 30.10

Households still migrating by land category

1994 Region	n	%
All Rangelands	216	32.5
Highlands	1	10.0
Steppe	148	36.5
Badia	67	26.9

This pattern is strongly associated with feed availability; subsidized feeds have allowed householders to become more sedentary. If the price of feeds rises substantially, it is inevitable that producers will either cease production or begin migration.

3.5.4 Reclassifying migration patterns

In the light of the responses to the survey and broader discussions with producers, a more comprehensive classification of migration was evolved. This suggests the following six categories;

(i)   Owners whose herd is always resident in one place;

(ii)   Owners whose herd is mostly resident in one place, but who occasionally move it to pasture in a year when the rains are good;

(iii)   Owners who move their herds every year to pasture, according to a reasonably regular schedule ('transhumants"?);

(iv)   Owners whose herd is on the move all the time over the Jordanian rangelands ("pure nomads"?);

(v)   Owners whose herd is on the move all year, but stay within a reasonably small ambit (e.g., 50 km radius); and

(vi)   Owners who move their herds across the border to other countries.

It is perfectly possible to be a nomad and farm, because it is easy to rent both land and agricultural labour. It is also possible to be a nomad in the badia and to have a settled family with a farm and children going to school. Indeed, because of the potential to have more than one wife, some pastoralists maintain two distinct families with two distinct lifestyles.

3.5.5 Surrogate migration

The gradual development of national borders and the increasing difficulty of seeking pasture in other countries has stimulated the development of a number of subterfuges to circumvent the inevitable restriction on access to pasture.

One of the most intriguing mechanisms for persisting with cross-border migration is the use of re-sale rings. Essentially, if an owner wishes his herd to make use of pasture in another country, he "sells" it to another pastoralist, who herds it while the pasture is available. When the pasture is exhausted, the herd is "'sold" back to the owner. Such rings may involve more than one country, and animals may move in large circles crossing from Syria to Jordan, Saudi Arabia and Iraq. For obvious reasons, no information is available on to the extent of this practice.

3.6 Land and land rights

Land rights can be effectively divided into two categories: rights over farmland and rights in the rangeland. In principle, tenure in farmed areas is related to patrilineal inheritance. Owners with rights in such land usually inherit it from their family. This land can in principle be bought and sold.

However, rangeland is, legally at least, controlled by the Government and the construction of buildings and ploughing up for farms is controlled. In reality, however, the boundary between "rangeland" and private farmland is constantly shifting due to pioneer agricultural settlement which can confer title to land.

3.6.1 Two views of land tenure

There are essentially two views of land tenure in the rangeland areas: "complex" and "simple". Rights in pasture are viewed, especially by anthropologists, as highly elaborated and sanctioned by traditional society. Numerous inter-locking systems of rights existed in the past and development can only be effective if these are respected or strengthened. The alternative view, the "simple" one, is that although tenure may exist in theory it is non-functional today. In other words, although pastoralists can explain their rights in a region of pasture these rights cannot be made operational, except through agriculture or related types of land development. Traditional tenure has to all intents and purposes broken down.

3.6.2 Collapse of rights in rangeland

Traditional theory holds that rights to pasture are not held by individuals and that, in principle, all producers are free to exploit it. This theory has not been operative through much of the history of this area (Nesheiwat, 1991). The evolution of the hema system essentially allocated pastures to individual subgroups, where authority was exercised via a sheikh.

Several key elements of the hema system allowed it to survive for many centuries, for the following reasons:

(i)   a high degree of militarization of society which allowed violent retribution against rule-breakers;

(ii)   the slow pace of movement to a given pasture (on foot);

(iii)   the fact that herding was done more directly by the owners of the animals; and

(iv)   actual herd sizes were smaller implying less competition for pastures.

These conditions have all been transformed within the last half-century: the Bedu have come under control of central Government; they have acquired trucks to transport animals; herding is largely done by hired shepherds; and herd sizes are now very large.

Many individuals or families perceive themselves as having rights in rangeland and can classify an area as their "traditional" grazing area. However, this does not mean they have any mechanism to prevent outside herds from coming in and exploiting the grazing. In general, this pattern seems quite acceptable because of the uncertain nature and inter-annual fluctuation of forage resources. If you do not allow someone to graze "your" area this year, in another year your herds may have access blocked elsewhere.

In the same way, there is a strong resistance to private or individual ownership of the rangeland. While notions of rights subsist in a conveniently ambivalent form, they can persist. If private ownership meant the erection of fences across the rangelands, there would be considerable resistance.

4. CONCLUSIONS AND POLICY IMPLICATIONS

4.1 The rangelands: producers' views

No project to manage the rangelands can succeed effectively without the particﬁipation of the users. To this end, the opinions of community leaders were sampled as part of the community questionnaire. This consisted of a series of open-ended questions relating to economic changes, problems observed within the rangeland and potential solutions. The answers were coded and the elements that cast light on producers' attitudes are analyzed in this section.

4.1.1 Rangeland degradation: who is responsible?

One of the most striking responses to the question of who was responsible for rangeland degradation was the uniformity with which community leaders attributed degradation to low rainfall. Most (66%) respondents considered the rainfall to be responsible for the state of the range. Much fewer (27%) attributed the problem to a surplus of animals. A significant number (46%), especially in the steppe and western badia, considered that ploughing up the land for irrigated agriculture was a major source of degradation. In a sense, this is a less a problem of degradation and more one of change of use. Figure 30.3 shows the percentage responses concerning the problems of the rangeland.

Figure 30.3

Perceived problems of the rangelands

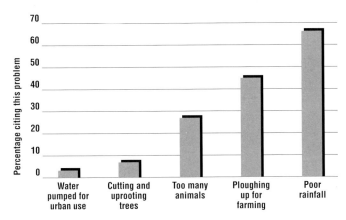

Source: IFAD Survey

One problem may be that livestock producers are probably used to inferring the rainfall from the state of the range. Since they do not measure it, they gauge rangefall from the plant cover. As the plant cover declines, so they estimate the decreasing rainfall.

Few respondents mention the cutting and uprooting of woody vegetation, but this unfortunately does not mean that it is not a real problem. Since those being questioned are also mainly responsible for this practice, they are unlikely to blame themselves. The pumping of water for urban use is a very real concern in limited areas, notably in the Azraq oasis and the Wadi Mujib.

The principal conclusion that can be drawn from is that only a small proportion of livestock producers accept responsibility for the state of the rangelands. Most attribute it to external forces which they are unable to control. Until producers demonstrate a clear awareness of their own role in bringing about the present situation, it will be difficult to involve them in the management of rangeland through selective destocking.

4.1.2 Management and authority structures

Bedu society has always been noted for its ideology of equality, both in terms of equal access to leaders and in the system of justice. Lancaster (1981) noted that the power of the sheikhs is always mediated through the consent of the tribe. While tribal groups were bound together by a common ideology, this system could function effectively.

However, once pastoralists began to function within the framework of the modern state, they were subject to the demands of conflicting authority structures.

The combination of the changing state and the growth of economic individualism has had the effect of breaking down allegiances within tribal groups. During interviews with individual householders, many spoke against the authority of the traditional leaders.

Following this, pastoralists with grievances tend to look to "government" for assistance or redress. Table 30.11 shows a summary of the bodies that community leaders had dealt with in matters relating to rangeland. It should not be assumed that the result of their dealings was positive.

Table 30.11

Existing authorities with which community leaders dealt n=85

	No.	%
Governor	43	50.6
Member of Parliament	14	16.5
Ministry of Agriculture	72	84.7
Tribal leader	31	36.5

Asking a speculative question such 'who would you work with?' invites an answer influenced by the interviewee's perception of the interviewer. It proved nearly impossible to disentangle the fact that teams were from the Ministry of Agriculture with a positive response. Presumably, if the interviewing team had been from either a cooperative organization or a non-governmental organization (NGO), this would have elicited a substantially more positive response (Figure 30.4)

Figure 30.4

Existing authorities with which community leaders dealt

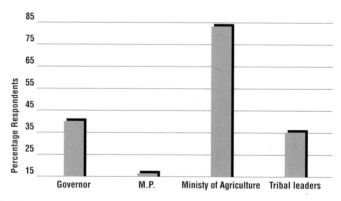

Source: IFAD Survey

Perhaps more interesting is the negative responses; very few interviewees put much faith in tribal associations. This is probably a good indicator of the breakdown of traditional authority. Table 30.12 shows the institutions that community leaders claimed they could work with in the event of a project to improve rangeland.

Table 30.12

Authorities with which community leaders would work n=85

	No.	%
Cooperatives	28	32.9
Tribal associations	16	18.8
Ministry of Agriculture	75	88.2
Others	11	12.9

4.2 A conservation ethos

One of the principal conclusions of the survey is that by and large livestock producers do not feel responsible for the condition of the rangeland. Moreover, their dependence on it as a feed supply is limited; they have thus little or no economic motivation to conserve it. Therefore, to conserve the Jordanian rangelands, the strategy of a project should be to make good the economic loss to livestock producers represented by the withdrawal of this resource. This is similar, in principle, to the 'set-aside' approach for farmland in Europe.

It is important to recognize that it is not in the immediate economic interest of individual producers to conserve the rangeland. Indeed, most of them see it as the task of government to help them exploit it still further. Despite this, the benefits of rangeland conservation remain in the larger national interest and probably the long-term interests of producers.

Individual studies have shown that protection of rangeland areas increases biomass, increases biotic diversity of both fauna and flora and increases the moisture-holding capacity of the soil (Hatough, et al., 1986). The development of reserved areas and use such as the Dana reserve, As-Shaumari at Azraq, suggests there is local pressure for conservation and that this can be seen as beneficial.

Whether a rangeland is "overgrazed" will inevitably remain controversial, as the long-term climatic cycles make it difficult to establish the "natural" condition of the range. In addition, the virtual disappearance of the species of wild ruminants that grazed in substantial numbers until the turn of the century mean that the present system of intense pressure form small ruminants cannot be considered to replace "natural grazing".

However, there is little doubt that such heavy pressure from just two species, aided by mobility through the use of water-trucks and lorries, represents a poor management strategy. Biomass is never allowed to reach development, plants may never reach the phase of setting seed and habitats for small fauna are virtually eliminated. Studies at Dana have shown that with dissected terrain, larger mammals can also survive.

In cases where wild fauna actually become a predator on the flocks, the two world views come directly into conflict. As in Dana, a number of sheep producers reported predation by wolves on their flocks in the northern hammada desert. Losses were not great, at perhaps 10 sheep from a herd of one thousand. Nonetheless, as far as the owners were concerned, these were losses, and their solution was to shoot the wolves. The Asiatic wolf is now extremely rare throughout the whole of the Middle East and, in national terms, may be considered a priority for conservation.

Resolving the conflict between these opposing attitudes is similar to the issues of conservation of biodiversity against maximum use by ruminants. As far as the Bedu are concerned, the diversity of species and even the development of biomass is simply an irrelevancy in the business of producing sheep. Yet, there must sometimes be larger national priorities and wider concerns may sometimes displace local needs.

5. RECOMMENDATIONS

Recommendations from the survey fall into two categories, immediate and long-term, which are summarized below.

5.1 Immediate

- Action should be taken to prevent the uprooting of woody vegetation for firewood. This is best done through a combination of public awareness and the facilitation of gas supplies in remote areas.
- A strategy should be adopted to encourage the bringing to market of more mature animals, especially sheep, thereby reducing the need for large flocks. One possible strategy is a subsidy on animals over a certain weight.
- The use of feed supplements, mineral blocks and industrial by-products by herd-owners should be encouraged, since the poor nutrition of animals fed only on cereals is an important reason for herders whose animals subsist largely on feeds to continue using the rangeland in certain periods.
- The use of fertility drugs without strict veterinary supervision should be discouraged.
- Veterinary services should be monitored and improved, especially in regions

close to the western edge of the badia. Particular attention should be given to vaccination against bluetongue, PPR and foot-and-mouth-disease. The poor health of stationary animals is another reason for encouraging migration.

- A public awareness campaign should be mounted, focusing on the following issues:
- the rainfall situation and the consequent responsibility of producers for the situation of the rangelands;
- the dangers of plastic waste;
- a complete illustrated reference list of local and scientific names of all the useful plants of the badia should be prepared and circulated to all extension staff in this region. Without such a tool it is difficult to see how discussions about rangeland management can proceed at a more than superficial level; and
- a preliminary survey of the faunal resources of the rangeland area should be commissioned to help understand the conservation issues more clearly.

5.2 Long Term

The long-term objective of any rangeland rehabilitation project must be the assignation of demarcated regions of the rangeland to social groups for management. The traditions and culture of the users argue that individual ownership would be strongly resisted. Since it is not practical or economic to fence such large areas, prevention of incursions must be in the hands of the community of users.

Communities of users will only make the effort to police a large open area of this type if: the economic benefit of using it is substantially greater than at present; and they have effective support from the local regulatory authorities (e.g., police, forest rangers) to act against intrusive herds or even their own members overusing the resource.

Priority should be given to rangelands within reasonable access of farming communities, because the community is stable and the members remain in touch with one another and the associated rangelands are close enough to the village to be policed by its residents.

The following stages have to be applied:

(i)   Communities of users who are prepared to cooperate with a rangeland project must be identified. Ideally, these should be settled groups with a strong livestock orientation and a proven record of community cooperation on other issues;

(ii)   Rangeland areas with a tradition of association with a particular community ('facing areas") need to be identified, demarcated and gazetted;

(iii) The community needs to form or adapt an existing association to manage the rangeland;

(iv) The community association, in collaboration with the livestock and range departments, must establish a grazing capacity for their range and assign usage quotas to their members;

(v) The community must develop a system of levies on members to pay the cost of policing the area; and

(vi) The community association must develop, in collaboration with the police and range department, a procedure for dealing effectively with defaulting herds or producers.

References

Agricultural Policy Department. 1993. *The Agricultural Policy Charter.* Amman, Jordan.

Blench, R.M. 1995. *Jordan's rangelands: baseline socio-economic survey.* Report to IFAD, Near East and North Africa Division.

Chatty, D. 1986. *From camel to truck: The Bedouin in the modern world.* Vantage Press, New York.

Chatty, D. 1990. The current situation of the Bedouin in Syria, Jordan and Saudi Arabia and their prospects for the future. In: Salzman, C. and Galaty, J.G. *Nomads in a changing world.* Naples: Istituto Universitario Orientale. pp.123-138.

Draz, O. 1979. *Range land development and stabilization of nomadic sheep husbandry in the Hashemite Kingdom of Jordan.* Report to Ministry of Agriculture, Amman, Jordan.

Eisawi, D. 1985. Vegetation in Jordan. *Studies on the History and Archaeology of Jordan, II.* (ed. Adnan Hadidi). Amman, Jordan. pp.45-57.

Hatough, A.M.A., Eisawi, D.M.H. and Disi, A.M. 1986. The effect of conservation on wildlife in Jordan. *Environmental Conservation,* 13, 4:331-335.

IFAD. 1993. *Preparation Report: Jordan Rangelands Project.* Rome: IFAD Near East and North Africa Division.

Juneidi, M.J. and Abu-Zanat, M. 1993. *Jordan Agricultural Sector Review: Low Rainfall Zone.* USAID, Amman.

Lancaster, W. 1981. *The Rwala Bedouin today.* Cambridge University Press.

Lancaster, W. and Lancaster, F. 1990. Desert devices: the pastoral system of the Rwala Bedu. In: John G. Galaty, and Douglas L. Johnson, (eds) *The world of pastoralism: herding systems in comparative perspective.* 177-194. New York: Guilford Press and London: Belhaven Press. pp.177-194.

Lancaster, W. and Lancaster, F. 1991. Limitations on sheep and goat herding in the Eastern Badia of Jordan: and ethno-archaeological enquiry. *Levant,* XXIII:125-138.

Lancaster, W. and Lancaster, F. 1993. Sécheresse et stratégies de reconversion économique chez le bédouins de Jordanie. In: Bocco, R., Jaubert, R. and Metral, F. (eds). *Steppes d'Arabies, Etats, pasteurs, agriculteurs et commer(ants: le devenir des zones sèches.* Cahiers de l'IUED. Geneva.

Long, R.E. 1957. *Bioclimates of Eastern Jordan.* FAO, Rome.

Marx, E. 1978. Ministry of Agriculture. The ecology and politics of nomadic pastoralists in the Middle East. In: Weissleder, Wolfgang. *The nomadic alternative.* The Hague: Mouton.

Mountfort, G.R. 1965. *Portrait of a desert.* Collins, London.

Musil, A. 1928. *Manners and customs of the Rwala Bedouin.* American Geographical Society, New York.

Nabulsi, H., Harb, M. and Ababneh, M. 1993. *Jordan Agricultural Sector Review: Integrated Livestock.* USAID, Amman.

Nesheiwat, K.S. 1991. *Socio-economic aspects of the traditional Hema system of arid land management in Jordan.* FAO, Rome.

Park, P. 1955. *Technical report on range improvement, development and management for the Hashemite Kingdom of Jordan.* Report to Ministry of Agriculture, Amman, Jordan.

Omar, S.A.S. 1991. Dynamics of range plants following 10 years of protection in arid rangelands of Kuwait. *Journal of Arid Enviromments,* 21:99-111.

Shehadeh, N. 1985. The climate of Jordan in the past and present. In: Hadidi, A (ed.). *Studies on the History and Archaeology of Jordan, II.* ed. Adnan Hadidi. Amman, Jordan. pp. 25-37.

Swenne, A. 1992. *Feeding/herding behaviour and feeding/herding opportunities of sheep and goats in the Shaubak area.* GTZ report, Veterinary Epidemiology Project, Ministry of Agriculture, Amman, Jordan.

Tuttle, V.F. 1971. *Range management programme for Jordan.* Report to Ministry of Agriculture, Amman, Jordan.

United States Agency for International Development (USAID) 1992. *Policy Review: Low rainfall zone.* Amman: Ministry of Agriculture.

1/ *The survey was conducted for the Ministry of Agriculture under the auspices of IFAD and commissioned by the Project Controller, M.A. Hassani, (at that time) of the Near East and North Africa Division. I would like to acknowledge discussions with William Lancaster, British Institute for Archaeology and History, Amman;, Prof. Dawud El-Eisawi, Department of Botany, University of Amman; Roderick Dutton, and; Antoine Swenne, Consultants and; Sherifa Zein Bint Nasser and Mohamed Sha'abaz, respectively; directors of finance and research of the Jordanian Badia Development Project. The survey was presented in Amman on 25th April 1995, in the form of a working draft, and I would like to thank those present for their constructive comments on the text. Vehicles and personnel were provided by the Ministry of Agriculture without whose support such a large survey would have been impossible. The survey team is listed below.*
I would especially like to thank Mohammed Qublan and Khalid Hwadi for their additional work in checking field data and for conducting extra missions to complete the geographic spread of the survey. Data was entered by Smart Systems, Amman, during the course of the survey and then checked by the survey personnel. Special thanks to Bilal Al-Haq for work on the database beyond the call of duty.

Name	Position
Roger Blench	Mission Leader
Karim Nesheiwat	Senior Enumerator
Mahmud Abu-Sittir	Senior Enumerator
Abdelhadi Falahat	Enumerator
Khalid Hwadi	Enumerator
Maha Salameh Arabiat	Enumerator
Mahmud Al-Souob	Enumerator
Mohammed Al-Rousan	Enumerator
Mohammed Fushaikat	Enumerator
Mohammed Qublan	Enumerator
Sana' Halasa	Enumerator

International Livestock Research Institute: mandate, programme and potential contribution to rangeland improvement in the WANA region

3 1

A. Lahlou Kassi

Synopsis

This paper reviews the work of the International Livestock Research Institute (ILRI) and traces the origin of the centre. The relevance of its programme to the West Asia and North Africa (WANA) region is outlined.

Key Points

1. *Within the Consultatitive Group on International Agricultural Research (CGIAR), the International Livestock Research Institute (ILRI) was established in 1995 by merging the former International Livestock Centre (ILCA) for Africa and the International Labaratory for Research on Animal Diseases (ILRAD). ILRI has a global mandate for research on livestock in sub-Saharan Africa, Asia, Latin America and North Africa and West Asia.*

2. *The past research experience of ILRI was limited to tropical environments and production systems in sub-Saharan Africa. However, methodologies developed to analyze livestock production systems, assess and monitor range resources either on the field or by remote-sensing and aerial surveys of livestock population distribution, have global relevance and could help in building a research programme on rangeland improvement in the Gulf countries.*

1. INTRODUCTION

The Consultative Group on International Agricultural Research (CGIAR), which supports a network of international research centres, among which the International Livestock Research Institute (ILRI) is the newest, was founded in the early 1970s, principally to address the problems of food insecurity in developing countries.

The CGIAR, in its new strategic plan, has further recognized that sustainable increases in agriculture and productivity should be addressed through both commodity improvements and the better conservation and management of natural resources, which is consistent with the objective of this workshop.

2. THE INTERNATIONAL LIVESTOCK RESEARCH INSTITUTE: MANDATE AND PROGRAMMES

2.1 ILRI Mandate

With its founding in 1995, ILRI's initial programmes have been built on the basis of two decades of experience of the former livestock research centres of the CGIAR, the International Laboratory for Research on Animal Diseases (ILRAD) and the International Livestock Center for Africa (ILCA). ILRAD conducted primarily laboratory-based strategic research on the two major disease complexes, trypanosomiasis and tick-borne diseases, affecting livestock in sub-Saharan Africa and other developing regions. ILCA has concentrated on the biological, agro-ecological and socio-economic constraints to livestock production systems in Africa, primarily through applied research on farming systems.

In contrast, ILRI has specifically been given a global mandate for research (including Sub-Saharan Africa, Latin America, Asia, North Africa and West Asia) to improve animal performance through: technological research and conservation of animal genetic diversity in developing regions; the sustainable productivity of major livestock and crop-livestock systems; the technical and economic performance of the livestock sector; and the development, transfer and utilization of research-based technology by national programmes and their client farmers.

2.2 ILRI programmes

As ILRI re-evaluates its initial programmes and develops its global agenda, the centre has used a number of mechanisms to define research priorities and activities. As part of this process, global and regional consultations were convened in 1995 and 1996. From these consultations, a number of key themes for research emerged, some of which were cross-cutting across regions (Table 31.1). The priority research areas to be highlighted included:

Table 31.1

Desertification phenomena and identification possibilities from remotely sensed data evaluated for the Bishri Mountain area

Research area	SE Asia	South Asia	LAC*	WANA**	SSA***
Productivity/sustainability of crop-livestock systems	4 [1,2]	4 [2]		4	4
Plantation/tree/livestock systems	4	4	4		
Natural resource management		4		4	4
Animal breed improvement	4 [3]	4 [3]			
Genetics of disease resistance	4			4	4
Livestock biodiversity		4	4	4	4
Animal health/diagnostics/ epidemiology/integrated control	4			4	4
Systems analysis/methodologies		4	4		
Livestock policy analysis		4	4	4	4
Feed utilization		4	4	4	4
Forage biodiversity		4	4		

Source: ILRI 1996)

1 : uplands; 2 : lowlands; 3 : buffalo

* LAC - Latin America and Caribbean
** WANA - West Asia and North Africa
*** SSA - Sub-Saharan Africa

(i)   natural resource management;

(ii)   development of control strategies for diseases of economic importance;

(iii)   conservation and utilization of genetic biodiversity in animals and plants;

(iv)   improvement of mixed crop-livestock smallholder farming systems;

(v)   policy studies examining market structures, technology adoption, impacts of policy on livestock production and access to livestock services; and

(vi)   improved feed resource utilization.

While ILRI is still in a transition period, and the present research focus is largely on sub-Saharan Africa (in accordance with the 1995-1998 Medium-Term Plan), research will commence in Asia and, funds permitting, extend into Latin America and the WANA region in the future.

ILRI priority programmes under the 1995-1998 Medium term Plan are shown in Box 31.1.

| Box 31.1 | Biodiversity (Conservation, Characterization) |

Box 31.1

ILRI Priority
Programmes
(1995 – 1998
Medium-term
Plan)

Biodiversity (Conservation, Characterization)
- Animal genetic resources
- Forage genetic resources

Production Systems Research
- Production systems analysis and impact assessment (economic, social and environmental)
- Integrated crop-livestock systems sub-Saharan Highlands; desert margins in humid Asia; Semiarid Asia, LAC, West Asia and North Africa (WANA)

Utilization of Tropical Feed Resources
- Rumen ecology
- Nutritional evaluation of tropical feeds

Animal Health Improvement
- Genetics of disease resistance
- Development of disease control technologies
- Implementation of disease control technologies Livestock Policy Analysis
- Resource management policies, institutions, and livestock development
- Policies, technologies and livestock input and output markets

Strengthening collaboration with national agricultural research service (NARS)
- Training and information services
- Collaborative research networks

2.3 ILRI experience in natural resource management of livestock

The research experience of ILRI is limited to tropical environments and production systems in sub-Saharan Africa, and thus, is not directly transferable to the Gulf countries. However, methodologies developed to analyze livestock production systems, assess and monitor range resources, either in the field or by remote sensing, and aerial surveys of livestock population distribution have global relevance. Moreover, numerous ecological traits and production system characteristics are shared by the rangelands in the Gulf countries and the different arid and semi-arid regions of the Sahel in Mali, Niger, northern Nigeria, and the drier regions of Ethiopia, Kenya, Zimbabwe and Botswana, where ILRI (formerly ILCA) has acquired experience through livestock system studies.

2.4 Field surveys

The field survey methods used in production system studies have been collated and reviewed in a methodology manual (ILCA, 1990). In surveys of range resources, particular attention was given to the high spatial heterogeneity and temporal variability of range resources in the Sahel. Random stratified sampling techniques were designed, in order to get a robust evaluation of the standing herbage mass within the range site. This was achieved by calculating the weighted mean from the means established for each component range facies (based on geomorphology and species composition) and stratas (based on apparent density of the herbage), at a relative low sampling cost (Hiernaux, 1995).

An algorithm is provided to assess the level of micro-heterogeneity of the herbaceous layer mass or cover. The same approach was also used to estimate herbage species composition. Sahelian rangeland is mainly composed of annual plants whose composition is susceptible to large changes from year to year (Breman and Cissé, 1987; Hiernaux, 1996).

Trees and shrubs are generally sparsely distributed in the Sahelian rangelands, but they contribute significantly to livestock nutrition and wood production (Le Houérou, 1980). Methods used to assess foliage and wood masses include woody plant population quantitative survey techniques, which consist of exhaustive sampling of woody plants in circular plots distributed at regular intervals along the transect (Hiernaux, 1996). The radius of these plots was set inversely proportional to average plant density for the species or the category of woody plant surveyed, in order to reduce cost and assure equal precision. Foliage and wood masses are then calculated for each species using pre-established allometric relationships between masses and the crown area or trunk circumference (Cissé, 1980). The measure of the foliage mass of branchlet sub-samples allows correction of the foliage mass estimate for the seasonal phenology status (Hiernaux et al., 1994).

These methods were used to monitor both the seasonal fluctuations of foliage availability for animals and the inter-annual changes in population structure and composition with climate changes and management (Hiernaux et al., 1995). Similar sampling techniques were used for large-size perennial grasses, such as *Andropogon gayenus* in southern Sahel and *Panicum turgidum* and *Aristida pallida* in the driest ranges of northern Sahel.

2.5 Remote sensing and GIS

Photo-interpretation of aerial photographs were used to map soil and vegetation types, as well as land use, and this was overlaid with information on land tenure and management documented during ground surveys in Ogaden, Ethiopia,

Central Mali and Kenya. This technique is presently used for detailed mapping of land use at community land level, either for research or development purposes. For example, land use at the individual crop-field scale was mapped for three rural community territories in Niger for consecutive years from 1992 to 1995 (ILRI, 1996). The annual land-use maps were overlaid to basic information maps on soils and infrastructure establishing a geographic information system (GIS) in which livestock monitoring and household economic data are also included.

The objective of this particular application is to model the nutrient flows mediated by livestock in this crop-livestock system, in order to identify the management practices that will help agriculture intensification while reducing the risks of resource degradation in this agro-ecosystem.

Fine spatial resolution satellite data such as Landsat, Thematic Mapper and Spot were used to map soil and vegetation types using classic supervised classification techniques (Franklin, 1990). Because they are acquired daily, the coarser resolution data of the Advanced Very High Resolution Radiometer (AVHRR) on-board satellites of The National Oceanic and Atmospheric Administration (NOAA) were used to estimate the seasonal production of herbaceous vegetation. Standing herbage mass measured on the ground at monthly intervals during the growing season in rangeland sites of Niger (Justice and Hiernaux, 1986; Wagenaar and de Ridder, 1986), Mali (Hiernaux, 1988) and Kenya (Lamprey and de Leeuw, 1987), were used to calibrate linear regressions established between vegetation production and the cumulative Normalized Vegetation Index (NDVI) averaged over ten-day periods.

An algorithm has been designed (Hanan, et al., 1991) to correct the error on the estimate, due to the soil background reflectance. Further improvement of the method was obtained by combining a model approach of the herbage growth to seasonal changes of NDVI values (Mougin, et al., 1995). Other combinations of reflectance models and satelllite data were used to try and predict, from fine-resolution satellite data, the quantitative information on woody plant density, height and cover (Franklin and Hiernaux, 1991).

Systematic, low aerial survey techniques (de Leeuw and Milligan, 1984; ILCA, 1986) were used to quantify the spatial distribution of livestock species, together with variables of the environment (tree cover, herbaceous cover) and management (density of camps, land use). These surveys were repeated at different seasons to consider the seasonal dynamics of livestock and resource distributions in the Mali, Niger, Senegal and Ethiopian studies.

The overlay of spatially referenced data on livestock distribution, water resource soil and vegetation types over the maps of forage production derived from calibrated satellite data, were used to recommend management strategies

(RIM, 1987). Attempts were also made in Ethiopia to predict vegetation production from coarse-resolution satellite data (AVHRR and METEOSAT) in the short term, so that they could be used in an early warning system for management decision at the state or large district level (Durkin and Hendriksen, 1986).

3. CONCLUSION: THE POTENTIAL CONTRIBUTION OF ILRI RESEARCH EXPERIENCE TO RANGELAND IMPROVEMENT IN THE WANA REGION

Although these research findings are quite specific to production systems and ecoregions, some of the processes described and the models established have a wider relevance. This would apply, for example, to the impact of grazing by cattle, sheep and goats on the vegetation and soils that were measured in different semi-arid African ecosystems (Abel and Stocking, 1987; Hiernaux, et al., 1995). It would also apply to the assessment of the role of livestock in energy and nutrient cycling and in the spatial transfer of fertility through grazing and manure deposition analyzed in crop-livestock systems of semi-arid Niger (de Ridder and Wagenaar, 1986; Fernandez-Rivera et al., 1995; Zomda, et al., 1995). These system studies have also generated survey methodologies of wide potential application for pastoral surveys and programmes of natural resource management by livestock (de Leeuw, et al., 1992).

In conclusion, ILRI at present could provide methodology and expertise in range and livestock surveys, remote sensing, GIS and production system analysis.

Acknowledgement

I would like to express my appreciation to my colleague P. Hiernaux for providing me with relevant documents and publications for the preparation of this paper.

References

Abel, N. and Stocking, M. 1987. A rapid method for assessing rates of soil erosion from rangeland: an example from Botswana. *J. of Range Management,* 40, 5: 460-466.

Breman, H. and Cissé, A.M. 1977. Dynamics of Sahelian pastures in relation to drought and grazing. *Oecologia* (Berlin) No.28. pp.301-315.

Cissé, M.I. 1980. The browse production of some trees of the Sahel: relationships between maximum foliage biomass and various physical parameters. In: Le Houérou H.N. (ed) *Browse in Africa, the current state of knowledge.* ILCA, Addis Ababa. pp.205-210.

de Leeuw, P.N., Diarra, L. and Hiernaux, P. 1992. An analysis of feed demand and supply for pastoral livestock in the Gourma region of Mali. In: Behnke Jr, R.H. Scoones, I. and Kerven, C. (eds) *Range ecology at disequilibrium; Proc. of meeting on Savanna Development and Pasture Production,* Woburn Nov 1990, ODI, London. pp.136-152.

de Leeuw P.N. and Milligan, K. 1984. A review of integrated surveys for resource inventory and monitoring of pastoral production systems in sub-Saharan Africa. *ILCA Bulletin* 20:18-22.

de Ridder, N. and Wagenaar, K.T. 1986. Energy and protein balances in traditional livestock systems and ranching in eastern Botswana. *Agricultural Systems,* 20,1:1-16.

Durkin, J.W. and Hendriksen, B.L. 1986. *An algorithm to estimate crop growing period from AVHRR data.* First Australian AVHRR conference, Perth. pp. 22-24.

Fernandez-Rivera, S., Williams, T.O., Hiernaux P. and Powell, J.M. 1995. Faecal excretion by ruminants and manure availability for crop production in semi-arid west Africa. In: Powell *et al.,* (eds). *Livestock and sustainable nutrient cycling in mixed farming systems of sub-Saharan Africa.* ILCA, Addis Ababa, Ethiopia. pp.149-169.

Franklin, J. 1990. Land cover stratification using landsat thematic mapper data in Sahelian and Sudanian woodland and wooded grassland. *Remote Sensing of the Environment,* 32:124-136.

Franklin, J and Hiernaux, P. 1991. Estimating foliage and woody biomass in Sahelian and Sudanian woodlands using a remote sensing model. *Int. J. Remote Sensing* vol.12, 6, 1387-1404.

Hanan, N.P., Prince, S.D. and Hiernaux, P. 1991. Spectral modelling of multicomponent landscapes in Sahel. *Int. J. Remote Sensing.* Vol. 12, no 6. pp.1243-1258.

Hiernaux, P. 1988. Vegetation monitoring by remote sensing: progress in calibrating a radiometric index and its application in the Gourma, Mali. *ILCA Bulletin* 32:14-21.

Hiernaux, P. 1995. Spatial heterogeneity in Sahelian rangelands and resilience to drought and grazing. In: West N.E. (ed) Proceedings of the Fifth International Rangeland Congress, Society for Range Management, Denver. vol.1. pp.230- 231.

Hiernaux, P. 1996. *The crisis of Sahelian Pastoralism: ecological or economic?* ODI, London, Pastoral Develop. Network, 39a.

Hiernaux, P. 1996. *Does patchiness increase vegetation productivity, biodiversity and stability ? The case of the 'brousse tigree' in the Sahel.* Presented at the International Symposium on 'Banded vegetation patterning in arid and semi-arid environment, ecological processes and consequences for management', Paris, 2-5 April 96. (submitted to *Acta Oecologica*).

Hiernaux, P.Y., Cissé, M.I., Diarra, L. and de Leeuw, P.N. 1994. Fluctuations saisonnieres de la feuillaison des arbres et des buissons saheliens. Consequences pour la quantification des ressources fourrageres. *La Revue d'Elevage et de Medecine Veterinaire des Pays Tropicaux,* 47, 1:117-125.

Hiernaux, P., de Leeuw, P.N. and Diarra, L. 1995. The interactive effects of rainfall, nutrient supply and defoliation on the herbage yield of Sahelian rangelands in North East Mali. In: Powell et al., (eds). *Livestock and sustainable nutrient cycling in mixed farming systems of sub-Saharan Africa.* ILCA, Addis Ababa, Ethiopia: pp.149-169.

ILCA, 1986. Low aerial surveys. ILCA, Addis Ababa, ILCA Monographs No. 4.

ILCA, 1990. Livestock systems research manual. ILCA, Working Paper 1, Addis Ababa, Ethiopia, vol 1.

International Livestock Research Institute (ILRI). 1996. ILRI 1995: building a global research institute. ILRI, Nairobi, Kenya.

Justice, C.O. and Hiernaux, P. 1986. Monitoring the grasslands of the Sahel using NOAA/AVHRR data, Niger 1983. *Int J. Remote Sensing* 7 :1475-1497.

Lamprey, R.H. and de Leeuw, P.N. 1987. Monitoring East African vegetation with the use of NOAA/AVHRR imagery. UNEP/ILCA NOAA-AVHRR calibration project report 2, ILCA, Nairobi.

Le Houérou, H.N. 1980. Browse in Africa. The current state of knowledge. ILCA, Addis Ababa, Ethiopia.

Mougin, E., Lo Seen, D., Rambal, S., Gaston, A. and Hiernaux, P. 1995. A regional Sahelian grassland model to be coupled with multispectral satellite data. 1: validation. *Remote Sensing of the Environment,* 52:181-193.

Mougin, E., Lo Seen, D., Rambal, S., Gaston, A. and Hiernaux, P. 1995. A regional Sahelian grassland model to be coupled with multispectral satellite data. 2: Model simulations v. spectral measurements. *Remote Sensing of the Environment,* 52: 194-206.

Resource Inventory and Management, (RIM) 1987. Refuge in the Sahel. RIM, St Hellier, Jersey, UK.

Wagenaar, K.T. and de Ridder, N. 1986. Estimates of biomass production and distribution in the ILP project zone in 1985 based on satellite NDVI values. ILCA Addis Ababa, RSU Working Document 1.

Zomda, Z.C., Powell J.M., Fernandez-Rivera, S. and Reed, J. 1995. Feed factors affecting nutrient excretion by ruminants and the fate of nutrients when applied to soil. In: Powell et al., (eds). *Livestock and sustainable nutrient* cycling in mixed farming systems of sub-Saharan Africa. ILCA, Addis Ababa, Ethiopia. pp.227-243.

part V

*Setting the parameters
for the twenty-first century*

There are still a few options open to dryland inhabitants but these are being reduced as each year passes. This section tries to set some parameters for future generations to ensure inter-generational equity, while at the same time allowing the present generation to prosper, or at least survive.

Maintaining the viable use of marginal resources: the Environmental Support of Nomads (ESON) Project

32

A. Al-Gain

Synopsis

This paper outlines the Environmental Support of Nomads (ESON) Project of the Meteorology and Environmental Protection Agency of Saudi Arabia (MEPA). The Project relies on high-technology tools such as remote sensing and computer simulation.

Key Points

1. *The ESON Project is aimed at creating a major component of the United Nation's Environment Programme (UNEP) Action Plan to Combat Desertification, through the development of a rational technology for the utilization of marginal resources.*
2. *The ESON Project hopes to demonstrate that pastoral nomadism is the only major economically beneficial user of the vast marginal natural resources in the Kingdom of Saudi Arabia.*
3. *Nomads will benefit from the project by being provided with the technical information from high-technology facilities that allow them to make better decisions for managing the grazing resources, in a way that maximizes livestock production while at the same time minimizing the risk of land degradation.*
4. *A key to successful development of a programme to manage the Kingdom's marginal resources is to foster cooperation between the appropriate Government ministry and those other agencies concerned about the conservation of natural resources.*

1. INTRODUCTION

Pastoral nomadism in arid and semi-arid regions has evolved over many centuries as a rational response to a rainfall regime with low annual precipitation and erratic patterns. This traditional strategy of human and animal mobility has ensured maximum sustainable use of the marginal grazing resource, a resource that covers vast areas of Saudi Arabia. As pointed out by Al-Gain (1985), human intervention has occurred in recent times through settlement acculturation, subsidies, mechanized transport, increased availability of water and improved veterinary services. This intervention, plus a preferred demand for local livestock products, has encouraged livestock growers to introduce and concentrate numbers of animals that exceed the ability of the resource to provide sufficient forage. As a result, overgrazing has occurred in some areas which has tended to degrade the land and threaten long-term productivity.

2. COOPERATION: A KEY TO CONFLICT RESOLUTION

Initially, the ESON Project had been designed by MEPA as a pilot project to reverse the present trend, and hopefully, restore environmental equilibrium to the grazing resource. By using modern technological facilities, up-to-date procedures and quasi-real-time data, MEPA would provide the pastoralist with information that would allow him to maximize the use of the currently available grazing resource without endangering future productivity, i.e., in a sustainable manner.

Recent events, however, have presented MEPA with an opportunity to collaborate with the National Commission for Wildlife Conservation and Development (NCWCD) and the Ministry of Agriculture and Water (MAW), in a portion of north-central Saudi Arabia, in which the NCWCD plans to reintroduce wildlife. While the objectives of MEPA and NCWCD may appear to differ, MEPA aims for sustainable livestock production without land degradation while NCWCD would like to protect grazing areas for the reintroduction of wildlife, the ultimate goals are similar. The aim of all three agencies is the sustainable use of range resources for all purposes. It should also be mentioned that the practice of enclosing relatively small areas is supported by MEPA, as these enclosures represent control areas for MEPA studies. ESON's proposed objective, therefore, is to include the competition for the available grazing resource by domesticated livestock and wildlife in devising an overall grazing management system. MAW's interest in this study stems from the fact that MEPA intends to turn over the data and the results of the pilot study to MAW for their operational use in providing technical assistance to all of Saudi Arabia's rangelands.

3. ENVIRONMENTAL MONITORING

As a continuous review operation, monitoring is a major process that ESON scientists are using in the study. Monitoring is conducted on the ground, in the air and via satellites. This combination of technological tools makes it possible to provide services for the utilization of marginal resources that was not possible before.

3.1 Automatic weather stations

The installation of 25 automatic recording weather stations in the ESON study area will provide real-time data, such as rainfall, temperature and wind speed, reported via satellite transmission. This information will prove valuable to the forecasting of the rainfall-biomass relationship, so that the nomad can determine potential grazing sites and make an estimate of the amount of forage that will be produced following rainfall.

3.2 Aerial surveys

UNEP has pioneered a Global Environmental Monitoring System (GEMS) that uses a series of aerial surveys to evaluate vegetative cover and biomass, vegetation species composition, range condition, and areas in imminent danger of land degradation (UNEP, 1980). As used here, range condition is the "state of health", or potential productivity, of the rangeland. Range condition is a function of past management, such as the grazing intensity or the number of animals per unit of grazing area, and current weather, primarily precipitation. Thus, the future potential of the land to produce forage is dependent on today's range condition and grazing intensity and the future's precipitation regime. Seasonal forecasting, the concept of range condition and the use of aerial surveys are extremely useful management tools.

However, because of the relatively coarse spatial resolution of the satellite data, higher resolution data had to be obtained. This was done with the use of a specially designed aerial video system mounted in a light aircraft.

3.3 Seasonal forecasting model

MEPA is currently studying the use of numerical modelling of the atmosphere for making extended range prediction of the climate in the form of weekly, monthly and seasonal outlook. Multi-seasonal predictions based on dynamical modelling (unthinkable a short time ago) are nearly operational (McPherson, 1994). When completed with a rainfall biomass model, such forecasts will assist the pastoralist to estimate the number of animals for next season's grazing through adjustments that will accommodate livestock needs, while protecting the range resource from damage due to overgrazing.

3.4 Range forage model

It is the intent of the ESON study to use a physically based model to predict range forage production such as the one developed by Wight and Hanks (1981). In the event that site data are not available, then a statistical relationship between precipitation and forage yield will be used. The driving forces for either approach are weather variables, principally precipitation and temperature.

In conjunction with the seasonal forecast (meteorological) model, estimates can be made of the total amount of forage that is expected to be produced in a given area during the next season. Such predictions are particularly important during drought years. The advanced warnings enable pastoralists to make adjustments for balancing livestock needs with protection of the range resources from damage due to overgrazing, or help them in decision-making terms modify their a priori distribution to a posterior one.

3.5 System model

As with any system, the grazing management system transforms inputs into outputs. In this case, the inputs are the meteorological variables, principally water and energy, and the decisions or actions taken by man which will be based on the aforementioned anthropological studies. The outputs can be grouped into either economic, (primarily livestock products) or environmental (desertification, range condition.)

Range systems are dynamic which, for modelling purposes, require that the state of the system be defined at any time (Al-Haratani and Fogel, this volume; Fogel and Duckstein, 1978). For range ecosystems, the concept of range condition (as previously mentioned) is used to describe the state of the grazing management system at a given time. One means for evaluating range condition is the amount of forage currently produced in relation to what may be attainable under good management and favourable conditions (Smith, 1988). Thus, for example, if a particular range is in good condition, it does not necessarily follow that forage production will be good. The natural inputs of water and energy also have to be considered.

With a mechanism for predicting the future state of the system, the range condition (as stated above) and the use of a seasonal forecast model, a grazing system simulation model will be developed which integrates all the models.

4. DECISION-MAKING IN NOMADISM

Firstly, it must be stated that MEPA has no intention of making the decisions for nomads to manage their grazing lands. The ESON Project will provide the nomadic pastoralist with decision-aiding facilities conceptually updating *a priori* to posterior distributions (e.g., automatic weather stations) and will provide them with pertinent information on the management of grazing systems, including updated estimates of carrying capacities.

Simulation models provide the opportunity for evaluating the results or outputs of particular grazing management systems, both economic and environmental, without waiting for the results from a field study. A methodology is also needed that will compare the different alternatives and select the one that best meets the objectives, thus representing a balance between achieving environmental equilibrium and the particular bias of the nomads. Therfore, a decision or action taken by the nomad represents a trade-off between the economic and the environmental outputs of the system (Khalili, et al., 1988).

5. HUMAN RESOURCES COMPONENT: THE NOMAD

Most of the processes mentioned above are studies involving physical processes. MEPA also intends to look at the socio-economic aspects as human resources are a major component of the ESON Project. The project cannot succeed without an understanding of how the nomads functioned in the past prior to recent interventions and how they have adapted to a more modern society, and equally important what adjustments the nomads are willing to accept (Cole, 1979). In other words, the system must be designed with the nomad in mind. For example, a return to a modified form of the traditional hema system may prove to be the best option under certain conditions as this has, in the past at least, been accepted by the nomads.

The study site selected by MEPA includes areas in which the NCWCD proposes to re-introduce the Houbara Bustard (e.g., in the Al-Taysiyah area). Another area within the proposed extended ESON study area is the Mahazat as-Sayd Reserve, a large fenced area that will be used as a control site. Immediately to the east of the ESON site is a large agricultural area, in which irrigated wheat is the principal crop. Thus, the ESON study area will allow scientists to study the inter-relationships of three types of land use, namely: (i) for livestock products; (ii) for the protection of wildlife; and (iii) for agricultural crops. This concept may allow resolution of the competitive use of marginal resources for the benefit of all users.

6. CONCLUSIONS

Achieving sustainable production from a natural resources system is a difficult task, sometimes an impossible one. For one, there is the trade-off between economic benefits derived from utilizing the natural resources and the possible detrimental impacts associated with use. Then, there is the competition for a particular resource from different land uses. For Saudi Arabia's range resources, the problem becomes more complex. These resources are marginal and must be utilized in a way that minimizes land degradation, but still is able to provide economic returns to the user, a difficult task under the best of conditions.

MEPA is conducting a study, now nearly complete, to provide information for all users of the range resources, be they nomads, semi-nomads or wildlife managers, that will allow them to adopt grazing management practices for combating desertification. Such information obtained from a network of automatic recording weather stations, satellite imagery, aerial surveys and field observations are analyzed and used as inputs into simulation models. These computer models, which simulate the products of a grazing system for many grazing seasons, are used to test the long-term sustainability of a particular grazing practice or intervention. In addition, with the forthcoming capability for seasonal meteorological forecasting, users of the range will be in a better position to plan for the next grazing season's activities. Knowledge gained from this study should be useful for all land uses in a way that promotes long-term benefits.

In summary, major scientific accomplishments of the ESON study include:
- a new approach to determining the trend of rangeland desertification;
- increased capability for making seasonal weather forecasts;
- development of a range management simulation model to test the sustainability of a specific grazing practice or government intervention;
- a better understanding of changes in the lifestyles of nomads; and
- a specially designed aircraft video system for obtaining higher-solution data to help interpret the lower resolution satellite data, which is applicable for use in the more desertic areas.

References

Al-Gain, A. 1974. The in-situ development of the Bedouin nomads: a Bayesian decision analysis. *Ph.D. Dissertation.* University of Arizona. Tucson.

Al-Gain, A. 1985. *Integrated Resource Survey in Support of Nomads in Saudi Arabia - A Proposal.* Proceedings of an International Research and Development Conference, Arid Lands Today and Tomorrow, Tucson, Arizona. pp.1213-21.

Al-Haratani, E. and Fogel, M. 1997. A simulation model for evaluating long-term impacts of grazing practices. (this volume)

Cole, D.P. 1979. Pastoral nomads in a rapidly changing economy: The case of Saudi Arabia. *Pastoral Network Paper* 73. Overseas Development Institute. London.

Fogel, M. and Duckstein, L. 1978. *Desertification under natural uncertainties and man's activities: A decision model.* Presented at Bilateral United States-Argentinian Workshop on Droughts, 3-8 December. Mar del Plata, Argentina.

Fogel, M. and Hyun, K. 1990. *Simulating spatially varied thunderstorm rainfall.* Proceedings, International Symposium on Hydraulics/Hydrology of Arid Lands. San Diego, CA. pp. 513-518.

Khalili, D., Duckstein, L. and Fogel, M. 1988. A multi-objective discrete system representation of rangeland watersheds. *Water Resources Bulletin* 24(5): 1035 - 1040.

McPherson, R.D. 1994. The national centers for environmental prediction: operational climate, ocean and weather prediction for the 21st century. *Bulletin of the American Meteorological Society* 75(3): 363-373.

Smith, E.L. 1988. Successional Concepts in Relation to Range Condition Assessment. In: Tueller, P.T. (ed). *Vegetation science applications for rangeland analysis and management.* Kluwer Academic Publishers, Dordrecht, The Netherlands. pp. 113-134.

United Nations Environment Programme, (UNEP). 1980. The Global Environment Monitoring System. *GEMS PAC Information Series* No.1. Nairobi.

UNEP. 1992. Status of desertification and implementation of the United Nations Plan of Action to Combat Desertification. UNEP/GCSS 111/3. Nairobi, Kenya.

Wight, J.R. 1987. ERHYM-Il: Model Description and User Guide for the BASIC Version. USDA/ARS -59.

Wight, J.R. and Hanks, R.J. 1981. A water-balance, climate model for range herbage production. *J. of Range Management* 34(4); 307-31.

Setting the parameters for future generations: whither traditional range/livestock systems?

33

V.R. Squires and A.E. Sidahmed

Synopsis

This paper outlines some views about the benefits of using drylands in a sustainable way, and discusses some likely consequences of allowing further dryland degradation to occur. The long-term future of traditional nomadic pastoralism is discussed in the light of environmental, economic, social and political changes

Key Points

1. *Traditional lifestyles are under threat thoughout the world. Environmental, social political and economic changes will impact on nomadic pastoralism. The strongholds of nomadic and semi-nomadic pastoral systems are undergoing rapid evolution as market-based systems overtake them.*

2. *Pastoralism in the arid zone has always been severely constrained. The key constraints that have plagued pastoralism in the past include both the technical (animal health and nutrition) and the socio-political (land tenure, policy issues, religion) and economic (marketing).*

3. *Emerging problems include the conservation of the resource base (including biodiversity issues), the globalization of the world economy, the breakdown of tradition and potential impacts of climate change.*

4. *On a global basis, livestock production based on pure grazing systems is relatively unimportant, and also grows at the lowest rate. Pastoral systems production grows at 1%, mixed farming at 3% and industrial production at more than 7%. It is clear that the balance is changing in sub-Saharan Africa too and that intensification is on its way, although in certain areas horizontal expansion may still be an option.*

1. INTRODUCTION

At a time when traditional lifestyles are under threat throughout the world it seems appropriate to ask what future is there for traditional (non-commercial) range/livestock production systems? As the papers presented in Part IV of this volume show, the strongholds of nomadic and semi-nomadic pastoral systems are undergoing rapid evolution as market-based systems overtake them.

At the same time, concerns about the sustainability of the resource base have emerged with the ratification, by many nations, of international conventions on biodiversity and on desertification and drought. Many people are left to wonder if the environmental damage done to rangelands, especially on desert margins, will bring about the demise of traditional pastoralism. In general, ecosystems are grazed because they are not sufficiently productive or reliable to be cropped. This means that management must cope with low or unreliable production, complex semi-natural systems, large management units and greater economic risk.

2. CONSTRAINTS TO PASTORALISM IN THE ARID ZONE

Under the conditions of highly variable rainfall, traditional pastoral economies are in continuous disequilibrium. Rainfall, rather than grazing pressure, determines the following year's primary production (Behnke, et al., 1993). This disequilibrium conserves soil and vegetation, because grazing pressure is adjusted to the quantity of feed available. As long as mobility and flexibility of grazing is conserved, the annual vegetation especially can maintain its resilience. This resilience is the result of the way arid rangelands have been traditionally used (Box 33.1).

The key constraints that have plagued pastoralism in the past include both the technical (animal health and nutrition) and the socio-political (land tenure, policy issues, religion) and economic (marketing). These constraints deserve some elaboration, although the reader should refer to the excellent papers in Part IV of this volume for more detailed examples.

New socio-economic issues have arisen which impact on the way in which traditional societies view the future. Demands for education, better health, higher expectations for their children and a desire for a more techologically based lifestyle (radio, TV, satellite communications. motorized transport), have shifted priorities (Blench, this volume).

Changes in land tenure, security of access, reductions in internecine disputation, the emergence of stronger central governments and rising nationalism as globalization of trade and commerce takes hold, have all played their part (Ahmad, this volume). These shifts call for a different set of institutions, markets and policies. They also call for the development and adaptation of new

Box 33.1

Traditional
Nomadism:
A system under
threat

Pastoral nomadism in arid and semi-arid regions has evolved over many centuries as a rational response to erratic patterns of rainfall. This traditional strategy of human and animal mobility ensures maximized sustainable use of the grazing resource. although production is invariably low, the strategy (centered as it is on the nomads perception of production possibilities based on the average state of nature) has coped quite successfully with the underlying uncertainties of the arid-range ecosystem.

Traditionally, nomadism has tended to exploit the grazing resource at a technological level commensurate with the nature of the resource, i.e., the technology-resource calculus. The ecological constraints imposed on human exploitation of these rangelands for a particular technology have been identified as follows:

(i)   animal density is governed by consumable plant biomass;
(ii)   consumable biomass is determined by soil moisture;
(iii)   human populations are necessarily limited to low densities;
(iv)   the distribution of populations both animal and human is highly variable; and
(v)   herd composition depends on range condition and water availability.

Animal husbandry in arid zones has therefore always been extremely vulnerable to climatic periodicities, which causes profound insecurity among herders. However, contemporary pastoralism in arid regions has become increasingly precarious to the point where it is widely regarded as associated with a way of life that is largely doomed. Modern governments are invariably intolerant of the mobility of nomadic pastoralists and nomadism is widely regarded as anachronistic to modern statehood and a stigma of underdevelopment.

Attempts at development of pastoralism in arid regions, to improve its productivity and integration into the national economy, have generally involved a sedenterization of nomads; either inadvertently through provision of localized facilities or through active settlement schemes. As a consequence, the vital element of mobility (in the traditional sense) has been curtailed.

These innovations, together with the technological acculturation that accompanies them has meant that pastoralism is no longer at a level ecologically adjusted to the utilization of the grazing resource. This dissonance leads inevitably to resource degradation and lends support to those who advocate abandonment of nomadic stock-raising.
Source: Al Gain (1985)

technologies to make livestock production environmentally more benign. The scope is enormous and so is the task.

Emerging problems include the conservation of the resource base (including biodiversity issues), the globalization of the world economy, the breakdown of tradition, and the potential impacts of climate change. The challenge is to find ways of managing drylands that are more environmentally sustainable, economically viable and socially equitable than at present.

3. DRIVING FORCES IN ARID GRAZING SYSTEMS

Over the longer term, the fundamental driving force on natural resources is population pressure, especially from outside the arid range lands and their pastoral users. While population growth of the pastoral peoples has been rather low, the growth of non-pastoral groups in the arid and semi-arid regions has been among the highest in the world. This growth of other groups causes an increasing encroachment by arable farmers on the pastoral "key resource" sites, and constrains the critical mobility necessary to adjust to the disequilibrium conditions.

The increased population pressure also leads to water development and settlements in arid rangelands. Also within the system, the population pressure mounts, and causes land degradation. Thus, in spite of the resilience of the system, many pastoralists face a downward spiral of increased crop encroachment, increased fuelwood requirements and decreased grazing availability (Squires and Sidahmed, 1997). These forces contribute to impoverishment of the pastoral population and to land degradation. This trend is being exacerbated by drought, and vulnerability to drought is one of the main indicators of long-term environmental and social sustainability of these arid grazing systems.

Several policy pressures exacerbate the fundamental driving force of increasing population pressure (Box 33.2), including:

(i)   "stabilization" of the system. Often well intentioned policies sought (and still seek) to stabilize the "boom and bust" cycles, which traditionally existed between man, animals and vegetation in arid rangelands through settlement of pastoralists and attempts to regulate and control the stocking rate;

(ii) feed-subsidies for drought relief;

(iii) changes in access to land; "privatizing" communal areas, carving them up into small plots, which do not allow the necessary mobility; and

(iv) inappropriate incentives. Subsidized tractors and fuel, as well as supported producer prices for domestic cereal production, intensifies the encroachment of crops in the "key resource" sites of the arid zones.

4. WORLD DEMAND FOR FOOD, ESPECIALLY MEAT PRODUCTS

The massive appetite of the growing urban populations for meat, milk (and other livestock products) often translates into environmental damage and disruption of traditional patterns of livestock-raising (IFPRI, 1995). At the same time, livestock producers are forced into resource degradation where population pressure and poverty coincide, such as in marginal pastoral areas (Ngaido, this volume; Winrock, 1992).

<table>
<tr><td>

Box 33.2

Inappropriate price
and support policies

</td><td>

Feed subsidies have been one of the major policy tools of WANA governments to support the development of livestock production. These policies, often implemented as part of a drought-relief package to sheep owners, have become part of the production base of large and medium sheep feeders and have created many economic distortions. FAO (1988:15) found these economic distortions were translated into:

(i)   stagnation of prices for livestock products;
(ii)   slow evolution of the livestock sector and the emergence of non-viable production systems;
(iii)   stagnation of forage production;
(iv)   increase of imports of animal products; and
(v)   substitution of beef production for sheep production following the liberalization of the price of sheep meat when the prices of cattle milk and meat remained controlled.

Blench (1995) argues that in Jordan "the system of allocating feeds on per-head basis has created a major incentive to increase herd sizes". These inefficiencies have prompted policy-makers to suggest the removal of feed subsidies. They have now been removed in Jordan.

Source: Ngaido, et al. (this volume)

</td></tr>
</table>

On a global basis, production based on pure grazing systems is relatively unimportant, and grows also at the lowest rate. Pastoral system production grows at 1% per annum, mixed farming at 3% and industrial production at more than 7%. Despite their cost-effectiveness, traditional pastoralists will not supply much of the increased demand for animal products but the more favoured margins of the rangelands will be encroached upon by croplands (Grainger and Bradley, this volume). This can often lead to land degradation.

5. LAND DEGRADATION IN ARID REGIONS

Livestock production, mainly as a result of pressures in this process, has become an important factor in environmental degradation. Large land areas have become degraded through overcropping, overgrazing and the concomitant loss of vegetation. The most important degradation of land and vegetation is around settlements and water points. They are mostly in a radius of about 1 to 5 km of the actual waterpoint. However, assuming an average distance of about 10 to 30 km between waterpoints, the degraded area would amount, at most, to 5 to 10% of the total area.

Until recently, arid rangelands, more than any other system, have been associated with land degradation. The concept of "desertification" originated from a perception of degrading fringes of arid rangelands and advancing deserts. In addition, the arid grazing systems and pastoral production modes of the developing world have been described as inefficient and backward production systems.

These views have changed radically. Firstly, there is now evidence that in the arid zones the extent of land degradation is greatly exaggerated, and that we are dealing with a highly resilient ecosystem, as shown by the "expanding and contracting" Sahara found by Tucker et al. (1991), and the increasing per head and hectare livestock productivity of the Sahelian herds demonstrated in this study. Secondly, there is convincing evidence that traditional mobile production systems on arid rangelands are highly efficient (Ellis and Swift, 1988). Production of protein per ha of traditional nomadic pastoralists in Mali and Botswana is two or three-fold higher (and at a much lower cost in non-renewable fuel resources) than production from sedentary production systems or ranching, respectively, under similar climatic conditions in Australia and the US (Breman and de Wit, 1983; de Ridder and Wagenaar, 1984). In addition, arid grazing systems have often multiple uses, with wildlife and other plant products being important products.

Land degradation of semi-arid lands in the West Asia and North Africa (WANA) region, and in Africa and India, is caused by a complex set of factors involving pastoralists and their stock, crop encroachment in marginal areas and fuelwood collection. Changes in land tenure arrangements, settlement and incentive policies (e.g., subsidized barley) have undermined traditional land-use practices and contributed to degradation (Abdulla, this volume; Blench, this volume).

6. LIVESTOCK AND THEIR IMPACT ON THE GLOBAL ENVIRONMENT

Water availability in low-rainfall areas is affected by livestock. Land and water is polluted where animal concentrations are high.

Biodiversity may also be affected by extensive livestock production, although there are a large number of cases, showing increases in plant-biodiversity in well-balanced grazing systems, especially those using multi-species. The interaction between wildlife and livestock in these ecosystems is complex. Firstly, there is increasing evidence of complimentarity, and only limited competition of wildlife and livestock in grazing. The grazing "overlap" between most wildlife species and livestock is rather limited. The combination of livestock-raising and wildlife management often results in an equal or better species wealth than any of these activities done individually. Furthermore, in national parks in Kenya, where livestock are not permitted, biodiversity is decreasing, with an increase in unpalatable species and bush-encroachment. On the other hand, there are many degraded areas in Kenya, due to combined wildlife-livestock pressure.

The driving forces leading to losses in animal biodiversity are habitat destruction, species introduction and hunting (WRI, 1994). In addition, hunting and culling of wild-life were encouraged in the past, because wildlife in general was considered to be a reservoir of diseases, such as Rinderpest and Malignant Catarrhal fever, and vectors of disease, such as East Coast Fever, and trypanoso- miasis (Sere and Steinfeld, 1996). The control of the above-mentioned diseases has improved considerably and there is a much better understanding of which particular species harbour specific diseases, opening better opportunities for wild life-livestock integration.

An extensive review of grazing and production data of 236 sites worldwide, including many sites in the semi-arid zone, showed no difference in biomass production, species composition and root development in response to long-term grazing (Milchunas and Lauenroth, 1993).

The arid rangelands contain a variety of plant species used by wild and domestic herbivores. Le Houerou (1993) estimates that in Africa, there are perhaps as many as 3 500 plant species which feed the continent's herbivores, compared with less than 150 species which feed humans. There is thus no danger for an immediate irreversible loss of plant biodiversity. The mixed grazing systems (cattle, small ruminants, camels and wildlife) can stimulate plant diversity, and the vegetation is extremely resilient, most of the changes observed in the vegetation are a result of dry spells, and, therefore, are most likely to be temporary.

However, some would question whether irreversible degradation is occurring at all, and just what the role of livestock is in that process. Livestock do not move, produce or reproduce without human intervention. Livestock do not degrade the environment – humans do. As a result of these misconceptions about livestock development, institutions and governments continue to miss opportunities that would permit the livestock sector to make its full contribution to human welfare and economic growth. It should noted that livestock are an important source of gaseous emission, contributing to global warming, which is projected to increase by 1.8C worldwide over the next 35 years.

All these pressures on the environment are the result of a metamorphosis, where the role of livestock has altered due to rising and changing demands for livestock commodities and to a different perception of the environment (Sere and Steinfeld, 1996).

In essence, the conflict between livestock and environment is a conflict between different human needs and expectations. In many places, livestock production is growing out of balance with the environment or is under so much pressure that it leads to environmental degradation.

Finding the balance between increased food production and the preservation of the world's natural resources remains a major challenge. It is clear that food will have to be produced at less cost to the natural resource base than at present.

7. TECHNOLOGY AND POLICY OPTIONS

The prevailing combination of poverty and high population growth, that characterizes many countries of the semi-arid regions of the world, cannot be easily broken. The over-riding need is to stop the building-up of further human pressure in arid zones, through adequate population control and alternative employment generation policies.

As the second priority, external interventions in the system need to acknowledge the disequilibrium status of the pastoral systems in the arid zones, and respond to their need for flexibility and mobility. This means that attempts to regulate stocking rates need be stopped. Even apart from the technical flaws in the estimation of the carrying capacity, experience has shown that it is almost always impossible to enforce those stocking rates.

The third priority should be to empower traditional pastoral institutions and develop effective co-management regimes, forging partnerships between the state and a wide variety of users, with the state carrying the overall responsibility for arbitrating conflicting interests at the national level, and facilitating negotiation between the multiple stakeholders. Access to land is to be based on customary resource user rights, however, avoiding rigid territorial boundaries.

The fourth priority is the identification of effective drought management policies.

Finally, the fifth priority should be to establish appropriate incentive policies by:

(i)   increasing the costs of grazing on the range which can reduce animal pressure by promoting an earlier off-take;

(ii)   full-cost recovery, especially for water supply and animal health services. Water has been in many cases a free good supplied by the public sector (and frequently financed by the international donor community); and

(ii)   removing of price distortions for other agricultural inputs, in order to reduce the conversion of pastoral key resources into marginal cropland.

8. RESEARCH NEEDS

The key areas where research is urgently needed emerge from the above recommendations. They include the identification of :

(i)   appropriate indicators, which provide reliable information on the resource trends in the arid areas;

(ii)   appropriate methodologies for economic appraisals on the investment in converting such "key resources";

(iii)   the factors which lead to strong pastoral institutions; and

(iv)   sustainable drought preparedness plans, with particular emphasis on decentralized management and the design of appropriate banking and insurance schemes, and appropriate conflict resolution schemes.

9. WHITHER NOMADIC PASTORALISM?

In the light of the above observations and from an analysis of the papers presented in this volume (notably those in Part IV), we must conclude that traditional nomadic pastoralism will become less and less important. There will always be those who wish to utilize (exploit) the otherwise unusable forage and water resources of the drylands but social, economic and political pressures will see the demise of this way of life (Box 33.3).

Box 33.3

The future of nomadism

The Al-Taysiyah Bedouin, like other nomad groups, face a difficult future. On the one hand, public policy and the impacts of modernization have protected their livelihood from extinction, and they are able to survive at reasonable levels of economic well-being. They have responded to current economic incentives and have been able to overcome many of the constraints associated with the traditional livestock livelihood system. In many ways, modernization has transformed the Bedouin into a tent-dwelling rancher, with a capital intensive enterprise that hires outside labour and depends critically on market conditions as much as on range conditions. This transformation, however, has also changed the nature of nomad decision-making. Herd management strategies and grazing practices reflect the demands of short-term economic maximization rather than long-term conservation. Herd sizes are large, water is free, range access is open, and cash is needed to pay the expenses. This combination favours the short-term option on natural resource management that is observed among the Al-Taysiyah Bedouin.

At the same time, there is increasing competition for the Bedouin in a modern world. Urban residents with available capital are moving into livestock herding for profit. These capitalists seek the economic benefits without the rigours of the lifestyle. Other interests are competing for the desert, such as city recreationists. agriculturalists, and now the conservation interests such as the Wildlife Conservation Agency, which is in the process of claiming rangeland for the recuperation of wildlife species. Such pressures, combined with the exodus of young Bedouin to urban areas, will continue to place the Bedouin existence in jeopardy.

For policy-makers. the choices are equally challenging. In a society that values the Bedouin lifestyle for its cultural contribution to national identity, new solutions are needed to ensure the sustainability of this livelihood. It is inevitable that such sustainability will require a re-definition of the Bedouin place in their desert and in their society.

Source: Finan and Al-Haratani (this volume)

References

Abdulla, S. (this volume). Economic analysis of nomadic livestock operations in northern Saudi Arabia.

Ahmad, Y. (this volume). The socio-economics of pastoralism: a commentary on changing techniques and strategies for livestock management.

Alexandratos, N. (ed) 1995. World Agriculture: Towards 2010. FAO and John Wiley and Sons. Rome and Chichester.

Al Gain, A. 1985. Integrated resource survey in support of nomads in Saudi Arabia— a proposal. Proc. International Research and Development Conf. Arid Lands Today and Tomorrow. Tucson, Arizona, pp. 1213 -21.

Behnke, R.H. Jr., Scoones, I. and Kerven, C. (eds.) 1993. Range ecology at disequilibrium. New models of natural resource variability and pastoral adaptation in African savannas. Overseas Development Institute, London.

Blench, R. (this volume) Rangeland degradation and socio-economic changes among the Bedu of Jordan: results of the 1995 IFAD survey.

Bremen H. and de Wit, C. 1983. Rangeland productivity and exploitation in the Sahel. Science: 221:1341-1347.

Ellis, J.E. and Swift, D.M. 1988. Stability of the African pastoral ecosystems: Alternate pradigms and implications for development. J. Range Management 41: 450-459.

Finan, T.J. and Al-Harani, E.R. (this volume). Moderrn Bedouins: the transformation of traditional nomad society in the Al-Taysiyah region of Saudi Arabia.

Grainger, A. and Bradley, D. (this volume). A GIS-modelling approach to monitoring rangeland degradation and desertification.

International Food Policy Research Institute (IFPRI). 1995. A 2020 Vision for Food, Agriculture and the Environment. International Food Policy Research Institute. Washington, DC, USA.

Le Houérou, H.N. 1993. The grasslands of the Sahel. In: R.T. Coupland, (ed) Natural grasslands ecosystems of the world Vol 8b, Chap. 7 pp. 197-200.

Milchunas, D.G. and Lauenroth, W.K. 1993. Quantitative effects of grazing on vegetation and soils over a global range of environments. Ecological Monographs 63: 327-366.

Ngaido, T., Nordblom, T., Osman, A.E. and Gintzburger, G. (this volume). A policy shift toward sustainable resource development.

de Ridder, N. and Wegenaar, K. 1986. Energy and protein balances in traditional livestock systems and ranching in eastern Botswana. Agricultural Systems 20:1-16.

Sere, C. and Steinfeld, H. 1996. World livestock production systems - Current status, issues and trends. FAO Animal Production and Health Paper No. 127. Rome, Italy.

Squires, V.R. and Sidahmed, A.E. (in press) Livestock managemnent in dryland pastyoral systems: prospects and problems. Annals of the Arid Zone.

Tucker, C. Dregne, H.E. and Newcomb, W.W. 1991. Expansion and Contraction of the Saharan Desert from 1980 - 990. Science 253: 299.

Winrock International Institute for Agricultural Development. 1992. Assessment of Animal Agriculture in sub-Saharan Africa. Morrilton, Arkansas, USA.

World Resources Institute (WRI). 1994. World Resources 1992-1994. Basic Books Inc. New York.

annexes

Annex 1:
Summary of issues
and recommendations

1. WORKSHOP OBJECTIVES

The Recommendations Committee (Annex 2) discussed the outcome of the workshop and addressed each of the following specific workshop objectives:

Objective 1: identify more precisely the situation and development needs of pastoral nomads in rapidly changing economic circumstances;

Objective 2: explore how these technologies can be adapted to pastoral development within an integrated land management strategy and make cost-effective suggestions for their future adaptation to the needs of pastoral nomads. Present an up-to-date record of the capacity and potential of remote sensing techniques to provide environmental data to planners, administrators and hence to Pastoralists; and

Objective 3: draw lessons from the experiences gained in designing strategies and programmes for sustainable use, improvement and management of the rangeland resources.

2. ISSUES ARISING FROM THE WORKSHOP

(i)   What technologies for use in the region in future?
        - how can it be applied at the field level?

(ii)   Long term monitoring:
        - need for and nature of;
        - funding and support; and
        - methodologies.

(iii)   What future is there for nomadism?

(iv)   Characterization of desertification:
        - definition; indicators; and
        - irreversibility.

(v)   Definitional problems:
        - what are rangelands?
        - what are deserts?
        - where is the boundary?
        - sustainability?

(vi)   Policy issues and linkages:
        - policies are driven by factors external to rangelands.

(vii)   Alternative land use options for the semi desert rangelands.

(viii) Need for development of rangeland strategies:
- role of International Convention on Desertification.

(ix) Conservation, environmental protection and biodiversity issues.

(x) International conventions, policy implications and linkages:
- Desertification Control;
- Biodiversity; and
- Climate change.

3. THE ABOVE ISSUES WERE CATEGORIZED UNDER THREE HEADINGS

3.1 Policy issues and linkages

(i) Policies are driven by factors external to rangelands.

(ii) International conventions.

(iii) Cross border migration of people and livestock.

(iv) Regional cooperation.

3.2 Setting parameters for future generations

(i) What is the vision for the future?

(ii) What strategy to achieve this?

(iii) What role will new technologies play?

3.3 Definitional issues

(i) Terminology - desertification, rangelands, deserts, nomads.

(ii) Reversibility vs irreversibility.

(iii) Range condition.

(iv) Sustainability.

4. RESPONSE TO SPECIFIC OBJECTIVES

Objective 1

Identify more precisely the situation and development needs of pastoral nomads in rapidly changing economic circumstances.

There is an apparent major information gap and a consequent poor understanding of the problems. Without a good understanding of the current situation, sound and effective policies cannot be developed.

Problems don't exist in a vacuum. They must be seen in the context of the political, socio-economic and ecological situation. There is a need to know what information is available that is relevant to the situation. Information is fragmented and needs to be pulled together. There is a need to describe the problems in some meaningful way.

Goal setting is a key process. It is first necessary to clearly define the goal: either (a) preserve nomadic way of life; (b) preserve rangelands; or (c) find a compromise which promises sustainable use. There are trade-offs e.g. many fewer livestock on the rangelands but a higher consumption of barley in "feedlots".

Recommendations

1.1 Recognize that rangeland plays its part in the overall national economic development. For many regions of the country, there are few other economically viable and ecologically feasible land uses. Land use should be harmonized to avoid conflicts.

1.2 Prepare a review of current knowledge about users of the rangelands with a view to developing a profile of their social and economic status and their goals and needs. This background paper will be a statement of what is known and not known about the various rangeland users.

1.3 Conduct a nation-wide study to fill in our knowledge gaps, including updating the rangeland surveys to evaluate the status of vegetation and the current inventory of livestock by species and class of animal. Use this as a baseline to develop a long-term monitoring system.

1.4 Recognize that restricted area case studies are of limited value as a planning tool unless they are preceded by or complement a nationwide survey to provide their context.

1.5 Develop, in co-operation with the specialized international and regional institutions, scenarios for the rangelands and their users thereby exploring options and consequences for use by planners and decision makers.

1.6 Raise awareness among rangeland users of the consequences of the current level of utilization of the nation's natural resources – rangeland, soils, water etc. Increase stakeholder (landuser) involvement. Make greater use of media, especially radio.

1.7 Recognising that a lesson from this Workshop is that implementable policies require that users be involved in their formulation, develop a participatory approach to the formulation of the National Action Plan for rangelands. Establishment of rangeland associations is a good way to facilitate participatory planning.

1.8 Strengthen and improve regional co-operation, especially within GCC and the Near East and North African region. Foster links with the relevant organizations and agencies in other arid and semi arid regions.

Objective 2

Explore how these technologies can be adapted to pastoral development within an integrated land management strategy and make cost-effective suggestions for their future adaptation to the needs of pastoral nomads. Present an up-to-date record of the capacity and potential of remote sensing techniques to provide environmental data to planners, administrators and hence to Pastoralists.

A response to this objective was framed in the context of trying to develop an integrated land management strategy for a sustainable land use in the arid and semi arid regions, including GCC states, along the lines of the ESON project. The scope and purpose is set in the following recommendations:

Recommendations

2.1 Compile and harmonise existing data

2.1.1 System requirements:
- Use a 3-level approach (ground, aerial and satellite orbital level).
- Use a Multi-disciplinary approach including assessment and monitoring of changes over time of:
  - climate;
  - land use and land cover;
  - vegetation components (dominant species, palatable-non palatable, annuals/perennials);
  - soils characteristics, topography;
  - socio-economy, population mobility land availability;
  - land use policy;
  - climate-land surface-human impact-hydrology interaction;
  - grazing pressure (herd composition, distribution and size);
  - biomass supply-demand (productivity, production, consumption, demands);
  - wildlife and pest species e.g. plague locust; and
  - production economy, market structure and subsidy policy.
- Use the longest possible data series backwards and forwards.

2. 3 Suggested system set up
- Use GIS for multi level and multi scale data management, analyses and spatial modelling of resources supply-demand. Geocoded data.
- Use Remote sensing:
  - NOAA AVHRR and METEOSAT (high frequency observations, every day);
  - Landsat (low frequency multi temporal observations, every five years);
  - SPOT (low frequency multi temporal observations on a sampling basis);
  - Air photos and video (low frequency multi temporal observations on a sampling basis);
  - Light aircraft based observations (low frequency); and
- Complement with Ground observations and participatory research based on sampling strategies.

2.4 Scale perspectives
- Time perspectives (observation frequency varying with variables):
  - NOAA AVHRR and METEOSAT composites- every 10 days;
  - Precipitation observations - daily;
  - Vegetation cover - every 1-2 years;
  - Land use - every 5 years;
  - Population (people and herds) - every 5 to 10 years; and
  - Vegetation composition - every year.
- Spatial perspective: Multi-resolution 1 m - 10 km

2.5 Training and information dissemination
Identify target groups on different data observation and user/application levels:
- Farmers and herders;
- Communities;
- Governments;
- Multinational level;
- Media;

Objective 3

Draw lessons from the experiences gained in designing strategies and programmes for sustainable use, improvement and management of the rangeland resources.

Considerable effort was made at both the investigation and the development level to address the problems of the rangeland resources. The knowledge accumulated, however, was fragmented and offered localised and unsustainable solutions. The Recommendations Committee emphasised in its deliberations the importance of integration of resource management, policy support and community participation in future decision making processes.

Recommendations

3.1 Prevent further losses of rangeland to other uses by developing an integrated management system including the issuing of licenses for land use thereby bring rangelands in line with the permit system and regulations applicable to other activities at the national and regional levels. In the specific case of the Kingdom of Saudi Arabia it was recommended that the predominantly fragile rangelands should be devoted to the exclusive use by the mobile traditional pastoral nomads and to restrict access of the sedentary commercial sheep raisers to these resources.

3.2 Strengthen national Range Management institutions through the provision of the necessary personnel and funds. Establish environmental education in schools. Establish Natural Resource Management curricula (teaching and research) in the universities to provide qualified personnel to carry out the task of inventory, monitoring and management of the rangelands.

3.3 Ensure that rangeland rehabilitation is made part of the National Action Plan to combat desertification.

Annex 2: Recommendation committee members

METEOROLOGY AND ENVIRONMENTAL PROTECTION ADMINISTRATION (MEPA), JEDDAH

Mr Abdulwahab Dagag, D.G. Natural Resources
Dr Martin Fogel, Advisor, ESON Project
Dr Ziad Abu Ghararah, Senior Advisor
Dr Aslam Basumbul, Senior Advisor
Dr Azhari Fathalla, Consultant for D.G. E.P.G.D.
Dr Ehsanalla Khan, Water Quality Consultant

INTERNATIONAL

Dr J. Ellis, Colorado State University, Fort Collins, U.S.A.
Dr M. Andrew, AACM, Adelaide, Australia
Dr W. Wint, Oxford University, Oxford, U.K.
Dr C. Tucker, NASA, Greenbelt, MA, U.S.A.
Dr U. Hellden, University of Lund, Sweden
Dr J. Lichtenegger, European Space Agency, Frascati, Italy
Dr A. Ayoub, UNEP, Nairobi, Kenya

MINISTRY OF AGRICULTURE AND WATER

Mr A. G. Al-Shareef, National Agriculture and Water Research Centre, Riyadh
Dr M. A. El-Shorbagy, Rangeland Specialist, UNDP/FAO, Riyadh
Dr Farid Iskander, Rangeland Advisor (retired)

INTERNATIONAL FUND FOR AGRICULTURAL DEVELOPMENT (IFAD)

Mr. A. Slama, Director, Technical Advisory Division
Dr A. E. Sidahmed, Technical Advisor (Livestock & Rangeland) Management), Workshop Coordinator
Dr V. R. Squires, Consultant/Resource Person

Annex 3:
List of contributors

ABDALLA, Suliman H.
Rangeland Animal Development Research Centre;
Al Jouf, SAUDI ARABIA

AHMAD Yusuf J.
2141 Washington Ave. # 204
Washington, D.C. 20007 USA

AÏT BELAÏD, Mohamed
Royal Centre for Remote Sensing,
Rabat, MOROCCO

AL-EISA, Abdullazziz
Meteorology and Environmental Protection Administration (MEPA),
Jeddah, SAUDI ARABIA

AL-GAIN, Abdulbar
Meteorology and Environmental Protection Administration (MEPA)
Jeddah, SAUDI ARABIA

AL-HARATANI, Eisa
Meteorology and Environmental Protection Administration (MEPA)
Jeddah, SAUDI ARABIA

AL-NOORI, M.A
National Agriculture and Water Research Centre (NAWRC)
Ministry of Agriculture and Water (MAW)
P.O. Box 17285 Riyadh 11484, SAUDI ARABIA

AL-SHAREEF, A.
National Agriculture and Water Research Centre (NAWRC)
Ministry of Agriculture and Water (MAW)
P.O. Box 17285 Riyadh 11484, SAUDI ARABIA

AL SHAREEF, Abdu Gasem
Range and Forestry Department
Ministry of Agriculture and Water (MAW)
Riyadh, SAUDI ARABIA

AMER, Saud
Applied Research Corporation, EROS Data Center
Sioux Falls, South Dakota, USA

ANDREW, Martin H.
AACM International Pty Ltd, 11-13 Bentham Street
Adelaide, South Australia 5000, AUSTRALIA

AYOUB, A.T.
United Nations Environment Programme (UNEP)
P.O. Box 47074
Nairobi, KENYA

BASHIR, Magzoub Omer
International Centre of Insect Physiology and Ecology (ICIPE) , Field Station,
Port Sudan, THE SUDAN

BLENCH, Roger
Overseas Development Institute
Portland House, Stag Place
London SW1E 5DP, UK

BRADLEY, Daniel
School of Geography, University of Leeds
Leeds LS2 9JT UK

COUGHENOUR, Michael B.
Natural Resource Ecology Laboratory
Colorado State University
Fort Collins, Colorado, USA

ELLIS, Jim
Natural Resource Ecology Laboratory, Colorado State University,
Fort Collins, Colorado, USA

EL-SHORBAGY, M.A.
UNDP/FAO Range Management Expert
Range and Forestry Department
Ministry of Agriculture and Water (MAW)
Riyadh, SAUDI ARABIA

FARGHER, John D.
AACM International Pty Ltd,
11-13 Bentham Street, Adelaide,
South Australia 5000, AUSTRALIA

FFOLLIOTT, Peter F.
University of Arizona
Tucson, Arizona 85721, USA

FOGEL, Martin
Meteorology and Environmental Protection Administration (MEPA),
Jeddah, SAUDI ARABIA

GEERKEN, R.
Gesellschaft für Technische Zusammenarbeit (GTZ) GmbH,
65726 Escborn, P. O.Box 5180, GERMANY

GINTZBURGER, Gus
International Centre for Agriculture Research in the Dry Areas (ICARDA)
P.O.Box 5466
Aleppo, SYRIA.

GRAINGER, Alan
School of Geography, University of Leeds,
Leeds, LS2 9JT UK

HAJOOJ, Abdulla, H.
Rangeland Animal Development Research Centre,
Al Jouf, SAUDI ARABIA

HASSANALI, Ahmed
International Centre of Insect Physiology and Ecology (ICIPE)
Nairobi, KENYA

HAY, Simon I.
The Trypanosomiasis and Land-Use in Africa (TALA) Project,
University of Oxford, Department of Zoology
South Parks Rd., Oxford OX1 3PS, UK

HELLDEN, Ulf
University of Lund
Soelvegatan 13, S-223 62 Lund, SWEDEN

ILAIWI, M.
The Arab Centre for the Studies of Arid Zones and Dry Lands (ACSAD)
P. O. Box 2440, Damascus, SYRIAN ARAB REPUBLIC

JAJA, M.
General Organization for Remote Sensing (GORS),
P.O.Box 12556
Damascus, SYRIAN ARAB REPUBLIC

KAUFMANN, H.
GeoResearchcenter Potsdam, Telegrafenberg A17,
14473 Potsdam, GERMANY

LAHLOU KASSI, Abdellalif
International Research Institute
P.O Box 5689
Addis Ababa, ETHIOPIA

LE HOUEROU, Henri N.
327, Rue De Jussieu
F-34090, Montpellier, FRANCE

LICHTENEGGER, Jürg
ERS Data Utilization Section European space Agency (ESA/ESRIN),
Frascati, ITALY

MILLER, Shawn
University of Maryland, Department of Meteorology
College Park, Maryland, USA

NGAIDO, Tidiane
International Center for Agricultural Research in the Dry Areas (ICARDA)
P.O.Box 5466, Aleppo, SYRIAN ARAB REPUBLIC

NIANG, Amadou Moctar
Ecology Monitoring Centre
Rue Leon Gontran Damas
Dakar, SENEGAL

NICHOLSON, Sharon E.
Department of Meteorology
Florida State University
Tallahassee, Florida 32308, USA

NORDBLOM, Tom
International Centre for Agricultural Research in the Dry Areas(ICARDA)
P.O.Box 5466 Aleppo, SYRIAN ARAB REPUBLIC

OSMAN, Ahmed
International Center for Agricultural Research in the Dry Areas(ICARDA),
P.O.Box 5466 Aleppo, SYRIAN ARAB REPUBLIC

PACKER, Michael J.
The Trypanosomiasis and Land-use in Africa (TALA) Project,
University of Oxford, Department of Zoology
South Parks Rd, Oxford OX1 3PS, UK

ROEDER, H.
Gesellschaft für Technische Zusammenarbeit (GTZ) GmbH,
65726 Escborn, P. O. Box 5180, GERMANY

ROGERS, David J.
The Trypanosomiasis and Land-Use in Africa (TALA) Project,
University of Oxford, Department of Zoology
South Parks Rd, Oxford OX1 3PS, UK

SAMDANI, M. S.
National Agriculture and Water Research Centre (NAWRC)
Ministry of Agriculture and Water (MAW)
P.O. Box 17285, Riyadh 11484, SAUDI ARABIA

SANKARY, A.M
University of Aleppo, Institute for Agriculture,
P.O.Box 3481, Aleppo, SYRIAN ARAB REPUBLIC

SEGL, K.
GeoResearchcenter Potsdam, Telegrafenberg A17,
14473 Potsdam, GERMANY

SIDAHMED, Ahmed .E.
International Fund for Agricultural Development (IFAD),
Via del Serafico 127,
00142 Rome, ITALY

SIMIR, Ahmed
Rangeland Animal Development Research Centre,
Al Jouf, SAUDI ARABIA

SORKATI, Isam Abd El Rahim
Range Management Department,
Ministry of Agriculture, Port Sudan, THE SUDAN

SQUIRES, Victor R.
Dryland Management Consultant
497 Kensington Rd, Wattle Park
Adelaide, 5066, AUSTRALIA

TUCKER, Compton J.
Laboratory for Terrestrial Physics, Code 923
National Aeronautics and Space Administration (NASA)
Goddard Space Flight Center, Greenbelt, Maryland 20771, USA

TUELLER, Paul T.
Department of Environmental and Resource Sciences,
University of Nevada - Reno,
1000 Valley Road, Reno, Nevada 89512, USA

WINT, William
Environmental Research Group Oxford Limited,
P.O. Box 346
Oxford OX1 3QE, UK

colour plates

COLOUR PLATE 1

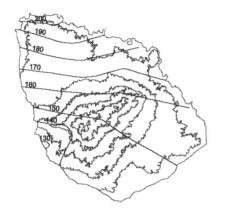

Rainfall (long-term annual average)

Watersheds and drainage pattern

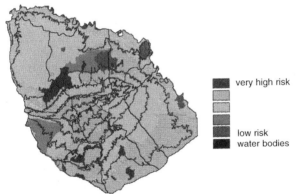

very high risk

low risk
water bodies

Erosion risk (based on lithologic units)

Location Map
TM-frame: 172/36 floated north
SPOT pan-frames: 125-126/279

Erosion and sedimentation of sands, strongly influenced by natural conditions such as rainfall, lithology, topography, drainage pattern and wind speed/direction.

Wadis that originate in the central Bishri Mts. within the slightly erodible units (mainly light red, minor dark red in the Erosion risk map) coinciding with steep slopes transport sand material down slopes continuously renewing resources for wind erosion. As long as water erosion dominates, only watersheds that share part of these areas are affected by sand accumulations (A,B,C,D,E).

Once the wadis reach the plains, leaving the wind protected valleys, south-easterly directed winds distribute the water-transported sand across watershed boundaries covering huge areas, especially in watersheds C and D, south-east, and those neighbouring them. In watersheds A and B, water and wind erosion are oriented opposite one another and eolian sands, therefore, are concentrated on smaller areas or are blown around the elevation of the Bishri Mts. (compare Color Plate 4.2). The natural processes were accelerated by cultivating the fragile soil system in the central part classified as a "high to very high" erosion risk.

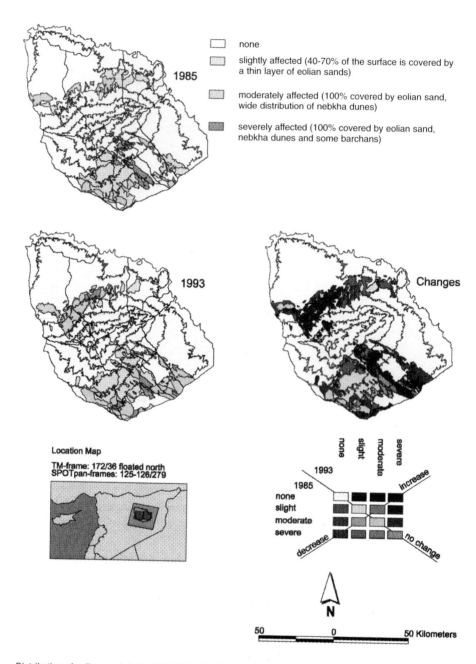

Distribution of eolian sands in the Bishri Mts. for the years 1985 and 1993, as visually interpreted from TM satellite data. Changes for the better (displayed in green in the change map) are due to the expansion of cultivation into the sand covered areas of 1985. Ploughing and stubbles of harvested barley fields destroy and obscure the typical spectral appearance of eolian sands and prevent their identification.

COLOUR PLATE 3

Biweekly maximum NDVI

24 July - 6 August 1992

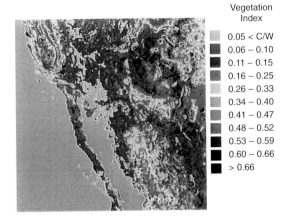

Vegetation
Index

0.05 < C/W
0.06 – 0.10
0.11 – 0.15
0.16 – 0.25
0.26 – 0.33
0.34 – 0.40
0.41 – 0.47
0.48 – 0.52
0.53 – 0.59
0.60 – 0.66
> 0.66

21 August - 3 September 1992

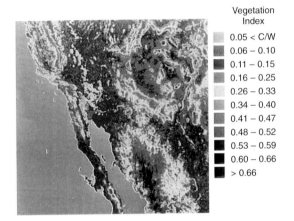

Vegetation
Index

0.05 < C/W
0.06 – 0.10
0.11 – 0.15
0.16 – 0.25
0.26 – 0.33
0.34 – 0.40
0.41 – 0.47
0.48 – 0.52
0.53 – 0.59
0.60 – 0.66
> 0.66

2-15 October 1992

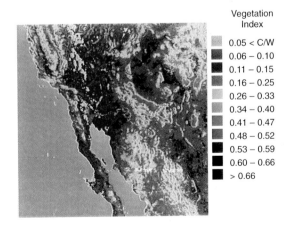

Vegetation
Index

0.05 < C/W
0.06 – 0.10
0.11 – 0.15
0.16 – 0.25
0.26 – 0.33
0.34 – 0.40
0.41 – 0.47
0.48 – 0.52
0.53 – 0.59
0.60 – 0.66
> 0.66

COLOUR PLATE 4

Predictions of all vegetation types in Nigeria

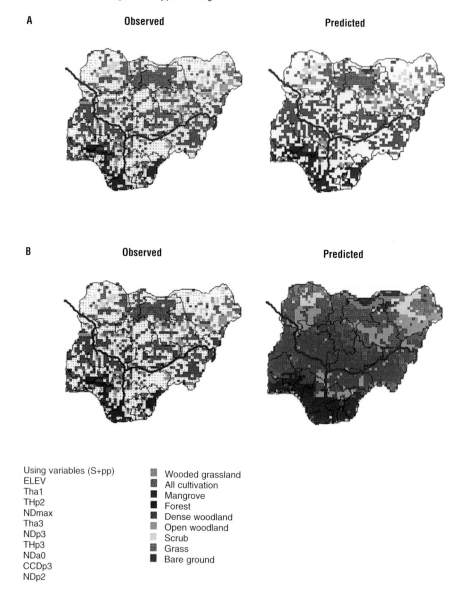

A   Observed   Predicted

B   Observed   Predicted

Using variables (S+pp)
ELEV
Tha1
THp2
NDmax
Tha3
NDp3
THp3
NDa0
CCDp3
NDp2

- Wooded grassland
- All cultivation
- Mangrove
- Forest
- Dense woodland
- Open woodland
- Scrub
- Grass
- Bare ground

(upper) Observed land-cover types in Nigeria (only those grid squares with > 60% coverage of a single land-cover type are shown) and the cover predicted from the set of satellite variables listed (details in Table 17.3). (lower) As for Colour Plate 4A, but with the predicted dominant vegetation cover for all grid squares, using the same set of satellite predictor variables.

COLOUR PLATE 5

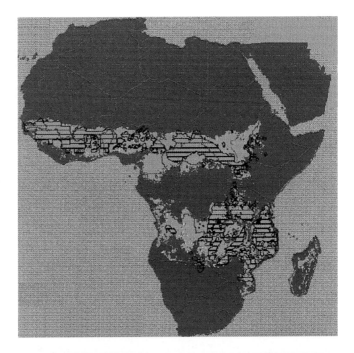

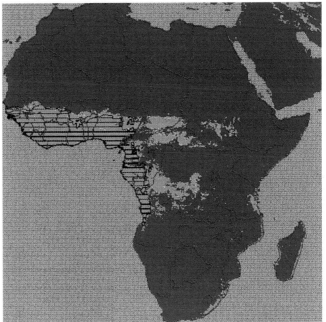

Observed (black lines) and predicted distributions of (a) *G. morsitans* and (b) *G.palpalis* (*s.l.*) in Africa. The predicted distributions are on a colour scale from red (low probability) to green (high probability).

COLOUR PLATE 6

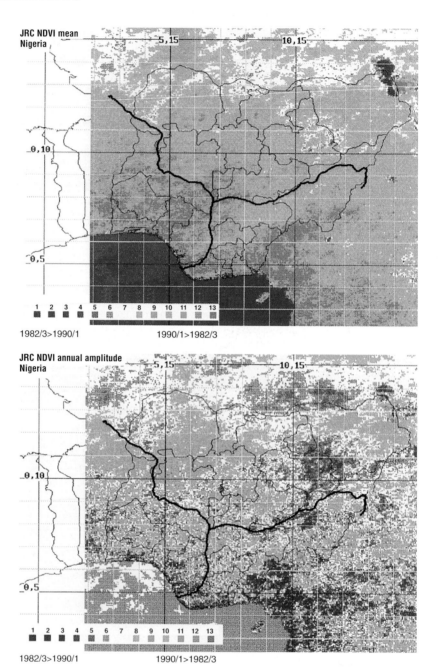

Land-cover change detection for Nigeria. The difference between NDVI Fourier variables for the early and late 1980s a) mean; b) amplitude of annual cycle. Increases in each variable over this period are indicated in green, decreases in red.

COLOUR PLATE 7

Vegetation map produced by supervised classification of the 1992 Spring image (Oujda, Morocco) (C) CNES/SPOT IMAGE (1992)/CRTS

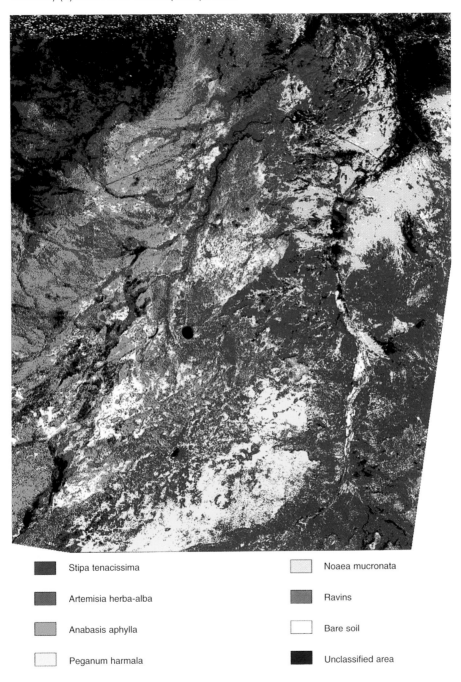

■ Stipa tenacissima	▨ Noaea mucronata
■ Artemisia herba-alba	■ Ravins
■ Anabasis aphylla	□ Bare soil
□ Peganum harmala	■ Unclassified area

COLOUR PLATE 8

Vegetation production for 1995

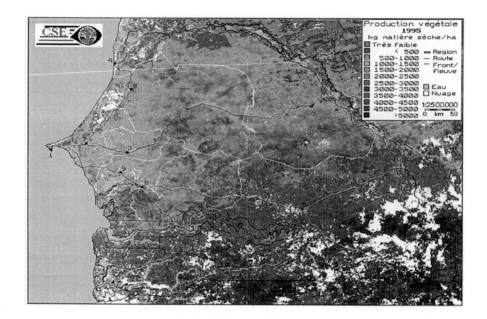